Photographer's Guide to the Sony DSC-HX80 and HX90V

Photographer's Guide to the Sony DSC-HX80 and HX90V

Getting the Most from Sony's Pocketable Superzoom Cameras

Alexander S. White

WHITE KNIGHT PRESS
HENRICO, VIRGINIA

Copyright © 2017 by Alexander S. White.

All rights reserved.

No part of this publication may be reproduced, stored in a retrieval system or transmitted in any form or by any means, electronic, mechanical, photocopying, recording or otherwise, without the prior written permission of the copyright holder, except for brief quotations used in a review.

The publisher does not assume responsibility for any damage or injury to property or person that results from the use of any of the advice, information, or suggestions contained in this book. Although the information in this book has been checked carefully for errors, the information is not guaranteed. Corrections and updates will be posted as needed at whiteknightpress.com.

Product names, brand names, and company names mentioned in this book are protected by trademarks, which are acknowledged.

Published by
White Knight Press
9704 Old Club Trace
Henrico, Virginia 23238
www.whiteknightpress.com
contact@whiteknightpress.com

ISBN: 978-1-937986-60-5 (paperback)
        978-1-937986-61-2 (ebook)

Printed in the United States of America

To my wife, Clenise.

Contents

INTRODUCTION 1

CHAPTER 1: PRELIMINARY SETUP 3

Charging and Inserting the Battery 3
Choosing and Inserting a Memory Card 4
Setting the Language, Date, and Time 7

CHAPTER 2: BASIC OPERATIONS 9

Introduction to Main Controls 9
    Top of Camera 9
    Back of Camera 9
    Front of Camera. 10
    Right Side of Camera 10
    Left Side of Camera 10
    Bottom of Camera 11
Taking Pictures in Auto Mode. 11
    Variations from Fully Automatic 13
        Photo Creativity Feature. 13
    Flash. 16
    Drive Mode: Self-Timer and Continuous Shooting 17
Overview of Movie Recording. 17
Viewing Pictures 19
    Reviewing While in Shooting Mode 19
    Reviewing Images in Playback Mode 19
    Playing Movies 19

CHAPTER 3: SHOOTING MODES 21

Intelligent Auto Mode 21
Superior Auto Mode 22
Program Mode 23
Aperture Priority Mode 24
Shutter Priority Mode 26

Manual Exposure Mode 27
Scene Mode 30
    Portrait 32
    Advanced Sports Shooting. 32
    Landscape. 33
    Sunset 33
    Night Scene 33
    Hand-Held Twilight 34
    Night Portrait 34
    Anti Motion Blur 34
    Pet 35
    Gourmet. 35
    Beach 35
    Snow 36
    Fireworks 36
    Soft Skin. 36
    High Sensitivity 36
iSweep Panorama Mode. 37
Memory Recall Mode 39

CHAPTER 4: SHOOTING MENU   41

Image Size 43
Aspect Ratio 45
Quality 46
Panorama Size and Panorama Direction 46
File Format 47
Record Setting 47
Drive Mode. 47
    Single Shooting. 48
    Continuous Shooting. 48
    Self-Timer 49
    Self-Timer (Continuous) 49
    Continuous Exposure Bracketing 49
    Single Exposure Bracketing 50
    White Balance Bracketing 50
    DRO Bracketing. 51
Bracket Settings 51
Flash Mode. 52
    Flash Off. 52
    Autoflash 52
    Fill-Flash 52
    Slow Sync 53
    Rear Sync 53
Flash Compensation. 54
Red Eye Reduction. 55
Focus Mode (Available as Menu Option on HX90V Only) 55
    Single-Shot AF 55
    Continuous AF 56
    DMF (HX90V Only) 57
    Manual Focus (HX90V Only) 57
Focus Area 59
    Wide. 59
    Center 59
    Flexible Spot 60
    Expand Flexible Spot 61
AF Illuminator 61

Exposure Compensation 61
ISO 62
    Multi Frame Noise Reduction 63
Metering Mode 64
White Balance 65
DRO/Auto HDR 68
Creative Style 71
    Adjusting Contrast, Saturation, and Sharpness 71
    Standard 72
    Vivid 72
    Portrait 72
    Landscape. 73
    Sunset 73
    B/W 73
    Sepia. 73
Picture Effect 73
    Off 74
    Toy Camera 74
    Pop Color 75
    Retro Photo 76
    Soft High-Key 76
    Partial Color 76
    High Contrast Monochrome 77
    Soft Focus 77
    HDR Painting 77
    Rich-Tone Monochrome 78
    Miniature Effect 78
    Watercolor 79
    Illustration. 79
Focus Magnifier (HX90V only). 79
High ISO Noise Reduction. 81
Center Lock-on AF 81
Smile/Face Detection 81
    Face Detection On (Registered Faces) 81
    Face Detection On 82
    Smile Shutter 82
Soft Skin Effect 83
Auto Object Framing 83
Scene Selection 84
Movie. 84
SteadyShot (Movies). 84
Auto Slow Shutter, Micref Level, and Wind Noise Reduction 84
Shooting Tip List 85
Memory Recall 85
Memory 85

Chapter 5: Physical Controls   87

Mode Dial 87
Shutter Release Button 87
Zoom Lever 87
Power Button 88
Built-in Flash and Flash Pop-up Switch 88
Electronic Viewfinder 88
AF Illuminator/Self-Timer Lamp 89
Control Ring (HX90V Only) 90
Playback Button 91

- Movie Button . . . 91
- Menu Button . . . 91
- Function Button . . . 92
  - Shooting Mode: Function Menu . . . 92
  - Quick Navi System . . . 93
  - Playback Mode: Send to Smartphone . . . 94
- In-Camera Guide/Delete Button . . . 94
- Control Wheel and Its Buttons . . . 96
  - Control Wheel . . . 96
  - Center Button . . . 97
  - Direction Buttons . . . 97
    - Up Button: Display . . . 97
    - Right Button: Flash Mode . . . 97
    - Down Button: Photo Creativity/Exposure Compensation . . . 98
      - Exposure Compensation . . . 98
    - Left Button: Self-Timer/Drive Mode . . . 100
- Tilting LCD Screen . . . 100
- Ports and Other Items on Sides and Bottom of Camera . . . 101

Chapter 6: Playback and Printing   103

- Normal Playback . . . 103
- Index View and Enlarging Images . . . 103
- Playback Screens . . . 105
- Deleting Images with the Delete Button . . . 106
- Playback Menu . . . 106
  - Delete . . . 107
  - View Mode . . . 108
  - Image Index . . . 108
  - Display Rotation . . . 109
  - Slide Show . . . 109
  - Rotate . . . 110
  - Enlarge Image . . . 111
  - 4K Still Image Playback . . . 111
  - Protect . . . 111
  - Motion Interval Adjustment . . . 111
  - Specify Printing . . . 112
  - Beauty Effect . . . 113

Chapter 7: Custom and Setup Menus   114

- Custom Menu . . . 114
  - Zebra . . . 114
  - MF Assist (HX90V Only) . . . 115
  - Focus Magnification Time (HX90V Only) . . . 115
  - Grid Line . . . 116
    - Rule of Thirds Grid . . . 116
    - Square Grid . . . 116
    - Diagonal Plus Square Grid . . . 117
  - Marker Display . . . 117
  - Marker Settings . . . 117
  - Auto Review . . . 118
  - Display Button . . . 119
  - Peaking Level (HX90V Only) . . . 121
  - Peaking Color (HX90V Only) . . . 122
  - Exposure Settings Guide . . . 122
  - Zoom Speed . . . 122

Contents | xi

    Zoom Setting 123
    Finder/Monitor 126
    Release without Card 126
    Self-portrait Timer 127
    Face Registration 127
    Write Date 128
    Function Menu Settings 128
    Custom Key Settings 129
        Control Ring (HX90V Only) 130
        Center Button 131
            Standard 132
            MOVIE 132
            Download Application 132
            Not Set 132
        Left Button 133
        Right Button 133
        Down Button 133
        In-Camera Guide Button 133
    Zoom Function on Ring (HX90V Only) 133
    Movie Button 134
Setup Menu 134
    Monitor Brightness 135
    Viewfinder Brightness 135
    Finder Color Temperature 135
    Volume Settings 135
    Audio Signals 136
    GPS Settings (HX90V Only) 136
        GPS On/Off 136
        GPS Auto Time Correction 137
        GPS Area Adjustment 137
        Use GPS Assist Data 137
        GPS Log Recording 137
    Upload Settings 138
    Tile Menu 138
    Mode Dial Guide 139
    Delete Confirmation 139
    Display Quality 140
    Power Save Start Time 140
    NTSC/PAL Selector (Cameras Sold in Europe and Other PAL Areas Only) . . . 140
    Function for VF Close 141
    Demo Mode 141
    HDMI Settings 141
        HDMI Resolution 142
        24p/60p Output 142
        HDMI Information Display 142
        CTRL for HDMI 143
    USB Connection 143
    USB LUN Setting 143
    USB Power Supply 144
    Language 144
    Date/Time Setup 144
    Area Setting 145
    Format 145
    File Number 146
    Select REC Folder 146
    New Folder 146
    Folder Name 147

Recover Image Database 147
Display Media Information 147
Version 148
Setting Reset 148

Chapter 8: Motion Pictures   150

Movie-Making Overview 150
Details of Movie Settings 150
   Movie-Related Shooting Menu Options 151
      File Format 151
         XAVC S HD 151
         AVCHD 151
         MP4 151
      Record Setting 151
         XAVC S HD 152
         AVCHD 152
            60i and 60p Video Formats 152
            24p Video Formats 153
         MP4 153
   Movie (Exposure Mode) 153
      Program Auto 154
      Aperture Priority 154
      Shutter Priority 155
      Manual Exposure 155
   SteadyShot (Movies) 156
   Auto Slow Shutter 157
   Micref Level 158
   Wind Noise Reduction 158
Effects of Mode Dial Position on Recording Movies 158
Effects of Other Shooting Menu Settings on Recording Movies 160
Effects of Physical Controls When Recording Movies 161
Summary of Options for Recording Movies 163
Other Settings and Controls for Movies 164
Movie Playback 164
   Motion Shot Feature 165
Editing Movies 166

Chapter 9: Wi-Fi, Applications, and Other Topics   168

Connections Using Wi-Fi and NFC 168
   Sending Images to a Computer 168
   Sending Images to a Smartphone 170
   Connecting with NFC 172
   Using a Smartphone or Tablet as a Remote Control 173
Wi-Fi Menu 176
   Send to Smartphone 176
   Send to Computer 176
   View on TV 177
   One-touch (NFC) 177
   Airplane Mode 178
   WPS Push 178
   Access Point Settings 178
   Edit Device Name 179
   Display MAC Address 179
   SSID/PW Reset 179
   Reset Network Settings 179

Applications and Application Menu 180
Other Topics 181
    Using the Superzoom Lens. 181
    Macro Photography 184
    Street Photography. 185
    Connecting to a Television Set 186

APPENDIX A: ACCESSORIES   187

Cases 187
Batteries and Chargers 188
Remote Controls. 189
External Flash and LED Light 191
External Video Recorder 192
External Audio Recorder. 192
Tripods 193

APPENDIX B: QUICK TIPS   194

APPENDIX C: RESOURCES FOR FURTHER INFORMATION   196

Books. 196
Websites and Videos. 196
    Digital Photography Review 196
    Reviews of the HX80 and HX90V. 196
    The Official Sony Site 197
    Other Resources 197

Index   **198**

Introduction

This book is a guide to the operation of the Sony Cyber-shot DSC-HX80 and DSC-HX90V digital cameras. This is the first time I am covering two camera models in the same book. I am doing this because it took me a while to get around to covering either of these models, which have both been on the market for a while, and their features are quite similar.

The major differences are that the HX90V has built-in GPS capability, a control ring around the lens, and manual focus, while the HX80 does not, and the HX80 lacks a few menu options that relate to those features. Note that there also exists a model called the HX90 which does not include the GPS capability of the HX90V but is otherwise the same model.

These cameras are classified as compact models, easily packed in luggage or carried on your person when traveling, but also equipped with strong optical zoom capabilities, with a 30x zoom range, from 24mm to 720mm. The cameras include many of Sony's excellent features for producing high-quality images with a variety of processing styles, including Picture Effect and Scene mode settings. They offer advanced shooting modes, several autofocus options, and high-definition video recording. Either of these models can readily serve as the only camera you would need for a vacation trip or for everyday photography needs.

My aim is to provide a complete guide to the features of the HX80 and HX90V, explaining how the features work and when you might want to use them. The book is aimed largely at beginning and intermediate photographers who are not satisfied with the official documentation and prefer a more user-friendly explanation of the cameras' controls and menus. For those seeking more advanced information, I discuss some topics that go beyond the basics, and I include in the appendices information about additional resources. I will provide updates and other information at my website, whiteknightpress.com, as warranted.

In structuring the book to discuss two camera models, I concentrate on the HX90V, which was the earlier of the models to be released, and I note any differences with the HX80. Where no differences are noted, the two cameras are essentially the same for any given control or feature. Except where noted otherwise, all illustrations in this book show display screens and menu screens of the HX90V. In some cases, those screens may differ slightly from the corresponding screens on the HX80, but those differences should not affect the usefulness of the illustrations.

Chapter 1: Preliminary Setup

When you purchase your Sony DSC-HX80 or DSC-HX90V, the box should contain the camera itself, battery, charger, wrist strap, micro USB cable, and several brief instruction pamphlets. There is no CD with software or user's guide; the software programs supplied by Sony are accessible through the Internet.

To install Sony's software for viewing and working with images and videos, go to the Internet address http://www.sony.net/pm, where you can download PlayMemories Home, a program for basic image editing, uploading, and management, available for both Mac and Windows-based computers. You might want to attach the wrist strap as soon as possible to help you keep a tight grip on the camera. The strap can be attached to the small mounting lug on the right side of the camera. I have never attached the strap, though, because the camera is so small that I can hold it firmly without much risk of dropping it, even without a strap.

Charging and Inserting the Battery

The Sony battery for these cameras is the NP-BX1. The standard procedure is to charge the battery while it's inside the camera. To do this, you use the supplied micro USB cable, which plugs into the camera and into the Sony charger or some other USB charging port.

There are pluses and minuses to charging the battery while it is inside the camera. On the positive side, you don't need an external charger, and the camera can charge automatically when it's connected to your computer. Also, many automobiles have USB slots where you can plug in your camera to keep up its charge. And, you can find many desktop or portable charging devices with USB ports, as discussed in Appendix A.

On the negative side, with this system you cannot charge a battery outside of the camera, so you cannot be charging a spare battery while using the battery that is inside the camera. One solution to this situation is to purchase at least one extra battery and a device that will charge your batteries externally.

With these two models, unlike some other Sony cameras, you can use the supplied battery charger as an AC adapter that will power the camera. So, if your battery runs completely down, you don't have to wait until you have recharged it to start using the camera again. You can plug the charger into the camera and into an AC outlet or USB power supply, and operate the camera directly from that power source. I'll discuss batteries, chargers, and other accessories in Appendix A.

To charge the battery, insert it into the camera and connect the charger. You first need to open the battery compartment door on the bottom of the camera and put in the battery. You can only insert it fully into the camera one way; what I do is look for the four gold-colored metal contact squares on the end of the battery and insert the battery so those four squares are positioned close to the front of the camera as the battery goes into the compartment, as shown in Figures 1-1 and 1-2. You may have to nudge aside the small blue latch that holds the battery in place, which is seen in Figure 1-3.

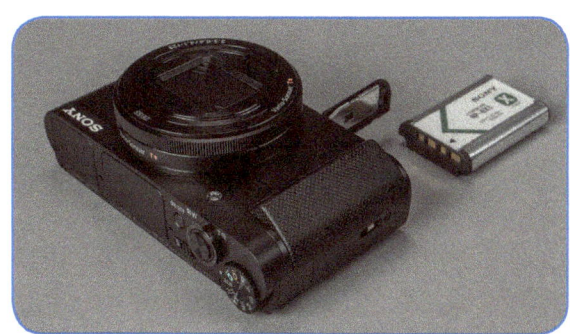

Figure 1-1. Battery Lined Up to Go Into Camera

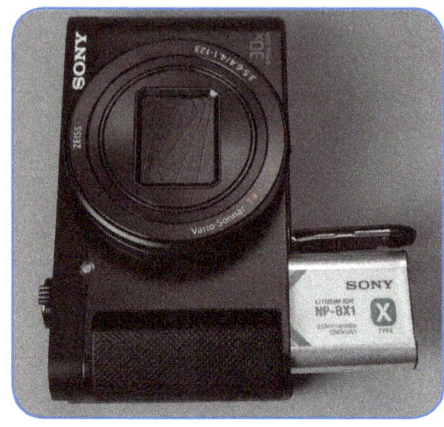

Figure 1-2. Battery Going Into Camera

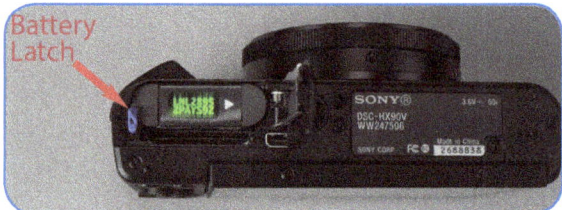

Figure 1-3. Battery Secured by Latch

With the battery inserted and secured by the latch, close the battery compartment door and slide the ridged latch on the door to the closed position. Then plug the larger, rectangular end of the USB cable into the corresponding slot on the provided AC charger, which is model number AC-UB10C (HX90V) or AC-UUD12 (HX80) in the United States. Plug the smaller end of the cable into the micro USB port on the upper part of the camera's right side as you hold it in shooting position, as shown in Figure 1-4.

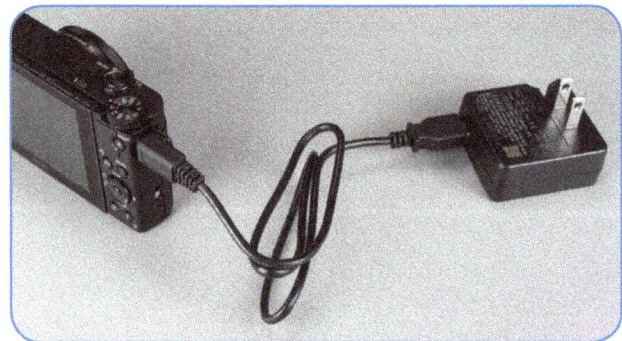

Figure 1-4. Battery Charger Connected to Camera

Plug the charger's prongs into a standard electrical outlet. (In countries other than the United States, the charger may come with a power cord that needs to be plugged into the charger and then into an outlet.) A small orange lamp to the right of the camera's charging port will light up steadily while the battery is charging; when it goes out, the battery is fully charged. The full charging cycle should take about 230 minutes. If the charging lamp flashes, that indicates a problem with the charger or a problem with the temperature of the camera's environment.

To charge the battery using a USB power supply such as a USB port on a laptop computer, plug the large end of the camera's USB cable into that power source and the small end into the charging port on the camera, while the camera is turned off.

Choosing and Inserting a Memory Card

The camera does not ship with a memory card. If you turn the camera on with no card inserted, you will see the message "NO CARD" in the upper left corner of the screen. If you ignore this message and press the shutter button to take a picture, don't be fooled into thinking that the camera is storing it in internal memory. The camera will temporarily store the image and play it back if you press the Playback button, but the image will not be permanently saved. (You cannot even operate the shutter with no card, if the Release w/o Card menu option is set to Disable, as discussed in Chapter 7.)

Some camera models have a small amount of built-in memory so you can take and store a few pictures even without a card, but the HX80 and HX90V do not have that safety net. (In an emergency, if you took one important picture with no card, you might be able to save it. First, don't turn off the camera. Second, play the image, and connect one end of a micro HDMI cable to the camera's HDMI port and the other end to a video capture device. Then capture the image to that device or to a computer connected to that device. I have done this using a Blackmagic Intensity Pro device, which saved the image to my computer. But that process is for emergencies only.)

To avoid the frustration of having a great camera that can't save images, you need to use a memory card. The HX80 and HX90V use two types of memory storage. First, they can use all varieties of SD cards, which are about the size of a postage stamp. These cards come in several varieties; some examples are shown in Figure 1-5.

The standard card, called simply SD, comes in capacities from eight megabytes (MB) to two gigabytes (GB). A higher-capacity card, SDHC, comes in sizes from four

GB to 32 GB. The newest, and highest-capacity card, SDXC (for extended capacity) comes in sizes of 48 GB, 64 GB, 128 GB, 256 GB, and 512 GB; this version of the card can have a capacity up to two terabytes (TB), theoretically, and SDXC cards generally have faster transfer speeds than the smaller-capacity cards. There also is a special variety of SD card called an Eye-Fi card, which I will discuss later in this chapter.

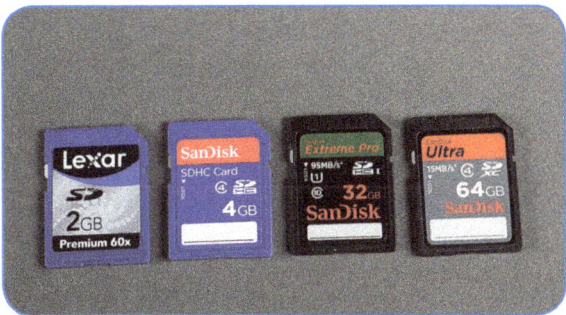

Figure 1-5. Various Sizes of SD Cards

These cameras also can use micro SD cards, which are often used in smartphones and other small devices. These smaller cards operate the same as SD cards, but you need an adapter to use this tiny card in the camera, as shown in Figure 1-6.

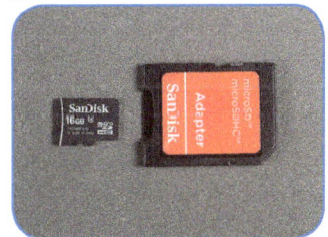

Figure 1-6. Micro SD Card with Adapter

In addition to using SD cards, the HX80 and HX90V, being Sony cameras, also can use Sony's proprietary storage devices, known as Memory Stick cards. These cards are similar in size and capacity to SD cards, but with a slightly different shape, as shown in Figure 1-7.

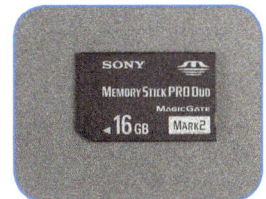

Figure 1-7. Sony Memory Stick Card

Memory Stick cards come in various types, according to their capacities. The ones that can be used in the HX90V are the Memory Stick PRO Duo, Memory Stick PRO-HG Duo, and Memory Stick Micro (M2). The Memory Stick Micro, like the micro SD card, requires an adapter.

There is an important limitation on your choice of a memory card. To record video using the XAVC S HD format, which provides the highest quality, you have to use a memory card with a capacity of 64 GB or more and speed of Class 10, UHS Speed Class 1, or faster. These specifications are not just recommendations; if you try to record using that video format on a card that does not meet the requirements noted above, the camera will display an error message, as shown in Figure 1-8, and will not record the video.

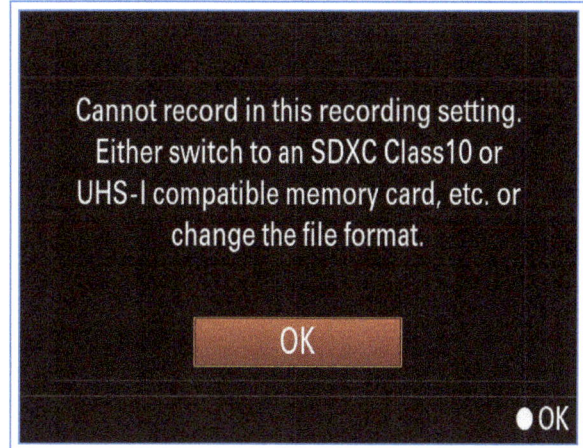

Figure 1-8. Error Message for Using Wrong Memory Card for Video

The XAVC S HD format is worth using if you want high-quality video, and it is a good idea to get one of the high powered cards that can support its use. Figure 1-9 shows several cards I have tested that can handle all video formats on the HX90V—the SanDisk Extreme PRO 64 GB SDXC card, rated in UHS Speed Class 1, the Lexar Professional 128 GB SDXC card, rated in that same speed class, the SanDisk Extreme 256 GB SDXC card, and the SanDisk Extreme PRO 512 GB card, both of which are rated in UHS Speed Class 3.

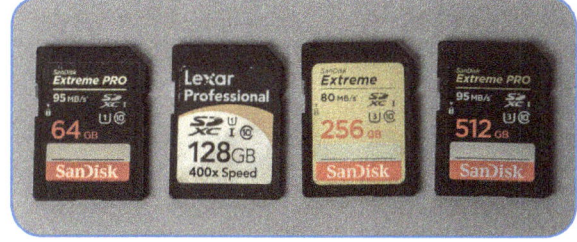

Figure 1-9. High-speed SD Cards for XAVC S HD Video

If you do not care about using the XAVC S HD video format, the factors to consider in choosing a card are capacity and speed. If you expect to record a good deal of HD video or very many high-quality still images, you should get a large-capacity card, but don't get carried away—the largest cards have such huge capacities that you may be wasting money purchasing them.

There are several variables to consider in computing how many images or videos you can store on a particular size of card, such as which aspect ratio you're using (3:2, 4:3, 16:9, or 1:1), image size, and quality. Here are a few examples of what can be stored on a memory card. If you're using the 4:3 aspect ratio and a card with a capacity of 16 GB, you can store about 2300 still images using the highest-quality Fine setting and Large size, or about 3250 images using the Standard setting for quality and Large for size. The numbers are proportionally higher for larger cards; you can fit about 4 times as many images on a 64 GB card as you can on a 16 GB card.

You can fit about 2 hours 35 minutes of the highest-quality XAVC S HD video on a 64 GB card, which is the smallest-size card you can use for that format. That same card will hold about 22 hours of video at the lowest-quality MP4 setting of 1280 x 720 pixels, which is still HD (high-definition) quality. Note, though, that the camera is limited to recording no more than about 29 minutes of video in any format in any one sequence. The highest-quality MP4 format (1920 x 1080 pixels at a bit rate of 28 megabits per second) can be recorded only for 20 minutes in one sequence, because of the four GB file size limit.

The other major consideration is the speed of the card. High speed is important to get good results for recording continuous bursts of images and the highest-quality video with this camera. You should try to find a card that writes data at a rate of six MB/second or faster to record HD video. If you go by the class designation, a Class 4 card should be sufficient for shooting stills, and a Class 6 card should suffice for recording video, except for the requirements discussed above for XAVC S HD video.

You also may want to consider using an Eye-Fi card. This special type of device looks like an ordinary SDHC card, but it includes a tiny transmitter that lets it connect to a Wi-Fi network and send images to your computer on that network as soon as the images are recorded by the camera. You also may be able to use Direct Mode, which lets the Eye-Fi card send your images directly to a computer, smartphone, tablet, or other device without needing a network, though Direct Mode can be tricky to set up.

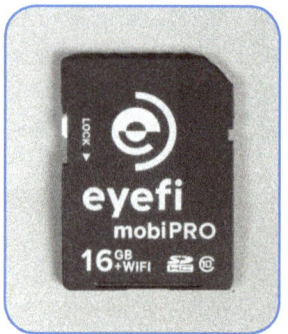

Figure 1-10. Eye-Fi mobiPRO SD Card

I have tested a 16 GB Eye-Fi mobiPRO card with the HX80 and HX90V, and it worked as expected. Within a few seconds after I snapped a picture with this card in either camera, the image appeared in the Pictures/Eye-Fi folder on my computer. This card, shown in Figure 1-10, can handle video files as well as still-image files.

Of course, with these cameras Sony has included built-in Wi-Fi capability, as discussed in Chapter 9, so you do not need to use an Eye-Fi card or the equivalent to transfer images wirelessly. If you already have one or more wireless SD cards, you should be able to use them in your HX80 or HX90V, but there are other options for wireless transfer that may make more sense.

If you decide to use a Memory Stick card and want to use it with a card reader, be sure you have a reader that can accept those cards, which, as noted above, are not the same shape as SD cards.

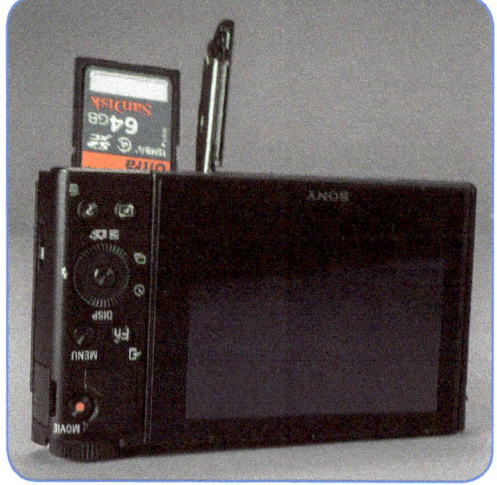

Figure 1-11. SD Card Going Into Camera

Once you have chosen a card, open the same door on the bottom of the camera that covers the battery compartment, and slide the card in until it catches. An SD card is inserted with its label pointing toward the back of the camera, as shown in Figure 1-11; a Memory

Chapter 1: Preliminary Setup | 7

Stick card is inserted with its label pointing toward the front of the camera, as shown in Figure 1-12.

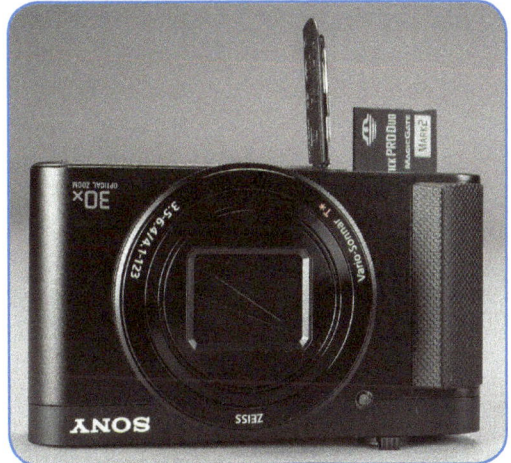

Figure 1-12. Memory Stick Card Going Into Camera

Once the card has been pushed down until it catches, close the compartment door and slide the latch to the outside position. To remove a card, push down on its edge until it releases and springs up, so you can grab it.

Although the card may work well when newly inserted in the camera, it's a good idea to format a card when first using it in the camera, so it will have the correct file structure and will have any bad areas blocked off from use. To do this, turn on the camera by pressing the power button, then press the Menu button at the center right of the camera's back. Next, press the Right button (right edge of the Control wheel on the camera's back) multiple times until the small orange line near the top of the screen is positioned under the number four, while the menu's highlight lines are on the toolbox icon, as shown in Figure 1-13.

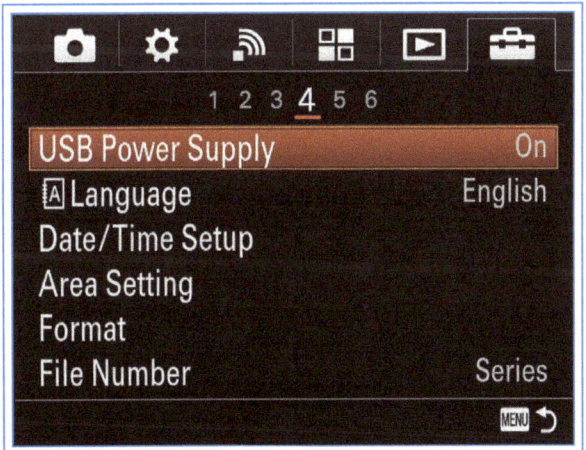

Figure 1-13. Screen 4 of HX90V Setup Menu

The toolbox icon stands for the Setup menu. The orange highlight bar should be on the top line of the menu, for the USB Power Supply command. Press the Down button (bottom edge of Control wheel) until the Format command is highlighted, then press the button in the center of the Control wheel (called the "Center button" in this book). On the next screen, seen in Figure 1-14, highlight Enter and press the Center button again to carry out the command.

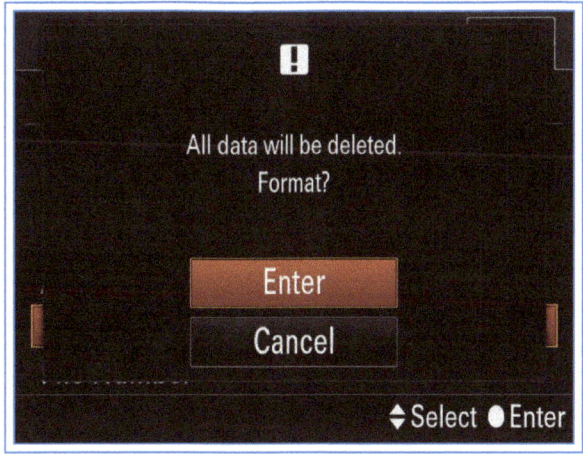

Figure 1-14. Format Confirmation Screen

Setting the Language, Date, and Time

You need to have the date and time set correctly before you take pictures, because the camera records that information invisibly with each image and displays it later if you want. It is, of course, important to have the date (and the time of day) correctly recorded with your digital images. The camera may prompt you to set the date and time the first time you turn it on, but if not, carry out this procedure.

First, follow the same steps with the menu as noted above, but this time highlight the Date/Time Setup item on screen 4 of the Setup menu. Then press the Center button to move to the next screen. On that screen, select the Date/Time item and press the Center button. You will see a screen like the one in Figure 1-15.

On that screen, press the Left and Right buttons or turn the Control wheel to move through the month, day, year, and time settings, and change them by pressing the Up and Down buttons. When you have made those settings, press the Center button to confirm. You can adjust the Daylight Savings Time and Date Format settings on the previous screen if you need to. Then press the Menu button one or more times to exit from the menu system.

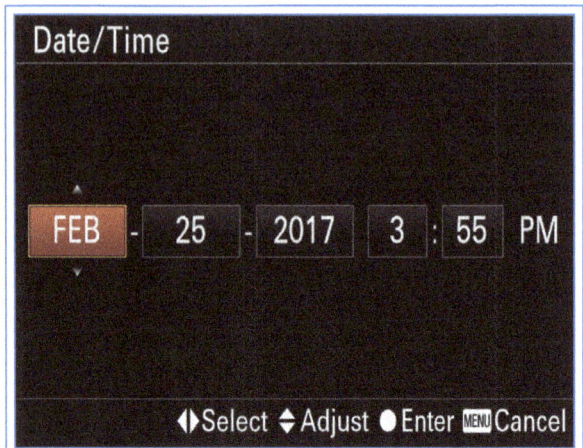

Figure 1-15. Screen for Setting Date and Time

If you need to change the language the camera uses for menus and other messages, press the Menu button as discussed above to enter the menu system, and navigate to screen 4 of the Setup menu, as shown in Figure 1-13. With the direction buttons, move if necessary to the Language item on the second line of the screen and press the Center button to select it. You then can select from the languages on the menu, as shown in Figure 1-16.

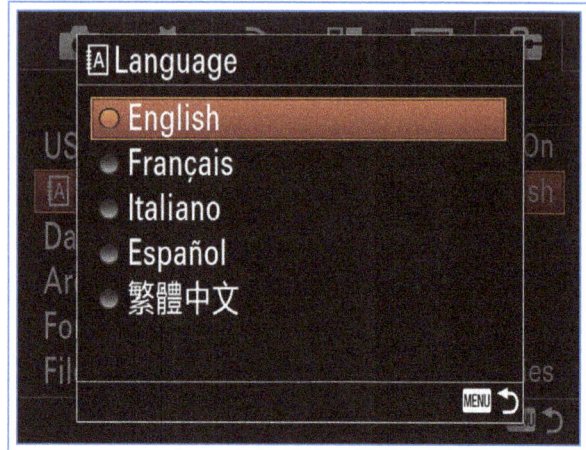

Figure 1-16. Screen for Selecting Language

Chapter 2: Basic Operations

Now that the camera has the correct time and date set and a charged battery inserted along with a memory card, I'll discuss the steps for basic picture taking. For now, I won't discuss details about various options and why you might choose one over another. I'll just describe a reasonable set of steps that will get your camera into action and will save a usable image or video to your memory card.

Introduction to Main Controls

Before I discuss options for setting up the camera using the menu system and controls, I will introduce the main physical features of the camera. I won't discuss all of the controls here; I will cover them in more detail in Chapter 5. As I mention each item for the first time, I will describe its position and function; you may want to refer back to these images for a reminder about each control. As I do throughout this book, I will use the HX90V for the illustrations, pointing out differences from the HX80 as appropriate.

Top of Camera

On top of the camera are some of the most important controls and other features, as shown in Figure 2-1.

The Mode dial selects a shooting mode for stills or video. For basic shooting without having to make other settings, turn the dial so the green camera icon is next to the white marker; this sets the camera to one of its most automatic modes. The large, black shutter release button is used to take pictures. Press it halfway to evaluate focus and exposure; press it all the way to take a picture. The zoom lever, surrounding the shutter button, is used to zoom the lens between its telephoto and wide-angle settings. The lever also is used to change the views of images in playback mode.

The power button turns the camera on and off. The flash is stored inside the top of the camera; to use it, you have to pop it up using the flash pop-up switch, marked with a lightning bolt, behind the power button. The two small microphone openings are where the camera records sound for movies. The electronic viewfinder is stored inside the left side of the camera; I will discuss it in the next section. The Control ring (HX90V only) is used to control manual focus, aperture, shutter speed, zoom, and other operations, depending on the shooting mode and various menu settings.

Back of Camera

Figure 2-2 shows the controls on the camera's back.

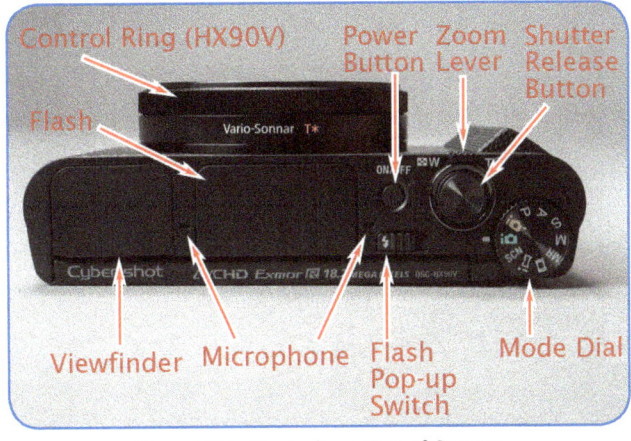

Figure 2-1. Controls on Top of Camera

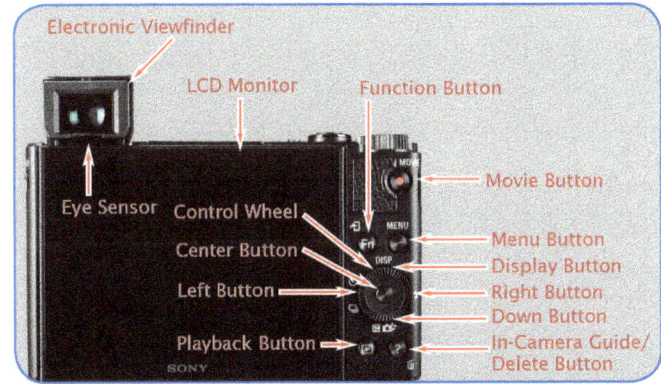

Figure 2-2. Controls on Back of Camera

The built-in electronic viewfinder (EVF) is stored inside the camera's top at the far left side until you pop it up using the Finder switch on the camera's left side. Underneath the viewfinder is a very small slot for the eye sensor, which detects the presence of your head for purposes of switching between the viewfinder and the LCD screen.

The Movie button starts or stops a video recording. The Menu button calls up the menu screens with settings for shooting and other values, such as control button functions, audio features, and others. In shooting mode, the Function (Fn) button calls up a menu of camera settings for easy access. In playback mode, it activates the Send to Smartphone command, if the command is available. The Playback button puts the camera into playback mode so you can view recorded images, and it also can turn the camera on, in playback mode. The In-Camera Guide/Delete button, marked with a question mark, can be programmed to call up any one of numerous functions. By default, in shooting mode it calls up shooting tips and help screens with information about menu options. In playback mode, it always serves as the Delete button for erasing images.

The Control wheel rotates to set values such as aperture and shutter speed and to navigate through menus. Its four edges also act as buttons when you press them, to control items like flash mode, exposure compensation, continuous shooting, and the display screen. The Center button confirms selections, among other functions. The LCD screen—which displays the live view along with the camera's settings and plays back recorded images—can rotate 180 degrees forward to let you take a self-portrait. The screen also can be set at an intermediate position to let you view scenes from unusual angles.

Front of Camera

Figure 2-3 shows the items on the camera's front.

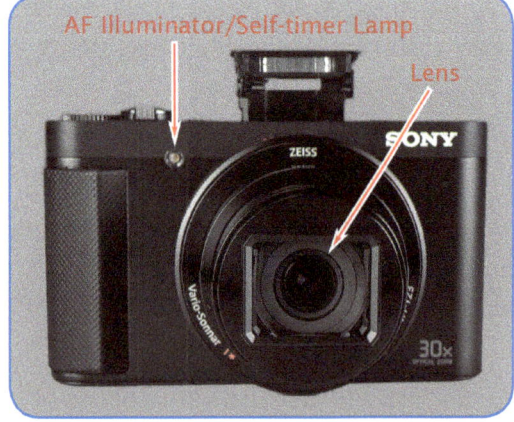

Figure 2-3. Items on Front of Camera

The AF Illuminator/Self-timer Lamp signals operation of the self-timer and provides illumination so the camera can use its autofocus system in dark areas. The lens has a 35mm equivalent focal length range of 24mm to 720mm and an aperture range of f/3.5 to f/8.0. (The actual focal length range of the lens is 4.1mm to 123mm; the "35mm equivalent" range is commonly used to state the focal length in a way that can easily be compared to lenses of other cameras.)

Right Side of Camera

On the right side of the camera is a small flap marked Multi. Under that flap is the Multi port or terminal, shown in Figure 2-4, where you connect the micro USB cable that is supplied with the camera to charge the battery, to power the camera, to connect the camera to a computer to manage images, or to connect to a printer to print images directly from the camera. You also can connect a wired remote control to this port, as discussed in Appendix A.

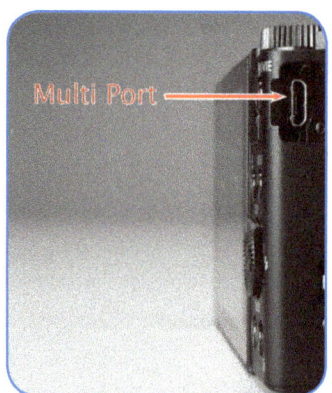

Figure 2-4. Multi Port on Right Side of Camera

Left Side of Camera

The left side of the camera, shown in Figure 2-5, has two items of interest.

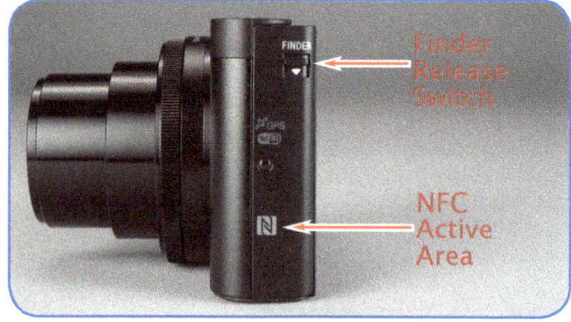

Figure 2-5. Items on Left Side of Camera

This is the location of the Finder release switch, which you press down to release the electronic viewfinder so it will pop up. You then have to pull the viewfinder eyepiece backward to its extended position so you can see the live view through the camera's lens. When you are finished with the viewfinder, press the eyepiece back into the housing. You can then press the viewfinder down into the camera's body. When you do this, the camera will turn off or stay powered on, depending on the setting of the menu option called Function for VF Close, the first item on screen 3 of the Setup menu.

On the HX90V only, there is a GPS logo on this side of the camera, indicating that this model has the ability to add geographical location information to your images. I will discuss that capability in Chapter 7.

The left side of the camera is the location of the NFC (near field communication) area, marked by a fancy letter N, where you touch the camera against a smartphone or tablet with NFC capability to establish a Wi-Fi connection automatically. I will discuss this feature in Chapter 9. There also is a Wi-Fi logo, indicating that the camera has the ability to connect wirelessly to smartphones and other devices, as I will discuss in Chapter 9.

BOTTOM OF CAMERA

Finally, as shown in Figure 2-6, on the bottom of the camera are the tripod socket, the battery/memory card compartment, the HDMI port, and the speaker that produces sound for videos. There also is one other item that can't be seen unless the battery compartment is open—the access lamp, located at the outside edge of the compartment, as shown in Figure 2-7.

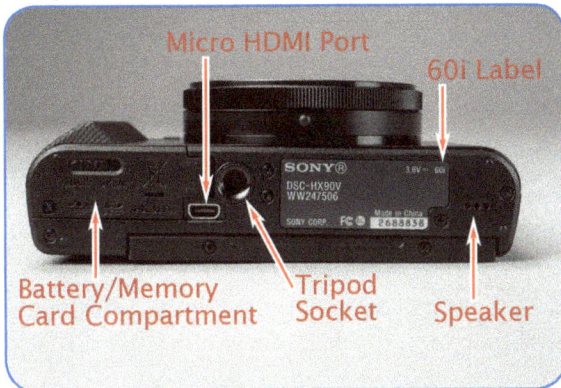

Figure 2-6. Items on Bottom of Camera

That red lamp lights up when the camera is writing data to the memory card. When the camera has taken a long series of continuous shots, the lamp may stay illuminated for several seconds. During that time, do not remove the battery or the memory card.

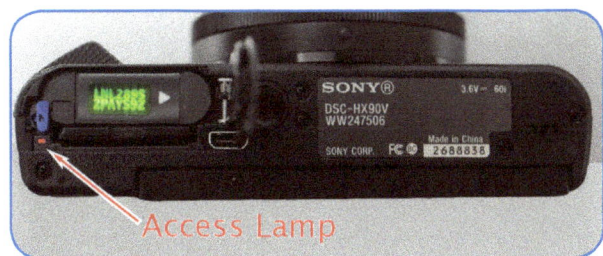

Figure 2-7. Red Access Lamp Inside Battery Compartment

The HDMI port is for connecting the camera to an HDTV to view images and videos. You can also use this port to output a video signal to a video recorder, or to a monitor so you can view the shooting information from the camera in shooting mode.

Taking Pictures in Auto Mode

Now I'll discuss how to use these controls to take still pictures and videos. Here's a list of steps to take if you want to set the camera to one of its most automatic modes and let it make (almost) all decisions for you. This is a good approach if you need to grab a quick shot without fiddling with too many settings.

1. Press the power button on top of the camera. The LCD screen will light up as the camera turns on.

2. Turn the Mode dial so the green camera icon is next to the white indicator line, as shown in Figure 2-8.

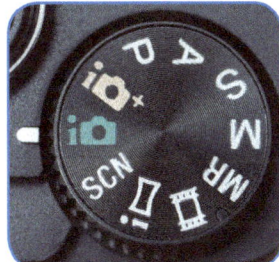

Figure 2-8. Mode Dial at Intelligent Auto

This sets the camera to the Intelligent Auto shooting mode. If you see the help screen that describes the mode (called the Mode Dial Guide), as seen in Figure 2-9, press the Center button to dismiss it. (You can dispense with that help screen altogether using the Mode Dial Guide option on screen 2 of the Setup menu, as discussed in Chapter 7.)

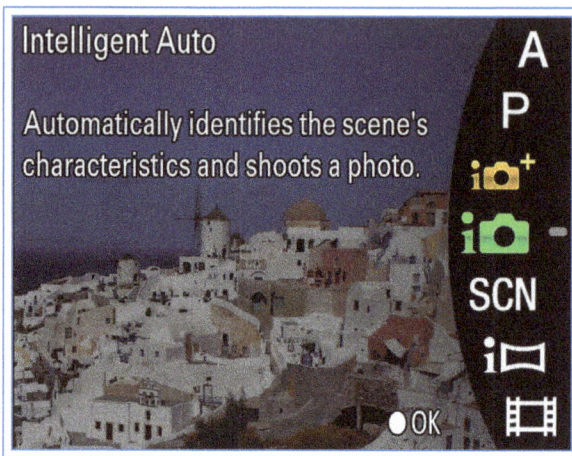

Figure 2-9. Mode Dial Guide for Intelligent Auto Mode

Smile/Face Detection	Off
Soft Skin Effect	Off
Auto Object Framing	Off
SteadyShot (Movies)	Standard
Auto Slow Shutter	On
Micref Level	Normal
Wind Noise Reduction	Off
Shooting Tip List	No setting needed
Memory	No setting needed

If you don't want to make all of these settings, don't worry; you are likely to get good images even if you don't adjust most of these settings at this point. Several of the settings apply only to video recording, but I have listed settings for them anyway, in case a video opportunity arises and you need to press the red button to make a recording. I have omitted some settings that are not available for adjustment in this shooting mode.

3. Press the Menu button to activate the menu system. As I discussed in Chapter 1, navigate through the menu screens by pressing the Right and Left buttons. You can tell which menu screen is active by looking at the small orange line (cursor) beneath the numbers. When a given screen is selected, navigate up and down through the options on that screen by pressing the Up and Down buttons or by turning the Control wheel right or left.

4. When the orange selection bar is on the option you want, press the Center button to select that item. Then, pressing the Up and Down buttons or turning the Control wheel, highlight the value you want to set for that option, and press the Center button to confirm it. You can then continue making menu settings; when you are finished with the menu system, press the Menu button to go back to the live view, so you can take pictures.

5. Using the procedure described in Step 4, make the settings shown in Table 2-1 using the menu system.

Table 2-1. Suggested Settings for Intelligent Auto Mode Still Images

Image Size	L: 18M
Aspect Ratio	4:3
Quality	Fine
File Format	MP4
Record Setting	1920 x 1080 60p 28M
Drive Mode	Single shooting
Flash Mode	Autoflash
Red Eye Reduction	Off
Focus Mode (HX90V only)	Single-shot AF
AF Illuminator	Auto
Center Lock-on AF	Off

6. Press the Menu button again to make the menu disappear, if it hasn't done so already.

7. If you are shooting in dark conditions, press the flash pop-up switch to the right. That switch is located on top of the camera behind the power button. Then press the Right button on the Control wheel, marked with a lightning bolt. A vertical menu will appear at the left side of the screen, as shown in Figure 2-10.

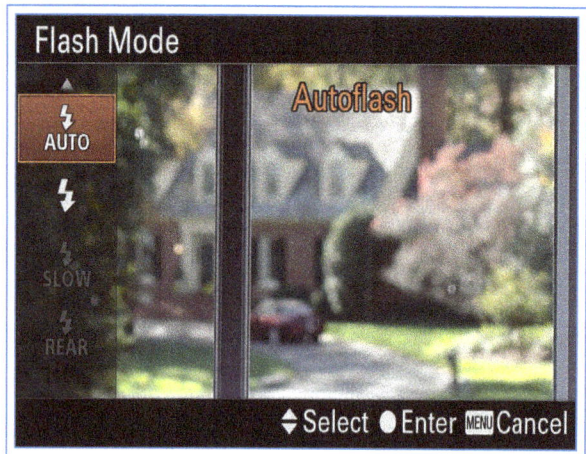

Figure 2-10. Flash Mode Menu

8. Make sure Autoflash is highlighted with the orange selection block. If it is not, press the direction buttons or turn the Control wheel to highlight it, so the Flash Mode is set to Autoflash. Press the Center button to dismiss this menu. (Table 2-1 includes

the menu setting for Flash Mode; using the Right button is another way to make that setting.)

9. Using a procedure like that in Steps 7 and 8, press the Left button, marked with a timer dial and an icon for a stack of images, and make sure the top option, showing a single rectangular frame, is selected, as shown in Figure 2-11. This sets the camera to take single shots, rather than continuous bursts. (This is the same setting shown for Drive Mode in Table 2-1.)

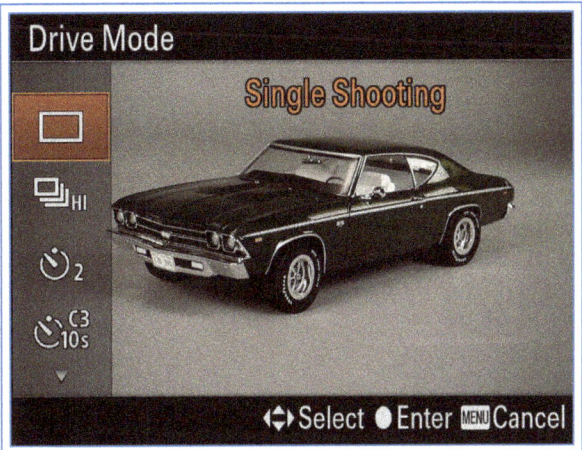

Figure 2-11. Drive Mode Set to Single Shooting

10. Aim the camera and compose the picture. Locate the zoom lever and push it to the left, toward the letter "W" on the camera, for a wider-angle shot, or to the right, toward the letter "T," to get a telephoto, zoomed-in shot.

11. Once the picture looks good, gently press the shutter button halfway and pause there. You should hear a beep and see one or more green focus brackets or small squares on the LCD, indicating sharp focus. Also look for a green disc in the extreme lower left corner of the screen. If that green disc lights up steadily, the image is in focus; if it blinks, the camera was unable to focus. In that case, you can re-aim and see if the autofocus system does better from a different distance or angle.

12. After you have made sure the focus is sharp, push the shutter button all the way to take the picture.

Variations from Fully Automatic

Although the camera takes care of the basic settings for you when it's set to Intelligent Auto mode, you can still make a number of adjustments to fine-tune the shooting process when the camera is in this automatic mode or the Superior Auto shooting mode. (The Superior Auto mode, designated by the tan-colored camera icon on the mode dial, is very similar to the Intelligent Auto mode.)

Photo Creativity Feature

The Photo Creativity feature, available only in the Intelligent Auto and Superior Auto modes, is a simple way to make adjustments to the appearance of still images and videos. I can understand why Sony presents these adjustments in this way, making them easy to use and giving them non-technical names such as "Brightness" and "Color," rather than "exposure compensation" and "white balance." However, it is somewhat confusing (to me, at least) that these same adjustments are made using different controls in the other, less-automatic shooting modes.

In any event, for now I will discuss how to make these adjustments in the Intelligent Auto and Superior Auto modes. In Chapter 3, I will discuss all of the shooting modes, and in Chapters 4 and 5 I will discuss how to make similar settings in the more advanced shooting modes. For example, I will discuss white balance in Chapter 4, where I discuss the White Balance option on the Shooting menu, and I will discuss exposure compensation in Chapter 5, in connection with the button that controls that function (the Down button, in the bottom position on the Control wheel).

With that introduction, here are details about how to make various settings in the two most automatic shooting modes using the Photo Creativity feature.

To use the Photo Creativity feature, press the Down button on the Control wheel—the button marked with the plus and minus icon and the camera icon with three plus signs at its right side, as shown in Figure 2-2 earlier. When you press that button, you will see some new icons and virtual controls appear on the display, as shown in Figure 2-12.

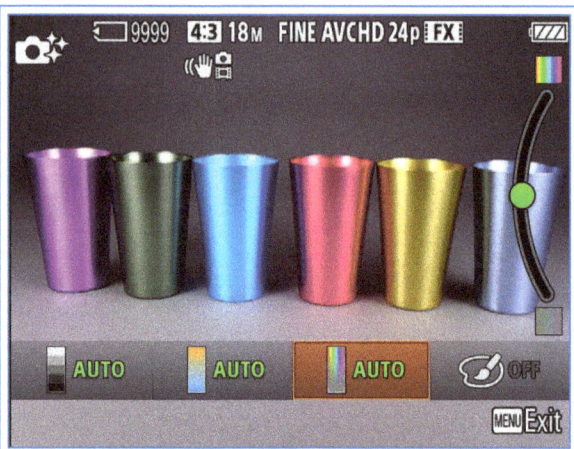

Figure 2-12. Photo Creativity Screen

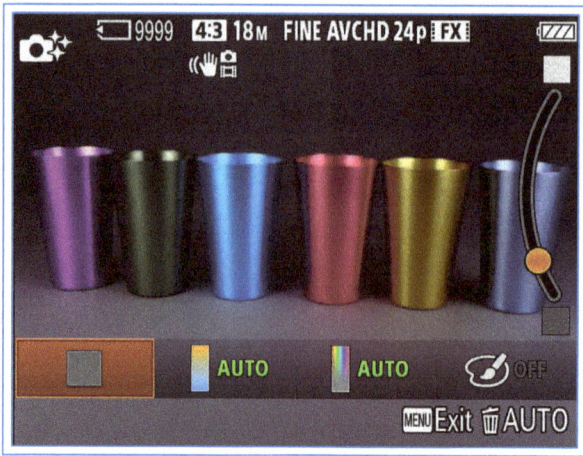

Figure 2-13. Brightness Slider Moved Toward Bottom of Scale

At the bottom of the screen are four blocks, each with an icon representing a setting. When the blocks first appear, each of the three blocks at the left should show the word AUTO, and the block at the far right, with an icon of an artist's palette and brush, should say OFF. Use the Right and Left buttons to move through these four blocks; each one will be highlighted in orange when it is selected.

You can keep pressing the Right or Left button to wrap around to the other side of the group of icons if you want. For example, when the artist's palette is highlighted, you can press the Right button one more time to move directly to the block at the far left of the screen.

When one of the blocks is highlighted in orange, you can change the value for that setting by turning the Control wheel or by pressing the Up or Down button to move an indicator disc or icon along a curved scale at the right side of the display. The display will change as appropriate to show the effect of your adjustment. For example, if you move the Color slider to the top of the curved scale, the image will appear more reddish, or "warm."

With the first three blocks, as you turn the wheel, a disc will move along the scale at the right of the screen. The disc will be green at first, but it will turn orange once the setting is changed. Also, the appearance of the icon for that block will change to show how the setting is changing, as seen in Figure 2-13.

When a block is first selected, a label for its setting will appear briefly on the screen and then disappear. The settings that are controlled by the four blocks are as follows, from left to right:

Brightness. The indicator disc starts in the middle of the scale. As you turn the Control wheel to move the disc higher, the image gets brighter; as it moves lower, the image darkens. In technical terms, this setting controls exposure compensation, which can be used in situations when the normal exposure calculated by the camera would not be ideal. For example, if a dark-colored subject, such as a bunch of grapes, is photographed against a white background, the camera's automatic exposure control is likely to underexpose the dark object, because the camera takes into account the broad expanse of white tones in the image and decreases the exposure level. With the Brightness control, you can increase the brightness level so the subject will appear properly exposed, as shown in Figure 2-14.

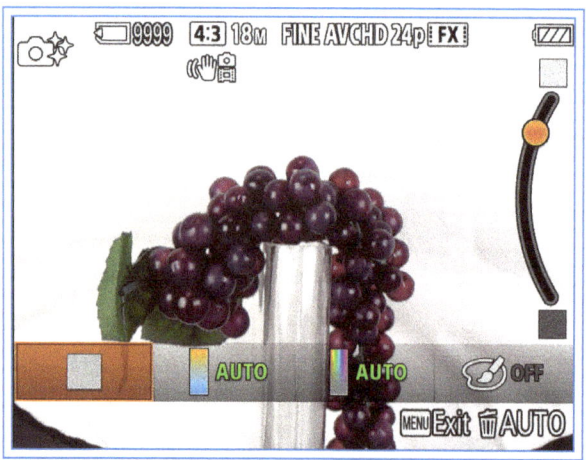

Figure 2-14. Brightness Level Adjusted Upward

Chapter 2: Basic Operations | 15

Color. This second setting from the left lets you adjust the white balance of images, though Sony uses the term "Color" to simplify things. As I will discuss in Chapter 4, the white balance setting adjusts the camera's processing of colors according to the color temperature of the light source. For example, light from incandescent bulbs has a lower color temperature than light from a bright blue sky. The lower color temperatures are considered "warmer," with a reddish or yellowish cast, and the higher ones yield colors that are considered "cooler," with a more bluish appearance. (In this case, "warm" and "cool" have to do with the appearance, rather than the actual temperature, of the subjects.)

With this setting, again, the normal value is in the center of the curved scale. To make the colors of the scene appear cooler, or more bluish, turn the Control wheel to the left to move the indicator disc toward the bottom of the scale; reverse that process to make the colors warmer, or more reddish. Figure 2-15 shows the Color setting adjusted to the bluish side.

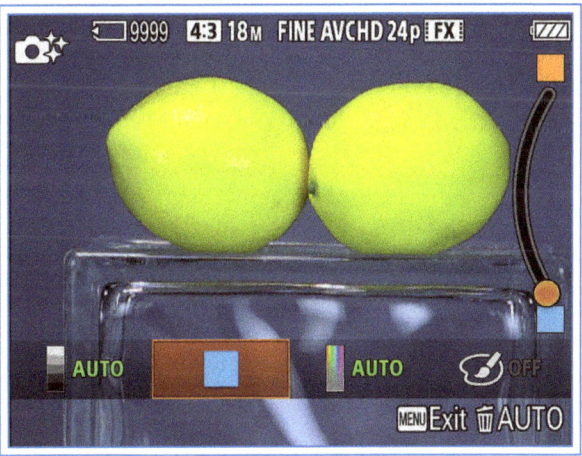

Figure 2-15. Color Slider Adjusted to Bluish Side

This adjustment does not change the actual white balance setting, which is fixed at Auto White Balance (AWB) for the automatic shooting modes; it merely tweaks the setting toward the warm or cool end of the scale. In some other shooting modes, as discussed in Chapter 4, you can make more precise adjustments to the camera's white balance through the White Balance menu option.

Vividness. The third setting from the left lets you adjust the intensity, or saturation, of colors in your images.

Again, the standard setting is in the middle of the scale; move the disc upward for more intense colors and downward for softer, less-saturated colors. In the more advanced shooting modes, you can adjust saturation in finer detail, along with contrast and sharpness, using the Creative Style menu option, as discussed in Chapter 4. Figure 2-16 shows Vividness set to its maximum.

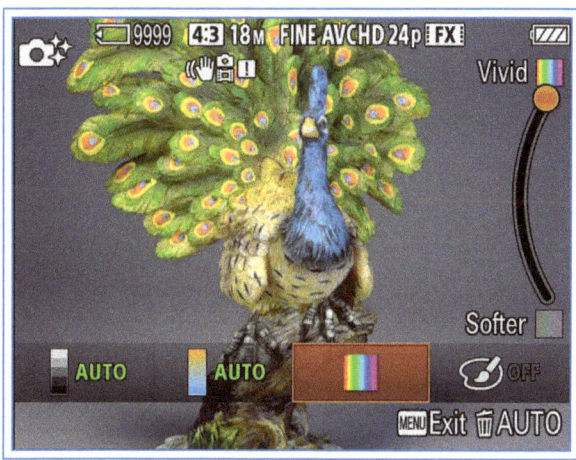

Figure 2-16. Vividness Slider Adjusted to Maximum Value

Picture Effect. The final option at the right, marked with an artist's palette, gives you access to the following settings: Toy Camera, Pop Color, Posterization Color, Posterization B/W, Retro Photo, Soft High-key, Partial Color: Red, Partial Color: Green, Partial Color: Blue, Partial Color: Yellow, and High Contrast Monochrome. These settings can produce dramatic effects, as indicated by their labels. The same settings are available through the Picture Effect item on the Shooting menu in advanced shooting modes, though there are some settings available through that menu item that cannot be made from the Photo Creativity system, such as different varieties of the Toy Camera setting as well as settings such as Watercolor and Illustration. I will discuss those settings and provide examples in Chapter 4.

You can combine more than one Photo Creativity setting to achieve various effects. For example, if you activate the Partial Color effect using the rightmost block at the bottom of the screen, you can then move the highlight to the Color or Vividness block and change the tint or intensity of the color that you selected for the Partial Color effect. Or, you can decrease the exposure of the image and also decrease the intensity of the colors by using the Brightness and Vividness controls together.

When you have moved a setting's control to the position you want, leave it there and take the picture with the control still on the screen. (Or, as noted above, you can go to another setting and adjust it as well before taking the picture.) Don't press the Menu button, because doing that will cancel the setting you just made.

To reset a setting to its original value, highlight its block and press the In-Camera Guide/Delete (?) button. For the first three blocks, this action will reset the indicator to its default value at the middle of the scale. For the Picture Effect setting, this action will turn the selected effect off, leaving no effect active. To reset all four blocks at once, turn the Mode dial to another shooting mode (such as Scene or Program), then back to the green camera icon for Intelligent Auto (or the tan icon for Superior Auto), and press the Down button to return to Photo Creativity. To exit from the Photo Creativity screen, press the Menu button.

Photo Creativity is a useful feature, and it is convenient to select one or more of its options while the camera is in Intelligent Auto or Superior Auto mode, so you don't have to invest too much effort into figuring out what settings to use. However, if you want to exercise more control over the settings, you can use one of the more advanced shooting modes with menu options and controls that let you make more precise adjustments.

Flash

Each of these camera models has a convenient built-in flash unit, which you may want to use on a regular basis. In Chapter 4 I'll provide details about the Flash Mode and Flash Compensation settings, as well as the prevention of "red eye" effects. In Appendix A, I'll discuss using external flash units, even though the camera has no flash shoe.

It's important to remember that the flash unit cannot pop up on its own, even if the flash mode is set to Fill-flash, which requires the flash to fire. You have to use the flash pop-up switch on top of the camera to release the flash before it can fire.

For this discussion, I'm assuming the camera is set to Intelligent Auto mode. In some other situations, such as with some of the Scene mode settings, the Flash menu will not appear; you will see an error message if you press the Right button when the shooting screen is active, whether the flash unit is popped up or not.

In Intelligent Auto mode, with the flash unit popped up, press the Right button once to call up the Flash Mode menu, then press the Up and Down buttons or turn the Control wheel to select a flash mode from that list. Press the Center button to confirm the selection. (As was discussed earlier, you also can summon the Flash Mode menu from the Shooting menu: Flash Mode is on the second screen of the Shooting menu. See Chapter 4 for a discussion of all items on the Shooting menu screens.)

The vertical menu at the left of the screen, shown earlier in Figure 2-10, has icons for the five flash modes—a lightning bolt with the "no" sign crossing it out, for Flash Off; a lightning bolt with the word "Auto," for Autoflash; a lightning bolt alone, for Fill-flash (meaning the flash will always fire); a lightning bolt with the word "Slow," for Slow Sync; and a lightning bolt with the word "Rear," for Rear Sync. When the camera is in Intelligent Auto mode, the last two choices will be dimmed; if you highlight one of them and press the Center button, the camera will display a message saying you cannot make that selection in this shooting mode.

I discussed earlier how to choose Autoflash. If you choose Fill-flash instead, you will see the lightning bolt icon on the screen at all times when the flash is popped up and the detailed display screen is selected. With this setting, the flash will fire regardless of whether the camera's exposure system believes flash is needed. You can use this setting when you are certain you want the flash to fire, such as in a dimly lighted room. This setting also can be of use in outdoor settings, such as when the sun is shining and you want to reduce the shadows on your subject's face. I will provide an illustration of the use of Fill-flash in Chapter 4.

When the camera is set for certain types of shooting, such as continuous shooting or using the self-timer with multiple shots, the flash is forced off and cannot be used. In some cases, such as with the Night Scene setting of Scene mode, you cannot even get the Flash Mode menu to appear; if you press the Flash button, the camera will display a message saying the flash is not available in that shooting mode, as shown in Figure 2-17.

Chapter 2: Basic Operations | 17

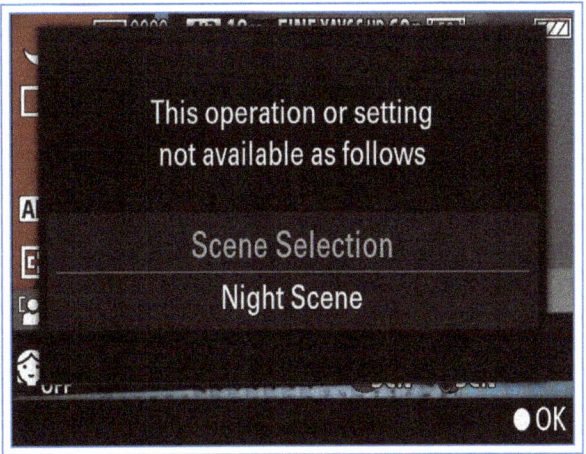

Figure 2-17. Error Message When Flash Mode Unavailable

If you set the Mode dial to P, for Program mode, and then press the Flash button to select a flash mode, you will see the same five options for Flash Mode on the menu, but this time the Flash Off and Autoflash options will be dimmed because those selections are not available in that shooting mode.

In summary, when using Intelligent Auto (or Superior Auto) mode, if you don't want the flash to fire because you are in a museum or similar location, you can select the Flash Off mode. You also can just leave the flash stored inside the camera, so it cannot pop up and fire.

If you want to let the camera decide whether to fire the flash, you can select Autoflash mode. To make sure that the flash will fire no matter what, you can select Fill-flash mode. In Chapter 4, I'll explain the other flash options, Slow Sync and Rear Sync, and I'll discuss some other flash-related topics. For now, you have the basic information you need to select a flash mode when the camera is set to the Intelligent Auto or Superior Auto shooting mode.

Drive Mode: Self-Timer and Continuous Shooting

The Drive Mode menu option includes more adjustments you can make when using Intelligent Auto mode. If you press the Control wheel's Left button, which is marked with a timer dial and an icon that looks like a stack of images, the camera will display a vertical menu for Drive Mode, as shown earlier in Figure 2-11.

Navigate through these options by pressing the Up and Down buttons or by turning the Control wheel.

I will discuss the Drive Mode menu options more fully in Chapter 4. For now, you should be aware of a few of the choices. (I will skip over some others.) If you select the top option, represented by a single rectangular frame, the camera is set for single shooting mode; when you press the shutter button, a single image is captured. With the second option, whose icon looks like a stack of images, the camera is set for continuous shooting and takes a rapid burst of images while you hold down the shutter button. You can use the Left and Right buttons to choose from Hi or Lo for the speed of shooting.

If you choose the third option, whose icon is a timer dial with a number beside it, the camera uses the self-timer. Use the Left and Right buttons to choose two, five, or 10 seconds for the timer delay. After the timer has been set, press the shutter button. The shutter will be released after the specified number of seconds. The 10-second or five-second delay is useful when you need to place the camera on a tripod and join a group photo; the two-second delay is useful to make sure the camera is not jiggled by the action of pressing the shutter button. The two-second setting helps greatly when you are taking a picture for which focusing is critical, such as an extreme closeup. I will discuss the use of the self-timer and other Drive Mode options in more detail in Chapter 4.

The Drive Mode options also can be reached as the third item on screen 2 of the Shooting menu.

There are other settings that can be made when the camera is set to Intelligent Auto or Superior Auto mode, including Image Size, Aspect Ratio, Quality, Face Detection, and others. I included suggested settings for those items in Table 2-1 earlier in this chapter, and I will discuss the details of those settings in Chapter 4.

Overview of Movie Recording

Now I'll discuss recording a short movie sequence with these cameras. With the camera powered on, turn the Mode dial to select Intelligent Auto mode (green camera icon). There is a special Movie mode setting marked by the movie-film icon on the Mode dial, but you don't have to use that mode for shooting movies; I'll discuss the use of that option and provide more details about movie-recording options in Chapter 8.

Press the Menu button to get access to the menu system, and press the Right or Left button, if necessary, enough times to move the orange cursor under the number two while the camera icon for the Shooting menu is highlighted, as shown in Figure 2-18.

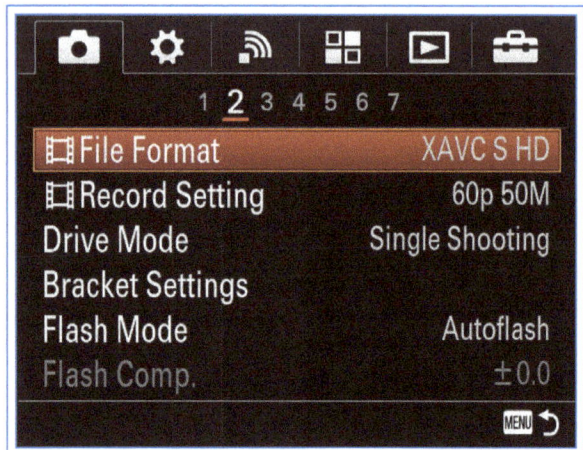

Figure 2-18. Screen 2 of Shooting Menu

The main movie-related menu items are located on the Shooting menu; there is no separate Movie menu.

On this second Shooting menu screen, highlight File Format and press the Center button to go to the submenu with three choices for the format of movie recording. For now, be sure the third option, MP4, is highlighted; that format provides good quality for your videos without requiring a special memory card and is easy to edit or upload using a computer. (As discussed in Chapter 1, if you select XAVC S HD for the movie format, you have to use a memory card with a capacity of at least 64 GB and a speed of Class 10 or greater.) The AVCHD setting provides excellent quality but can be challenging to edit and work with using a computer.

For the rest of the settings, I will provide a table like the one included earlier in this chapter for shooting still images. The settings shown in Table 2-2 are standard ones for shooting high-quality movies.

Table 2-2. Suggested Shooting Menu Settings for Movies in Intelligent Auto Mode

File Format	MP4
Record Setting	1920 x 1080 60p 28M
Focus Mode (HX90V only)	AF-S
SteadyShot (Movies)	Standard
Auto Slow Shutter	On
Micref Level	Normal
Wind Noise Reduction	Off

There are other Shooting menu settings that affect movie recording; I will discuss that topic in Chapter 8. If you are going to be shooting a scene that includes people's faces, you may want to go to the Smile/Face Detection line on screen 5 of the Shooting menu and set the Face Detection item to On. You can leave the other items set as they were for shooting still images, as listed in Table 2-1 for still shooting.

Once you have made the above settings, aim the camera at your subject, and when you are ready to start recording, press and release the red Movie button at the upper right corner of the camera's back. (If you see an error message, go to the last screen of the Custom menu, marked by a gear icon, and set the Movie Button option to Always.)

The screen will display a red REC icon in the lower left corner of the display, above a counter showing the elapsed time in the recording, as shown in Figure 2-19.

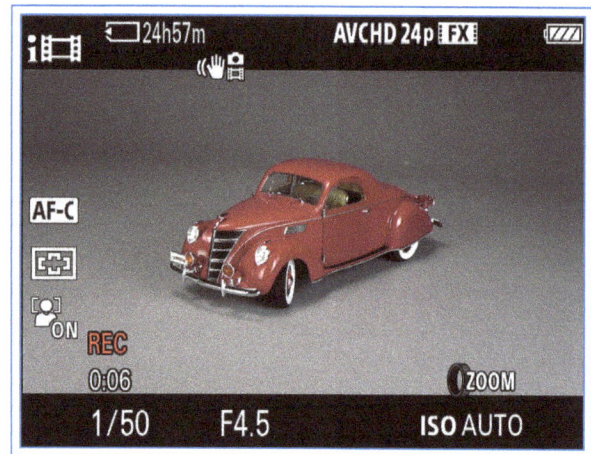

Figure 2-19. REC Icon on Screen During Video Recording

Hold the camera as steady as possible (or use a tripod), and pan (move the camera side to side) slowly if you need to. The camera will shoot until it reaches a recording limit, or until you press the Movie button again to stop the recording. (The maximum time for continuous recording of any one scene is about 29 minutes with most recording formats.) Don't be too concerned about the level of the sound that is being recorded, because you do not have much control over the audio volume while recording using the built-in microphone. I will discuss options for audio recording in Chapter 8.

The camera will automatically adjust exposure as lighting conditions change. You can zoom the lens in and out as needed, but you should do so sparingly if at all, to avoid distracting the audience and to avoid putting the sounds of zooming the lens on the sound track. When you are finished, press the Movie button again, and the recording will end.

Those are the basics for recording video with these cameras. I'll discuss movie options further in Chapter 8.

Viewing Pictures

Before I talk about more advanced settings for taking still pictures and movies, as well as other topics, I will discuss the basics of viewing your images in the camera.

Reviewing While in Shooting Mode

When you take a still picture, it will appear on the camera's display for a short time, if you have the Custom menu's Auto Review option set to turn on this function. I'll discuss details of that setting in Chapter 7. By default, a new image stays on the screen for two seconds. If you prefer, you can set that display to last for five or 10 seconds, or to be off altogether.

Reviewing Images in Playback Mode

To review images taken previously, enter playback mode by pressing the Playback button, to the lower left of the Control wheel. To view all still images and movies for a particular date, go to screen 1 of the Playback menu (marked with a triangle icon), set the View Mode option to Date View, and press the Center button on the selected date. If you prefer, you can set View Mode to show only stills, only MP4 movies, only AVCHD movies, or only XAVC S HD movies.

Once you choose a viewing option, you can scroll through images and movies by pressing the Left and Right buttons or by turning the Control wheel. Hold down the Left or Right button to move quickly through the items. You can enlarge the view of a still image by moving the zoom lever on top of the camera toward the T position, and you can scroll around in the enlarged image using the four direction buttons.

Press the zoom lever repeatedly in the other direction, toward the wide-angle setting, to return the image to normal size. You can immediately return an image to normal size by pressing the Center button or the Menu button.

When viewing an image at normal size, press the zoom lever once to the left to see an index screen with either nine or 25 thumbnail images, depending on a Playback menu option. Another press of the lever to the left brings up either a calendar screen for selecting images or videos by date, or a screen for selecting a folder, depending on the View Mode option in effect. I'll discuss other playback options in Chapter 6.

To switch among views with varying amounts of information for your recorded images, press the Display button (Up button on the Control wheel) until the view you prefer is shown.

Playing Movies

To play movies in the camera, move through your files by the methods described above until you find the movie you want to play. You should see a triangular playback icon inside a circle, as shown in Figure 2-20.

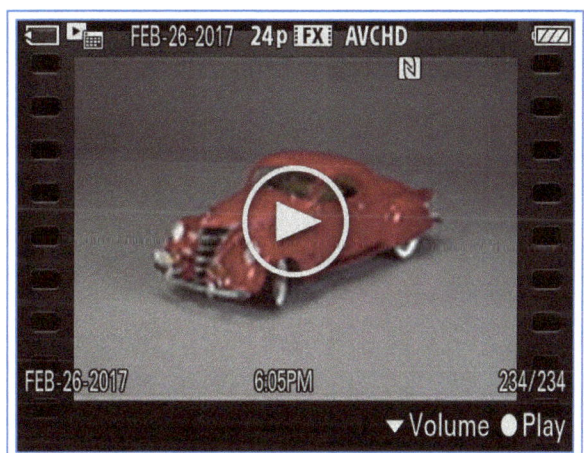

Figure 2-20. Movie Ready to Play in Camera

Press the Center button to start the movie playing. Then, as shown in Figure 2-21, you will see prompts at the bottom of the screen showing the controls you can use, including the Center button to pause. (You may have to press the Display button to show the icons.)

You also can press the Down button to bring up a more detailed set of controls on the screen, as shown in Figure 2-22.

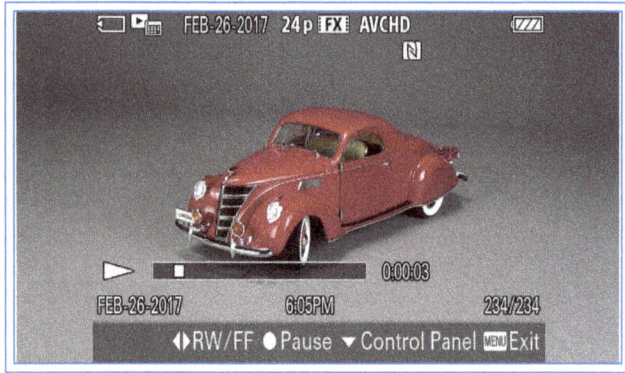

Figure 2-21. Initial Movie Playback Controls

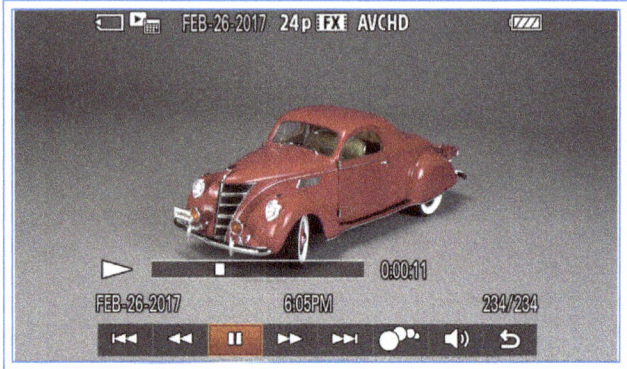

Figure 2-22. Detailed Movie Playback Controls

To change the volume, pause the movie and press the Down button to bring up the detailed controls; then navigate to the speaker icon, next to last at the right of those controls. Press the Center button to select volume, then use the Control wheel or the Right and Left buttons to adjust the volume. You also can adjust the volume before a movie starts playing, by pressing the Down button to bring up the volume control. To exit from playing the movie, press the Playback button. (I'll discuss other movie playback options in Chapter 8.)

To play your movies on a computer or edit them with video-editing software, you can use the PlayMemories Home software that is provided through the Sony web site. You also can use any program that can deal with AVCHD and MP4 video files, such as Adobe Premiere Elements, Adobe Premiere Pro, Final Cut Express, Final Cut Pro, iMovie, or Windows Movie Maker, depending on what type of computer you are using.

Movies recorded using the XAVC S HD format are saved as files with the .mp4 extension, and, in my experience, can be imported and edited with standard software that uses those files, such as iMovie for the Mac and Movie Maker for Windows-based computers. However, those files can be quite large, so you may need a computer with a large and fast storage drive and a powerful processor to edit those files efficiently.

Chapter 3: Shooting Modes

The Sony HX90V and its sister model provide many options and settings for both still images and movies. These options are selected by choosing a shooting mode as well as various menu options and other settings. I will discuss shooting modes in this chapter, Shooting menu options in Chapter 4, and settings with physical controls in Chapter 5.

To record still images, you need to select one of the available shooting modes on the Mode dial: Intelligent Auto, Superior Auto, Program Auto, Aperture Priority, Shutter Priority, Manual exposure, Scene Selection, iSweep Panorama, or Memory Recall. (The other mode on the dial is for recording movies.) So far, I have concentrated on procedures using Intelligent Auto mode. This chapter will discuss all of the shooting modes, starting with a review of the first one.

Intelligent Auto Mode

This is the mode to select for a quick shot when you don't have time to deal with settings such as ISO, white balance, aperture, shutter speed, or metering method. It's a good mode to choose when you hand the camera to someone to take a photo of you and your companions.

To set this mode, turn the Mode dial to the green camera icon, as shown in Figure 3-1.

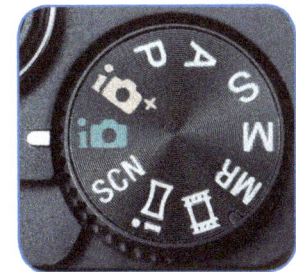

Figure 3-1. Mode Dial at Intelligent Auto

When you do this, the camera may display the Mode Dial Guide screen, showing Intelligent Auto Mode selected on a graphic Mode dial display, as seen in Figure 3-2. If the Mode Dial Guide option on screen 2 of the Setup menu is turned off, the camera will not automatically display the Mode Dial Guide.

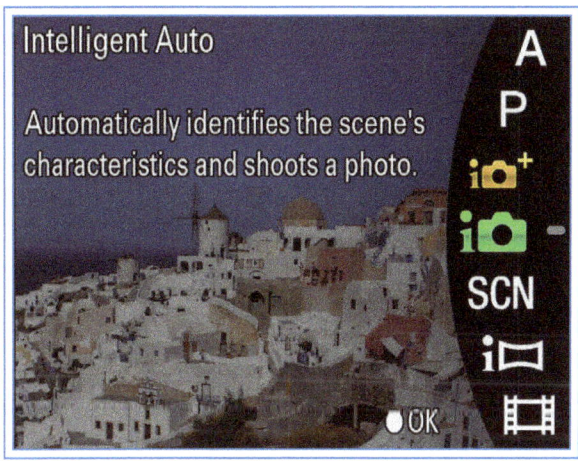

Figure 3-2. Mode Dial Guide Screen for Intelligent Auto Mode

In Intelligent Auto mode, the camera makes several decisions for you and limits your options in some ways. For example, you can't set the ISO or white balance to any value other than Auto, and you can't choose a metering method or use the Picture Effect option to alter the appearance of images. You can, however, use quite a few features, as discussed in Chapter 2, including the Photo Creativity options, continuous shooting, Flash Mode, Face Detection, and others.

In this mode (and Superior Auto mode, discussed next), the camera uses its programming to try to figure out what subject or scene you are shooting. Some subjects the camera will try to detect are Infant, Portrait, Night Portrait, Night Scene, Landscape, Backlight, Low Light, Spotlight, and Macro. It also will try to detect certain conditions, such as whether a tripod is in use, whether the subject is moving, and the brightness of the lighting, and it will display icons for those factors. So, if you see different icons when you aim at various subjects in this shooting mode, that means the camera is evaluating the scene for factors such as brightness, backlighting, the presence of human subjects, and the like, so it can use the best settings for the situation. Face detection must be turned on for the camera to recognize faces with the Infant setting or any of the Portrait settings.

For Figure 3-3, the camera evaluated a scene with a mannequin's head and appropriately used its Portrait setting. The Portrait scene-recognition icon is seen in the upper left corner of the screen.

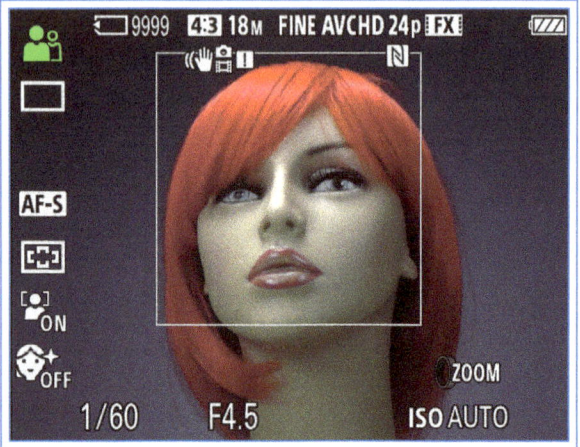

Figure 3-3. Scene Recognition for Portrait Setting

Figure 3-4 shows the use of automatic scene recognition for a knight figurine closer to the lens. The camera interpreted the scene as a macro, or closeup shot, and switched automatically into Macro mode, indicated by the flower icon. In addition, the camera correctly detected that it was attached to a tripod, as indicated by the tripod icon to the lower right of the macro symbol.

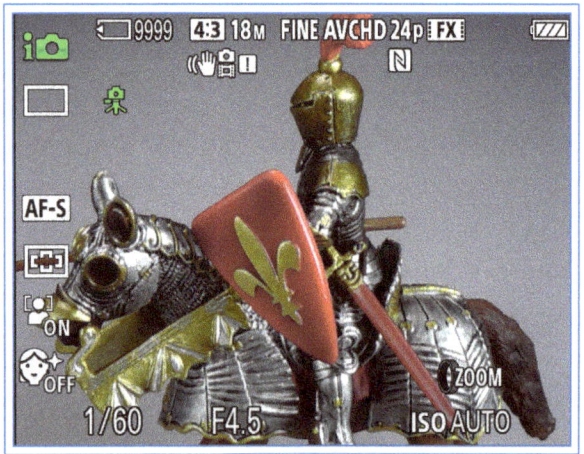

Figure 3-4. Scene Recognition for Macro Setting

Of course, scene recognition depends on the camera's programming, which may not interpret every scene the same way you would. If that becomes a problem, you may want to make individual settings using one of the more advanced shooting modes, such as Program, Aperture Priority, Shutter Priority, or Manual. Or, you can use the SCN setting on the Mode dial and select a Scene mode setting that better fits the current situation.

Superior Auto Mode

With many compact cameras, there is only one largely automatic shooting mode. These Sony cameras, however, provide you with two choices, both of which provide high degrees of automation but which have one significant difference. The second version of Auto mode, called Superior Auto, is designated on the Mode dial by the icon of a tan-colored camera with the letter "i" and a plus sign next to it, as shown in Figure 3-5.

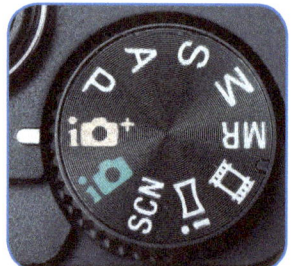

Figure 3-5. Mode Dial at Superior Auto

Superior Auto mode includes all functions of Intelligent Auto mode, and adds one extra feature. In Superior Auto mode, as in Intelligent Auto mode, the camera uses its scene recognition capability to determine what subject matter or conditions are present, such as a portrait, a dimly lit scene, and the like. For many of these subjects, the camera operates the same way as in Intelligent Auto mode.

However, with situations involving dimly lit or backlit scenes, the camera takes a different approach: It will take a rapid burst of shots and combine them internally into a single image with higher quality than would be possible with a single shot. The higher quality can be achieved because the camera generally has to raise the ISO setting to a fairly high level, which introduces visual "noise" into the image. By taking multiple shots and then merging them, the camera can average out and cancel some of the noise, thereby increasing the quality of the resulting image.

One problem with this system is that you, the photographer, can't control when the camera uses this burst shooting technique. The camera will evaluate the lighting and use this technique if the lighting appears to be excessively dark or if backlighting is detected.

When the camera believes this option is appropriate, it fires a quick series of shots; you will hear the rapid firing of the shutter. Then, it will take longer than usual for the camera to process the multiple shots into a single image; you will likely see a message saying "Processing" on the screen for several seconds. When the camera is using this operation, which Sony calls "Overlay," you will see a small white icon in the upper left corner of the display that looks like a stack of frames with a plus sign at its upper right corner, as shown in Figure 3-6.

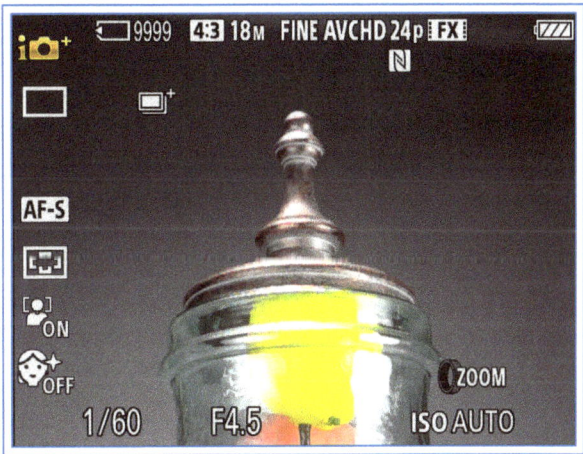

Figure 3-6. Overlay Icon in Upper Left Corner of Display

I have not found much advantage from using the Superior Auto setting. However, the overlay feature may improve the quality of an image, so it is not a bad idea to set the camera to the Superior Auto mode when you are shooting in low-light or backlit conditions. As a general rule, though, I prefer to use a mode such as Program, discussed below, and set my own values for items such as DRO, HDR, ISO, and metering mode.

Program Mode

Choose this mode by turning the Mode dial to the P setting, as shown in Figure 3-7.

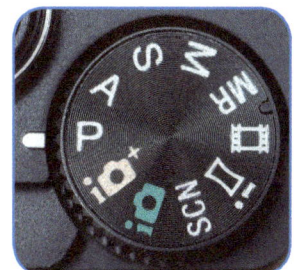

Figure 3-7. Mode Dial at Program

Program mode (also called Program Auto mode) lets you control many settings on the camera, apart from shutter speed and aperture, which the camera chooses on its own. You can override the automatic exposure to a fair extent by using exposure compensation, as discussed in Chapter 5, as well as exposure bracketing, discussed in Chapter 4, and Program Shift, discussed later in this section. You don't have to make a lot of decisions if you don't want to, because the camera will make reasonable choices as defaults. The camera can choose a shutter speed as long as one second or as short as 1/2000 second. It can use apertures from f/3.5 to f/6.4. (Sony has limited the range of aperture settings in this mode; in other modes, the aperture can be set to its most narrow value of f/8.0.)

The Program Shift function, which is available only in Program mode, works as follows. When you aim the camera at your subject, the camera will display its chosen settings for shutter speed and aperture in the lower left corner of the display. At that point, turn the Control wheel on the back of the camera. The values for shutter speed and aperture will change, if possible under current conditions, to different values for both settings while keeping the same overall exposure of the scene.

(HX90V only) You also can use the Control ring (the large ring around the lens) to make this setting, if the Control Ring option is set to the Standard setting through the Custom Key Settings item on screen 4 of the Custom menu, as discussed in Chapter 7. If you use the Control ring for Program Shift, you will see two circular scales on the display, with shutter speed and aperture values that shift as you turn the ring. (A similar display is visible at the bottom of the screen if you use the Control wheel, but only if the Exposure Settings Guide menu option is turned on through screen 2 of the Custom menu.)

With the Program Shift option, the camera "shifts" the original exposure to any of the matched pairs that appear as you turn the Control wheel. For example, if the original exposure was f/3.0 at 1/30 second, you may see equivalent pairs of f/4.0 at 1/25, f/4.5 at 1/20, and f/5.0 at 1/15, among others. When Program Shift is in effect, the P icon in the upper left corner of the screen will have an asterisk to its right, as shown in Figure 3-8.

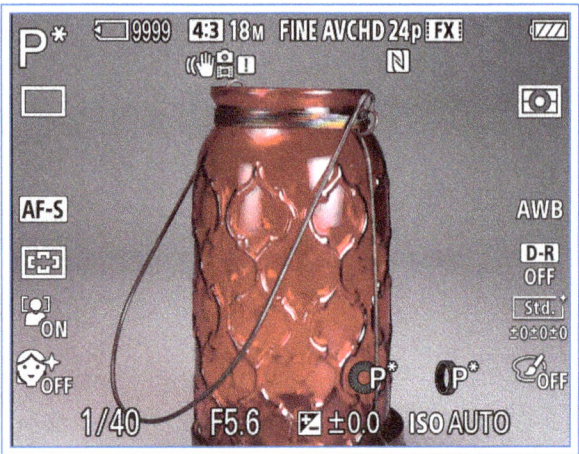

Figure 3-8. Program Shift Icon on Display Screen

To cancel Program Shift, turn the Control wheel or Control ring (HX90V only) until the original settings are back in effect or release the flash by pressing the flash pop-up button. (Program Shift cannot function when the flash is in use.)

Program Shift is useful if, for example, you want to let the camera make the original exposure setting but you want a faster shutter speed to stop action or a wider aperture to blur the background. Of course, if you need to use a particular shutter speed or aperture, you probably should use Aperture Priority mode or Shutter Priority mode. However, Program Shift is a good option to have when you're taking pictures quickly using Program mode and you need a fast way to tweak the settings somewhat.

One important aspect of Program mode is that it expands the choices available through the Shooting menu, which controls many of the camera's settings. You will be able to make choices involving ISO sensitivity, metering method, DRO/HDR, white balance, Creative Style, and others that are not available in the Auto or Scene modes. I won't discuss those settings here; see Chapter 4 for information about all of the different selections that are available.

Aperture Priority Mode

You set the camera to the Aperture Priority shooting mode by turning the Mode dial to the A setting, as shown in Figure 3-9. In this mode, you select the aperture setting and the camera will select a shutter speed that will result in normal exposure, if possible.

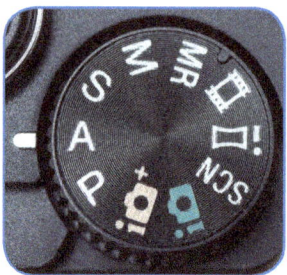

Figure 3-9. Mode Dial at Aperture Priority

The main reason to choose this mode is so you can select an aperture to achieve a broad depth of field, with objects in focus at different distances from the lens, or a shallow depth of field, with only one object in sharp focus and other parts of the image blurred to reduce distractions. With a narrow aperture (higher f-stop number) such as f/8.0, the depth of field will be relatively broad; with a wider aperture such as f/3.5, it will be shallower, resulting in the possibility of a blurred background.

In Figure 3-10 and Figure 3-11, I made the same shot with two different aperture settings. I focused on the apple in the foreground in each case. For Figure 3-10, the aperture of the camera was set to f/3.5, the widest setting available.

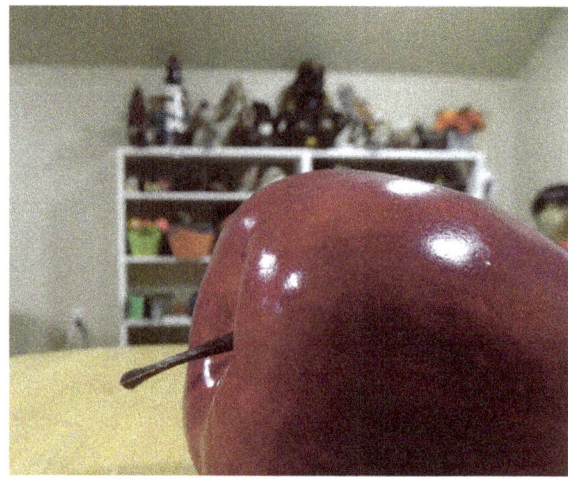

Figure 3-10. Aperture Set to f/3.5

With this setting, because the depth of field at this aperture was somewhat shallow, the objects in the background are blurry. I took Figure 3-11 with the camera's aperture set to f/8.0, the narrowest possible, resulting in a broader depth of field, and consequently bringing the background into somewhat sharper focus.

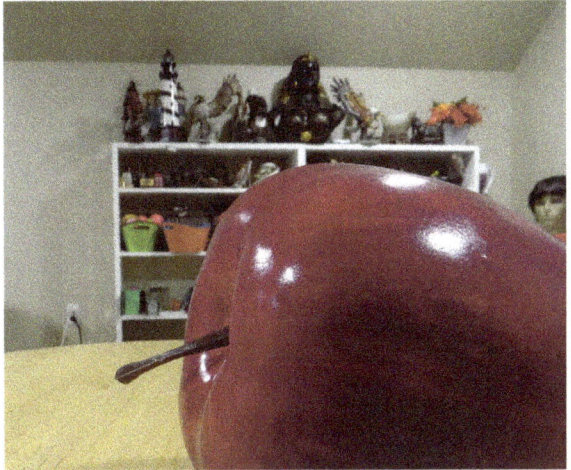

Figure 3-11. Aperture Set to f/8.0

With cameras like the HX80 and HX90V, which have a fairly small digital sensor and do not have a very wide maximum aperture, the blurred-background effect from a wide aperture is not that dramatic, because of the laws of optics. You can achieve a much more noticeable effect of this sort using a camera with a larger sensor and a wider aperture range, such as any camera from the Sony RX100 series or a full-frame camera such as the Sony RX1R II. However, these two photos illustrate the general effects of varying your aperture by setting it wider (lower numbers) when you want to blur the background and narrower (higher numbers) when you want to enjoy a broad depth of field and keep subjects at varying distances in sharp focus.

The blurred background look, sometimes called "bokeh," can be useful to isolate your subject by de-emphasizing a distracting background. Even with a small-sensor camera such as the HX80 or HX90V, you can achieve this effect by zooming the lens to a telephoto setting, such as 100mm or more, getting as close to the subject as possible, and separating the subject from the background as much as possible. Figure 3-12 is an image I took using that approach, to illustrate the bokeh effect more dramatically than is possible by just varying the aperture.

Here are the steps to set the aperture. After moving the Mode dial to the A setting, use the Control wheel to change the aperture. As you turn the wheel, the camera will display a sliding scale of values at the bottom of the screen, if the Exposure Settings Guide option on the Custom menu is turned on.

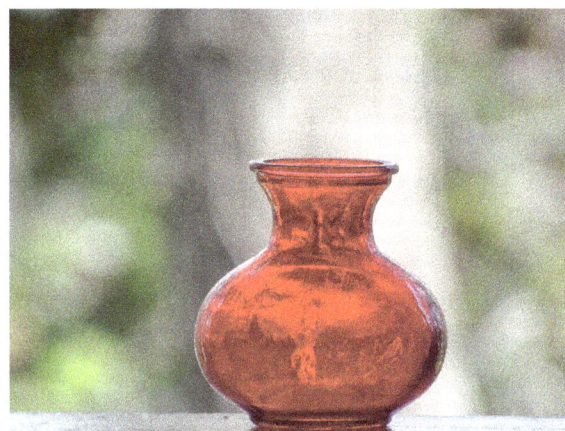

Figure 3-12. Blurred Background Example Using Zoom Effect

(HX90V only) You also can use the Control ring to set the aperture. If the Control ring does not change the aperture, check the setting for the Control Ring in the Custom Key Settings item on the Custom menu, as discussed in Chapter 7; that menu option has to be set to Standard or Aperture for the ring to carry out this function. If you use the Control ring to set the aperture, the camera will display a circular scale showing the changing aperture values, as seen in Figure 3-13, and the selected value will also appear in the bottom center of the screen.

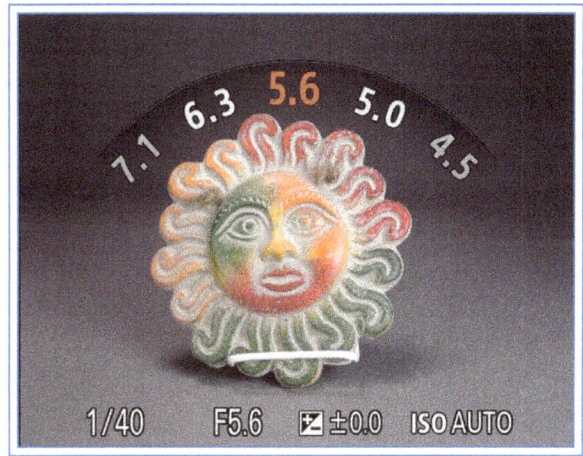

Figure 3-13. Display When Control Ring Sets Aperture (HX90V)

The available aperture settings range from f/3.5 to f/8.0, though the widest settings, such as f/3.5, are available only at the wide-angle focal lengths, as discussed later in this section. In Aperture Priority mode, the camera can select shutter speeds from 1/2000 second to eight seconds.

Although, in most cases, the camera will be able to select a corresponding shutter speed that results in a normal exposure, there may be times when this is not possible. For example, if you are taking pictures in a very bright location with the aperture set to f/3.5, the camera may not be able to set a shutter speed fast enough to yield a normal exposure. In that case, the fastest possible shutter speed (1/2000) will flash on the display to show that a normal exposure cannot be made using the chosen aperture. The camera will let you take the picture, but it may be too bright to be usable.

Similarly, if conditions are too dark for a good exposure at the aperture you have selected, the slowest possible shutter speed (8", meaning eight seconds) will flash.

In situations where conditions are too bright or dark for a good exposure, the camera's display will become bright or dark, giving you notice of the problem.

As I noted earlier, not all apertures are available at all times. The widest aperture, f/3.5, is available only when the lens is zoomed out to its wide-angle setting (zoom lever moved toward the W). At the highest zoom levels, the widest aperture available is f/6.4.

To see an illustration of this point, here is a quick test. Zoom the lens out by moving the zoom lever all the way to the left, toward the W label. Then select Aperture Priority mode and set the aperture to f/3.5. Now zoom the lens in by moving the zoom lever to the right. After the zoom is finished, the aperture will have changed to f/6.4 because that is the limit for the aperture at the full-telephoto zoom level. (The aperture will change back to f/3.5 if you zoom back to the wide-angle setting.)

Because of the small sensor and limited aperture range of these cameras, Aperture Priority mode is not necessarily the best choice for many photographs. However, if you want to blur the background of a portrait somewhat, or you want to ensure that the depth of field for a group photo is as large as possible, keeping all subjects in sharp focus, it is useful to be able to select the appropriate aperture yourself.

Shutter Priority Mode

In Shutter Priority mode, you choose the shutter speed and the camera will set the corresponding aperture to achieve a proper exposure of the image if it can.

In this mode, designated by the S position on the Mode dial, as shown in Figure 3-14, you can set the shutter to be open for a time ranging from 30 seconds to 1/2000 of a second. If you are photographing fast action, such as a baseball swing or a hurdles event at a track meet, and you want to stop the motion with a minimum of blur, you should select a fast shutter speed, such as 1/1000 of a second.

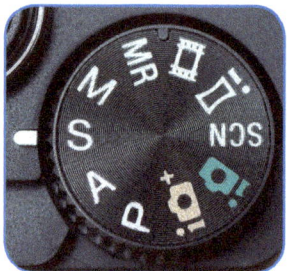

Figure 3-14. Mode Dial at Shutter Priority

To illustrate the effects of different shutter speeds, I photographed a cup of uncooked rice being poured into a transparent pitcher, using very different shutter speeds for two different images. For Figure 3-15, I set the shutter speed to 1/1000 second. In that image, you can see many of the individual grains of rice appearing as if they are frozen in mid-air.

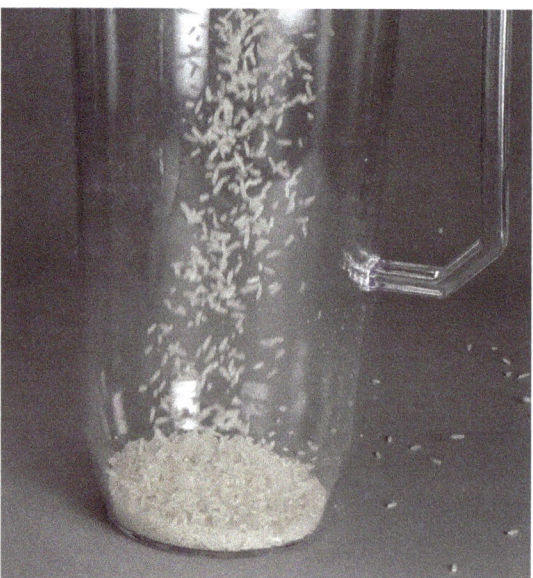

Figure 3-15. Shutter Speed Set to 1/1000 Second

For Figure 3-16, I used a much slower shutter speed of 1/30 second, which made the grains of rice appear in a continuous stream, almost like a flow of milk.

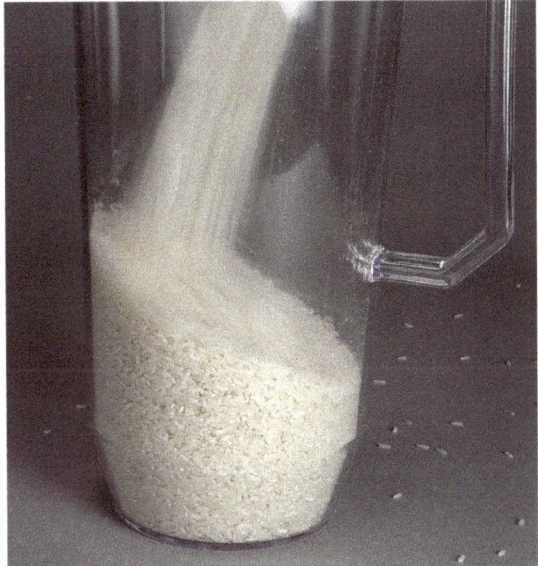

Figure 3-16. Shutter Speed Set to 1/30 Second

Choose this mode by turning the Mode dial to the S position, as seen in Figure 3-14. Select the shutter speed by turning the Control wheel. As with Aperture Priority mode, the camera will display a sliding scale of values as you turn the Control wheel to set the shutter speed, if you have the Exposure Settings Guide option turned on in the Custom menu.

(HX90V only) You also can set the shutter speed by turning the Control ring. The Control Ring function must be set to Standard or Shutter Speed using the Custom Key Settings option on the Custom menu for the ring to control shutter speed. The camera will display a circular scale when you use the Control ring to make the setting.

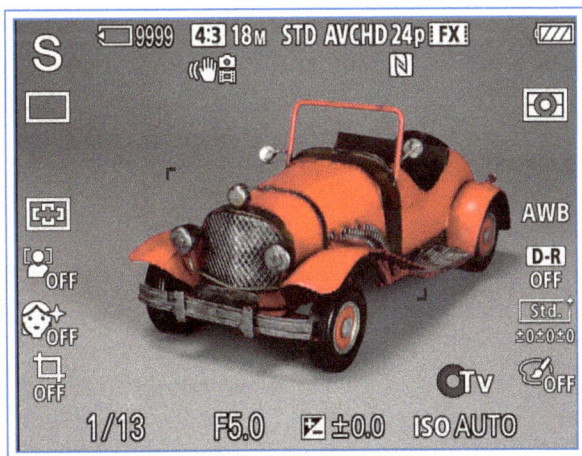

Figure 3-17. Shutter Speed Display on HX80 Camera

Although the Mode dial uses the letter "S" to stand for Shutter Priority, on the detailed display screen, as shown in Figure 3-17 on the HX80, the camera uses the notation Tv in the lower right corner, next to the icon showing that the Control wheel can be used to make this setting. (On the HX90V, there will be icons for the Control ring's function as well.) Tv stands for time value, a notation often used for this shooting mode.

As you cycle through various shutter speeds, the camera will select the appropriate aperture to achieve a proper exposure, if possible. As I discussed in connection with Aperture Priority mode, if you select a shutter speed for which the camera cannot select an aperture for a normal exposure, the display will change appearance to indicate how dark or light the resulting shot will be, and the aperture reading at the bottom of the display will flash. The flashing aperture means that proper exposure at that shutter speed is not possible at any available aperture, according to the camera's calculations.

For example, if you set the shutter speed to 1/320 second in a fairly dark indoor environment, the aperture number (which will be f/3.5, the widest setting, if the zoom is set to wide angle) may flash, indicating that proper exposure is not possible, and the display may be quite dark. As I discussed for Aperture Priority, you can still take the picture if you want to, though it may not be usable. A similar situation may take place if you select a slow shutter speed (such as four seconds) in a relatively bright location.

Manual Exposure Mode

One of the features of the HX80 and HX90V that distinguish them from simpler cameras is their fully manual exposure mode, a great tool for photographers who want to have full control over exposure decisions.

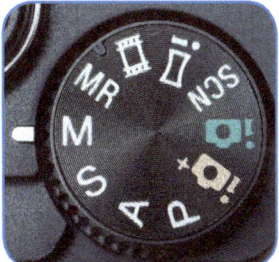

Figure 3-18. Mode Dial at Manual Exposure

To control exposure manually, set the Mode dial to the M indicator, as shown in Figure 3-18. You now have to control both shutter speed and aperture by setting them yourself. With the HX80, you need to use the Control wheel to adjust both aperture and shutter speed. To do that, press the Down button to switch between the two selections. When you press the Down button, either the shutter speed number or the aperture number on the display will turn orange for about 10 seconds to show that that value is currently being controlled by the Control wheel. Also, the label beside the gray icon for the Control wheel in the lower right corner of the display will change between Av (for aperture value) and Tv (for time value) when you press the Down button to switch the wheel's function. Figure 3-19 shows the HX80 display when the Control wheel is controlling shutter speed.

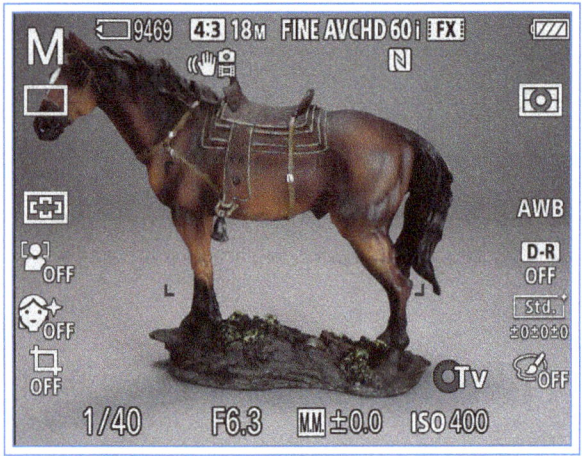

Figure 3-19. Display When Control Wheel Sets Shutter Speed (HX80)

(HX90V only) If you want, you can control both aperture and shutter speed using the Control wheel, as described above. However, you also have the option of using the Control ring to adjust the aperture, as long as the Control ring item for the Custom Key Settings menu option is set to Standard or Aperture. In that case, turn the Control ring to set the aperture and turn the Control wheel to set the shutter speed.

As you adjust shutter speed and aperture, a third value, to the right of the aperture value, also may change. That value is a positive, negative, or zero number. The meaning of the number is different depending on the current ISO setting. (In Chapter 4, I'll provide more details about the ISO setting, which controls how sensitive the camera's sensor is to light. With a higher ISO value, the sensor is more sensitive and the image is exposed more quickly, so the shutter speed can be faster or the aperture more narrow, or both.)

To set the ISO value, press the Menu button to access the Shooting menu, go to the third screen, and highlight the ISO item. Press the Center button to bring up the ISO menu, as shown in Figure 3-20, and scroll through the selections using the Up and Down buttons or by turning the Control wheel.

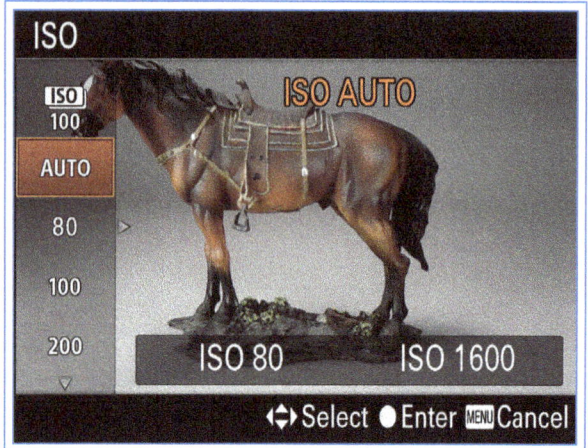

Figure 3-20. ISO Menu

Choose a low number like 80 or 100 to maximize image quality when there is plenty of light; use a higher number in dim light. Higher ISO settings are likely to cause visual "noise," or graininess, in your images. Generally speaking, you should try to set ISO no higher than 800 to ensure the highest image quality.

If the ISO value is set to a specific number, such as 100, 200, or 800, then, in Manual exposure mode, the icon at the bottom center of the display is a box containing the letters "M.M.," which stand for "metered manual," as shown in Figure 3-19.

In this situation, the number next to the M.M. icon represents any deviation from what the camera's metering system considers normal exposure. So, even though you are setting the exposure manually, the camera will let you know whether the selected aperture and shutter speed will produce a standard exposure.

If the aperture, shutter speed, and ISO values you have selected will result in a darker exposure than normal, the M.M. value will be negative, and vice-versa. This value can vary only by +2.0 or -2.0 EV (exposure value) units; after that, the value will flash, meaning the camera considers the exposure excessively abnormal.

Of course, you can ignore the M.M. indicator; it is there only to give you an idea of how the camera would

Chapter 3: Shooting Modes

expose the image. You very well may want part or all of the scene to be darker or lighter than the metering would indicate to be "correct."

As with Aperture Priority and Shutter Priority modes, the camera's display will become unusually bright or dim to indicate that current settings would result in an abnormal exposure.

If, instead of a specific value, you have set ISO to Auto ISO, the icon at the bottom center of the screen changes. In this situation, the camera displays the exposure compensation icon, which contains a plus and minus sign, as shown in Figure 3-21.

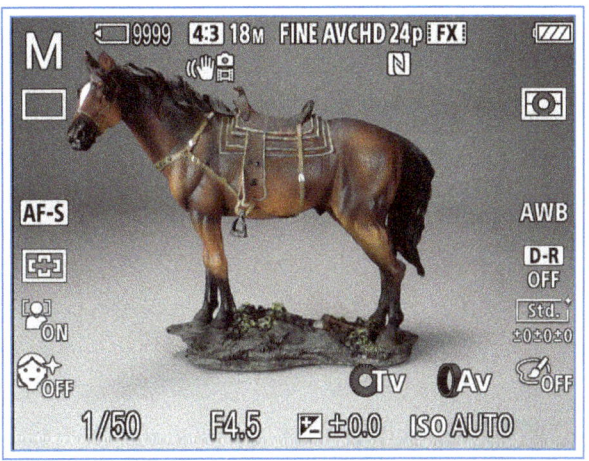

Figure 3-21. Manual Exposure Display When Auto ISO in Effect

The reason for this change is that, when you use Auto ISO in Manual exposure mode, the camera can likely produce a normal exposure by adjusting the ISO. There is no need to display the M.M. value, which shows deviation from a normal exposure. Instead, the camera lets you adjust exposure compensation, so you can set the exposure to be darker or brighter than the camera's autoexposure system would produce.

To set exposure compensation in Manual mode, you cannot use the ordinary control for that purpose—the Down button—because that button toggles the function of the Control wheel for controlling aperture or shutter speed, as discussed above. To control exposure compensation in Manual mode, you can use the Exposure Compensation item on screen 3 of the Shooting menu, or you can assign exposure compensation to the Center, Left, Right, or In-Camera Guide button. You make that assignment using the Custom Key Settings option on the last screen of the Custom menu, as discussed in Chapter 7. You also can use the Function menu to adjust exposure compensation, if that adjustment has been included in that menu, as discussed in Chapter 7.

(HX90V only) You also can assign exposure compensation to the Control ring using the Custom Key Settings menu option.

With Manual exposure mode, the settings for aperture and shutter speed are independent of each other. When you change one, the other one stays unchanged until you adjust it manually. But the effect of this system is different depending on whether you have selected a specific value for ISO as opposed to Auto ISO.

If you select a numerical value for ISO, which can range from 80 to 3200 or even higher when Multi Frame Noise Reduction is selected for the ISO setting, the camera leaves the creative decision about exposure entirely up to you, even if the resulting photograph would be washed out by excessive exposure or underexposed to the point of near-blackness.

However, if you select Auto ISO for the ISO setting, then, as discussed above, the camera will adjust the ISO to achieve a normal exposure if possible. In this case, Manual exposure mode becomes like a different shooting mode altogether. You might call this the "aperture and shutter speed priority mode," because you are able to set both aperture and shutter speed but still have the camera adjust exposure automatically by changing the ISO value.

The ability to use Auto ISO in Manual exposure mode is very useful. For example, suppose you are taking photographs of a craftsman using tools in a dimly lighted area. You may want to use a narrow aperture such as f/7.1 to achieve a broad depth of field and keep the tools and other items in focus, but you also may want to use a fast shutter speed, such as 1/100 second, to freeze action. If you use Aperture Priority mode, the camera will choose the shutter speed; with Shutter Priority mode, the camera will choose the aperture, and with Program mode, the camera will choose both values. Only by using Manual exposure mode with Auto ISO can you choose both aperture and shutter speed and still have the camera find a good exposure setting automatically.

Even with the ability to use Auto ISO, though, there may be situations in which the camera cannot produce a normal exposure. This could happen if you have limited the range of the Auto ISO setting by setting a narrow range between the minimum and maximum settings for Auto ISO. It also could happen if you have chosen extreme settings for aperture and shutter speed, such as 1/500 second at f/8.0 in dark conditions. In such situations, the ISO Auto label and the exposure compensation value at the bottom of the display will flash, indicating that a normal exposure cannot be achieved with these settings.

The range of apertures you can set in Manual mode is the same as for Aperture Priority mode: f/3.5 to f/8.0. (As in other modes, the widest aperture available is f/6.4 when the lens is zoomed in.)

The range of shutter speeds in Manual mode is the same as for Shutter Priority mode: 1/2000 second to 30 seconds.

I use Manual exposure mode often, for various purposes. One use is to take images at different exposures to combine into a composite HDR image, as seen in Figure 3-22, where I took four photos of the same subject at different exposure levels, and merged them into the final image using Photomatix HDR (high dynamic range) software, to achieve this exotic appearance. I will discuss HDR images in Chapter 4.

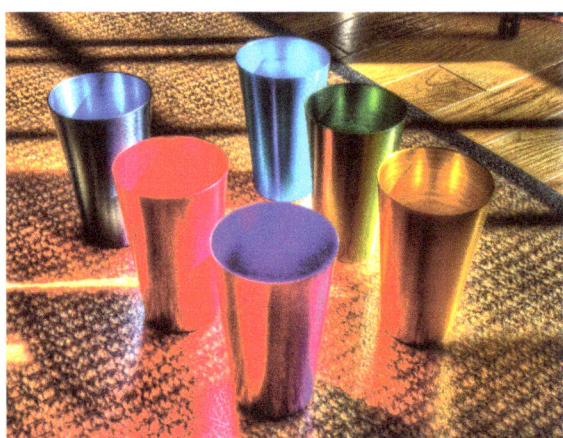

Figure 3-22. HDR Image From Several Manual Exposure Shots

I also use Manual mode when using external flash with the camera, as discussed in Appendix A, because the external flash does not interact with the camera's autoexposure system.

Manual mode also is useful for some special types of photography, such as making silhouettes or other images in which you need to control the exposure in unusual ways.

Scene Mode

Unlike other modes, Scene mode does not have a single defining feature, such as permitting control over one or more aspects of exposure. Instead, when you select Scene mode and then choose a scene type within that mode, you are telling the camera what sort of environment the picture is being taken in and what type of image you are looking for, and you are letting the camera make the decisions as to what settings to use to produce that result.

With most scene types, you cannot select several options that are available in the advanced shooting modes, such as Creative Style, Picture Effect, Metering Mode, White Balance, Focus Area, and ISO. There also are some settings that are available with certain scene types but not others, as discussed later in this chapter.

Although some photographers may feel that Scene mode limits creative decisions, I find it useful. You don't have to use the scene types only for their labeled purposes; some of them may offer settings that are useful for scenarios you regularly encounter.

You select Scene mode by turning the Mode dial to the SCN indicator, as shown in Figure 3-23.

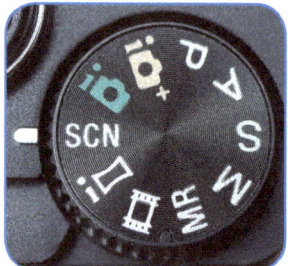

Figure 3-23. Mode Dial at SCN Setting

Now, unless you want to use the setting that is already in place, you need to pick one from the list of 15 scene types. There are several ways to do this, depending on current menu settings.

If Mode Dial Guide is turned on through screen 2 of the Setup menu, then, whenever you turn the Mode dial to the SCN setting and press the Center button, the Scene Selection menu in Figure 3-24 appears.

Chapter 3: Shooting Modes | 31

If Mode Dial Guide is not turned on, or if the camera is already in Scene mode, you can use the Shooting menu to call up the Scene Selection screen. Navigate to screen 6 of the Shooting menu and choose the Scene Selection item, as shown in Figure 3-25.

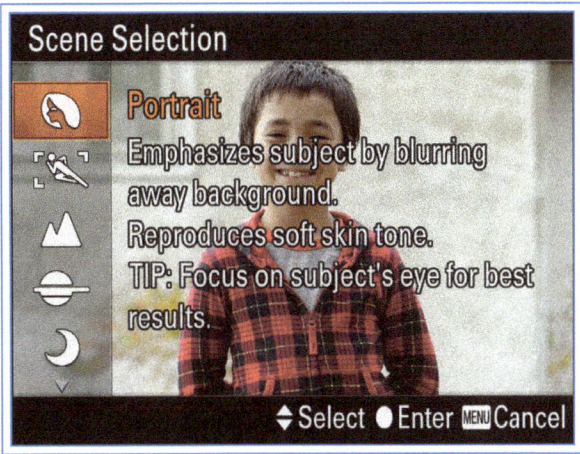

Figure 3-24. Scene Selection Menu

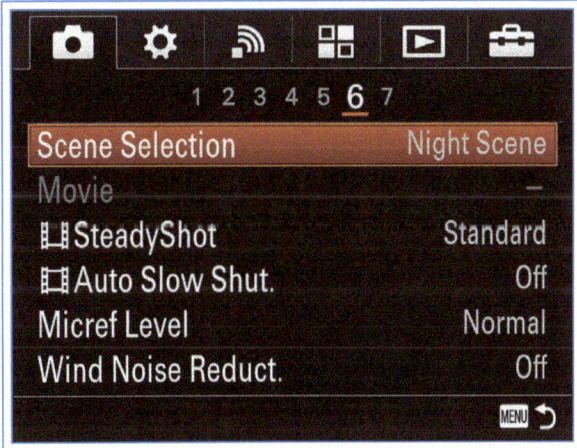

Figure 3-25. Scene Selection Option on Shooting Menu

Once the Scene Selection menu is displayed, scroll through the 15 selections using the Up and Down buttons or the Control wheel. Press the Center button to select a setting and return to the shooting screen. You will see an icon representing that setting in the upper left corner of the display. (You may need to press the Display button to see the screen that shows the scene setting icon; the icon will disappear after a few seconds on some display screens.) For example, Figure 3-26 shows the display when the Gourmet setting is selected.

For each scene type the camera displays a screen with a description of the setting's uses as you move the selector over it, as shown in Figure 3-24, so you are not left to puzzle out what each icon represents. As you press the Up or Down button or turn the Control wheel to move the selector over the other scene types, when you reach the bottom or top edge of the screen, the selector wraps around to the first or last setting and continues going.

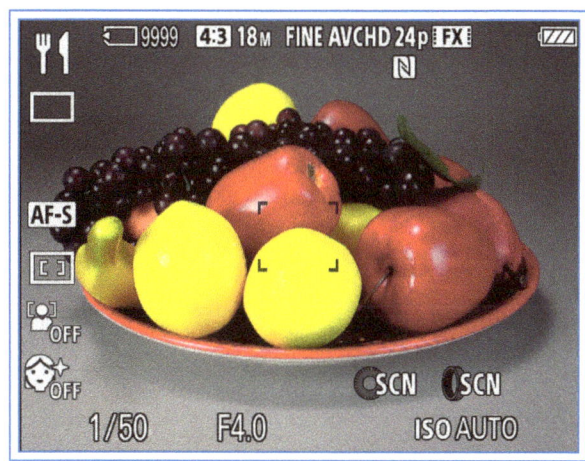

Figure 3-26. Icon for Gourmet Scene Type on Shooting Screen

There is one more way to select a scene type, which is the easiest of all. You can turn the Control wheel in Scene mode to change scene types. With that option, the camera cycles through the various scene icons in the upper left corner of the display.

(HX90V only) If the Control ring is set to its Standard setting, when the shooting screen is displayed in Scene mode, you can turn the Control ring to cycle through the various scene types. You will see a circular display as the ring turns, as shown in Figure 3-27.

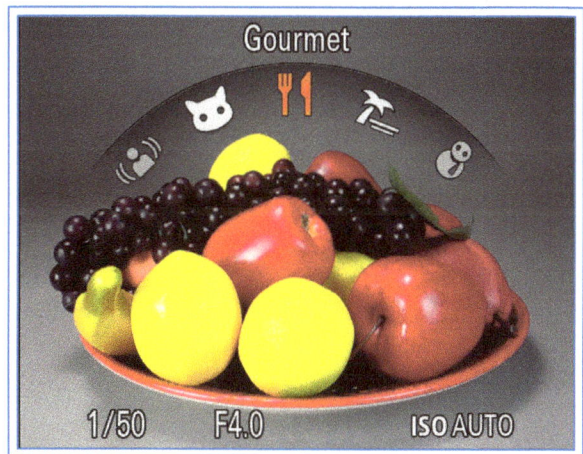

Figure 3-27. Display When Control Ring Selects Scene Types (HX90V)

After you stop turning the ring, the icon for the selected scene type will appear in the upper left corner. (If you are using manual focus or DMF (Direct Manual Focus) this will not work, because the Control ring will adjust focus and will not be available to display scene types.)

That's all you have to do to select a scene type. But you need to know something about each option to decide whether it's one you would want to use. In general, each scene type carries with it a variety of values, including things like focus mode, flash status, range of shutter speeds, sensitivity to various colors, and others.

Note that some settings are designed for certain types of shooting, rather than particular subjects such as sunsets or fireworks. For example, the Anti Motion Blur and High Sensitivity settings are designed for difficult shooting environments, such as dimly lighted areas.

Portrait

The Portrait setting is designed to produce flesh tones with a softening effect, as shown in Figure 3-28. You should stand fairly close to the subject and set the zoom to fill the frame. If you have the Auto Object Framing option turned on through the Shooting menu, the camera may re-frame the portrait for you.

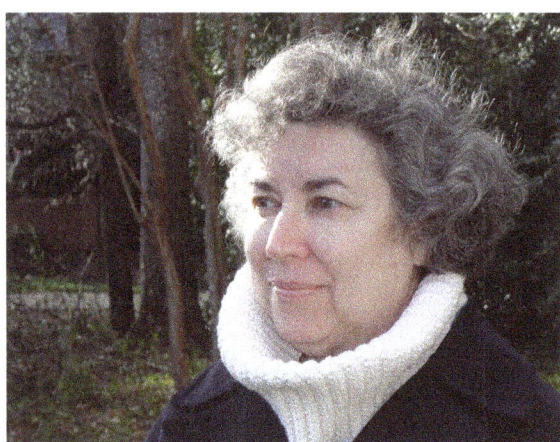

Figure 3-28. Portrait Example

The camera will try to use a wide aperture to blur the background. You can use Autoflash or Fill-flash if you want to even out the lighting or reduce shadows on your subject's face. If you want to improve the lighting, consider using off-camera flash with a softbox attachment.

If you are shooting a portrait in front of a busy background, such as a house, try to position the subject's head in front of a plain area, such as a light-colored wall, so the head will be seen clearly.

You can use the self-timer, but you cannot use bracketing or continuous shooting. You can use the self-portrait timer feature if it is turned on through the Custom menu. To use that feature, flip the LCD screen up so it is facing in the same direction as the lens, and turn the camera so the lens is facing you. Press the shutter button as you see your face, and the shutter will fire after a three-second on-screen countdown.

Note that there is another portrait-oriented Scene mode setting called Soft Skin, which is available if you want to soften the subject's skin more than the Portrait setting does. That setting is discussed later in this section.

Advanced Sports Shooting

The Advanced Sports Action setting is for use when lighting is bright and you need to freeze the action of athletes, children at play, pets, or other subjects. The camera may set a high ISO value so it can use a fast shutter speed to stop action. If you turn on continuous shooting, you can hold down the shutter button and capture a burst of images to increase your chances of capturing the action at a perfect moment. You can use either of the two speeds of continuous shooting, but you cannot use the self-timer or exposure bracketing. (I'll discuss the Drive Mode options in Chapter 4.)

The camera turns on continuous autofocus, so it adjusts focus automatically as the subject moves. You cannot change that setting. The camera tries to predict the position of the subject based on its current motion, in order to adjust focus properly. The flash is disabled with this setting.

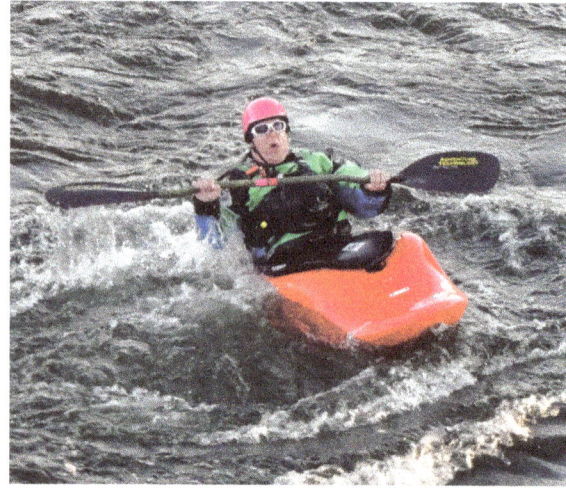

Figure 3-29. Advanced Sports Shooting Example

In Figure 3-29, I used the Advanced Sports Shooting option to photograph a kayaker as he or she navigated some rapids on the James River. I turned on high-speed continuous shooting, and caught this action shot as the kayaker worked the paddle.

Landscape

Landscape is a Scene mode setting I use often. It is convenient to turn the Mode dial to the SCN position and pull up the Landscape setting when I'm at a scenic location. The camera lets you use Fill-flash in case you want to shoot an image of a person as part of your composition, and it boosts the brightness and intensity of the colors somewhat. Otherwise, it limits your choices; you cannot use continuous shooting, but you can use the self-timer. Figure 3-30 is an example taken using the Landscape setting for a shot of several bridges from the side of the river.

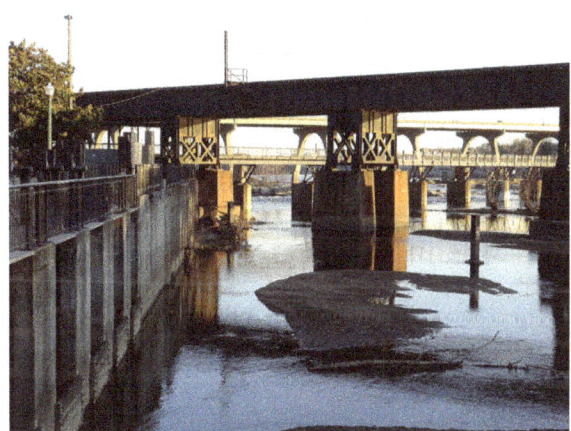

Figure 3-30. Landscape Example

Sunset

This setting enhances reddish hues. You can use Fill-flash to take a portrait with the sunset or sunrise in the background. You cannot use continuous shooting, but you can use the self-timer. As I noted earlier, you don't have to limit this, or any Scene mode setting, to the subject its name implies. If you are photographing reddish leaves in autumn, you might use this option to create an enhanced view of the brightly colored foliage.

In Figure 3-31, I used the Sunset option to photograph the sky at sunset on a cloudy night. The camera enhanced the red tones fairly dramatically.

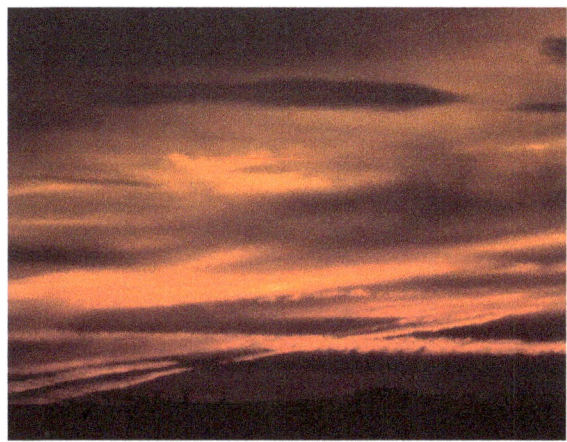

Figure 3-31. Sunset Example

Night Scene

The Night Scene option is designed to preserve the natural look of an evening setting. The camera disables the use of the flash completely; if the scene is quite dark, you should use a tripod to avoid camera motion during the long exposure that may be required. You cannot use continuous shooting, but you can use the self-timer. This setting is good for landscapes and other outdoor scenes after dark when flash would not help. The camera does not raise the ISO or use multiple shots, as it does with other modes used in dim lighting, such as Anti Motion Blur and Hand-held Twilight.

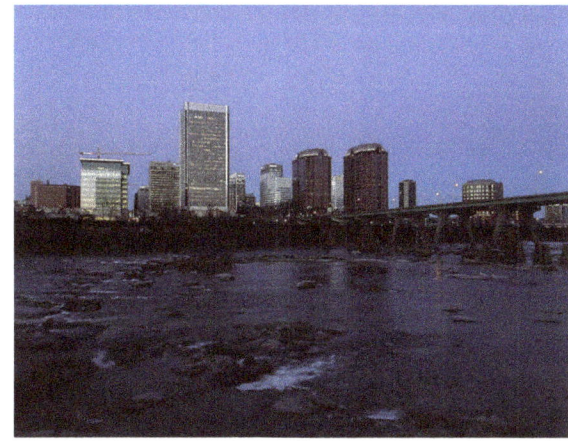

Figure 3-32. Night Scene Example

In Figure 3-32, I used the Night Scene setting to photograph the downtown skyline not long after sunset. Because the camera managed to use a shutter speed of 1/4 second, I was able to hand-hold the camera without introducing noticeable motion blur.

Hand-Held Twilight

This scene type is for taking pictures in low light without flash or tripod. With this special setting, the camera may boost the ISO to a higher level so it can use a fast shutter speed, and it takes a rapid burst of four shots. The camera combines these shots internally into one composite image to counteract the effects of high ISO, which often causes visible "noise," or grain, in an image.

Although the camera tries to select frames with minimal motion blur, the final result with this setting is more likely to show motion blur than a shot made with the Anti Motion Blur setting, discussed later in this section.

Hand-held Twilight is a good option if you are shooting a landscape or other static subject when you cannot use a tripod or flash and the light is dim. If you can use a tripod, you might be better off using the Night Scene setting, discussed above. Or, if you don't mind using flash, you could just use Intelligent Auto, Program, or one of the more ordinary shooting modes. Hand-held Twilight is a useful option when it's needed, but it will not yield the same overall quality as a shot at a lower ISO with the camera on a steady support.

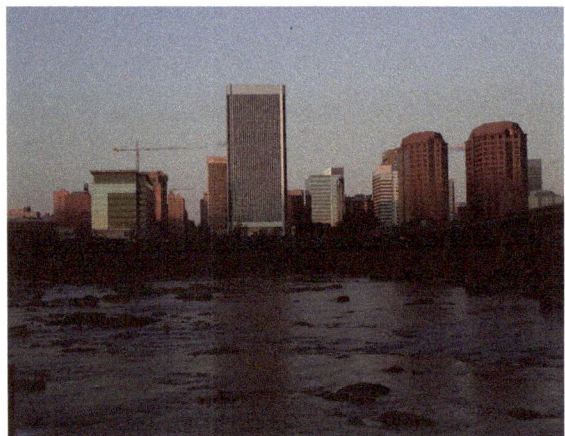

Figure 3-33. Hand-held Twilight Example

In Figure 3-33, I used this setting for another shot of the city skyline a few minutes after sunset, without using a tripod.

Night Portrait

This night-oriented setting is for situations when you are taking a portrait and are willing to use the camera's built-in flash. The main differences from the settings discussed above are that with Night Portrait, the camera takes only one shot and it activates the flash, in Slow Sync mode. You cannot set the Flash Mode to Flash Off. (However, you can leave the flash unit retracted, and the camera will let you take the shot without flash.) You can use the self-timer, but not continuous shooting.

I will discuss Slow Sync in more detail in Chapter 4. Basically, with this setting, the camera uses a slow shutter speed, so that as the flash illuminates the portrait subject, there is enough time for natural light to illuminate the background also. You can use the self-timer, but not continuous shooting. Because of the slow shutter speed, you should use a tripod if possible to avoid motion blur.

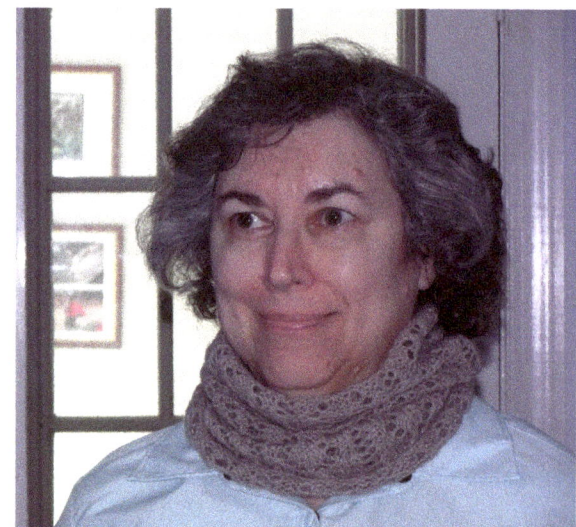

Figure 3-34. Night Portrait Example

In Figure 3-34, I used this setting for a portrait indoors after dark, with some ambient light in the background. I used the flash, and the camera set the shutter speed to 1/4 second, an exposure long enough to allow some of the background lighting to appear.

Anti Motion Blur

As noted earlier, this Scene mode setting is not meant for a particular subject, but for a certain type of situation. This option is useful when the lighting is dim or the lens is zoomed in to a telephoto setting. In either of those situations, the image is subject to blurring because of camera motion. In dim lighting, blurring can happen when the camera uses a slow shutter speed to expose the image properly, because it can be hard to hold the camera steady enough for a sharply focused shot longer than about 1/30 second. In the telephoto case, any camera motion is exaggerated because of the magnification of the image.

To counter the effects of this blurring, with Anti Motion Blur the camera raises the ISO to a higher-than-normal level so the camera can use a fast shutter speed and still let in enough light to expose the image properly. Because higher ISO settings result in increased visual noise, the camera takes a rapid burst of four shots and combines them internally into a single image with reduced noise. The camera also counteracts blur from motion of the subject to a fair extent, by analyzing the shots and rejecting those with motion blur as much as possible.

Anti Motion Blur is useful as the light is fading if you don't want to use flash. It is similar to the Hand-held Twilight setting, discussed above, but the camera is likely to use a higher ISO value with this option, which may result in more noise in the image. For Figure 3-35, I used this setting to capture an image of a couple of people visiting a store at an outdoor shopping mall after dark.

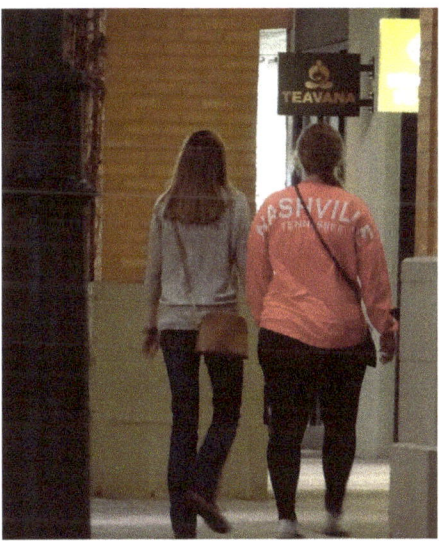

Figure 3-35. Anti Motion Blur Example

You should not expect good results if you use this setting with fast-moving subjects, because the camera will not be able to eliminate motion blur. With slower-moving subjects, though, the HX80 and HX90V can do a good job of reducing or avoiding blur. With this setting, you cannot set the Drive Mode options except for the self-timer, and you cannot use the flash.

Pet

The Pet setting is for taking photos of cats, dogs, and other animals. It is similar to Advanced Sports Shooting in that the flash is off by default but can be set to Fill-flash. The Pet option, though, lets you use the Soft Skin Effect item on the Shooting menu. I would recommend that you use the Pet setting when you are shooting a relatively posed or calm shot of your dog, cat, or other pet; if the animal is running around, you might be better off with the Advanced Sports Shooting selection, which lets you use continuous shooting.

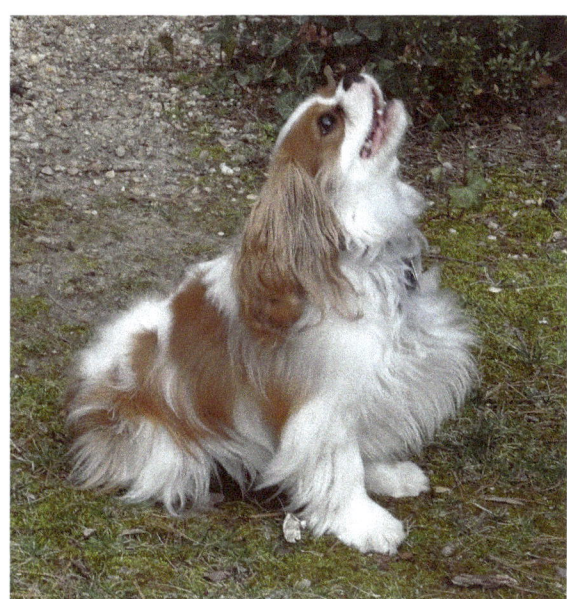

Figure 3-36. Pet Example

I used this setting for Figure 3-36, a shot of our family's high-spirited spaniel, after my wife convinced her to sit still for a few seconds.

Gourmet

The Gourmet setting, according to Sony, is meant to let you shoot food so that it looks "delicious." In terms of settings, the camera increases the brightness and vividness of colors to enhance the appearance of food. This setting is useful for people who write food blogs, or who like to record their meals for posterity. The camera lets you have the flash either forced off or set to Fill-flash. Continuous shooting is not available, but you can use the self-timer. In Figure 3-37, the color and brightness enhancements of this setting gave a boost to an image of a bowl of artificial fruit.

Beach

The Beach setting is intended to let you get clear images under the bright conditions of a sunny day at the seashore. The camera boosts the brightness and vividness of colors, and lets you use Fill-flash if necessary to overcome harsh shadows. You can use the self-timer if you want.

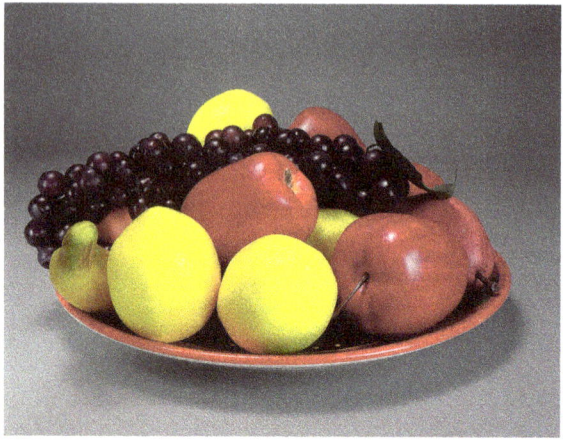

Figure 3-37. Gourmet Example

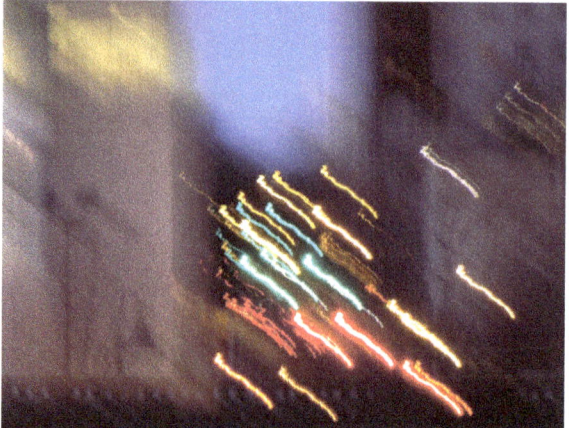

Figure 3-38. Fireworks Example

Snow

The Snow setting is similar to the Beach option, brightening and intensifying colors. You can use Fill-flash or the self-timer. I have not found much difference between the results from using the Beach and Snow settings.

Fireworks

This scene type is designed to capture vivid images of fireworks bursts. It sets the camera to a two-second shutter speed and intensifies colors. If you can, you should set the camera on a tripod or other sturdy support. The camera disables the flash and continuous shooting, but you can use the self-timer.

This setting is one you can also use as an alternative to the Night Scene setting when you are using a tripod after dark. You might want to try this approach to take advantage of the different color processing that the camera uses with this option. In Figure 3-38, I used this setting for a hand-held shot of traffic lights using a high zoom setting from a considerable distance. Because of the two-second shutter speed and the unavoidable shaking of the camera, the result was this abstract set of colored lights.

Soft Skin

The Soft Skin scene setting is designed for taking portraits with a skin-smoothing effect to remove wrinkles and blemishes from the subject's face. The camera turns on the Soft Skin menu option, which appears on screen 5 of the Shooting menu, set to the Mid level, but you can change it to the Lo or Hi setting. You cannot turn the Soft Skin option completely off.

You can use Autoflash, Fill-flash, or the self-timer if you wish. In Figure 3-39, I used this setting for a portrait similar to that in Figure 3-28, to show the comparison between the two settings.

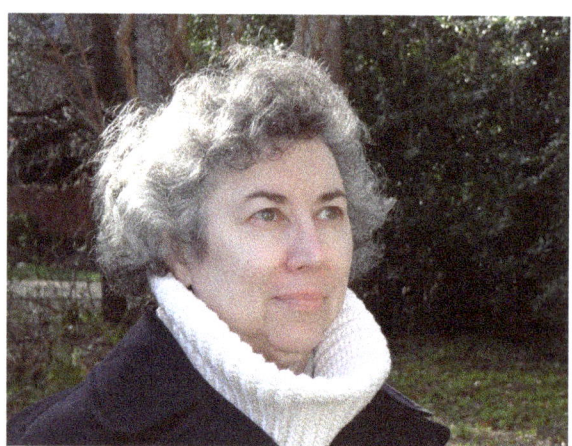

Figure 3-39. Soft Skin Example

High Sensitivity

This final Scene mode setting is another option for low-light shooting. The camera disables the flash and continuous shooting, but it allows use of the self-timer. The camera is likely to use an ISO of 3200 or higher, up to a maximum of 12800 if the light is dim enough to require it. When the ISO is at a lower level, up to 3200, the camera takes only a single shot. At ISO levels above 3200, the camera takes four shots and combines them in order to minimize visual noise, as it does with the Hand-held Twilight and Anti Motion Blur settings.

If you need to shoot in dim light without a tripod and produce an image that is as smooth and noise-free as possible, you probably should use Hand-held Twilight or Anti Motion Blur instead of High Sensitivity. However, there might be occasions when you don't mind the grainy, noisy appearance that a high ISO can bring. It's good to have various choices available when you are confronted with a dimly lit location.

Note that you cannot set the ISO to 12800 with the ISO setting on the Shooting menu; as discussed in Chapter 4, the highest setting available on that menu is 3200. To get the camera to use the 12800 value for ISO, you have to use the Multi Frame Noise Reduction setting on the ISO menu or this High Sensitivity setting of Scene mode.

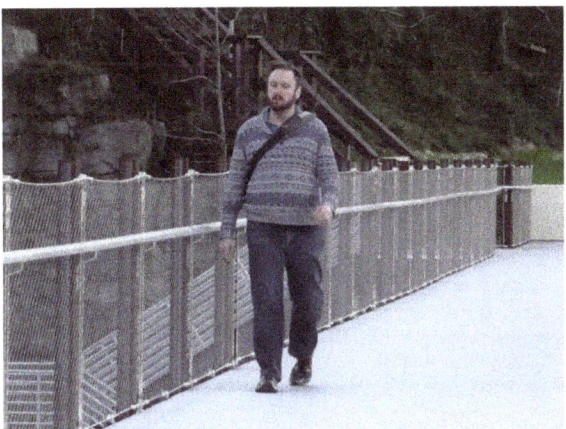

Figure 3-40. High Sensitivity Example

In Figure 3-40, I used the High Sensitivity setting to photograph a man coming toward me on a pedestrian bridge across the river. The camera set the ISO to 1600 with a shutter speed of 1/80 second, so I was able to take the photograph without a tripod.

iSweep Panorama Mode

The next setting on the Mode dial is designed for the shooting of panoramic images. The HX80 and HX90V, like many other Sony cameras, have an excellent capability for automating the capture of panoramas. If you follow the fairly simple steps involved, the camera will stitch together a series of images internally to create a wide (or tall) view of a scenic vista or other subject that lends itself to panoramic depiction.

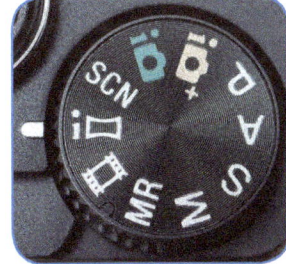

Figure 3-41. Mode Dial at iSweep Panorama

On the Mode dial, select the icon that looks like a squeezed rectangle with a letter "i" beside it, as seen in Figure 3-41. You will see a message telling you to press the shutter button and move the camera in the direction of the arrow that appears on the screen, as shown in Figure 3-42.

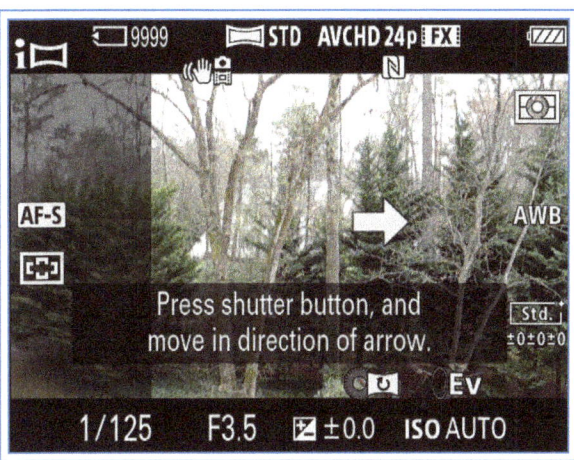

Figure 3-42. Message to Press Shutter for Panorama Shot

At that point, you can follow the directions and likely get excellent results. However, the camera also lets you make several choices for your panoramic images using the Shooting menu. Press the Menu button, and you will go to the menu screen that is currently displayed.

Navigate to the Shooting menu, which limits you to fewer choices than in most other shooting modes because several options are not appropriate for panoramas. For example, the Image Size, Aspect Ratio, and Quality settings are dimmed and unavailable. Also, options such as Drive Mode, Flash Mode, and Focus Area are of no use in this situation and cannot be selected. In addition, you will not be able to zoom the lens in; it will be fixed at its wide-angle position. (If the lens was zoomed in previously, it will zoom back out automatically when you switch the Mode dial to the iSweep Panorama selection.)

You will, however, see two options on the first screen of the Shooting menu that are not available for selection in any other shooting mode: Panorama Size and Panorama Direction, as shown in Figure 3-43.

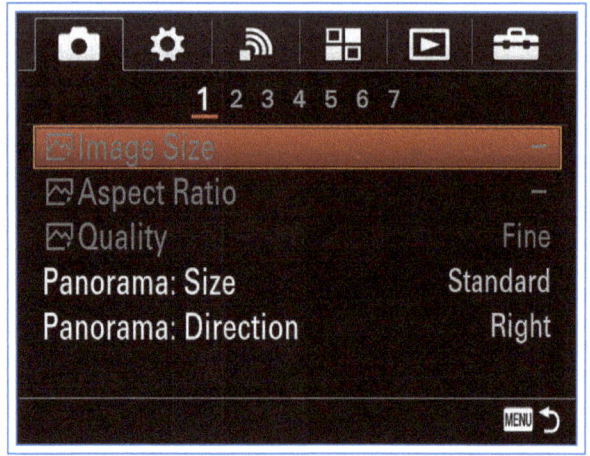

Figure 3-43. Panorama Size and Direction on Shooting Menu

Panorama Size has three options: Standard, Wide, and 360°. With Standard, a horizontal panorama will have a size of 4912 by 1080 pixels, which is a resolution of about 5.3 megapixels (MP). If you choose Wide, a horizontal panorama will have a size of 7152 by 1080 pixels, resulting in a resolution of about 7.7 MP. If you choose 360°, the panorama's size will be 11520 by 1080, a resolution of about 12.4 MP.

A vertical panorama at the Standard setting is 3424 by 1920 pixels, or about 6.5 MP; a vertical panorama at the Wide setting is 4912 by 1920 pixels, or about 9.4 MP.

The Panorama Direction option selects Right, Left, Up, or Down for the direction in which you will sweep the camera. You also can turn the Control wheel to change the direction, so you will not have to use the Shooting menu for that purpose.

(HX90V only) If the Control ring is set to the Standard option through the Custom Key Settings item on the Custom menu and you are not using manual focus or DMF, you can also turn the Control ring, and the camera will cycle through the four arrows for the four panorama directions.

You can use the Direction settings with different orientations of the camera to get different results than usual. For example, if you set the direction to Up and hold the camera sideways while you sweep it to the right, you will create a horizontal panorama with 1920 pixels in its vertical dimension rather than the standard 1080.

Those are the main settings for most panoramas. There are a few other options you can select for panoramas on the Shooting menu, including Focus Mode (HX90V only), Metering Mode, White Balance, and Creative Style. I will discuss all of these menu options in Chapter 4. My preferred settings for shooting panoramas are the ones shown in Table 3-1, at least as a starting point.

Table 3-1.	Suggested Settings for Panoramas
Focus Mode (HX90V only)	Single-shot AF
Metering Mode	Multi
White Balance	Auto White Balance
Creative Style	Standard

One other setting you can make when shooting panoramas is exposure compensation, which is set using the Down button on the Control wheel. I will discuss that function in Chapter 5. In the context of shooting panoramas, this feature can be useful because the camera will not change the exposure if the camera is pointed at areas with varying brightness. For example, if you start sweeping from a dark area on the left, the camera will set the exposure for that area. If you then sweep the camera to the right over a bright area, that part of the panorama will be overexposed and possibly washed out in excessive brightness. To correct for this effect, you can reduce the exposure using negative exposure compensation. In this way, the initial dark area will be underexposed, but the brighter area should be properly exposed. Of course, you have to decide what part of the panorama is the most important one for having proper exposure.

Another way to deal with this issue is to point the camera at the bright area before starting the shot and press the shutter button halfway to lock the exposure, and then go back to the dark area at the left and start sweeping the camera. In that way, the exposure will be locked at the proper level for the bright area.

Once you have made the settings you want, follow the directions on the screen. Press and release the shutter button and start moving the camera at a steady rate in the direction you have chosen. I tend to shoot my panoramas moving the camera from left to right, but you may have a different preference. You will hear a steady clicking as the camera takes multiple shots during the sweep of the panorama. A white box and arrow will proceed across the screen; your task is to finish the camera's sweep at the same moment that the box and arrow finish their travel across the scene. If you move the camera either too quickly or too slowly, the panorama will not succeed; if that happens, just try again.

Panoramas usually work best when the scene does not contain moving objects such as cars or pedestrians because when items are in motion, the multiple shots are likely to capture images of the same object more than once in different positions.

It is advisable to use a tripod if possible so you can keep the camera steady in a single plane as it moves. If you don't have a tripod available, you might try using the electronic level that is built into the camera. You have to activate the level with the Display Button option on the Custom menu, as discussed in Chapter 7. Then press the Display button until the screen with the electronic level appears. Make sure the outer tips of the level stay green as much as possible, and the resulting panorama should benefit from the level shooting.

In addition to exposure, as discussed above, focus and white balance are fixed as soon as the first image is taken for the panorama.

When a panoramic shot is played back in the camera, it is initially displayed at a small size so the whole image can fit on the display screen. You can press the Center button to make the panorama scroll across the display at a larger size, using the full height of the screen.

Figure 3-44 is a sample panorama, shot from left to right using the Standard setting for Panorama Size.

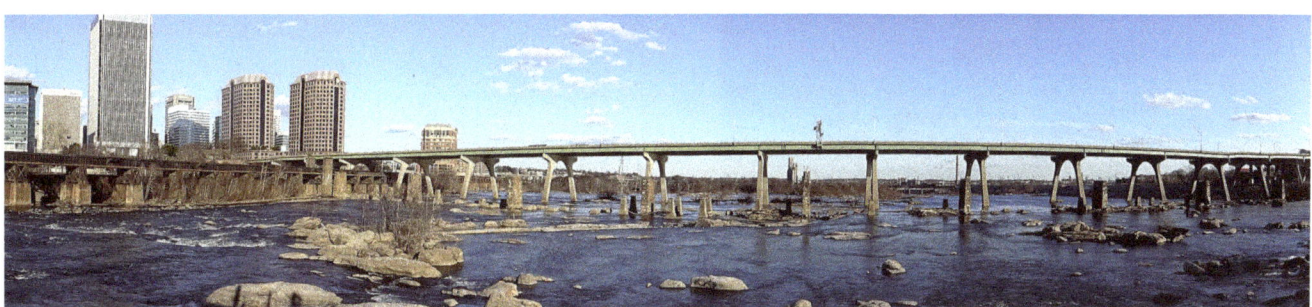

Figure 3-44. Sample Panorama: James River, Richmond, Virginia

Memory Recall Mode

There is one more shooting mode left to discuss, apart from Movie mode, which I will discuss in Chapter 8. This last mode, called Memory Recall, is a powerful tool that gives you expanded options for your photography.

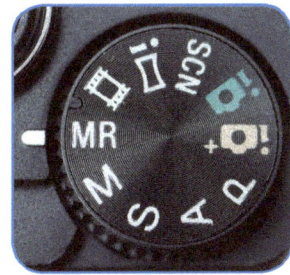

Figure 3-45. Mode Dial at Memory Recall

When you turn the Mode dial to the MR position (shown in Figure 3-45) and then select one of the three groups of settings that can be stored there, you are, in effect, selecting a custom-made shooting mode that you create with your own favorite settings.

You can set up the camera just as you want it—with stored values for items such as shooting mode, shutter speed, aperture, zoom amount, white balance, ISO, and other settings—and later recall all of those values instantly just by turning the Mode dial to the MR position and selecting one of the three stored memory registers on the Memory Recall screen, depending on which one you used to store the settings. With these cameras, unlike some other camera models, you can store settings for any shooting mode, including the Intelligent Auto and Scene modes.

Here is how this works. First, set up the camera with all of the settings you want to recall. For example, suppose you are going to do street photography. You may want to use a fast shutter speed, say 1/250 second, in black and white, at ISO 1600, using continuous shooting with autofocus, Large and Fine images, and shooting in the 4:3 aspect ratio.

The first step is to make all of these settings. Set the Mode dial to Shutter Priority and use the Control wheel to set a shutter speed of 1/250 second. Then press the Menu button to call up the Shooting menu and select L for Image Size, 4:3 for Aspect Ratio, and Fine for Quality. Then choose continuous shooting (Hi speed) for Drive Mode. Next, set ISO to 1600, and set the white balance to Daylight. Next, move to the Creative Style option and select the B/W setting, for black and white. You also may want to push the zoom lever all the way to the left for wide-angle shooting. You can set any other available Shooting menu options as you wish, but the ones listed above are the ones I will consider for now.

Once these settings are made, navigate to the Memory item, shown in Figure 3-46, which is the final item on the last screen of the Shooting menu.

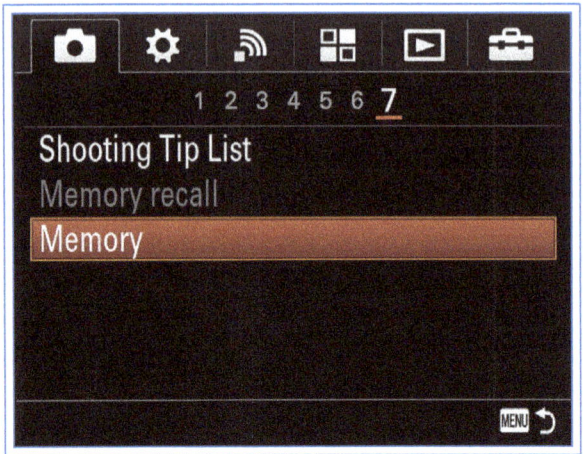

Figure 3-46. Memory Item on Shooting Menu

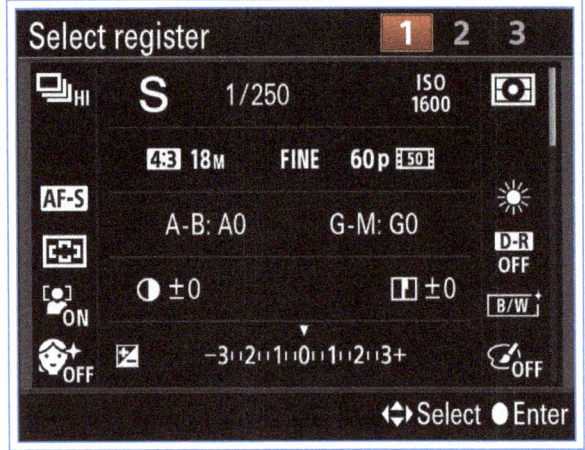

Figure 3-47. Memory Screen with Registers and Settings

After you press the Center button, you will see a screen like the one in Figure 3-47, showing icons and values for all of the settings currently in effect.

The words Select Register appear at the upper left of the screen, and the indicators 1, 2, and 3 at the upper right. In the example shown here, the number 1 is highlighted. Now press the Center button, and you will have selected Register 1 to store all of the settings you just made.

Note the short gray bar at the right side of the Memory screen shown in Figure 3-47. That bar indicates that you can scroll down through other screens to see additional settings that are in effect, such as ISO Auto Maximum and Minimum, AF Illuminator, Center Lock-on AF, and several others. Use the Up and Down buttons to scroll through those screens.

Next, to check how this worked, try making some very different settings, such as setting the camera for Manual exposure with a shutter speed of one second, Creative Style set to Vivid, continuous shooting turned off, the zoom lever moved all the way to the right for telephoto, and Quality set to Standard. Then turn the Mode dial back to the MR position and press the Center button while the number 1 is highlighted for Register 1. You will see that all of the custom settings you made have instantly returned, including the zoom position, shutter speed, and everything else. You can then continue shooting with those settings.

This is a wonderful feature, and it is more powerful than similar options on some other cameras, which can save menu settings but not values such as shutter speed and zoom position, or can save settings only for the less-automatic shooting modes, but not the Scene and Auto modes. What is also quite amazing is that if you now switch back to Manual exposure mode, the camera will restore the settings that you had in that mode before you turned to the MR mode. (The position of the zoom lens will not revert to where it was, though.)

You can store settings from the Shooting menu, as well as the aperture, shutter speed, exposure compensation, and optical zoom settings. So, for example, you could set up one of the three memory registers to recall Scene mode using the Gourmet setting, with the lens zoomed back to its wide-angle position. In that way, you could be ready for shooting a plate of food on a moment's notice. A Program Shift setting cannot be stored.

This feature is powerful and useful. With a twist of the Mode dial and the press of a button, you can call up a complete group of settings tailored for a particular type of shooting. It is worth your while to experiment with this feature and develop various groups of settings that work well for your shooting needs.

Chapter 4: Shooting Menu

Much of the power of the Sony HX80 and HX90V comes from options on the Shooting menu, which gives you many ways to control the appearance of images and how you capture them. (Sony calls this menu the Camera Settings menu, but I have chosen to call it the Shooting menu in this book, to distinguish it from other menus that also involve camera settings.)

Depending on your preferences, you may not have to use the Shooting menu too much. You may prefer to use the camera's physical controls, with which you can make several settings, or you may use the Scene or Auto mode settings, which choose many options for you. However, it's nice to have this degree of control if you want it, and it is useful to understand the settings you can make. In addition, with these cameras, more than with many other models, you can control a fair number of settings on the Shooting menu even when the camera is in a Scene or Auto mode. Therefore, it is well worth exploring this powerful menu.

The available menu options can change depending on the setting of the Mode dial. For example, if the camera is set to Intelligent Auto mode, the Shooting menu options are limited because that mode is for a user who wants the camera to make many decisions without input. If the camera is in iSweep Panorama mode, the options are limited because of the specialized nature of that mode. For this discussion, I'm assuming you have the camera set to Program mode, because with that mode you have access to most of the options on the Shooting menu.

Turn the Mode dial on top of the camera to P, which represents Program mode, as shown in Figure 4-1. Enter the menu system by pressing the Menu button and move through the screens of the menu system by pressing the Right or Left button on the Control wheel. With each press of one of those buttons, the small orange line (cursor) at the top of the screen moves underneath a number that represents a menu screen.

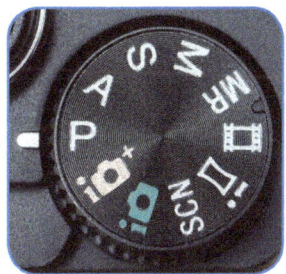

Figure 4-1. Mode Dial at Program

When the menu system first appears, the cursor should sit beneath the number one while the camera icon, which represents the Shooting menu, is highlighted in the group of icons at the top of the screen, as shown in Figure 4-2. If a different screen is displayed, use the Right and Left buttons to navigate to that first screen. As you keep pressing the Right button, the cursor will move through all seven screens of the Shooting menu.

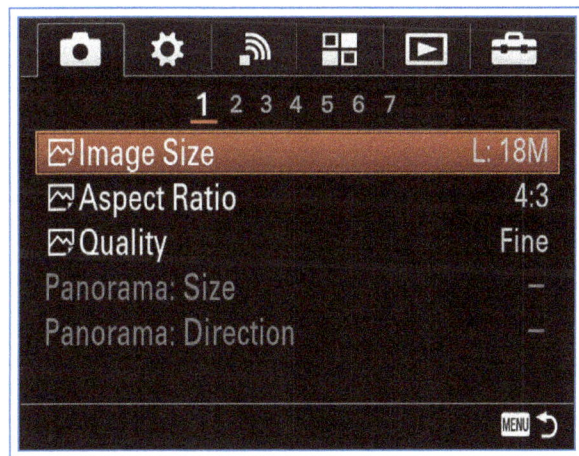

Figure 4-2. Screen 1 of Shooting Menu

Depending on how your camera is set up, you may see a group of six blocks, called "tiles" by Sony, when you press the Menu button, as shown in Figure 4-3. If you see that screen, move through the tiles using the direction buttons or the Control wheel, and press the Center button to select a menu's tile. You will then see a screen like that in Figure 4-2. (You can turn off the Tile Menu option through the Setup menu, as discussed in Chapter 7.)

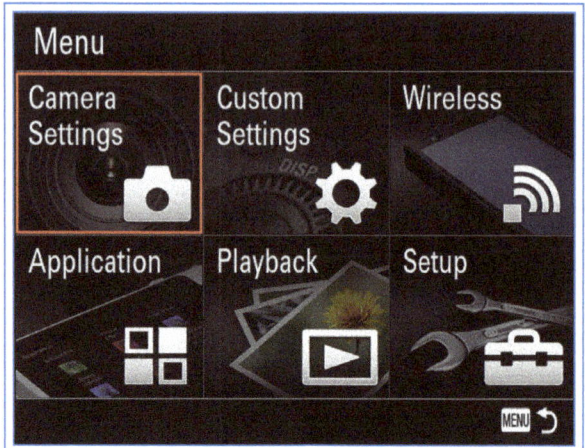

Figure 4-3. Menu Display When Tiled Menu Option is Turned On

As you move through the menu screens, after the Shooting menu comes the Custom menu, marked by a gear icon, then the Wi-Fi menu, headed by a wireless network icon. The last three menus are the Application menu, designated by a set of black and white blocks; the Playback menu, marked by a triangle icon; and, finally, the Setup menu, marked by a toolbox icon.

To navigate quickly through the six menu systems, you can press the Up button to move the orange highlight block into the line of menu icons at the top of the screen. When one of those icons is highlighted, you can use the Left and Right buttons to navigate directly from one menu system to another without going through the various screens of each menu.

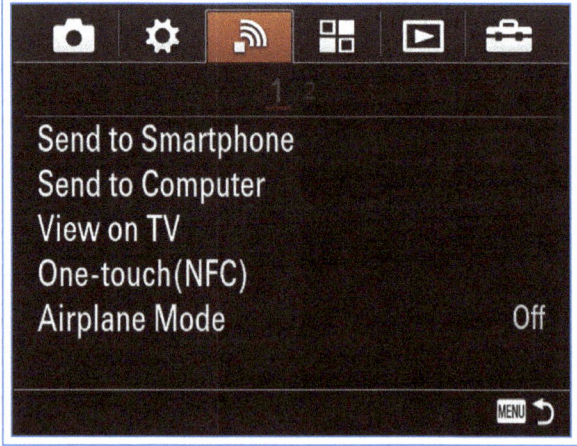

Figure 4-4. Wi-Fi Menu Icon Highlighted

For example, in Figure 4-4 the Wi-Fi menu icon is highlighted. From there, you can press the Left button twice to move the highlight to the camera icon for the Shooting menu at the far left, as shown in Figure 4-5.

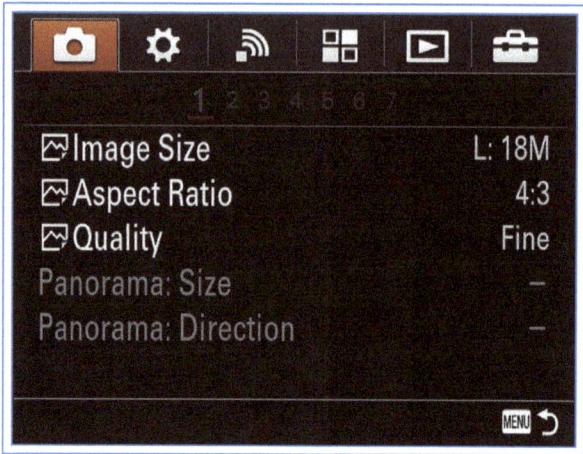

Figure 4-5. Shooting Menu Icon Highlighted

Then you can press the Down button to move the highlight into the list of items on screen 1 of the Shooting menu, as shown earlier in Figure 4-2.

In this chapter, I am going to discuss only the Shooting menu; I will discuss the other five menus in Chapter 6 (Playback), Chapter 7 (Custom and Setup), and Chapter 9 (Wi-Fi and Application).

The Shooting menu contains many options divided into seven numbered screens. In most cases, each option (such as Image Size) occupies one line, with its name on the left and its current setting (such as L:18M) on the right. In other cases (such as Scene Selection, Movie, and Memory Recall), there may be only a small dash or nothing at all on the right side of the screen, meaning the selection is not currently applicable. For example, if the camera is in Program mode, the Scene Selection item on the Shooting menu will be followed by a dash because you cannot select a scene type in Program mode.

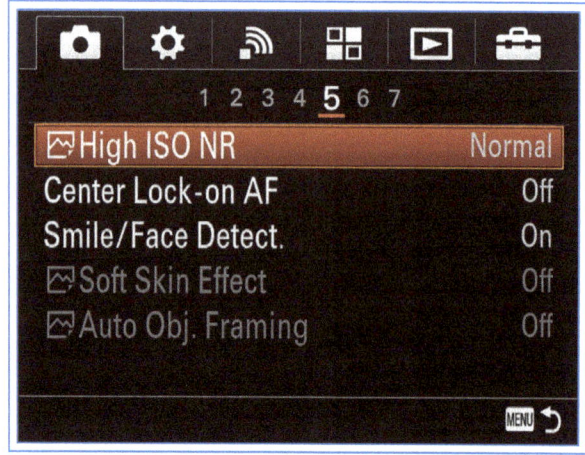

Figure 4-6. Menu Screen with Two Items Dimmed

Chapter 4: Shooting Menu | 43

You also will see that some items on the menu screens are dimmed, as the Soft Skin Effect and Auto Object Framing options are in Figure 4-6, for example. This means those options are not available for selection in the current context. In this case, continuous shooting was turned on, and that setting conflicts with the two settings that are dimmed, so they cannot be selected.

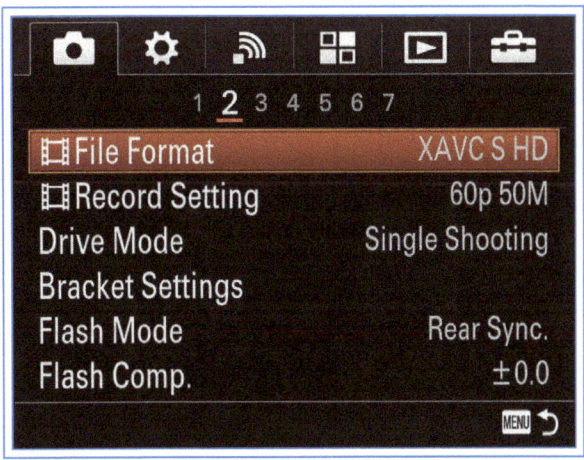

Figure 4-7. Menu Screen with Icons for Movie-Related Items

In addition, some items are preceded by an icon that indicates whether they are used for still images or movies. For example, Figure 4-7 shows screen 2 of the Shooting menu for the HX90V, on which the first two items apply only for movies, as indicated by the movie-film icons preceding those menu items. Figure 4-8 shows screen 3 of the menu, which has one item, AF Illuminator, marked by a still-image icon because it applies only for still photography.

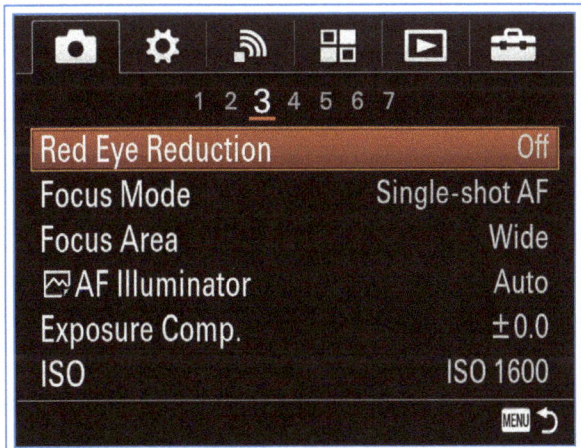

Figure 4-8. Menu Screen with Icon for Stills-Related Item

To follow the discussion below of the options on the Shooting menu, leave the shooting mode set to Program, which gives you access to most of the options on that menu. (I'll also discuss the options that are available in other modes as I come to them.) I'll start at the top of screen 1 of the Shooting menu for the HX90V and discuss each option on the way down the list for each of the seven screens of this menu. I will point out items that are not available on the HX80.

Image Size

This first option on the Shooting menu is related to the next two entries on the menu, Aspect Ratio and Quality, to control the overall appearance and "quality" of your images, in a broad sense. The Image Size setting controls the size in pixels of a still image recorded by the camera. Each of these cameras has a digital sensor with a maximum effective resolution, or pixel count, of about 18 megapixels. The sensor is capable of recording a still image with 4896 pixels, or individual points of light, in the horizontal direction and 3672 pixels vertically. When you multiply those two numbers together, the result is about 18 million pixels, often referred to as megapixels, MP, or M.

The resolution of still images is important mainly when it comes time to enlarge or print your images. If you need to produce large prints (say, eight by 10 inches or 20 by 25 cm), then you should select a high-resolution setting for Image Size. You also should choose the largest Image Size setting if you may need to crop out a small portion of the image and enlarge it for closer viewing. For example, if you are shooting photos of wildlife and the animal or bird you are interested in is in the distance, you may need to enlarge the image digitally to see that subject in detail. In that case, also, you should choose the highest setting for Image Size.

The available settings for Image Size are L, M, S, and VGA, for Large, Medium, Small, and VGA, as shown in Figure 4-9. When you select one of the first three options, the camera displays a setting such as L:18M, meaning Large: 18 megapixels. The number of megapixels changes depending on the Aspect Ratio setting, discussed below. This is because when the shape of the image changes, the number of horizontal pixels or the number of vertical pixels changes also to form the new shape.

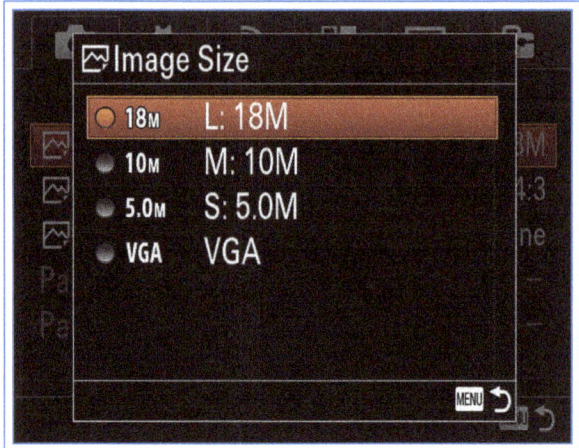

Figure 4-9. Image Size Menu Options Screen

For example, if the Aspect Ratio setting is 4:3, the maximum number of pixels is used because 4:3 is the aspect ratio of the camera's sensor. However, if you set Aspect Ratio to 16:9, the number of horizontal pixels (4896) stays the same, but the number of vertical pixels is reduced from 3672 to 2752 to form the 16:9 ratio of horizontal to vertical pixels. When you multiply those two numbers (4896 and 2752) together, the result is about 13 million pixels, which the camera states as 13M, as seen in Figure 4-10.

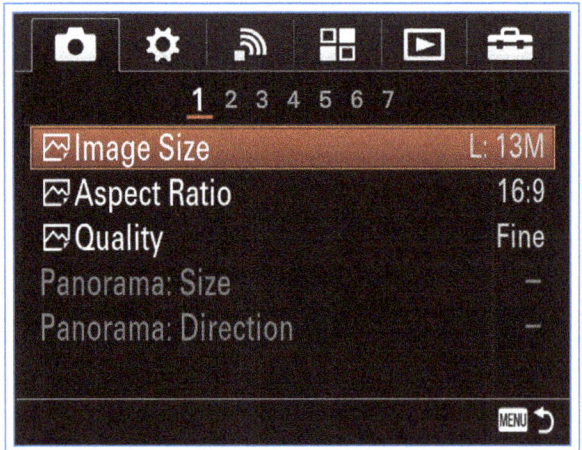

Figure 4-10. Shooting Menu Screen 1 with Aspect Ratio Set to 16:9

The VGA option, the smallest size possible, is available only if Aspect Ratio is set to 4:3. Otherwise, this choice does not even appear on the menu option for Image Size. VGA stands for video graphics array, the designation used for older-style computer screens, which have a 4:3 aspect ratio. The pixel count for this setting is very low—just 640 by 480 pixels, yielding a resolution of 0.3 M, much less than one megapixel. This very small size is suitable if you need to send images by e-mail or need to store a great many images on a memory card.

One of the few reasons to choose an Image Size smaller than L is if you are running out of space on your memory card and need to keep taking pictures in an important situation. Table 4-1 shows approximately how many images can be stored on a 16 GB memory card for various settings. (These numbers are somewhat different from those discussed in Chapter 1, which come from the Sony users guide. The numbers here come from readings taken with a freshly formatted card in my camera, for comparison.)

Table 4-1.	Number of Images That Fit on a 16 GB Card (Image Size vs. Quality at 4:3 Aspect Ratio)			
	Large	Medium	Small	VGA
Fine	2394	3497	5283	9999+
Standard	3423	4861	6944	9999+

As you can see, if you are using a 16 GB memory card, which is not a very large size these days, you can fit about 2400 images on the card even at the maximum settings of 4:3 for Aspect Ratio, Large for Image Size, and Fine for Quality. If you limit the image quality to Standard, you can fit about 3400 images on the card. If you reduce the Image Size setting to Small, you can store more than 5,000 images. I am unlikely ever to need more than about 300 or 400 images in any one session, unless I shoot a number of bursts, especially bursts using the highest speed. So, a 16 GB card should be adequate for most purposes, unless you plan to shoot a lot of HD video. (Of course, as noted in Chapter 1, if you use the XAVC S HD format for recording video, you need to use a high-speed memory card with a capacity of 64 GB or more.)

If space on your memory card is not a consideration, then I recommend you use the L setting at all times. You never know when you might need the larger-sized image, so you might as well use the L setting and be safe. Your situation might be different, of course. If you were taking photos purely for a business purpose, such as making photo identification cards, you might want to use the Small setting to store the maximum number of images on a memory card and reduce expense. For general photography, though, I rarely use any setting other than L for Image Size. (One exception could be when I want to increase the range of the optical zoom lens without losing image quality; see the discussion of Smart Zoom and related topics in Chapter 7.)

Aspect Ratio

This second option on the Shooting menu lets you choose the shape of your still images. The choices are the default of 4:3, as well as 3:2, 16:9, and 1:1, as shown in Figure 4-11.

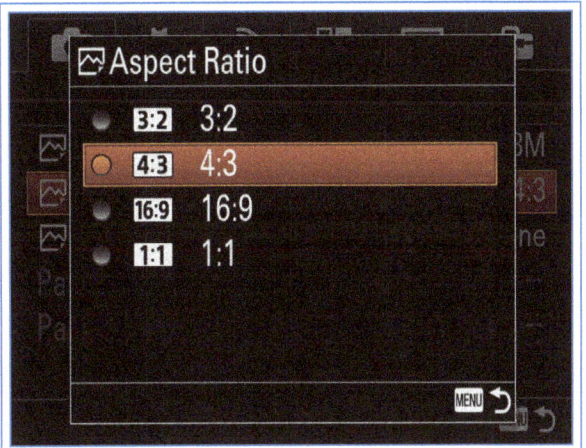

Figure 4-11. Aspect Ratio Menu Options Screen

These numbers are the ratio of units of width to units of height. For example, with the 16:9 setting, the image is 16 units wide for every nine units of height. The aspect ratio that uses all pixels on the image sensor is 4:3 for this camera; with any other aspect ratio, some pixels are cropped out. So, if you want to record every possible pixel, you should use the 4:3 setting. If you shoot using the 4:3 aspect ratio, you can always alter the shape of the image later in editing software such as Photoshop by cropping away parts of the image. However, if you want to compose your images in a certain shape and don't plan to do post-processing in software, the aspect ratio settings of this menu item can help you frame your images in the camera using the appropriate aspect ratio on the display.

For each of the aspect ratios discussed below, I am including an image I took using that setting in the same location at the same time, to give an idea of what the different aspect ratios look like.

The default 4:3 setting, used for Figure 4-12, includes the maximum number of pixels, and is in the shape of a traditional (non-widescreen) computer screen, so if you want to view your images on that sort of display, this may be your preferred setting. As I noted earlier

in discussing Image Size, if you want to use the VGA setting for Image Size, the camera must be set to the 4:3 aspect ratio.

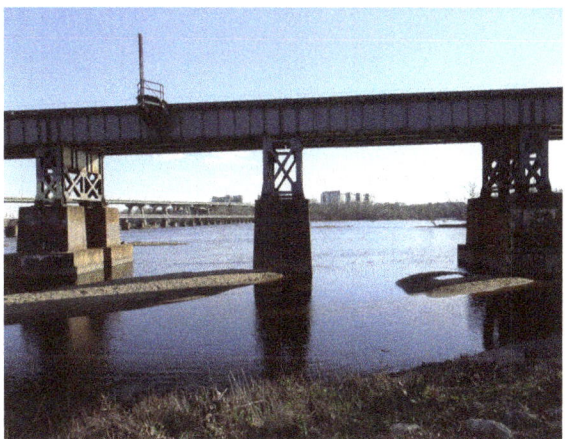

Figure 4-12. Aspect Ratio 4:3

The 3:2 setting, shown in Figure 4-13, is the ratio used by traditional 35mm film. This aspect ratio can be used without cropping to make prints in the common U.S. size of six inches by four inches (15 cm by 10 cm). With this setting, some pixels are lost at the top and bottom of the image.

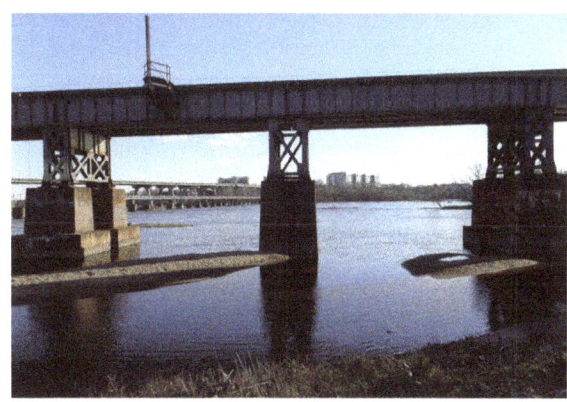

Figure 4-13. Aspect Ratio 3:2

The 16:9 setting, illustrated in Figure 4-14, is the "widescreen" option, like that found on many modern HD television sets. You might use this setting when you plan to show your images on an HDTV set. Or, it might be suitable for a particular composition in which the subject matter is stretched out in a horizontal arrangement. With this setting, some pixels are cropped out at the top and bottom.

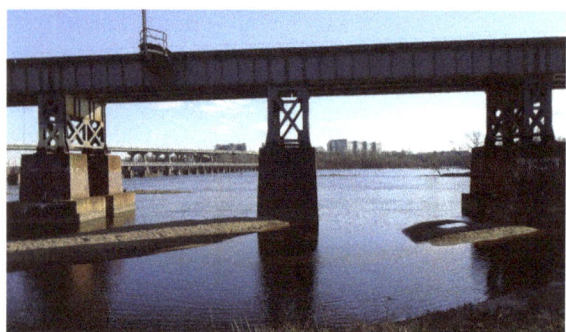

Figure 4-14. Aspect Ratio 16:9

The 1:1 ratio, illustrated in Figure 4-15, produces a square shape, which some photographers prefer because of its symmetry and because the neutrality of the shape leaves open many possibilities for composition. With the 1:1 setting, the camera crops pixels from the left and right sides of the image.

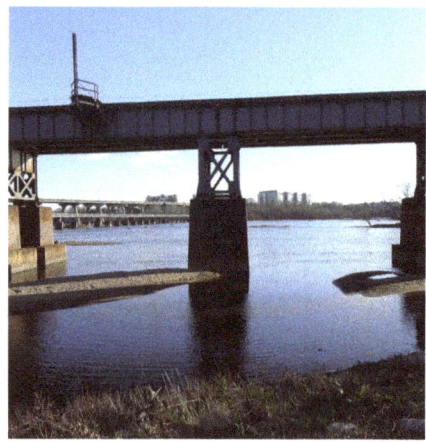

Figure 4-15. Aspect Ratio 1:1

The Aspect Ratio setting is available in all shooting modes except iSweep Panorama. However, although you can set Aspect Ratio when the camera is in Movie mode (Mode dial turned to movie-film icon), that setting will have no effect until you switch to a mode for taking still images, such as Program mode. When the Mode dial is set to the Movie position, you cannot take still images.

Quality

The Quality setting, below Aspect Ratio, is one of the basic Shooting menu options for still images. The choices are Fine and Standard, as shown in Figure 4-16.

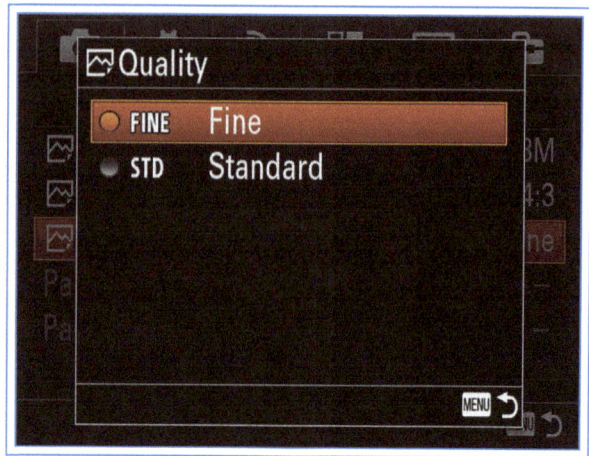

Figure 4-16. Quality Menu Options Screen

The term "quality" in this context concerns the way in which digital images are processed in the JPEG format, which these cameras use for all of their still images. JPEG is an acronym for Joint Photographic Experts Group, an industry group that created the JPEG standard. JPEG images are digitally "compressed" to reduce their size without losing too much information or detail from the picture. However, the more an image is compressed, the greater the loss of detail and clarity in the image. The JPEG files for this camera come in two varieties: Fine and Standard. The Fine setting provides the least compression. Images captured with the Standard setting undergo more compression, resulting in smaller files with somewhat reduced quality.

I strongly recommend that you choose the Large size and Fine quality, unless you need to conserve storage space on your memory card or on your computer.

Panorama Size and Panorama Direction

The last two commands on this screen of the Shooting menu are available only when the Mode dial is set to the iSweep Panorama position. I discussed these settings in Chapter 3, in connection with that shooting mode. These options let you select the size and direction of shooting for panoramas you take in that mode. You also can change the direction of shooting by turning the Control wheel.

HX90V only: When the Control ring is set to its Standard setting through the Custom Key Settings option on screen 4 of the Custom menu, you can set the panorama direction by turning that ring (unless you are using manual focus or DMF, which take over the use of the ring).

The next menu options are on screen 2 of the Shooting menu for the HX90V, shown in Figure 4-17.

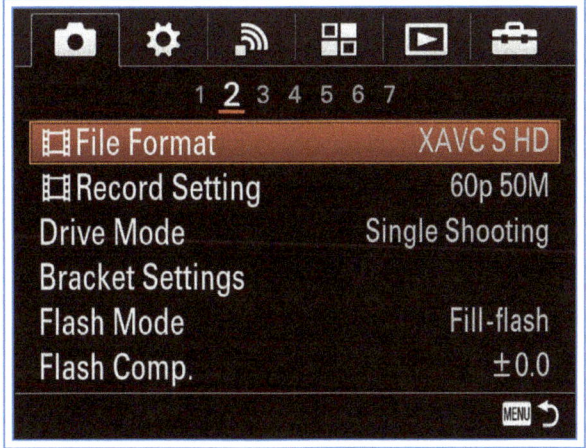

Figure 4-17. Screen 2 of HX90V Shooting Menu

File Format

This first option on screen 2 of the Shooting menu is preceded by a movie-film icon, meaning it applies only for movies. I will discuss this option in Chapter 8. For now, you should know that XAVC S HD gives the highest quality but is available only if you use a memory card with a capacity of 64 GB or greater and rated in Speed Class 10 or UHS Speed Class 1 or greater. The AVCHD option yields very high quality and MP4 gives somewhat lower quality but can be easier to work with for editing. The choice you make for this setting depends to a large extent on the type of video you are recording, as discussed in Chapter 8.

Record Setting

This next option on screen 2 of the Shooting menu is related to the File Format option, discussed above. The available options for Record Setting will change, depending on what you select for File Format. I will discuss the details of this option in Chapter 8. For now, if you want the highest quality for MP4 video, choose the top option, 1920 x 1080 60p 28M. These options will be different if you choose XAVC S HD, AVCHD, or MP4 for File Format. They also will be different if you are using the PAL system for video recording, the system used in much of Europe and some other locations.

For example, the top option for MP4 in that case is 1920 x 1080 50p 28M. In this book, I will discuss the video options that are applicable for the NTSC system, as used in the United States, Japan, and elsewhere. (If you have a camera that was sold in the United States, it should have come with the NTSC system and cannot be changed to PAL. If you have a camera that was sold in Europe or another PAL area, it may have a menu option that lets you change between PAL and NTSC. That option is discussed in Chapter 7.)

Drive Mode

This next menu option gives access to continuous shooting and related features of the camera, for shooting bursts of images, bracketing exposures, and using the self-timer. You can also get access to this menu option by pressing the Drive Mode button (Left button), as discussed in Chapter 5, unless that button has been assigned to a different function using the Custom Key Settings option on the Custom menu. Or, you can get access to these options through the Function menu or the Quick Navi system, as also discussed in Chapter 5.

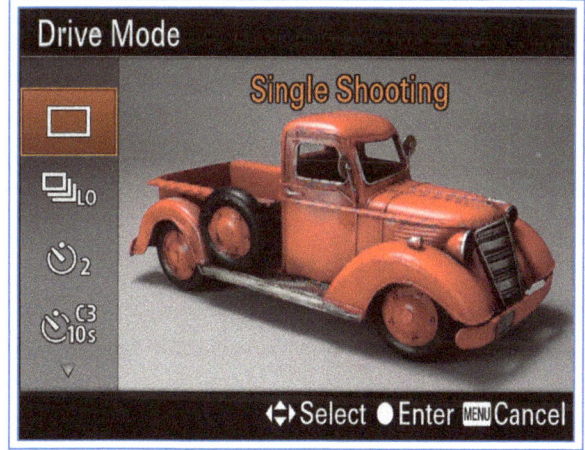

Figure 4-18. Drive Mode Menu

When you highlight the Drive Mode option and press the Center button, the menu in Figure 4-18 appears, with eight choices: Single Shooting, Continuous Shooting, Self-timer, Self-timer (Continuous), Continuous Exposure Bracketing, Single Exposure Bracketing, White Balance Bracketing, and DRO Bracketing. You have to scroll down for the last four choices.

Details for each of these Drive Mode settings are discussed below.

Single Shooting

This is the normal mode for shooting still images. Select this top choice on the Drive Mode menu to turn off all continuous shooting. In some cases, having one of the continuous-shooting options selected makes it impossible to use other settings, such as Soft Skin Effect and Auto Object Framing. If you find you cannot make a certain setting, select single shooting to see if that removes the conflict and fixes the problem.

Continuous Shooting

Continuous shooting, sometimes called burst shooting, is useful in many contexts, from shooting an action sequence at a sporting event to taking a series of shots of a person in order to capture changing facial expressions. I often use this setting for street photography to increase my chances of catching an interesting shot.

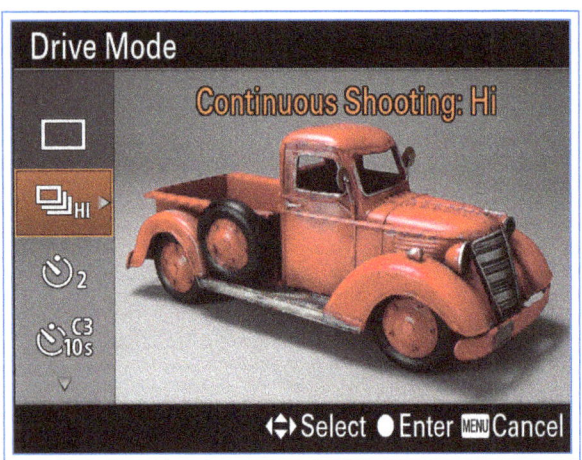

Figure 4-19. Icon for Continuous Shooting Highlighted

To use burst shooting, use the Down button or the Control wheel to move the highlight to the second icon on the Drive menu, for continuous shooting, as shown in Figure 4-19. Then use the Left and Right buttons to select either Hi or Lo for the speed of continuous shooting. Once the desired speed is highlighted, press the Center button to confirm the selection and the camera will return to the shooting screen.

With the Hi setting, the camera will shoot up to 10 images in a burst at a rate of up to 10 frames per second; with Lo, it will shoot 10 images at up to two frames per second. Focus and exposure will be fixed with the first shot, and the camera will not make adjustments even if the distance to the subject or the lighting changes.

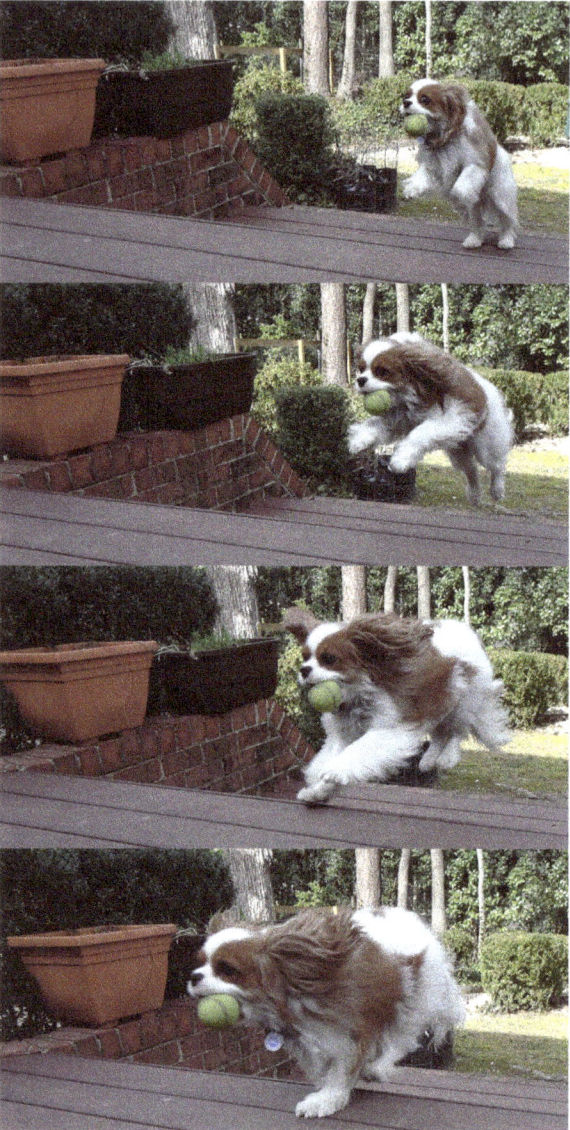

Figure 4-20. Series of Continuous Shooting Images

Figure 4-20 is a composite that combines four images I took using high-speed continuous shooting. These images of our family dog running show how a quick burst of shots can stop action. I used Shutter Priority mode with a shutter speed of 1/500 second in order to stop the action with a minimum of motion blur.

The continuous shooting options are not available with iSweep Panorama mode or with any settings in Scene mode other than Sports Action. They also are not available with certain Picture Effect settings: Soft Focus, HDR Painting, Rich-tone Monochrome, Miniature, Watercolor, and Illustration; with the Multi

Frame Noise Reduction setting for ISO; or when the Smile Shutter or Auto HDR setting is being used.

SELF-TIMER

The next icon down on the menu of Drive Mode options represents the self-timer, as shown in Figure 4-21.

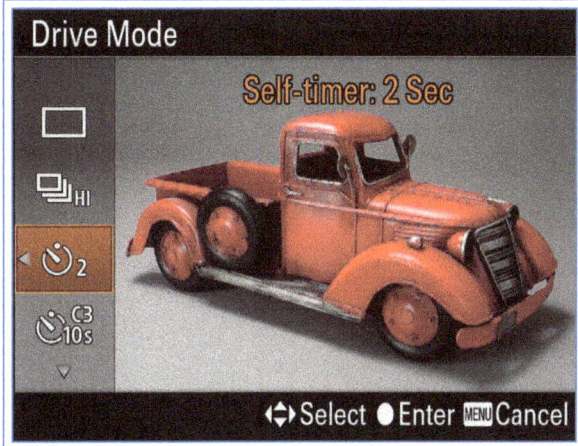

Figure 4-21. Icon for Self-timer Highlighted

The self-timer is useful when you need to participate in a group photograph. You can place the camera on a tripod, set the timer for five or 10 seconds, and insert yourself into the group before the shutter clicks. The self-timer also is helpful when you don't want to cause blur by jiggling the camera as you press the shutter button.

For example, when you're taking a macro shot very close to the subject, focusing can be critical, and any bump to the camera could cause motion blur. Using the self-timer gives the camera a chance to settle down after the shutter button is pressed, before the image is recorded.

The self-timer option presents you with three choices: 10 seconds, five seconds, and two seconds. When the self-timer icon is highlighted, press the Left or Right button on the Control wheel to choose one of these options by highlighting it and pressing the Center button to select it. After you make this selection, the self-timer icon will appear in the upper left corner of the display with the chosen number of seconds (10, 5, or 2) displayed next to the icon. (If you don't see the icon, press the Display button until the screen with the various shooting icons appears.)

Once the self-timer is set, when you press the shutter button, the timer will count down for the specified number of seconds and then take the picture. The reddish lamp on the front of the camera will blink, and the camera will beep during the countdown.

The self-timer is not available in iSweep Panorama mode, with the Advanced Sports Shooting setting of Scene mode, or for recording a movie with the Movie button.

SELF-TIMER (CONTINUOUS)

The next item down on the Drive Mode menu, shown in Figure 4-22, is another variation on the self-timer.

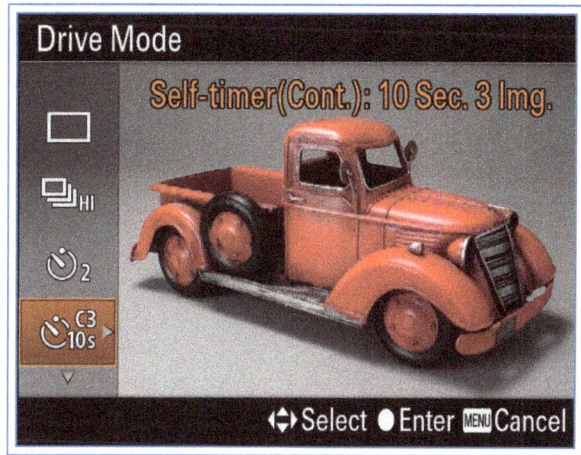

Figure 4-22. Icon for Self-timer (Continuous) Highlighted

With this option, the camera takes multiple shots after the countdown ends. You can choose any of the three time intervals, and the camera will take a quick series of three shots after the specified delay. When you highlight this option, you will see a horizontal triangle indicating that, using the Left and Right buttons, you can select one of the three options. For example, the option designated as C3/2S sets the camera to take three shots after the timer counts down for two seconds; C3/10S sets it for three shots after a 10-second delay.

This option is useful for group photos; when a series of shots is taken, you increase your chances of getting at least one shot in which everyone is looking at the camera and smiling.

CONTINUOUS EXPOSURE BRACKETING

This next option on the Drive Mode menu, shown in Figure 4-23, sets the camera to take three images with one press of the shutter button but with a different exposure level for each image, giving you a greater chance of having one image that is properly exposed.

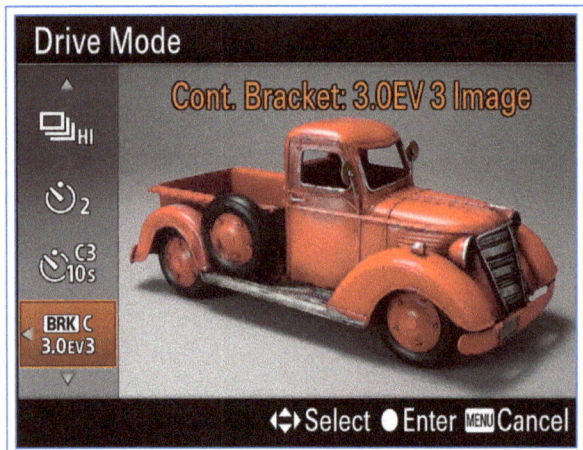

Figure 4-23. Icon for Continuous Exposure Bracketing Highlighted

When you highlight this option, you will see a horizontal triangle meaning that you can use the Left and Right buttons to select one of five combinations of the difference in exposure value and the number of images in the bracket. The choices include exposure value (EV) intervals of 0.3, 0.7, 1.0, 2.0, or 3.0.

The decimal numbers represent the difference in EV among the three exposures that the camera will take. For example, if you select 0.7 EV as the interval for the three exposures, the camera will take three shots—one at the metered exposure level; one at a level 0.7 EV (or f-stop) below that, resulting in a darker image; and one at a level 0.7 EV above that, resulting in a brighter image. If you want the maximum exposure difference among the shots, select 3.0 EV as the interval for the three shots.

Once you have set this option as you want it and composed your scene, press and hold the shutter button and the camera will take the three shots in rapid succession while you hold down the button.

The first exposure will be at the metered value, the second one underexposed by the selected interval, and the third one overexposed to the same extent. You can change this order using the Bracket Settings menu option, discussed later in this chapter.

You can use exposure compensation, in which case the camera will use the image with exposure compensation as the base level, and then take exposures that deviate under and over the exposure of the image with exposure compensation.

If you pop up the flash and set it to fire, using the Fill-flash setting for example, the flash will fire for each of the bracketed shots and the exposure will be varied, but you have to press the shutter button for each shot, after the flash has recycled. (The orange dot to the right of the flash icon on the screen shows when the flash is ready to fire again.) With this approach, the camera will vary the output of the flash unit rather than the exposure value of the images themselves.

When using Manual exposure mode with ISO set to Auto, the camera adjusts the ISO setting to achieve the different exposure levels for the multiple images. If ISO is set to a specific value, the camera varies the shutter speeds for the multiple shots.

SINGLE EXPOSURE BRACKETING

The next option is similar to the previous one, except that you have to press the shutter button for each shot; the camera will not take multiple shots while you hold down the shutter button. You have the same choices for the EV interval. You might want to choose this option when you need to pause between shots for some reason, such as if you are using a model who needs to have some costume or makeup adjustments for each exposure. It also could be useful if you want to look at the resulting image after each shot to see if you need to make further adjustments to your settings.

Apart from using individual shutter presses, this option works the same as continuous exposure bracketing. For example, you can use flash and you can change the order of the exposures using the Bracket Settings menu option.

None of the bracketing options—exposure, white balance, or DRO—is available in the Intelligent Auto, Superior Auto, Scene, or iSweep Panorama shooting modes.

WHITE BALANCE BRACKETING

The next option on the Drive Mode menu, White Balance Bracket, whose icon is highlighted in Figure 4-24, is similar to Continuous Exposure Bracketing, except that the value that is varied for the three shots is white balance rather than exposure.

Using the Left and Right buttons, select either Lo or Hi for the amount of deviation from the normal white balance setting. Then, when you press the shutter button (you don't have to hold it down), the camera will take a series of three shots—one at the normal setting; the next one with a lower color temperature, resulting in a "cooler," more bluish image; and the last one with a higher color temperature, resulting in a "warmer," more reddish image. When you use this form of bracketing, unlike exposure bracketing, you will hear only one shutter sound because the camera takes just one image, with one quick shutter press, and then electronically creates the other two exposures with the different white balance values.

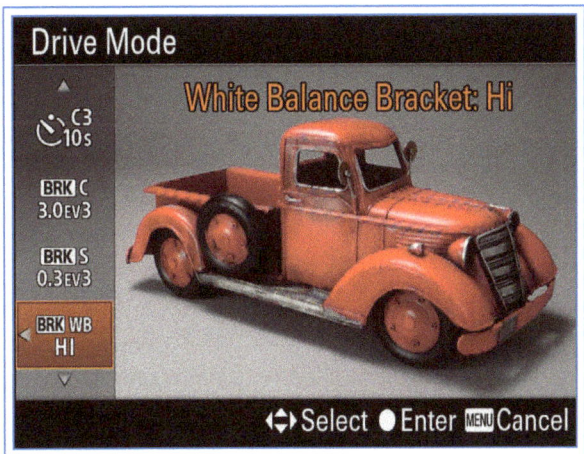

Figure 4-24. Icon for White Balance Bracketing Highlighted

You can change the order of exposures using the Bracket Settings option, discussed later in this chapter.

DRO Bracketing

This final option on the Drive Mode menu, whose icon is shown in Figure 4-25, sets the camera to take a series of three shots at different settings of the DRO (dynamic range optimizer) option.

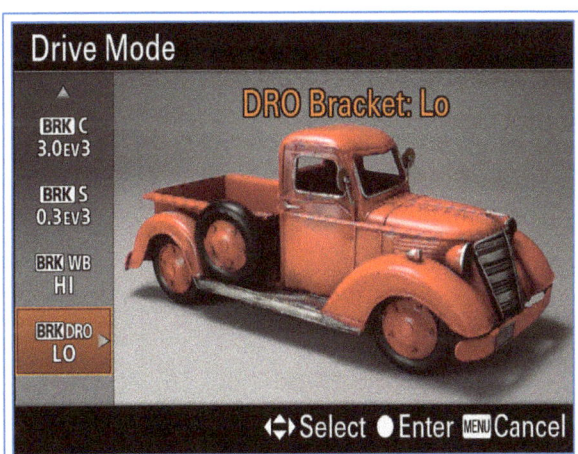

Figure 4-25. Icon for DRO Bracketing Highlighted

I'll discuss DRO later in this chapter. Essentially, DRO alters the camera's image processing to even out the contrast between shadowed and bright areas. It can be difficult to decide how much DRO processing to use, and this option gives you a way to experiment with several different settings before you decide on the amount of DRO for your final image.

As with White Balance Bracket, you can select Hi or Lo for the DRO interval. Also, as with White Balance Bracket, you only need to press the shutter button once, briefly; the camera will record the three different exposures electronically. The order of these exposures is not affected by the Bracket Order menu option.

Bracket Settings

The next option on this menu screen lets you adjust two settings for how bracketed exposures are taken. When you select Bracket Settings, you will see two sub-options: Self-timer During Bracket, and Bracket Order, as shown in Figure 4-26.

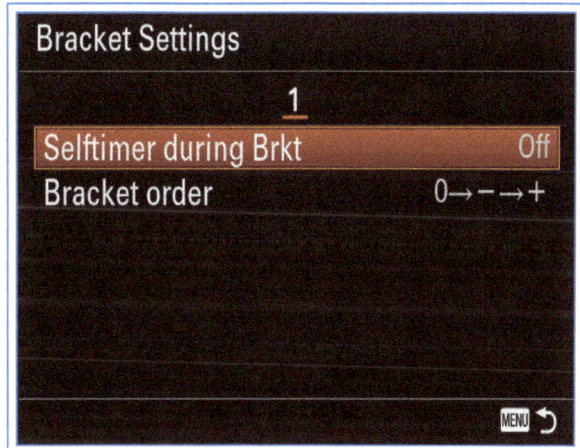

Figure 4-26. Bracket Settings Menu Options Screen

The first choice, Self-timer During Bracket, lets you use the self-timer with bracket shooting. Without this option you could not use bracketing and the self-timer at the same time, because they are selected by different options on the Drive Mode menu. With this menu option, you can have the self-timer set for two, five, or 10 seconds before the first bracket shot is triggered, or you can leave the self-timer turned off. This setting turns on the self-timer for any type of bracket shooting you choose—exposure, white balance, or DRO.

The second sub-option, Bracket Order, lets you alter the sequence of the bracketed shots. As shown in Figure 4-27, there are two choices. The first one is the default setting, with which the first shot is at the normal setting, the next is more negative (or with lower color temperature), and the last one is more positive (or with higher color temperature). If you choose the second option, the images are shot in a strictly ascending series, moving from the most negative setting to the most positive setting.

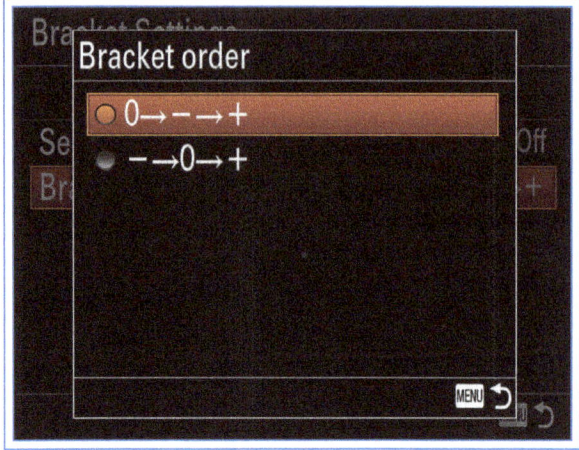

Figure 4-27. Bracket Order Menu Options Screen

The Bracket Order option affects the order for exposure bracketing and white balance bracketing, but not for DRO bracketing.

Flash Mode

In Chapter 2, I discussed the use of the camera's built-in flash, which is controlled with the Flash Mode menu option. As I discussed earlier, that option can be reached by pressing the Flash button, which is the Right button on the Control wheel. (That button assignment can be changed using the Custom Key Settings option on the Custom menu.) Flash Mode also is available as this option on the Shooting menu.

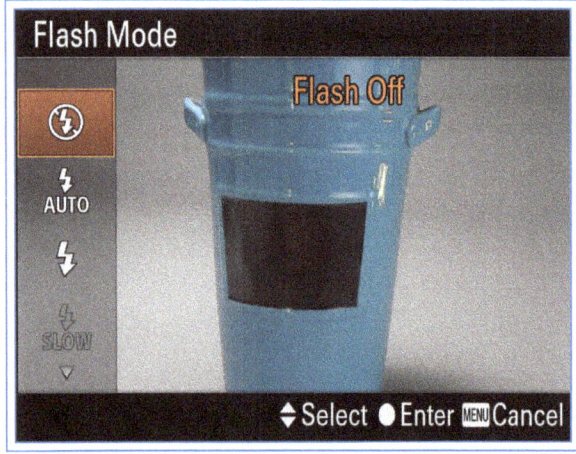

Figure 4-28. Flash Mode Menu

There are five options on the Flash Mode menu—Flash Off, Autoflash, Fill-flash, Slow Sync, and Rear Sync—the first four of which are shown in Figure 4-28. The Slow Sync option is dimmed on this screen, because that setting is not available for selection in the Intelligent Auto shooting mode, illustrated here. There is no shooting mode in which all five options are available. Here is a brief summary of the options I discussed in Chapter 2, followed by a discussion of the ones I did not discuss there.

FLASH OFF

To make sure the flash will not fire, choose Flash Off. This is a good choice when you are in a museum or other place where you don't want the flash to fire, or if you know you will not be using flash. It also can be helpful to avoid depleting a battery that is running low. This option is available in Intelligent Auto mode, Superior Auto mode, and with the Portrait, Landscape, Sunset, Pet, Gourmet, Beach, Snow, and Soft Skin settings of Scene mode. Of course, you also have the option of just not raising the flash with the flash pop-up switch, which will have the same effect as using this Flash Mode option.

AUTOFLASH

With Autoflash, you leave it up to the camera to decide whether to fire the flash. The camera will analyze the lighting and other aspects of the scene and decide whether to use flash without further input from you. This selection is available only in Intelligent Auto mode, Superior Auto mode, and with the Portrait and Soft Skin settings of Scene mode.

FILL-FLASH

With Fill-flash, you are making a decision to use flash no matter what the lighting conditions are. If you choose this option, the flash will fire every time you press the shutter button, if the flash is popped up. This is the setting to use when the sun is shining and you need to soften shadows on a subject's face, or when you need to correct the lighting when a subject is backlit.

For example, for Figure 4-29, I took two shots of a mannequin outdoors on a sunny day, with the mannequin's head partly in the sun and partly shaded. For the left image I left the flash turned off, and for the right one I used Fill-flash. The shot with flash is more evenly lighted, with the harsh shadows reduced.

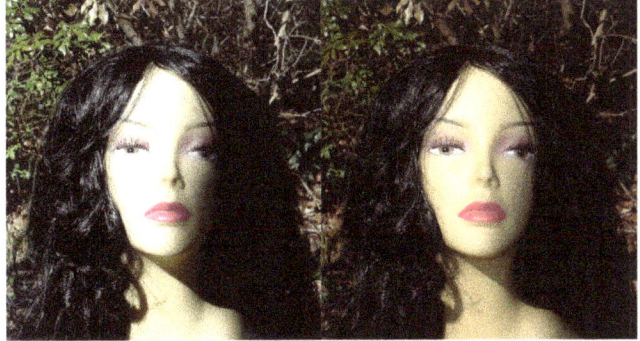

Figure 4-29. Fill-flash Example

With this option, the camera uses what could be called "Front Sync," as opposed to Rear Sync, the last option on the Flash Mode menu, discussed later in this section. Fill-flash is available with all shooting modes except Movie and iSweep Panorama, and these Scene mode settings: Advanced Sports Shooting, Night Scene, Hand-held Twilight, Night Portrait, Anti Motion Blur, Fireworks, and High Sensitivity.

Slow Sync

Slow Sync is one of the settings I did not discuss in detail in Chapter 2. This option is designed for use when you are taking a flash photograph of a subject at night or in dim lighting. With this setting, the camera uses a relatively slow shutter speed so the ambient (natural) lighting will have time to register on the image. In other words, if you're in a fairly dark environment and fire the flash normally, it will likely light up the subject (such as a person), but because the exposure time is short, the surrounding scene may be black. If you use the Slow Sync setting, the slower shutter speed allows the surrounding scene to be visible also.

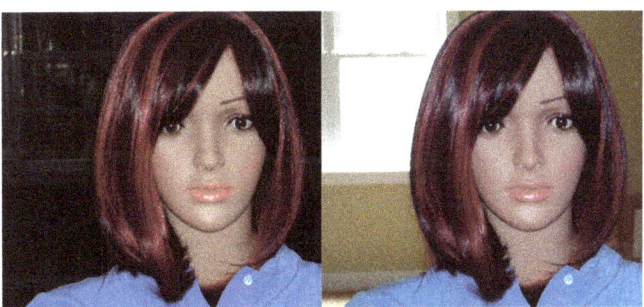

Figure 4-30. Slow Sync Example

I took the two images in Figure 4-30 with identical lighting and camera settings, except that I took the left image with the flash set to Fill-flash and shutter speed at 1/640 second, and I took the right image with the flash set to Slow Sync, resulting in a longer shutter speed of 1/4 second. In the left image, the flash illuminated the mannequin in the foreground, but the background is dark. In the right image, the room beyond the mannequin is illuminated by ambient light because of the slower shutter speed.

When you use Slow Sync, you should use a tripod because the camera may choose a slow shutter speed, such as three seconds or longer. Note that you can choose Slow Sync even in Shutter Priority mode. If you do so, you should select a slow shutter speed because the point is to use a slow shutter speed to light the background with ambient light. With Shutter Priority mode you can choose the shutter speed, but it would not make sense to select a relatively fast one, such as, say, 1/30 second. The same consideration applies for Manual exposure mode, in which you also can select Slow Sync.

Slow Sync is available only in the Program, Aperture Priority, Shutter Priority, and Manual exposure modes. With the Night Portrait setting of Scene mode, Slow Sync is set by the camera and cannot be changed.

Rear Sync

The last setting for Flash Mode is Rear Sync. You should not need this option unless you encounter the situation it is designed for. If you don't activate this setting (that is, if you select any other flash mode in which the flash fires), the camera uses the unnamed default setting, which could be called "Front Sync." In that case, the flash fires very soon after the shutter opens to expose the image. If you choose the Rear Sync setting instead, the flash fires later—just before the shutter closes.

Rear Sync helps avoid a strange-looking result in some situations. This issue arises, for example, with a relatively long exposure, say one-half second, of a subject with lights, such as a car or motorcycle at night, moving across your field of view. With normal (Front) sync, the flash will fire early in the process, freezing the vehicle in a clear image. However, as the shutter remains open while the vehicle keeps going, the camera will capture the moving lights in a stream extending in front of the vehicle. If, instead, you use Rear Sync, the initial part of the exposure will capture the lights in a trail that appears behind the vehicle, while the vehicle itself is not frozen by the flash until later in the exposure. With Rear Sync in this particular situation, if the lights in question are taillights that look more natural behind the vehicle, the final image is likely to look more natural than with the Front Sync (default) setting.

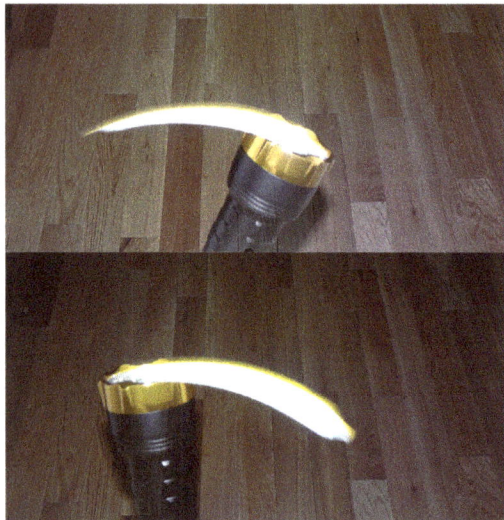

Figure 4-31. Rear Sync Example

The images in Figure 4-31 illustrate this concept using a flashlight. I took both pictures using the built-in flash, with a shutter speed of 1/4 second. For each shot, I waved the flashlight from right to left. In the top image, using the normal (Fill-flash) setting, the flash fired quickly, making a clear image of the flashlight at the right of the image, and the light beam continued on to the left during the long exposure to make a light trail in front of the flashlight's path of movement.

In the bottom image, using Rear Sync, the flash did not fire until the flashlight had traveled all the way to the left, and the trail of light from its beam appeared behind the flashlight's path of motion. If you are trying to convey a sense of natural movement, the Rear Sync setting, as seen here, is likely to give you better results than the default setting.

A good general rule is to use Rear Sync only when you have a definite need for it. Using this option makes it harder to compose and set up the shot, because you have to anticipate where the main subject will be when the flash finally fires late in the exposure process. But, in the relatively rare situations when it is useful, Rear Sync can make a dramatic difference. Rear Sync is available in the more advanced shooting modes: Program, Aperture Priority, Shutter Priority, and Manual exposure.

Flash Compensation

This menu item lets you control the output of the camera's built-in flash unit. This function works similarly to exposure compensation, which is available by pressing the Down button in the more advanced shooting modes. (Exposure compensation is discussed in Chapter 5.) The difference between the two options is that flash compensation varies only the brightness of the light emitted by the flash, while exposure compensation varies the overall exposure of a given shot, whether or not flash is used.

Flash compensation is useful when you are using flash but don't want the subject overwhelmed with light. I often use this setting when I am shooting a portrait outdoors with the Fill-flash setting to reduce shadows on the subject. With a bit of negative flash compensation, I can keep the flash from overexposing the image or casting a harsh light on the subject's face. On a very bright day, I can use positive flash compensation to help the flash overcome harsh shadows.

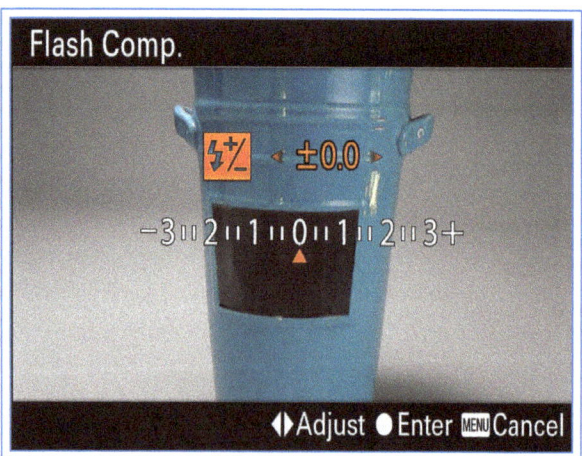

Figure 4-32. Flash Compensation Adjustment Screen

To use this option, highlight it on the menu screen and press the Center button, then, on the next screen, shown in Figure 4-32, press the Left and Right buttons or turn the Control wheel to set the amount of positive or negative compensation you want.

Whenever the flash unit is popped up, an icon will appear in the upper right corner of the display showing the amount of flash compensation in effect, as shown in Figure 4-33, even if it is zero. Be careful to set the value

Chapter 4: Shooting Menu | 55

back to zero when you are done with the setting, because any setting you make will stay in place even after the camera has been powered off and back on again.

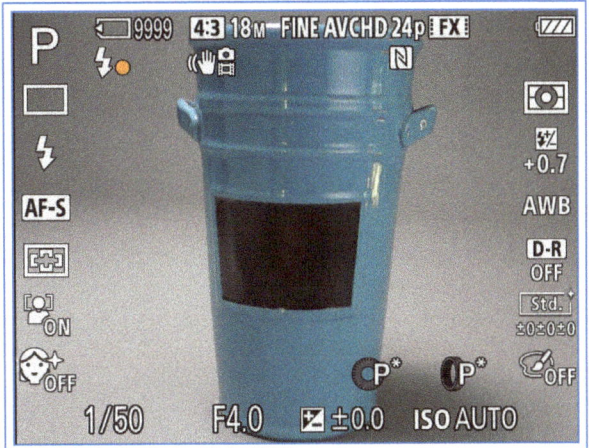

Figure 4-33. Flash Compensation Icon on Shooting Screen

The Flash Compensation option is not available for selection on the menu in the Intelligent Auto, Superior Auto, Scene, or iSweep Panorama modes.

The next menu options are on screen 3 of the Shooting menu on the HX90V, shown in Figure 4-34.

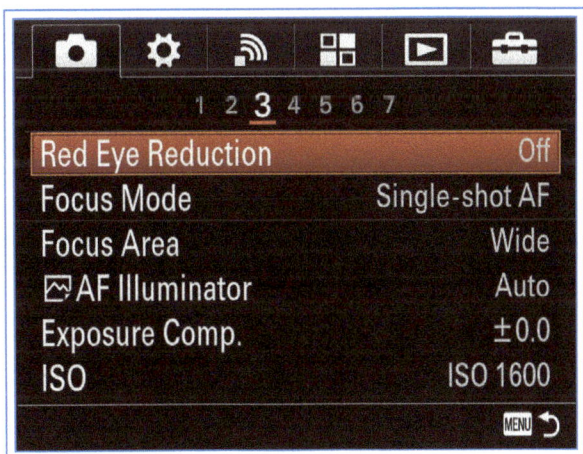

Figure 4-34. Screen 3 of HX90V Shooting Menu

Red Eye Reduction

This first option on screen 3 of the Shooting menu is designed to combat "red eye"—the eerie red glow in human eyes that appears in images when on-camera flash lights up the blood vessels on the retinas. This menu item can be set to either On or Off. If it is turned on, then, whenever the flash is used, it fires a few times before the actual flash that illuminates the image. The pre-flashes cause the subject's pupils to narrow, reducing the ability of the later, full flash to bounce off the retinas and produce the unwanted red glow in the eyes.

I prefer to leave this option turned off and deal with any red eye effects using editing software. However, if you will be taking flash photos at a party, you may want to use this menu option to minimize the occurrence of red eye effects in the first place.

Focus Mode (Available as Menu Option on HX90V Only)

The Focus Mode option, whose main screen is shown in Figure 4-35, lets you select the method the camera uses for focusing.

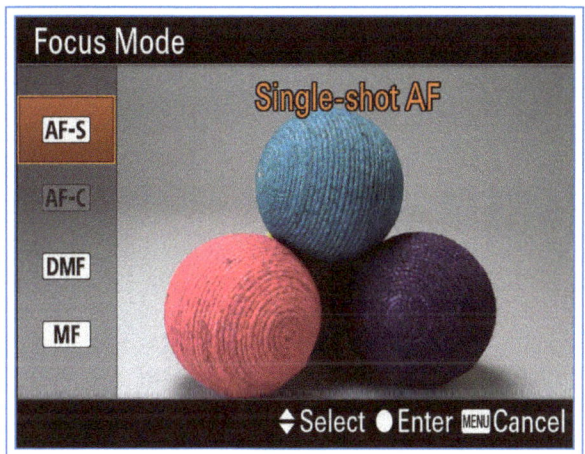

Figure 4-35. Focus Mode Menu Option (HX90V)

Although the Focus Mode menu option is available for adjustment only on the HX90V camera, some of the following discussion applies to the HX80 also. In particular, the discussion of single-shot AF applies to both models, because that is the main focus mode for the HX80, even though you cannot change it. Continuous AF is dimmed on this menu and cannot be selected when shooting still images but it is still an important option to discuss for both models, because the camera automatically turns on continuous AF when shooting movies and in the Advanced Sports Shooting setting of Scene mode. DMF (direct manual focus) and MF (manual focus) are available only with the HX90V.

Single-Shot AF

The first Focus Mode option is single-shot AF, indicated by the AF-S icon. As noted above, this is the main focus option for shooting still images for both camera models. On the HX80, you cannot change this setting.

On the HX90V, you can choose direct manual focus or manual focus instead, as discussed later in this section.

With this option, the camera tries to focus on the scene using the focus area that is selected using the Focus Area menu option, discussed below. When you press the shutter button halfway down, the camera will lock in the focus and keep it locked as long as you keep the button pressed halfway.

Once you press the shutter button halfway down, you will see one or more green focus brackets on the screen indicating the point or points where the camera achieved sharp focus, as shown in Figure 4-36, and you will hear a beep (unless beeps have been turned off through the Setup menu, as discussed in Chapter 7).

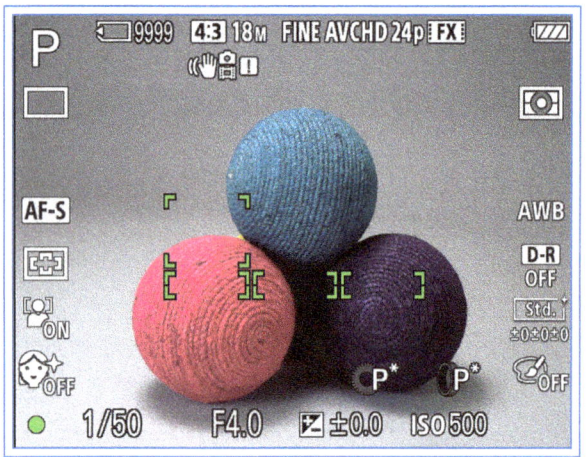

Figure 4-36. Green Brackets Indicating Good Focus

In addition, a green disc in the lower left corner of the display will light up steadily, indicating that focus is confirmed. If focus cannot be achieved, the green disc will blink and no focus brackets will appear on the screen.

Once you have pressed the shutter button halfway to lock focus, you can use the locked focus on a different subject that is at the same distance as the one the camera originally locked its focus on. For example, if you have focused on a person at a distance of 15 feet (4.6 m), and then you decide you want to include another person or object in the scene, once you have locked the focus on the first person by pressing the shutter button halfway down, you can move the camera to include the other person or object in the scene as long as you keep the camera at about the same distance from the subject. The focus will remain locked at that distance until you press the shutter button the rest of the way down to take the picture.

Continuous AF

The next option for Focus Mode, Continuous AF, is designated by the AF-C icon on the menu. As noted above, you cannot turn on this option for still shooting with either of these camera models. With the HX90V, you can choose between this option and manual focus for movie recording, but not for still shooting. With both camera models, continuous AF is automatically turned on when the Scene mode is set to Advanced Sports Shooting.

With this option, as with Single-shot AF, the camera focuses continuously before you press the shutter button. The difference with this mode is that the camera does not lock the focus when you press the shutter button halfway. Instead, focus will continue to be adjusted if the subject moves or the distance to the subject changes through camera motion. You will not hear a beep or see any brackets to confirm focus. Instead, the green disc in the lower left corner of the display will change its appearance to show the focus status.

If the green disc is surrounded by curved lines, as shown in Figure 4-37, that means focus is currently sharp but is subject to adjustment if needed.

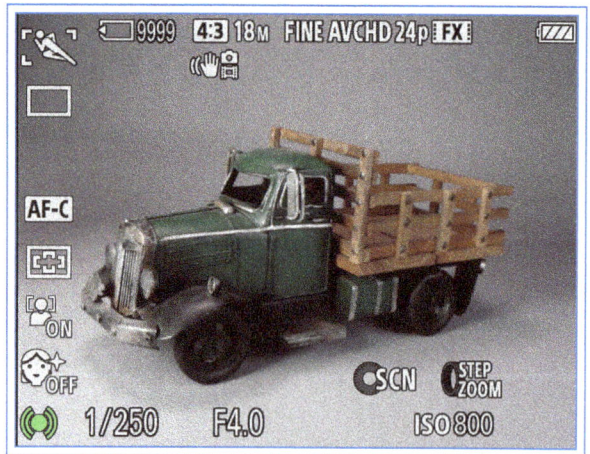

Figure 4-37. Disc and Curves for Continuous AF Adjustment

If only the curved lines appear, that means the camera is still trying to achieve focus. If the green disc blinks, that means the camera is having trouble focusing.

This focusing mode can be useful when you are shooting a moving subject. With this option, you can get the camera to fix its focus on the subject, but you don't have to let up the shutter button to refocus; instead, you can hold the button down halfway until the instant when you take the picture. In this way, you may save some time, rather than having to keep starting the focus and exposure process over by pressing the shutter button halfway again.

DMF (HX90V Only)

The third option for Focus Mode is DMF, which stands for direct manual focus. This feature lets you use a combination of autofocus and manual focus. DMF can be helpful if you are shooting an extreme closeup of a small object, when focus can be critical and hard to achieve. With the DMF option, you can start the focusing process by pressing the shutter button halfway down. The camera will make its best attempt to focus sharply using the autofocus mechanism. Then you can use the camera's manual focusing mechanism (turning the Control ring, as discussed below in this section) to fine-tune the focus, concentrating on the parts of the subject that you want to be most sharply focused.

Another time DMF can be useful is when you are shooting a scene with objects at varying distances and you want to focus on one of the more distant ones. In that case, you can start out using manual focus, adjusting it for the most important object, to let the camera know which item to focus on. Then you can press the shutter button halfway to let the camera take over and use autofocus to improve the sharpness of the focus.

When DMF is activated, you can turn on the Peaking Level feature on the Custom menu, as discussed below, and it will function for autofocus as well as for manual focus. In addition, you can use the MF Assist feature with DMF. That feature is discussed below in connection with manual focus. If you use MF Assist with DMF, you have to hold the shutter button halfway down while turning the Control ring to focus, in order for the screen to be enlarged. If you turn the Control ring without holding the shutter button halfway, the focus will be adjusted, but without the enlargement of the screen.

Manual Focus (HX90V Only)

The final selection on the Focus Mode menu is manual focus. As I indicated in the discussion of DMF, there are various situations in which you may achieve sharper focus by adjusting it on your own rather than by relying on the camera's autofocus system. Those situations include shooting extreme closeups; shooting a group of objects at differing distances; or shooting through a barrier such as glass or a wire fence.

Also, manual focus gives you the freedom to use a soft focus effect purposely. As I will discuss later in this chapter, the HX90V includes a setting on the Picture Effect menu called "Soft Focus," which adds a pleasing softness to your image. If you would rather create this effect on your own by controlling the focus directly, you can set the camera for manual focus and defocus all or part of the subject in precisely the way you want.

Using manual focus with the HX90V is quite easy. All you have to do is turn the Control ring—the large ring around the lens, next to the camera's body. This action is intuitive, and it is similar to the way most lenses were focused in the days before autofocus existed.

In addition, there are several functions available to assist with your manual focusing. I will discuss those menu options in Chapter 7, but I will briefly describe them here so you can get started with manual focus.

The first option, MF Assist, is turned on or off through the second option on screen 1 of the Custom menu. With MF Assist turned on, whenever you start turning the Control ring to adjust focus in manual focus mode, the image on the display is magnified 7.7 times, as shown in Figure 4-38, so you can more clearly check the focus.

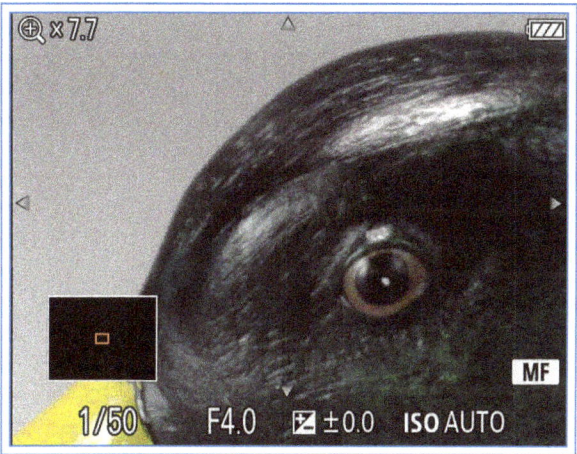

Figure 4-38. MF Assist In Use

Once the magnified image is displayed, if you press the Center button, the image is magnified further to 15.3 times normal. Press the Center button again to return to the 7.7-times view and press the shutter button halfway to return the display to normal size. You can adjust how long the magnified display stays on the screen using the Focus Magnification Time option, which is directly below MF Assist on the Custom menu. I prefer to set the time to No Limit, so the magnification does not disappear just as I am getting the focus adjusted as I want it. With the No Limit setting, the magnification remains on the screen until you dismiss it by pressing the shutter button halfway.

If you don't want the camera to enlarge the image as soon as you start focusing, you can use the Focus Magnifier option instead of MF Assist. You can activate Focus Magnifier through screen 4 of the Shooting menu, or you can assign it to a control button using the Custom Key Settings option on screen 4 of the Custom menu. You can set the Center, Left, Right, Down, or In-Camera Guide button to activate the Focus Magnifier option.

Once Focus Magnifier is activated, a small orange frame appears on the screen, as shown in Figure 4-39.

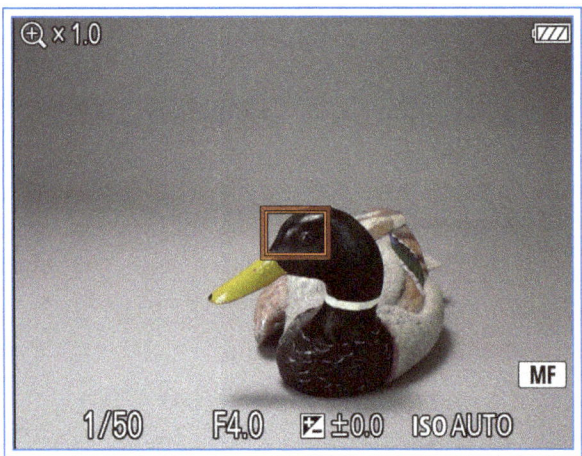

Figure 4-39. Focus Magnifier Frame In Use

You can move that frame around the screen with the Control wheel or the direction buttons. The frame represents the area that will be magnified when you press the Center button. By pressing the Center button, you can switch magnification to various levels.

You can use both MF Assist and Focus Magnifier, though I see no need to do so. My preference is to use only the MF Assist option. I prefer not to go through the steps to turn on the Focus Magnifier option, which does not add that much to the focusing options. However, when I am faced with a challenging task such as shooting in dim lighting, I sometimes use the Focus Magnifier option because it is easier to deal with that situation by being able to see the subject clearly at its

normal size and selecting the focus point before using magnification and starting to focus.

The HX90V provides one more aid to manual focusing, called Peaking Level, the third item on screen 2 of the Custom menu. That option can be turned off, or it can be set to Low, Mid, or High. When Peaking Level is turned on to any of those levels, then, when you are using manual focus or DMF, the camera places bright pixels around the areas of the image that it judges to be in focus. Figure 4-40 shows a screen without Peaking, and Figure 4-41 shows it with Peaking Level set to Mid.

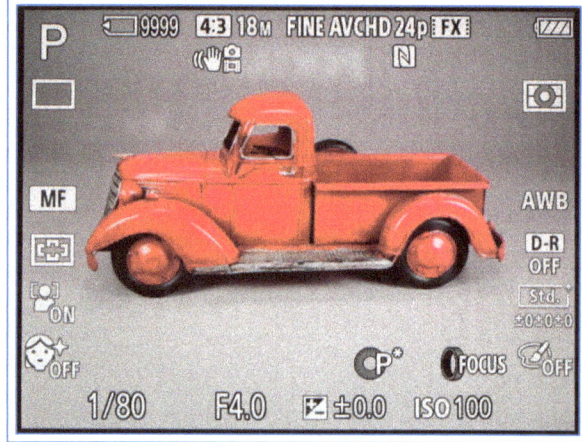

Figure 4-40. Peaking Example: Peaking Off

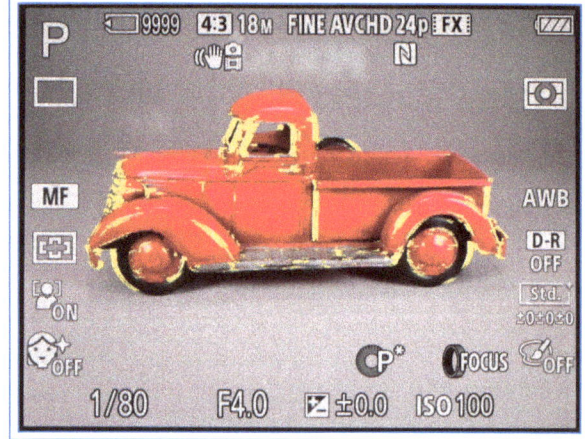

Figure 4-41. Peaking Example: Peaking Mid

Besides setting the intensity of this display, you can set its color—white, red, or yellow—using the Peaking Color option on the Custom menu. I find Peaking to be especially useful in dark conditions because the Peaking effect contrasts with the dark display. Also, as noted above, Peaking works with both the autofocus and manual focus aspects of the DMF option. I will discuss Peaking further in Chapter 7.

Focus Area

The next option on this menu screen, Focus Area, lets you choose what area the camera focuses on when using autofocus.

(HX90V only) The Focus Area option is applicable when the camera uses single-shot AF or direct manual focus. If you select direct manual focus, you can use autofocus in the same way as with single AF, so DMF is the same as single AF with respect to Focus Area. I will discuss the following options assuming that you are using single AF or DMF as your focus mode.

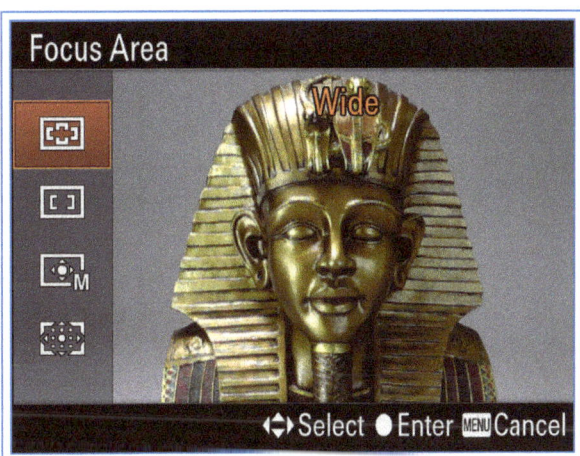

Figure 4-42. Focus Area Menu Options Screen

The choices for Focus Area are Wide, Center, Flexible Spot, and Expand Flexible Spot. Figure 4-42 shows the icons for these options, from top to bottom.

WIDE

With Wide, the camera uses multiple focus zones and tries to detect one or more items within the scene to focus on based on their locations. The camera initially displays a large, black focus frame in the center of the display. When it has achieved sharp focus on one or more items, the camera displays a green frame indicating the focus point. You may see one or several green frames, depending on how many focus points are detected at the same distance. An example with multiple frames is shown in Figure 4-43.

If the camera has difficulty picking out a subject to focus on, it will display a large, dotted frame in the center of the image, as shown in Figure 4-44. The camera also uses this type of frame when it is using Clear Image Zoom or Digital Zoom, which are discussed in Chapter 7.

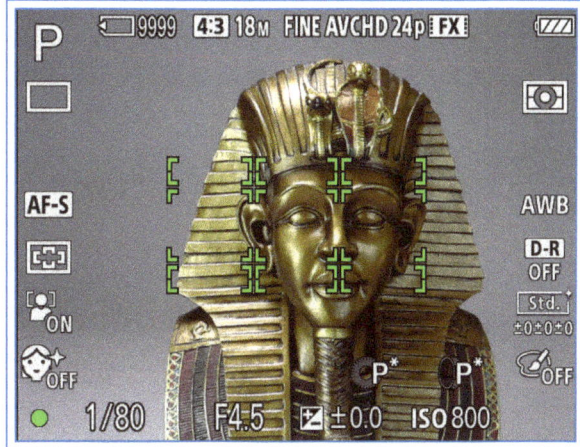

Figure 4-43. Focus Brackets for Wide Focus Area Setting

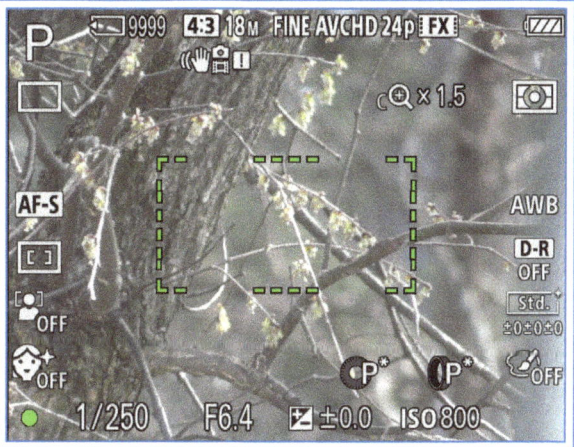

Figure 4-44. Large, Dotted Focus Frame

When you are using single autofocus, the Wide option is excellent for shots of landscapes, buildings, and the like. In continuous autofocus mode (used only with movie recording and with the Advanced Sports Shooting setting of Scene mode), the camera does not display any focus frames with the Wide setting, even after focus is achieved. The camera tries to focus on the subjects that appear to be the main ones.

CENTER

If you select Center for the Focus Area setting, the camera places a black focus frame in the center of the display, as shown in Figure 4-45, and focuses on whatever it finds within that frame.

When you press the shutter halfway, if the camera can focus it will beep and the frame will turn green. This option is useful for an object in the center of the scene.

Even if you need to focus on an off-center object, you can use this setting. To focus on an object at the right, center that object in the focus frame and press the shutter button halfway to lock focus. Keeping the button pressed halfway, move the camera so the object is on the right, and press the button to take the picture.

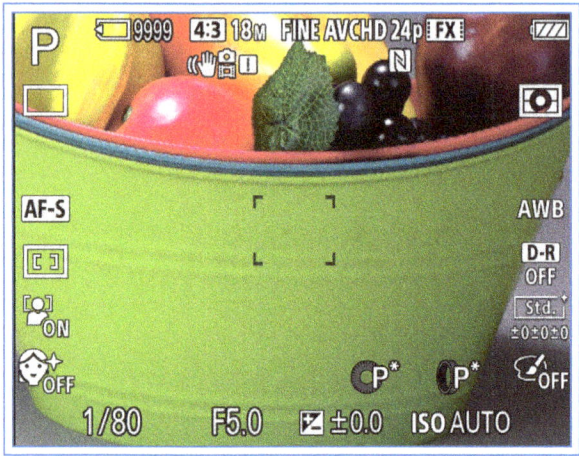

Figure 4-45. Focus Frame for Center Focus Area Setting

Flexible Spot

The Flexible Spot option gives you more control over the focus area, with a frame you can move around the screen and resize. When you highlight this option on the Shooting menu, the camera displays the screen shown in Figure 4-46.

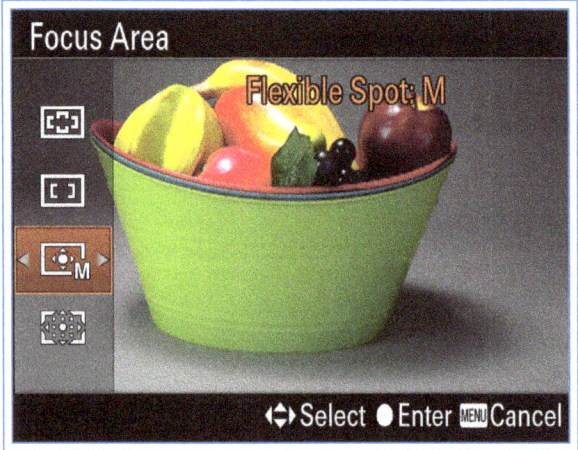

Figure 4-46. Icon for Flexible Spot Option Highlighted

On this screen, press the Right or Left button to select the size of the Flexible Spot focus frame: L, M, or S, for Large, Medium, or Small. After choosing a size, press the Center button and you will see a screen like that in Figure 4-47, with an orange focus frame of that size with arrows pointing to the four edges of the display.

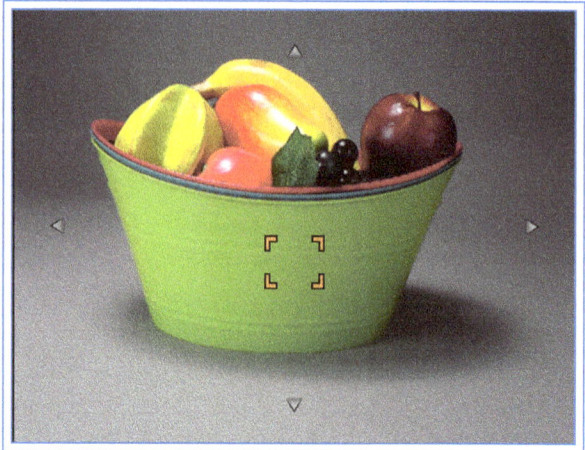

Figure 4-47. Flexible Spot Frame Ready to Be Moved

Use the four direction buttons to move the frame around the display, and turn the Control wheel to change the frame's size. When the frame is located and sized as you want it, press the Center button to fix it in place. The camera will display a black frame of the chosen size in the chosen location. When you press the shutter button halfway to focus, the focus frame will turn green when focus is sharp.

This frame operates the same way as the frame for the Center option, except for the ability to change the location and size. To return the frame quickly to the center of the screen, press the In-Camera Guide (Delete) button while the frame is activated for moving, and it will jump back to the center of the display.

This option is useful for focusing on a particular point, such as an object at the far right, without having to move the camera to place a focus frame over that object. This might help if you are using a tripod, for example, and need to set up the shot with precision, focusing on an off-center subject. If the subject is small, using the smallest focus frame can make the process even easier.

One problem with the Flexible Spot menu option is that it can be cumbersome to move the frame again once you have fixed it in place. One way to do this is to select the Focus Area menu option and repeat all of the steps discussed above. There are a couple of quicker ways to move the frame, though.

The easiest way to do this is to go to the last screen of the Custom menu and select the Custom Key Settings option. On the next screen, select Center Button, and assign the Standard setting to that button. Then, whenever Flexible Spot is in effect, just press the

Center button on the shooting screen, and the screen for moving the focus frame will appear. You can quickly use the direction buttons to move the frame where you want it, or you can press the In-Camera Guide (Delete) button to center it. You also can turn the Control wheel to change the size of the focus frame.

If you want to use the Center button for some other operation, you can assign Focus Area to the Left, Right, Down, or In-Camera Guide button using the Custom Key Settings menu option. Then, when you press the assigned button, the camera displays the menu for specifying the Focus Area option. Or, you can assign Focus Area to the Function menu, which is called up by pressing the Function button. I will discuss that menu in Chapter 7.

My preference is to assign the Standard setting to the Center button. Then, to move the focus frame, I just press that button and it is an easy matter to adjust the frame's location and size. I will discuss the Custom Key Settings options further in Chapter 7.

Expand Flexible Spot

This next option is a variation on the previous one, Flexible Spot. It operates the same way, with a couple of differences. First, the frame is small and cannot be resized. Second, because the Control wheel is not needed to resize the frame, it can move the frame around the screen. (You also can use the direction buttons to move the frame.)

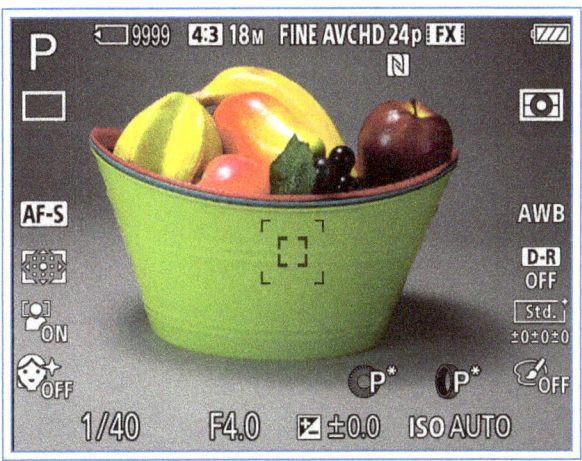

Figure 4-48. Expand Flexible Spot Focus Frame in Use

When you use this frame to fix the focus for your shot, the camera will first try to focus on a subject within the frame. If it cannot find a subject to focus on in that small area, it will expand its scope and try to focus on a subject within the area immediately surrounding the frame. That area is outlined by four small brackets outside the corners of the focus frame, as shown in Figure 4-48.

This option can be of use when you want to focus on a small area, but don't want the focusing to fail if focus can't be achieved in that exact spot.

AF Illuminator

The AF Illuminator menu item gives you the option of disabling the use of the reddish lamp on the front of the camera for autofocusing for still images. By default, this option is set to Auto, which means that when you are shooting in a dim area, the camera will turn on the lamp briefly if needed to light up the subject and assist the autofocus mechanism in gauging the distance to the subject. If you would rather make sure the light never comes on for that purpose—to avoid causing distractions in a museum or other sensitive area, or to avoid alerting a subject of candid photography—you can set this option to Off. In that case, the lamp will never light up for focusing assistance, though it will still illuminate if the self-timer is activated.

Exposure Compensation

This next option on the Shooting menu gives you a second way to adjust exposure compensation. As I discuss in Chapters 2 and 5, the primary way to adjust this option is by pressing the Down button, labeled with the exposure compensation icon, with its plus and minus signs. However, when the camera is set to Manual exposure mode, the Down button is used to toggle the function of the Control wheel between adjusting aperture and adjusting shutter speed.

Therefore, in that shooting mode, the Down button is not available for setting exposure compensation, and this menu option can be used for that purpose. (Another option when using Manual mode is to assign exposure compensation to the Control ring (HX90V only) or to a control button using the Custom Key Settings menu option, or to use the Function menu, as discussed in Chapter 7.) Note, though, that exposure compensation cannot be adjusted in Manual mode by any method unless ISO is set to Auto ISO.

When you use the Exposure Compensation menu option, there is no difference from the procedure when you press the Down button. Once the EV scale appears, use the Left and Right buttons or the Control wheel to set the amount of compensation, to make the image brighter or darker than it would be otherwise. Exposure compensation can be adjusted up to plus or minus 3.0 EV for still images, but only up to 2.0 EV in either direction for movies. Exposure compensation is not available in the Auto or Scene modes. In the two Auto modes, however, you can achieve the same effect using the Photo Creativity feature, as discussed in Chapter 2.

ISO

The next Shooting menu option is ISO. ISO is a measure of the sensor's sensitivity to light. When ISO is set to higher values, the camera's sensor needs less light to capture an image and the camera can use faster shutter speeds and narrower apertures. The problem with higher values is that their use produces visual "noise" that can reduce the clarity and detail in your images, adding a grainy, textured appearance.

In practical terms, you should shoot with low ISO values (around 100) when possible; shoot with high ISO settings (800 or higher) when necessary to allow a fast shutter speed to stop action and avoid motion blur, or when desired to achieve a creative effect with graininess.

With that background, here is how to set ISO on this camera. As is discussed in Chapters 5 and 7, with these cameras you can get quick access to certain important settings, such as ISO, using the Function menu, the Quick Navi system, using a control button that has the function assigned to it, or with the Control ring (HX90V only). However, you can also set ISO from the Shooting menu, and you can get access to some additional ISO settings only from this menu. So, it's important to know how to use this menu item.

After you highlight ISO on the menu, press the Center button to bring up the vertical ISO menu at the left of the screen, as seen in Figure 4-49. Scroll through the options by turning the Control wheel or by pressing the Up and Down buttons to select a value ranging from one of the top two options—Multi Frame Noise Reduction and Auto ISO—through 80, 100, 200, 400, and other specific values, to a maximum of 3200 at the bottom of the scale.

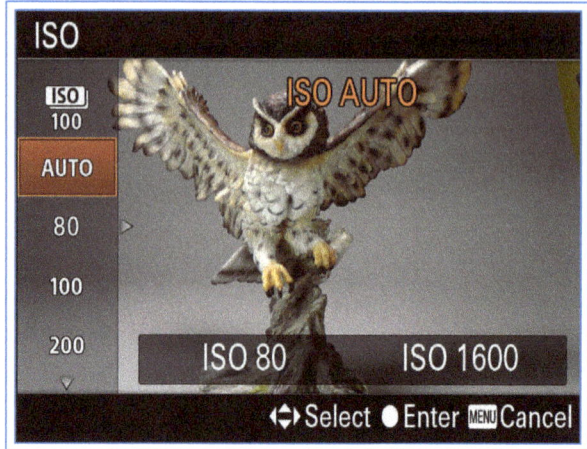

Figure 4-49. ISO Menu

(If you want to use an ISO value higher than 3200, you need to use the Multi Frame Noise Reduction feature, discussed below, or the High Sensitivity setting of Scene mode, discussed in Chapter 3.)

If you choose Auto ISO (the second option on the menu, highlighted in Figure 4-49), the camera will select a numerical value automatically depending on the lighting conditions and other camera settings. You can select both the minimum and maximum levels for Auto ISO. In other words, you can set the camera to choose the ISO value automatically within a defined range such as, say, ISO 200 to ISO 1600. In that way, you can be assured that the camera will not select a value outside that range, but you will still leave some flexibility for the setting.

To set minimum and maximum values, while the orange highlight is on the Auto ISO option, press the Right button to move the highlight to the right side of the screen, where there are two rectangles that are labeled (when highlighted) ISO Auto Minimum and ISO Auto Maximum, as shown in Figure 4-50.

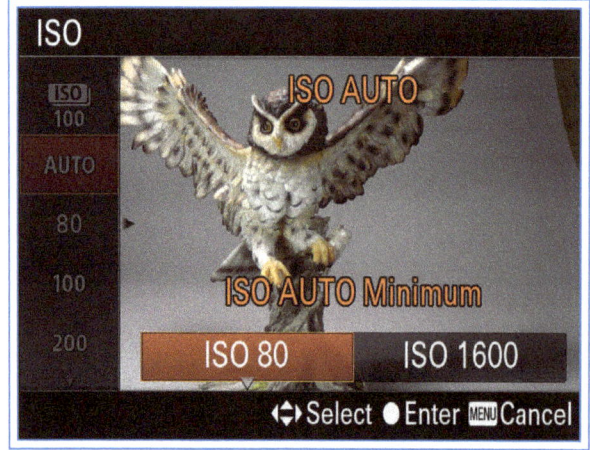

Figure 4-50. Screen to Set ISO Auto Minimum and Maximum

Move the highlight to each of these blocks in turn using the Right button and change the value as you wish, by pressing the Up and Down buttons or turning the Control wheel. You can set both the minimum and the maximum to values from 80 to 3200. When both values have been set, press the Center button to move to the shooting screen.

Once those values are set, the camera will keep the ISO level within the range you have specified whenever you select Auto ISO or the Auto setting for Multi Frame Noise Reduction, discussed below. Of course, you can always set a specific ISO value at any other level by selecting it from the ISO menu. In that case, the ISO Auto Minimum and Maximum settings have no effect.

Multi Frame Noise Reduction

The top item on the ISO menu, whose icon includes the ISO label and a stack of frames, as shown in Figure 4-51, is Multi Frame Noise Reduction (MFNR).

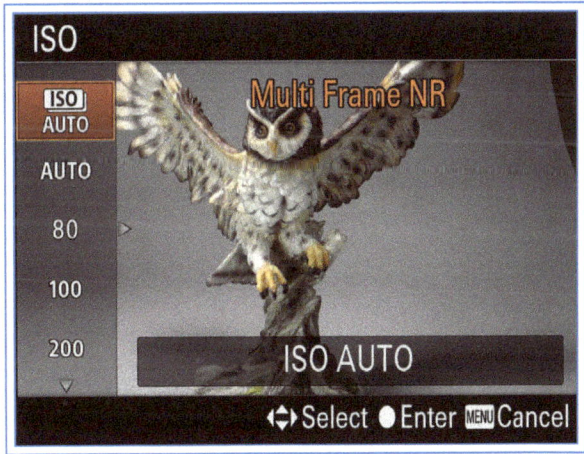

Figure 4-51. Icon for Multi Frame Noise Reduction Highlighted

This setting lets you set an ISO value as high as 12800, four times as high as the maximum value on the standard ISO menu. When you use MFNR, the camera takes multiple shots in a rapid burst and creates a composite image with reduced noise. The camera also attempts to select frames with minimal motion blur.

After you have selected MFNR, use the Right button to move the highlight to the first orange block on the right side of the screen, to choose the ISO setting to be used, as shown in Figure 4-52.

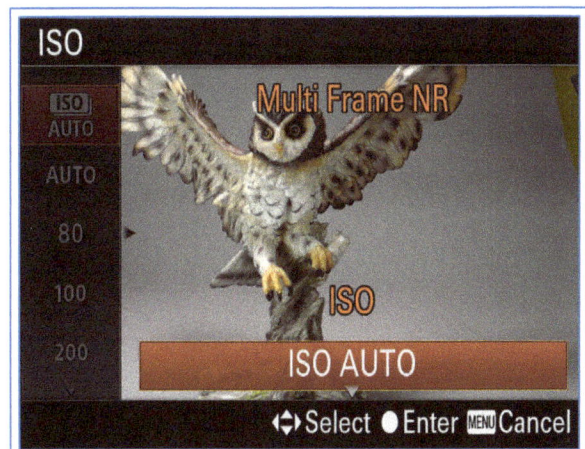

Figure 4-52. Screen to Select Value for MFNR Setting

Use the Up and Down buttons or turn the Control wheel to select a value, which can be Auto or a specific value from 100 all the way up to 12800. If you choose Auto, the camera will select an ISO value within the limits set for ISO Auto Minimum and Maximum, and it will take multiple shots using that value.

You cannot use the flash, DRO, or Auto HDR when MFNR is in effect. Also, MFNR is not compatible with the use of any Picture Effect settings or with video recording.

Using the MFNR setting is the only way to directly set the camera to an ISO level above 3200. (You can, however, use the High Sensitivity setting of Scene mode, in which case the camera may use a setting as high as ISO 12800 if it finds it necessary.) If you are faced with the prospect of taking pictures in an unusually dark environment, consider using the specialized MFNR setting, which really is more akin to a shooting mode than to an ISO setting.

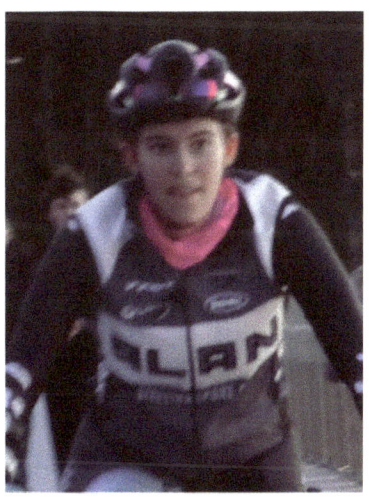

Figure 4-53. MFNR Example

In Figure 4-53, I used the MFNR setting to capture a shot of a bicyclist riding toward me after sunset. The camera set the ISO to 3200 and used a shutter speed of 1/20 second.

Here are some more notes on ISO. As I discussed in Chapter 3, with these camera models, unlike many other cameras, you can select Auto ISO in Manual exposure mode. In that way, you can set both the shutter speed and aperture, and still have the camera set the exposure automatically by varying the ISO level. In the two Auto shooting modes, Scene mode, and iSweep Panorama mode, Auto ISO is automatically set, and you cannot adjust the ISO setting.

My recommendation is to use Auto ISO for general snapshots when the main consideration is to have a properly exposed image. When you know you will need a fast shutter speed, select a high ISO setting as necessary. When you need to use a wide aperture to blur the background or a slow shutter speed to smooth out the appearance of flowing water, use a low ISO setting. When you are shooting in unusually dark conditions, consider using the MFNR setting with a high upper limit for ISO, even as high as 12800 in extreme cases.

Screen 4 of the HX90V's Shooting menu is shown in Figure 4-54.

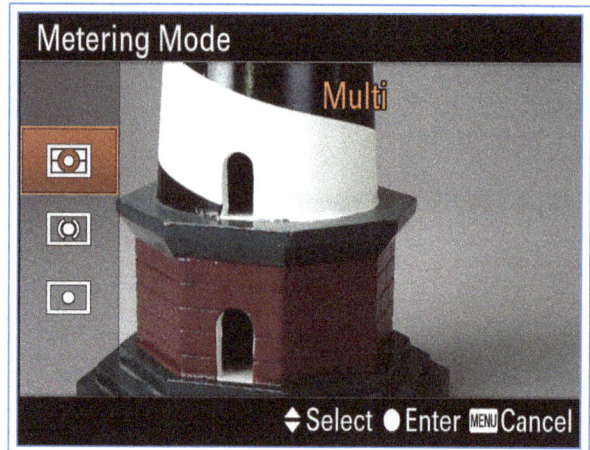

Figure 4-55. Metering Mode Menu Options Screen

This choice tells the camera's automatic exposure system what part of the scene to consider when setting the exposure. With Multi, the camera uses the entire scene that is visible on the display. With Center, the camera still measures all of the light from the scene, but it gives additional weight to the center portion of the image on the theory that your main subject is in or near the center. Finally, with Spot, the camera evaluates only the light that is found within the spot metering zone.

In Spot mode, the camera places a small circle in the center of the screen indicating the metered area, as seen in Figure 4-56.

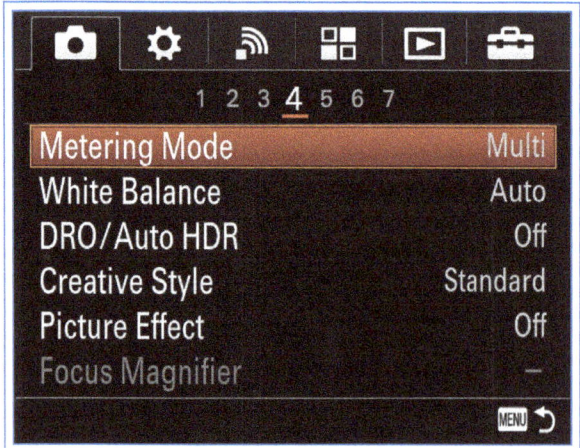

Figure 4-54. Screen 4 of HX90V Shooting Menu

Metering Mode

This option lets you choose among the three patterns of exposure metering offered by the camera—Multi, Center, and Spot—as shown in Figure 4-55.

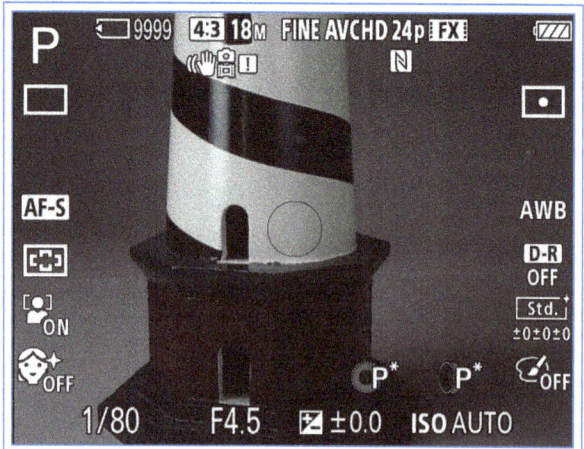

Figure 4-56. Spot Metering Circle In Use

With the Spot setting, you can see the effects of the exposure system clearly by selecting the Program exposure mode and aiming the small circle at various points, some bright and some dark, and seeing how sharply the brightness of the scene on the camera's display changes. If you try the same experiment using

Multi or Center mode, you will see more subtle and gradual changes.

If you choose Spot metering, the circle you will see is different from the rectangular frames the camera uses to indicate the Center or Flexible Spot Focus Area settings. If you make either of those Focus Area settings at the same time as the Spot metering setting, you will see both a spot-metering circle and an autofocus frame in the center of the LCD screen.

Be aware which one of these settings is in effect, if a circle or a frame is visible in the center of the screen. Remember that the circle is for Spot metering, and the rectangular bracket is for Center or Flexible Spot autofocus.

In the two Auto modes and all varieties of Scene mode, the only metering method available is Multi. That method also is the only one available when Clear Image Zoom or Digital Zoom is in use. (The conflict arises only when the lens is actually zoomed beyond the limit of optical zoom; at that point, the camera will change the metering method to Multi, and will change it back when the lens is zoomed back within the optical zoom limit.)

The Multi setting is best for scenes with relatively even contrast, such as landscapes, and for action shots, when the location of the main subject may move through different parts of the frame. The Center setting is good for sunrise and sunset scenes, and other situations with a large, central subject that exhibits considerable contrast with the rest of the scene. The Spot setting is good for portraits, macro shots, and other images in which there is a relatively small part of the scene whose exposure is critical. Spot metering also is useful when lighting is intense in one portion of a scene, such as when a concert performer is lit by a spotlight.

White Balance

The White Balance menu option is needed because cameras record colors of objects differently according to the color temperature of the light source illuminating those objects. Color temperature is a value expressed in Kelvin (K) units. A light source with a lower K rating produces a "warmer," or more reddish light. A source with a higher rating produces a "cooler," or more bluish light. Candlelight is rated about 1,800 K, indoor tungsten light (ordinary light bulb) is rated about 3,000 K, outdoor sunlight and electronic flash are rated about 5,500 K, and outdoor shade is rated about 7,000 K. If the camera is using a white balance setting that is not designed for the light source that illuminates the scene, the colors of the recorded image are likely to be inaccurate.

The HX90V and its sister model, like most cameras, have an Auto White Balance setting that chooses the proper color correction for any given light source. The Auto White Balance setting works well, and it will produce good results in many situations, especially if you are taking snapshots whose colors are not critical.

If you need more precision in the white balance of your shots, these cameras have settings for common light sources, as well as options for setting white balance by color temperature and for setting a custom white balance based on the existing light source.

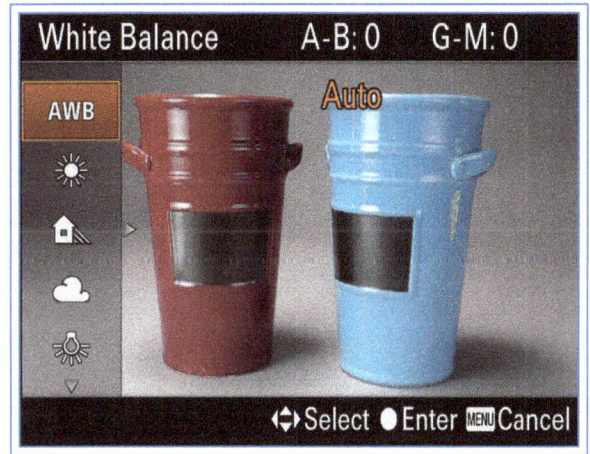

Figure 4-57. White Balance Menu

Once you have highlighted this menu option, press the Center button to bring up the vertical menu at the left of the screen, as shown in Figure 4-57.

Press the Up and Down buttons or turn the Control wheel to scroll through the choices on the first screen: Auto White Balance (AWB), Daylight (sun icon), Shade (house icon), Cloudy (cloud icon), and Incandescent (round light bulb icon).

The second screen includes Fluorescent Cool White (bulb icon, with 0), Fluorescent Day White (same, with +1), Fluorescent Daylight (same, with +2), Flash (WB with lightning icon), and Color Temperature/Filter (K and filter icon). When you scroll past that option, there is a Custom icon followed by a similar icon with the word "SET," which represents the option for setting a Custom value.

To select a setting, highlight it and press the Center button. Most of the settings describe a light source in common use. There are three settings for fluorescent bulbs, so you should be able to find a good setting for any fluorescent light, though you may need to experiment to find the best setting for a given bulb. For settings such as Daylight, Shade, Cloudy, and Incandescent, select the setting that matches the dominant light in your location. If you are indoors and using only incandescent lights, this decision will be easy. If you have a variety of lights turned on and sunlight coming in the windows, you may want to use either the Color Temperature/Filter setting or the Custom option.

The Color Temperature/Filter option lets you set the camera's white balance according to the color temperature of the light source. One way to determine that value is with a device like the Sekonic C-700 color meter.

A meter of that sort works well when you need extra accuracy in your white balance settings. If you don't want to use a meter, you can still use the Color Temperature/Filter option, but you will have to do some guesswork or use your own sense of color. For example, if you are shooting under lighting that is largely incandescent, you can use the value of 3,000 K as a starting point, because, as noted earlier in this discussion, that is an approximate value for the color temperature of that light source. Then you can try setting the color temperature figure higher or lower, and watch the camera's display to see how natural the colors look.

As you lower the color temperature setting, the image will become more "cool," or bluish; as you raise it, the image will appear more "warm," or reddish. Once you find the best setting, leave it in place and take your shots.

To make this setting, after you highlight the icon for Color Temperature/Filter, press the Right button to move the orange highlight to the right side of the camera's screen, so that it highlights the color temperature value bar, as shown in Figure 4-58.

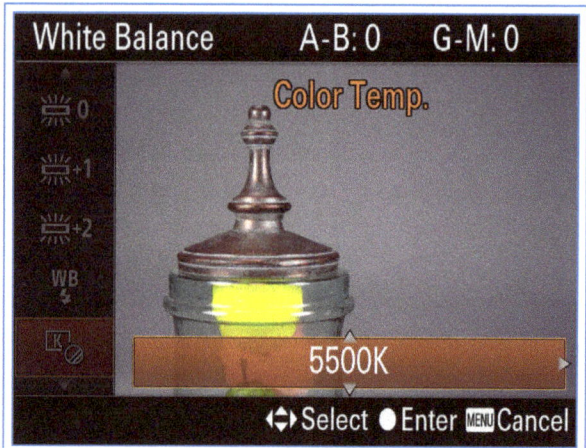

Figure 4-58. Screen to Set Color Temperature

Raise or lower that number by pressing the Up and Down buttons or by turning the Control wheel, and press the Center button to select that value.

If you don't want to work with color temperatures, you can set a Custom White Balance. This process can be confusing, because the Custom setting has two icons on the White Balance menu. The Custom icon, just below the Color Temperature/Filter icon, is used to set the camera to the currently stored Custom White Balance setting. The next icon, with the word "SET", is the one to use to get a new reading for the Custom setting using the camera's special procedure for setting that value. Before you can use the first Custom icon, you need to use the second Custom icon to set the Custom White Balance value as you want it.

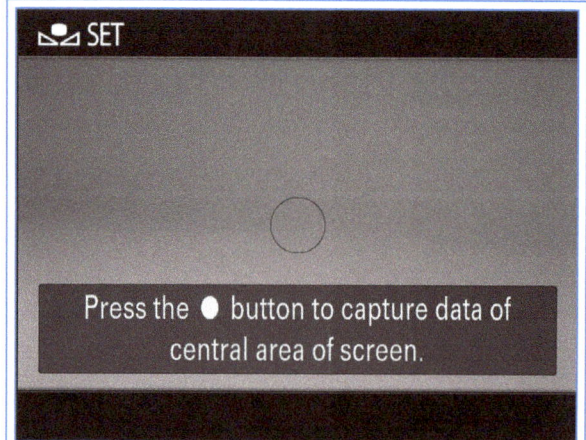

Figure 4-59. Screen to Set Custom White Balance

To set and store a Custom White Balance, highlight the SET icon at the bottom of the White Balance menu. Press the Center button to select this option, and the camera will display a message saying "Press the [Center] button to capture data of central area of screen," as shown in Figure 4-59. Aim the camera at a gray or white surface, lit by the light source you are measuring, that fills the circle on the screen. Press the Center button, and the camera will set the white balance.

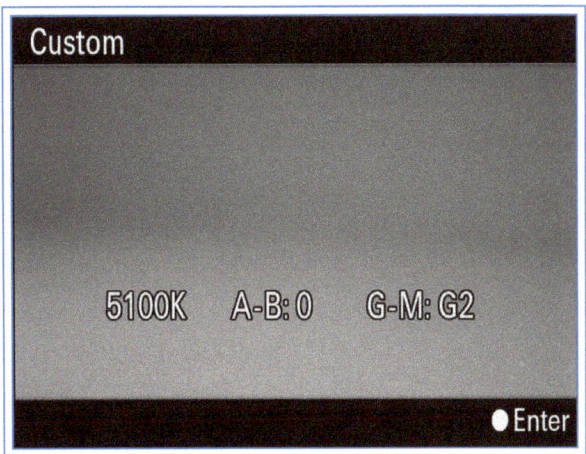

Figure 4-60. Results Screen for Setting Custom White Balance

The lower area of the screen will show the measured color temperature along with letters and numbers indicating variations along two color axes. If there is some variation, you will see an indication such as G-M: G2, meaning two units of variation toward green along the green-magenta axis, as shown in Figure 4-60.

Press the Center button to store the new Custom setting, replacing any existing setting. To use the Custom White Balance setting you saved, select the upper Custom icon on the White Balance menu. You can change the Custom setting whenever you want to, if you are shooting under different lighting conditions.

There is one more way to adjust the white balance setting by taking advantage of the two color axes discussed above. If you want to tweak the white balance setting to the nth degree, when you have highlighted your desired setting (whether a preset or the Custom setting), press the Right button, and you will see a screen for fine adjustments, as shown in Figure 4-61.

This screen has a pair of axes that intersect at a zero point marked by an orange dot. The axes are labeled G, B, M, and A for green, blue, magenta, and amber. You can now use all four direction buttons to move the orange dot along any of the axes to adjust these four values until you have the color balance exactly how you want it. Press the Center button to confirm the setting.

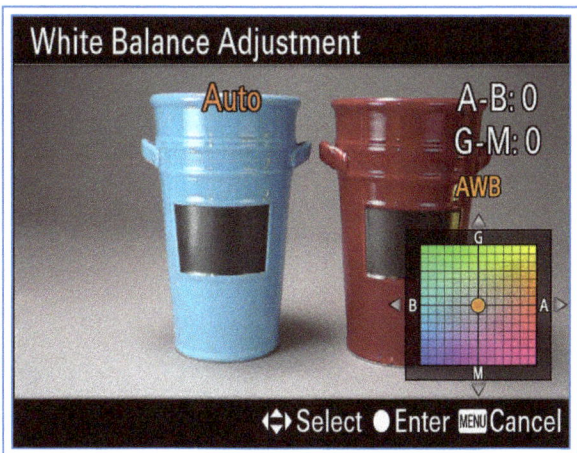

Figure 4-61. Color Axes for Fine-turning White Balance

If you prefer, you can turn the Control wheel to adjust the G-M axis, but you still need to press the Left and Right buttons to adjust the B-A axis. Be careful to undo any adjustments using these axes when they are no longer needed; otherwise, the adjustments will alter the colors of all of your images that are shot with this white balance setting in a shooting mode for which white balance can be adjusted, even after the camera has been powered off and then back on.

Before you decide to use the "correct" white balance in every situation, consider whether that is the best course of action to get the results you want. For example, I know of one photographer who generally keeps his camera set for Daylight white balance even when shooting indoors because he likes the "warmer" appearance that comes from using that setting. I don't necessarily recommend that approach, but it's not a bad idea to give some thought to straying from a strict approach to white balance, at least on occasion.

The White Balance menu setting is fixed to Auto White Balance in the Auto and Scene modes.

Before I leave this topic, I am including a chart in Figure 4-62 that shows how white balance settings affect images taken by the HX80 and HX90V. I took the photos in the chart with my HX90V under daylight-balanced artificial light using each available white balance setting, as indicated on the chart. Most of the settings yielded acceptable results. The only ones that clearly look incorrect for this light source are the Incandescent and possibly the Fluorescent Cool White setting. The other settings produced variations that might be appropriate, depending on how you plan to use the images.

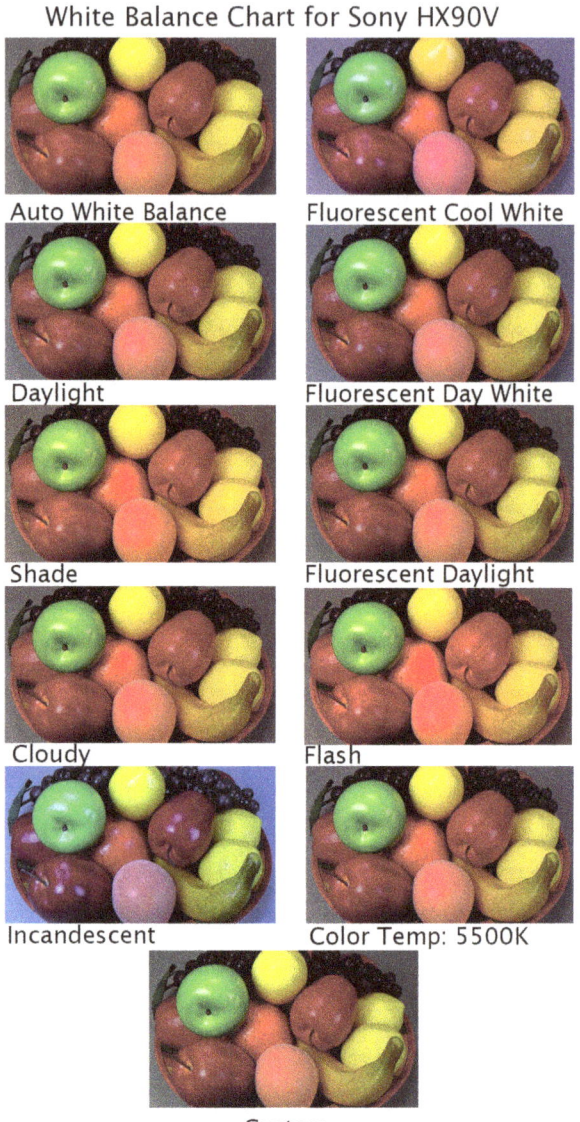

Figure 4-62. White Balance Comparison Chart

One way to deal with this situation is to use high dynamic range, or HDR techniques, in which multiple photographs of the same scene with different exposures are combined into a composite image that has clearly visible details throughout the entire scene. The HX80 and HX90V can take HDR shots on their own, or you can take separate exposures yourself and combine them in software on your computer into a composite HDR image. I will discuss the details of those HDR techniques later in this chapter.

The DRO (dynamic range optimizer) setting gives you another way to deal with the problem of uneven lighting, with special processing in the camera that can boost details in dark areas and reduce overexposure in bright areas at the same time, resulting in a single image with better-balanced exposure than would be possible otherwise. To do this, the DRO setting uses digital processing to reduce highlight blowout and pull details out of the shadows.

To use the DRO feature, press the Menu button and highlight this option, then press the Center button to bring the DRO/Auto HDR menu up on the camera's display, as shown in Figure 4-63. Scroll through the options on that menu using the Up and Down buttons or by turning the Control wheel.

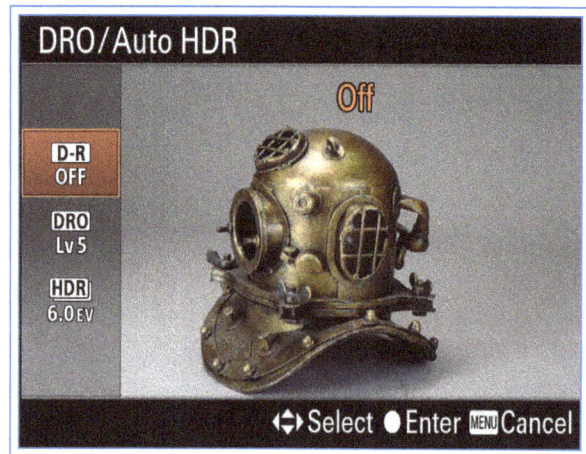

Figure 4-63. DRO/Auto HDR Menu Options Screen

DRO/Auto HDR

The next option on the Shooting menu lets you control the dynamic range of your shots using the DRO/HDR processing of the HX80 or the HX90V. These settings can help avoid problems with excessive contrast in your images. Such issues arise because digital cameras cannot easily process a wide range of dark and light areas in the same image—that is, their "dynamic range" is limited. So, if you are taking a picture in an area that is partly lit by bright sunlight and partly in deep shade, the resulting image is likely to have some dark areas in which details are lost in the shadows, or some areas in which highlights, or bright areas, are excessively bright, or "blown out," so, again, the details of the image are lost.

With DRO Off, no special processing is used. With the second choice, press the Right and Left buttons to move through the DRO choices: Auto, or Level 1 through Level 5. With the Auto setting, the camera analyzes the scene to pick an appropriate amount of DRO processing. Otherwise, you can pick the level; the higher the number, the greater the processing to even out contrast between light and dark areas.

Figures 4-64 through 4-66 are examples of the various levels of DRO processing, ranging from Off to Level 5.

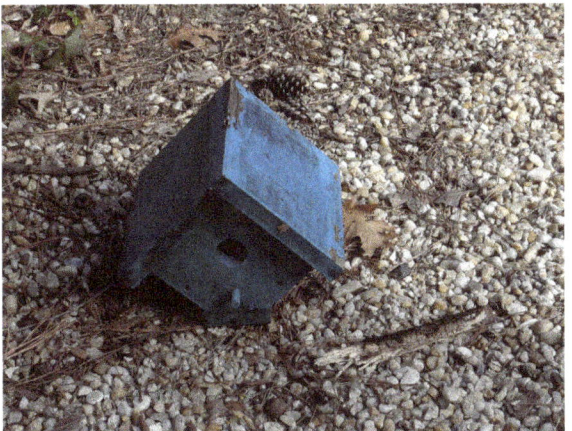

Figure 4-64. DRO Series: DRO Off

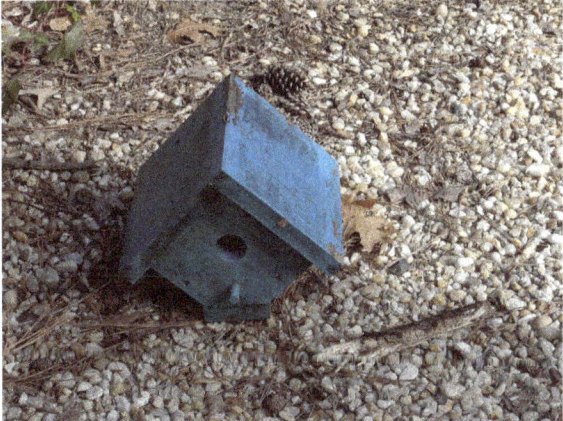

Figure 4-65. DRO Series: DRO LV3

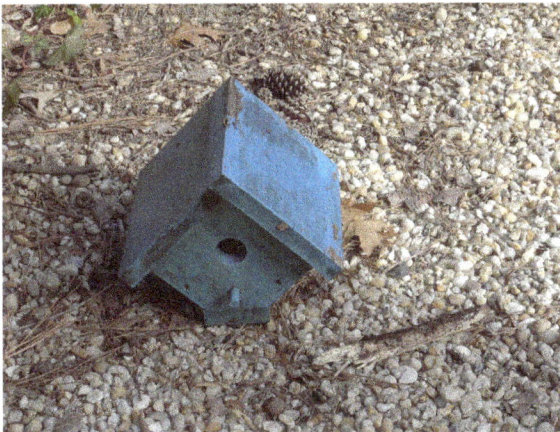

Figure 4-66. DRO Series: DRO LV5

As you can see, the greater the level of DRO used, the more evenly the camera processed the lighting in the scene, primarily by selectively enhancing details in the shadowy areas at the left. There is some risk of increasing visual noise in the dark areas with this sort of processing, but the HX80 and HX90V do not do badly in this respect; I have not seen increased noise levels in images processed with the DRO feature.

The final option for this item, HDR, involves in-camera HDR processing. With traditional HDR processing, the photographer takes two or more shots of a scene with contrasting lighting, some underexposed and others overexposed, and merges them using Photoshop or HDR software to blend differently exposed portions from all of the images. The end result is a composite HDR image with clear details throughout all parts of the image.

Because of the popularity of HDR, many makers have incorporated some degree of HDR processing into their cameras in an attempt to help the cameras even out areas of excessive brightness and darkness to preserve details. With the HX80 and HX90V, as with many modern cameras, Sony has provided an automatic method for taking multiple shots that the camera combines internally to achieve one HDR composite image. To use this feature, highlight the bottom option on the DRO/Auto HDR menu, as shown in Figure 4-67.

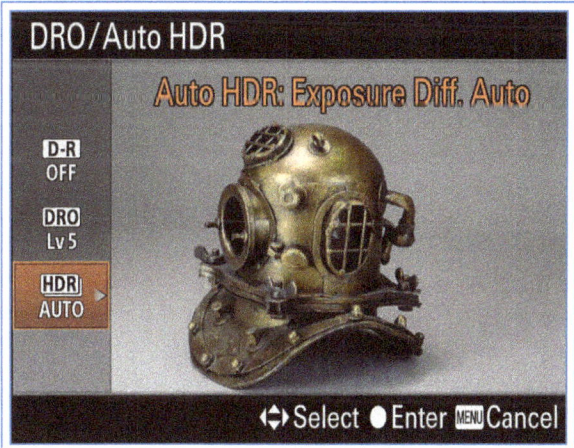

Figure 4-67. HDR Icon Highlighted on Menu

Press the Right and Left buttons to scroll through the various options for the HDR setting until you have highlighted the one you want, then press the Center button to select that option and exit to the shooting screen. The available options are Auto HDR and HDR with EV settings from 1.0 through 6.0.

If you select Auto HDR, the camera will analyze the scene and the lighting conditions and select a level of exposure difference on its own. If you select a specific level from 1.0 to 6.0, the camera will use that level as the overall difference among the three shots it takes.

For example, if you select 1.0 EV for the exposure difference, the camera will take three shots, each 0.5 EV level (f-stop) different in exposure from the next—one shot at the metered EV level, one shot at 0.5 EV lower, and one shot at 0.5 EV higher. If you choose the maximum exposure difference of 6.0 EV, then the shots will be 3.0 EV apart in their brightness levels.

When you press the shutter button, the camera will take three shots in a quick burst; you should either use a tripod or hold the camera very steady. When it has finished processing the shots, the camera will save the composite image as well as the single image that was taken at the metered exposure.

For Figures 4-68 through 4-71, I took shots of a garden pot in an area with both sunlight and shadows, to illustrate the effects of the HDR settings. For Figure 4-68, HDR was turned off; for Figure 4-69, HDR was set at 3.0EV; for Figure 4-70, HDR was set to its highest value, 6.0EV. The image with HDR at 6.0EV gave the best results in terms of pulling details out of the shadows.

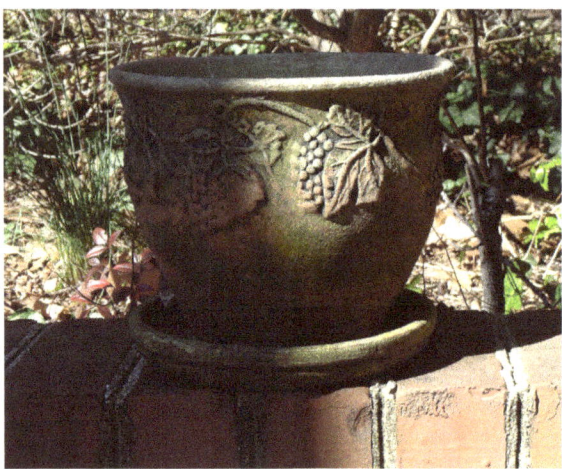

Figure 4-68. HDR Series: HDR Off

For comparison, I took several shots of the subject using a range of exposure levels in Manual exposure mode. I merged those images together in Photomatix Pro software and tweaked the result until I got what seemed to be the optimal dynamic range.

In my opinion, the HDR image done in software, shown in Figure 4-71, did a better job of evening out the contrast than the Auto HDR images processed in the camera. However, these images were taken under fairly extreme conditions. The in-camera HDR option is an excellent option for subjects that are partly shaded and partly in bright light, when you don't have the time or inclination to take multiple pictures and combine them later with HDR software into a composite image.

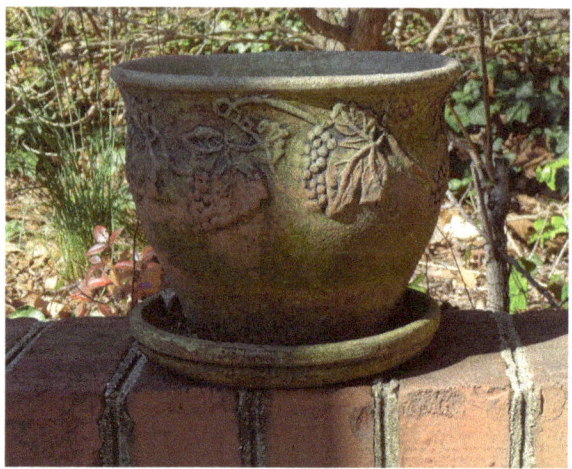

Figure 4-69. HDR Series: HDR EV3.0

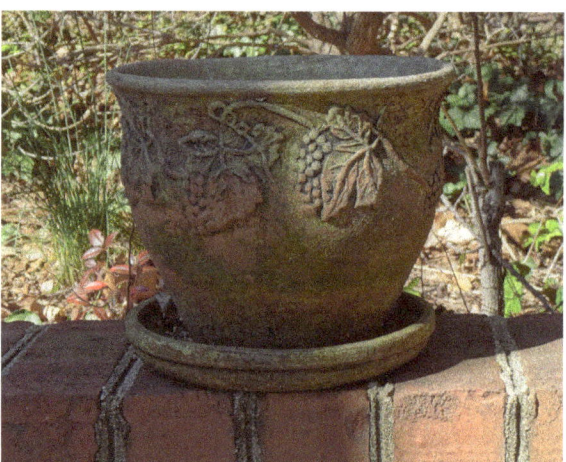

Figure 4-70. HDR Series: HDR EV6.0

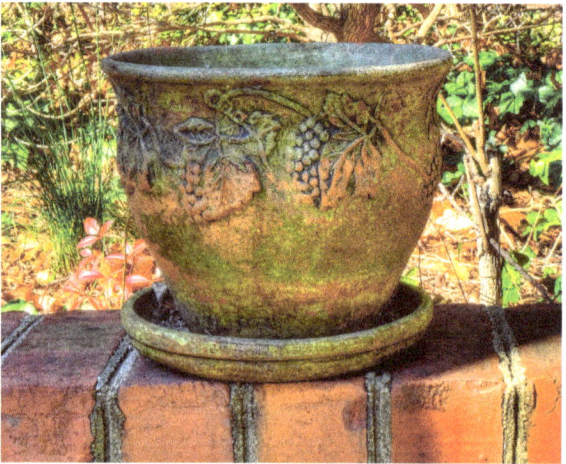

Figure 4-71. HDR Series: Photomatix Composite Image

My recommendation is to leave the DRO Auto setting turned on for general shooting, especially if you don't

Chapter 4: Shooting Menu

plan to do post-processing. If the contrast in lighting for a given scene is extreme, then try at least some shots using the Auto HDR feature.

If you plan to do post-processing, you can use Manual exposure mode or exposure bracketing to take shots at different exposures and merge them with Photoshop, Photomatix, or other HDR software.

You cannot adjust DRO and Auto HDR settings in the Auto, Scene, and iSweep Panorama modes. With the Sunset, Night Scene, Night Portrait, Hand-held Twilight, Anti Motion Blur, and Fireworks settings of Scene mode, DRO/Auto HDR is turned off. With other scene types, DRO is turned on. DRO/HDR cannot be used when Multi Frame NR or Picture Effect is active. You can use flash with these settings, but it will fire only for the first HDR shot, and it defeats the purpose of the settings to use flash, so you probably should not do so.

Creative Style

The Creative Style setting provides options for altering the appearance of your images with in-camera adjustments to their contrast, saturation (color intensity), and sharpness. Using these settings, you can add or subtract intensity of color or make subtle changes to the look of your images, as well as shooting in monochrome. Of course, if you plan to edit your images with software such as Photoshop, you can duplicate these effects at that stage. But, if you don't want to spend time processing images in that way, being able to alter the look of your shots using this menu option can be a useful capability.

To use this feature, Highlight Creative Style on the Shooting menu, and press the Center button to go to the next screen, as shown in Figure 4-72.

Using the Up and Down buttons or turning the Control wheel, scroll through the seven main settings: Standard, Vivid, Portrait, Landscape, Sunset, Black and White, and Sepia. If you want to choose one of these settings with no further adjustment, just press the Center button when your chosen option is highlighted.

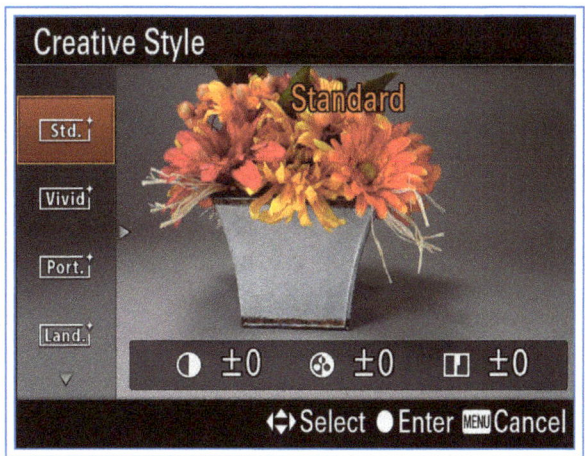

Figure 4-72. Creative Style Menu Options Screen

If you select an option other than Standard, you may notice a change on the camera's display in shooting mode. For example, if you choose Sepia or Black and White, the screen will have that coloration.

ADJUSTING CONTRAST, SATURATION, AND SHARPNESS

To fine-tune contrast, saturation, or sharpness for a Creative Style setting, move the highlight bar to the setting, such as Standard, Vivid, or Portrait, and press the Right button to put a new bar in the right side of the screen. You will see a label above a line of three icons with numbers at the bottom of the screen, as shown in Figure 4-73.

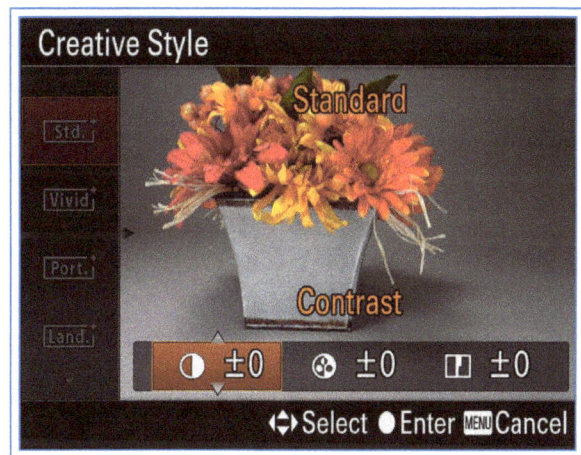

Figure 4-73. Creative Style Adjustments Screen

As you move the highlight over each icon with the Left and Right buttons, the label will change to show which value is active and ready to be adjusted. When the chosen value (contrast, saturation, or sharpness) is highlighted, use the Up and Down buttons or turn the

Control wheel to adjust the value upward or downward by up to three units. When the Black and White or Sepia setting is active, there are only two adjustments available—contrast and sharpness. Saturation is not available because it adjusts the intensity of colors and there are no colors to adjust for those two settings.

By varying the amounts of these three parameters, you can achieve a considerable range of different appearances for your images. For example, by increasing saturation, you can add punch and make colors stand out. By adding contrast and/or sharpness, you can impose a "harder" appearance on your images, making them look grittier and more realistic. When adjustments have been made, the camera indicates the amount of those adjustments above the Creative Style icon on the detailed shooting screen.

Creative Style Chart for Sony DSC-HX90V Camera

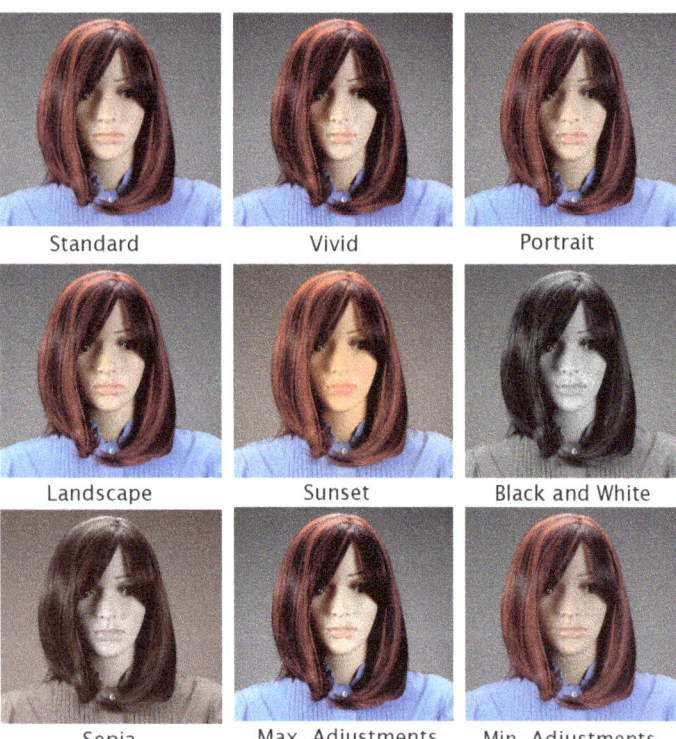

Figure 4-74. Creative Style Comparison Chart

The Creative Style comparison chart in Figure 4-74 includes at the lower right a pair of images in which the left shot was taken with the Standard setting with all three parameters adjusted to their maximums, and the right shot was taken with the same setting, but with the contrast, sharpness, and saturation all adjusted to their minimum levels of -3 units. As you can see, the left image is noticeably brighter, with a crisper look than the right one.

If you want to save your adjusted settings for future use, you can use the Memory option on the Shooting menu to save those settings as part of a set of options for the Memory Recall shooting mode, as discussed in Chapter 3.

The Creative Style option works with all shooting modes except the two Auto modes and Scene mode. This menu option cannot be used when the Picture Effect option is in use.

The chart in Figure 4-74 includes comparison photos showing each Creative Style setting as applied to the same subject under the same lighting conditions to illustrate the different effects you can achieve with each variation. General descriptions of these effects are provided after the comparison chart.

Standard

The Standard setting uses what Sony considers to be appropriate processing to give a pleasing overall appearance for everyday photographs, with some enhancements to make color photographs appear bright and sharp. This option is intended to be a good default setting for general purposes.

Vivid

The Vivid setting increases the saturation, or intensity, of all colors in the image. As you can see from the sample, it calls attention to the scene, though it does not produce very dramatic effects. The Vivid setting might work well if you want to emphasize the colors in images taken at a birthday party or at a carnival.

Portrait

The main feature of the Portrait setting is a reduction in the saturation and sharpness of colors to soften the appearance of skin tones. You might want to use this setting to take portraits that are flattering rather than harsh and realistic. Because this setting provides mid-range values for the colors and contrast, some photographers find this to be their favored Creative Style setting for general photography.

Landscape

With the Landscape setting, the camera increases all three values—contrast, saturation, and sharpness—to make the features of a landscape, such as trees and mountains, stand out with clear, sharp outlines. It is similar to Portrait in its processing of colors, but the sharper outlines and contrast might be too strong for portraits.

Sunset

With the Sunset option, the camera increases the saturation to emphasize the red hues of the sunset. In my opinion, this setting produces more changes in color images than any of the others.

B/W

This setting removes all color, converting the scene to black and white. Some photographers use this setting to achieve a realistic look for their street photography.

Sepia

This second monochrome setting also removes the color from the image, but adds a sepia tone that gives an old-fashioned appearance to the shot.

The camera also has settings for Portrait, Landscape, and Sunset in Scene mode, discussed in Chapter 3. However, the similar settings of the Creative Style option are available in the more advanced shooting modes, including Program, Aperture Priority, Shutter Priority, and Manual exposure, so you have access to settings such as ISO, Metering Mode, and others. And, as noted above, you can tweak Creative Style settings by fine-tuning contrast, saturation, and sharpness.

The Creative Style settings are of value to a photographer who needs to take numerous photographs with a certain appearance and process them quickly. For example, a wedding or sports photographer may not have time to process images in software; he or she may need to capture hundreds of images in a particular visual style and have them ready for a client or a publication without delay. For this type of application, the Creative Style settings are invaluable. The settings also are useful for any photographer who wants to maintain a consistent appearance of his or her images and is not satisfied with how the files look when captured with the factory-standard settings.

Picture Effect

The Picture Effect menu option includes a rich array of settings for shooting images with in-camera special effects. The Sony HX80 and HX90V give you a variety of ways to add creative touches to your shots, and the Picture Effect settings are probably my favorites.

The Picture Effect settings work in the advanced shooting modes, and are compatible with most other settings, apart from Creative Style. Therefore, with a Picture Effect setting turned on, you still have control over many of the most important settings, including Image Size, White Balance, ISO, and even, in most cases, Drive Mode. So, unlike the situation with the Scene mode settings, when you select a Picture Effect option, you are still free to control the means of taking your images as well as other aspects of their appearance.

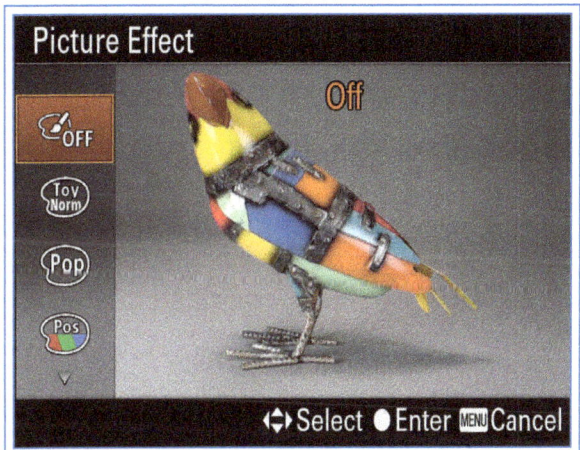

Figure 4-75. Picture Effect Menu

To use these effects, select the Picture Effect menu option as seen in Figure 4-75, and scroll through the choices at the left using the Control wheel or the Up and Down buttons.

Some selections have no other options, and some have sub-settings that you can choose by pressing the Left and Right buttons.

I will discuss each option in turn. In Figures 4-76 and 4-77, I provide charts with example images taken with each effect, all showing the same scene, for the purpose of comparison. Despite the fact that some settings are intended for other types of scenes, I believe the charts are useful to show how the various settings affect the same scene. After the charts, I will discuss each of the settings and provide a more individualized example image for each one.

Picture Effect Chart - Part 1

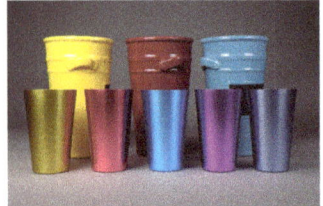
Off

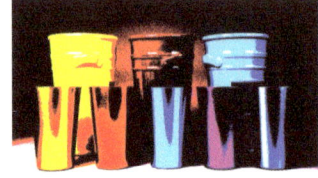
Posterization

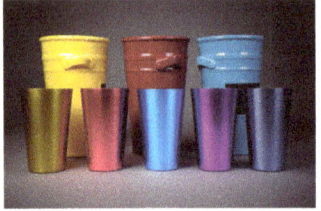
Toy Camera - Normal

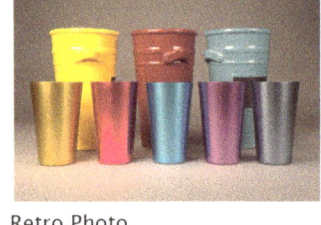
Retro Photo

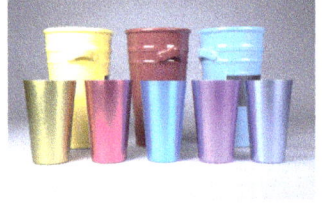
Pop Color

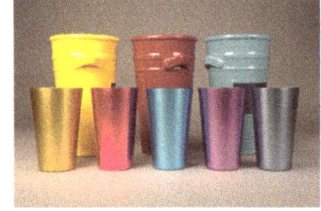
Soft High-key

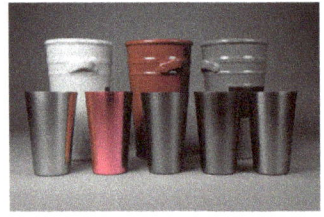
Partial Color - Red

Figure 4-76. Picture Effect Chart 1

Picture Effect Chart - Part 2

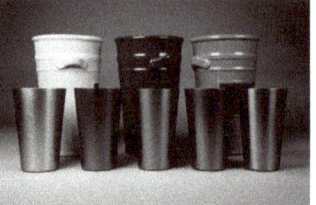
High Contrast Monochrome

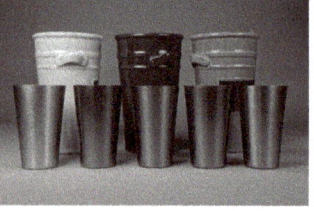
Rich-tone Monochrome

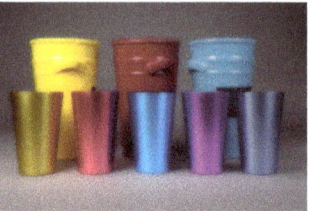
Soft Focus - Mid

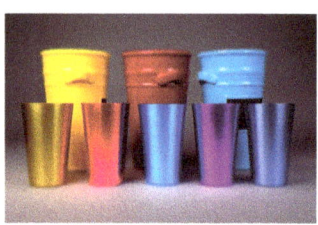
Miniature

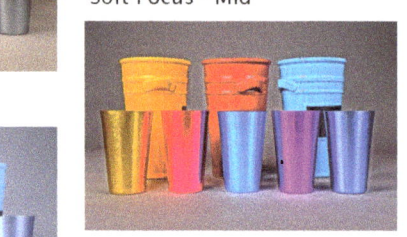
HDR Painting - Mid

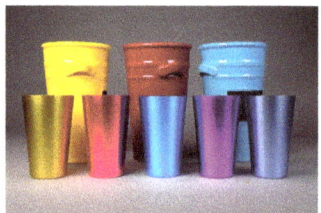
Watercolor

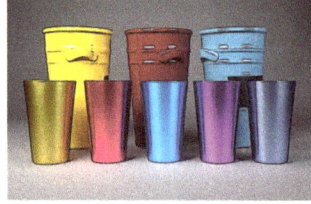
Illustration - Mid

Figure 4-77. Picture Effect Chart 2

Following are details about each of the settings.

OFF

The top setting on the Picture Effect menu is used to cancel all Picture Effect settings. When you are engaged in ordinary picture-taking or video shooting, you should make sure the Off setting is selected so that no unwanted special effects interfere with your images.

TOY CAMERA

The Toy Camera option is an alternative to using one of the "toy" film cameras such as the Holga, Diana, or Lomo, which are popular with hobbyists and artists who use them to take photos with grainy, low-resolution appearances. With all of the Toy Camera settings, the camera processes the image so it looks as if it were taken by a camera with a cheap lens: The image is dark at the corners and somewhat blurry.

The several sub-settings for Toy Camera, reached by pressing the Right and Left buttons, act as follows:

Normal: No additional processing.

Cool: Adjusts color to the "cool" side, resulting in a bluish tint.

Warm: Uses a "warm" white balance, giving a reddish hue.

Green: Adds a green tint, similar to dialing in an adjustment on the green axis for white balance.

Magenta: Similar to the Green setting, but adjustment is along the magenta axis.

Figure 4-78 is an image of a lighted fountain, taken with the Toy Camera Normal option.

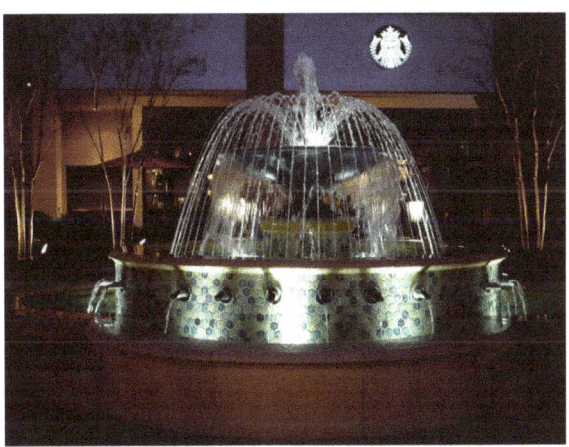

Figure 4-78. Toy Camera Example

Pop Color

This setting is meant to give a "pop art" feel through emphasis on bright colors. What you get with this setting is another way to add "punch" and intensity, along with added brightness, to your color images. In Figure 4-79, I used this option to enhance the color of orange plastic used to wrap firewood, in an attempt to emphasize the geometrical pattern of the wrapping.

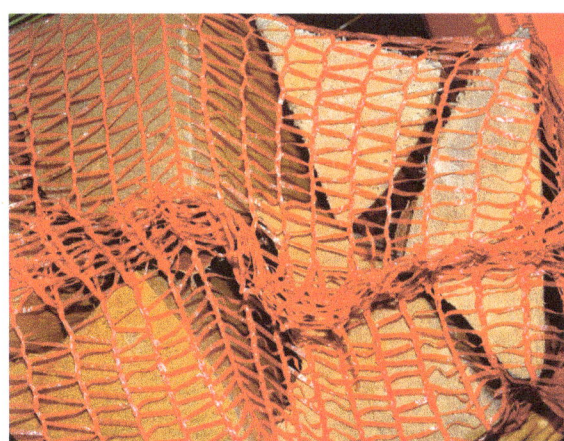

Figure 4-79. Pop Color Example

Posterization

This is a dramatic effect. Using the Right and Left buttons, you can choose to apply this effect in color or in black and white. In either case, the camera places extra emphasis on colors (or dark and light areas if you select black and white) and uses a high-contrast, pastel-like look. It is somewhat like an exotic type of HDR processing. The number of different colors (or shades of gray) used in the image is decreased to make it look as if the image were created from just a few poster paints; the result has an unrealistic but dramatic effect, as you can see in Figure 4-80, with its view of a pair of escalators in a shopping mall.

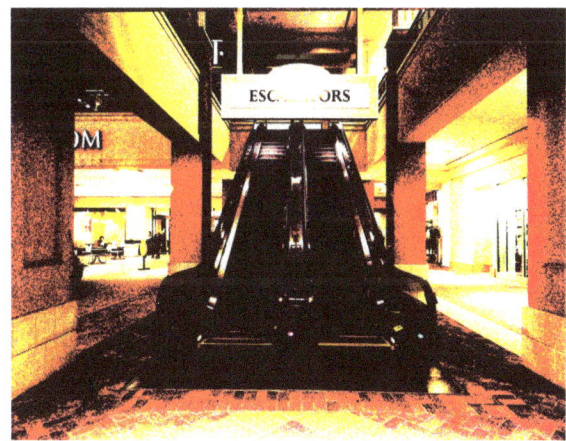

Figure 4-80. Posterization Example

Remember that with all Picture Effect options, you can adjust other settings, including white balance, exposure compensation, and others. With Posterization, you might use exposure compensation, which can change the appearance of this effect dramatically. I have found the results with this setting often are improved by using negative exposure compensation to avoid excessive brightness. I recommend using Posterization to achieve a striking effect, perhaps for a distinctive-looking poster or greeting card.

Retro Photo

With this setting, the camera uses sepia tint and reduced contrast to mimic the appearance of an aging photo. This effect is not as pronounced as the sepia effects I have seen on other cameras; with the HX80 and HX90V, a good deal of the image's original color still shows up, but there is subtle softening of the image with the sepia coloration.

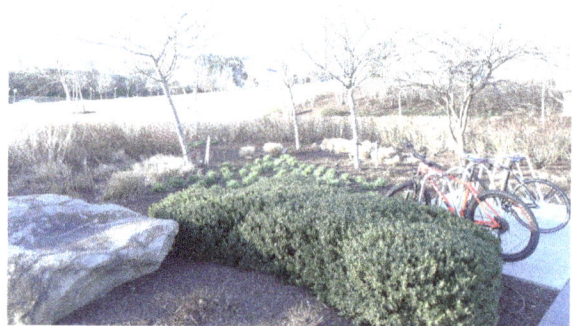

Figure 4-82. Soft High-key Example

Partial Color

The Partial Color effect lets you choose a single color to retain in an image; the camera reduces the saturation of all other colors to monochrome, so that only objects of that single hue remain in color in the image. I really enjoy this setting, which can be used to isolate a particular object with dramatic effect. In Figure 4-83, I used this option to isolate the blue umbrellas in a shopping mall seating area.

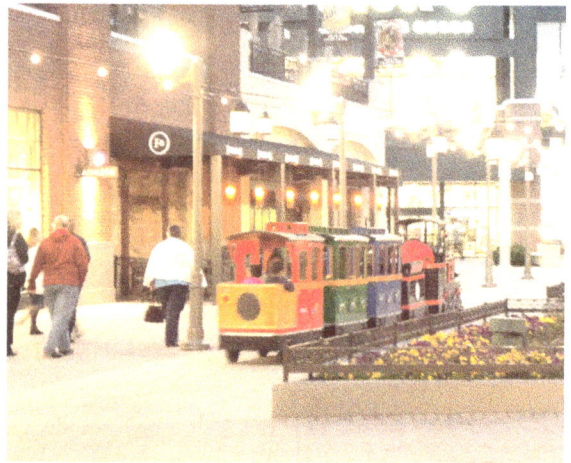

Figure 4-81. Retro Photo Example

In Figure 4-81 I used this effect for a scene of a miniature train carrying children at the shopping mall.

Soft High-Key

"High key" is a technique that uses bright lighting throughout a scene for an overall look with light colors and few shadows. With the HX80 and HX90V, Sony has added softness to give the image a light appearance without the harshness that might otherwise result from the unusually bright exposure.

In Figure 4-82, I used this setting for a shot of some landscaping outside a downtown office building, with the idea of making the scene to appear somewhat unearthly or surreal because of the excessively bright exposure and washed-out appearance.

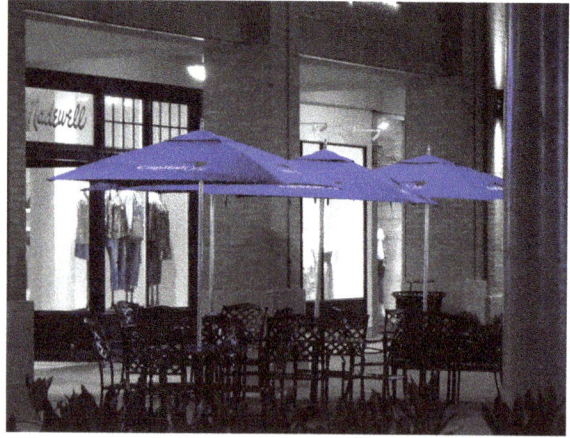

Figure 4-83. Partial Color Example

The choices for the color to be retained are red, green, blue, and yellow; use the Left and Right buttons to select one of those colors. When you aim the camera at your subject, you will see on the display what objects will show up in color.

There is no direct way to adjust the color tolerance of this setting, so you cannot, for example, set the camera to accept a broad range of reds to be retained in the image. However, if you change the white balance setting, the camera will perceive colors differently.

So, if there is a particular object that you want to depict in color, but the camera does not "see" it as red, green, blue, or yellow, you can try selecting a different white balance setting and see if the color will be retained. You also can fine-tune the white balance using the color axes to emphasize or minimize certain hues if you want to bring a particular object within the range of the color that will be retained.

By choosing a color that does not appear in the scene at all, you can take a straight monochrome photograph.

High Contrast Monochrome

This setting lets you take black and white photographs with a stark, high-contrast appearance. You might want to consider this setting for street photography or any other situation in which you are not looking for a soft or flattering appearance.

I used this setting for Figure 4-84, an image of a metal staircase and railing in a park, to emphasize the geometry of the structures.

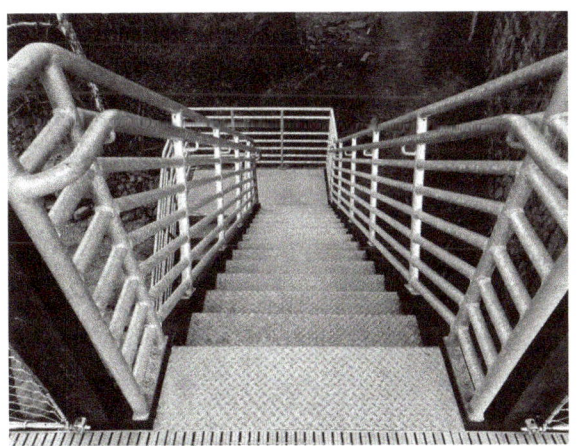

Figure 4-84. High Contrast Monochrome Example

Soft Focus

The Soft Focus effect is another setting that is variable; you can select either Lo, Mid, or Hi by pressing the Right and Left buttons to scroll through those options. This effect is quite straightforward; the camera blurs the focus to achieve a dreamlike aura. Note that this is the first of several Picture Effect settings that cannot be previewed on the screen; you have to take the picture and then play it back to see the results of the Soft Focus setting. As I noted earlier in this chapter, with the HX90V, you also have the option of setting Focus Mode to manual focus and defocusing the image to your own taste to achieve a similar effect.

I often find this effect to work well for images of people walking on a path. For Figure 4-85, I used this effect for that sort of composition when I spotted this couple walking in my direction.

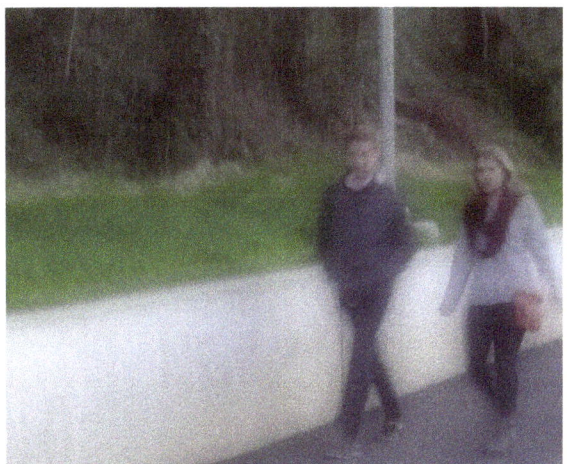

Figure 4-85. Soft Focus Mid Example

HDR Painting

The HDR Painting setting is similar to the HDR setting of the DRO/Auto HDR menu option. With this option, the camera takes a burst of three shots at different exposure settings and combines them internally into a single image to achieve even exposure over a range of areas with differing brightness. Unlike the more standard HDR setting, this one does not let you select the specific exposure differential for the three shots, but it lets you choose Lo, Mid, or Hi for the intensity of the effect. Also, it adds stylized processing to give the final image a painterly appearance.

I have often had good results with this setting when I shoot from an indoor area through a window on a sunny day, especially when there is a variety of colorful items outside. Because the camera takes multiple images with this effect, you can't preview the results on the screen before taking the picture. Using a tripod is advisable to avoid blur from camera motion while the three shots are being taken.

For Figure 4-86, I used this setting for a scene outside a downtown office building, where the colors and patterns seemed to lend themselves to this sort of treatment.

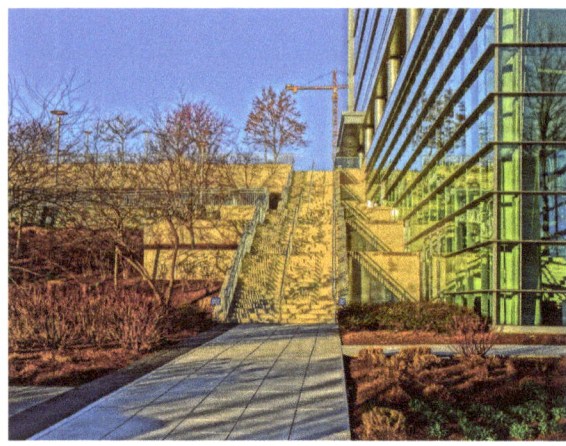

Figure 4-86. HDR Painting Mid Example

Rich-Tone Monochrome

The Rich-tone Monochrome setting can be considered as a black and white version of the HDR Painting setting. With this option, like that one, the camera takes a triple burst of shots at different exposures and combines them digitally into a single composite photo with a broader dynamic range than would otherwise be possible. Unlike the color setting, though, this one does not let you select the intensity of the effect. I used it in Figure 4-87 for a photo of the city skyline across the river. This effect seemed to emphasize the contrast between the river and the buildings

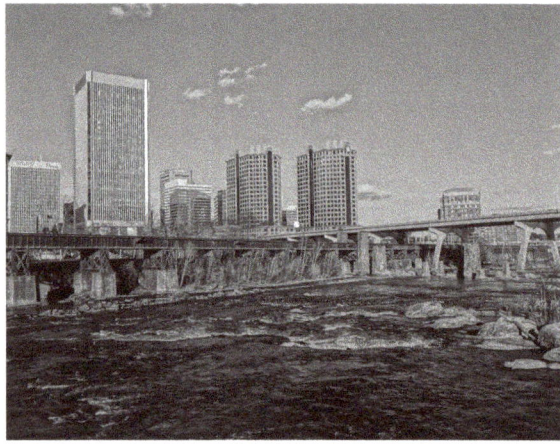

Figure 4-87. Rich-tone Monochrome Example

Miniature Effect

With the Miniature Effect option, the camera adds blurring at one or more sides or the top or bottom of an image to simulate the look of a photograph of a tabletop model or miniature. Such images often appear hazy in one or more areas, either because of the narrow depth of field of these closeup photos, or because of the use of a tilt-and-shift lens, which causes blurring at the edges.

For this feature to work well, you need an appropriate subject. I have found that this effect looks interesting when applied to something like a street scene or a train, which might actually be reproduced in a tabletop model. For example, if you are able to get a high vantage point above a road intersection or a railroad, you may be able to use this processing to make it look as if you had photographed a high-quality tabletop display.

After highlighting this option on the Shooting menu, press the Right and Left buttons to choose either Top, Middle (Horizontal), Bottom, Right, Middle (Vertical), Left, or Auto for the configuration of the effect. If you choose a specific area, that area will remain sharp. For example, if you choose Top, then, after you take the picture, the top area (roughly one-third) will remain sharp, and the rest of the image below that area will appear blurred. If you choose Auto, the camera will select the area to remain sharp based on the area that was focused on by the autofocus system and by the camera's sensing how you are holding the camera.

You will not see how the effect will alter the image while viewing the scene, though the camera will place gray areas on the parts of the image that will ultimately be blurred to give an idea of how the final product will look. In Figure 4-88, I used this setting for an image of parked cars on a road.

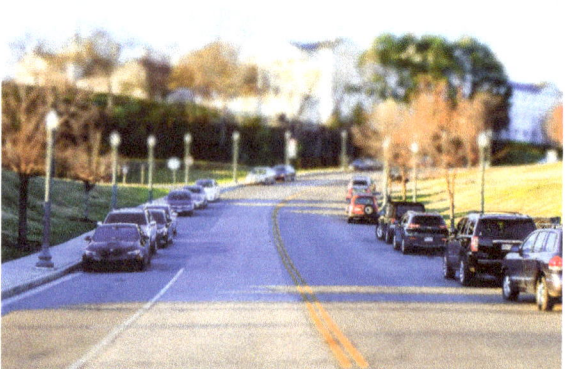

Figure 4-88. Miniature Effect Example

This effect can provide a lot of fun if you experiment with it; it can take some work to find the right subject and the best arrangement of sharp and blurry areas to achieve a satisfying result.

WATERCOLOR

The Watercolor effect blurs the colors of an image to make it look as if it were painted with watercolors that are bleeding together. You need to choose a subject that lends itself to this sort of distortion. For example, I have found that the faces of dolls and other figures can be pleasantly altered to have an impressionistic appearance; larger objects may not be affected significantly by this somewhat subtle effect. I have also had some pleasing results with plants and trees. In Figure 4-89, I used this option for a scene that included some colorful flags and a blue sky.

in the scene, especially if they are wearing clothes with bright colors.

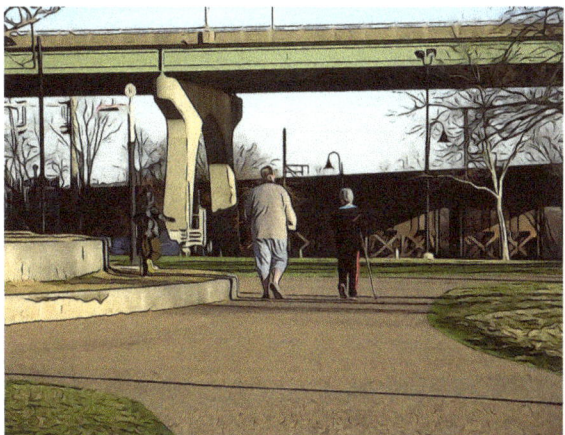

Figure 4-90. Illustration Mid Example

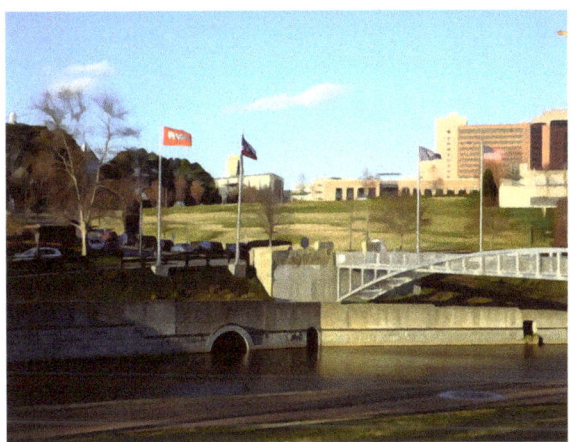

Figure 4-89. Watercolor Example

ILLUSTRATION

This final option for the Picture Effect setting is one of my favorites. This effect finds edges of objects in the scene and adds contrast to them, making the image seem like a pen-and-ink illustration that has been colored in. You can set the intensity of the effect to Lo, Mid, or Hi using the Right and Left buttons. If you choose a subject with edges that can be outlined and a repeating pattern, you can achieve a pleasing result. This is another effect whose final result you cannot judge while viewing the live scene; you need to see the recorded image to know what the actual effect will look like.

As you can see in Figure 4-90, taken with Illustration set to Mid, this effect can transform an ordinary view into a stylized image while leaving the scene recognizable. The images produced with this effect may be more suited as decorative items than as depictions of actual objects or locations, but their appearance can be very striking and unusual. I have found that this setting often produces good results when people are included

Here are some more notes about the Picture Effect settings. First, several of the options are not available for shooting movies. Those settings are Soft Focus, HDR Painting, Rich-tone Monochrome, Miniature Effect, Watercolor, and Illustration. If one of those effects is turned on when you press the Movie button, the camera will turn off the effect while the movie is being recorded, and turn it back on after the recording has ended. You also cannot use continuous shooting with any of those six effects. Note that you can activate several of the Picture Effect settings with the Photo Creativity feature in the two Auto shooting modes, as discussed in Chapter 2. However, Picture Effect is not available with the Scene mode or the iSweep Panorama mode. It also is not compatible with the Multi Frame Noise Reduction setting for ISO or with the DRO/HDR settings.

Focus Magnifier (HX90V only)

The Focus Magnifier option gives you a way to magnify a part of the shooting screen on the HX90V so you can evaluate the focus before capturing an image, when using manual focus. (It works differently for movies, as discussed below.) This option is similar to the MF Assist option on screen 1 of the Custom menu, which lets you enlarge the screen when using manual focus or DMF. However, the Focus Magnifier has some differences from MF Assist, as discussed below.

When you have set Focus Mode to manual focus or DMF (direct manual focus) for still photography, select this menu option and the camera places an orange frame on the display, as seen in Figure 4-91. You can move the frame to any position on the display using the direction buttons or the Control wheel.

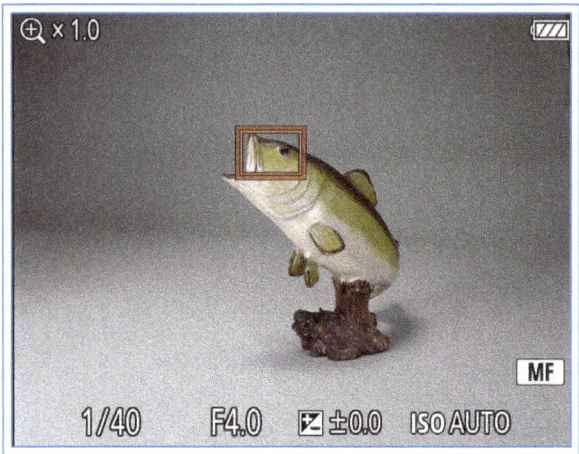

Figure 4-91. Focus Magnifier Frame In Use

When the frame is over the area where you want to check focus, press the Center button. The camera will enlarge the area within the frame to 7.7 times normal, as shown in Figure 4-92.

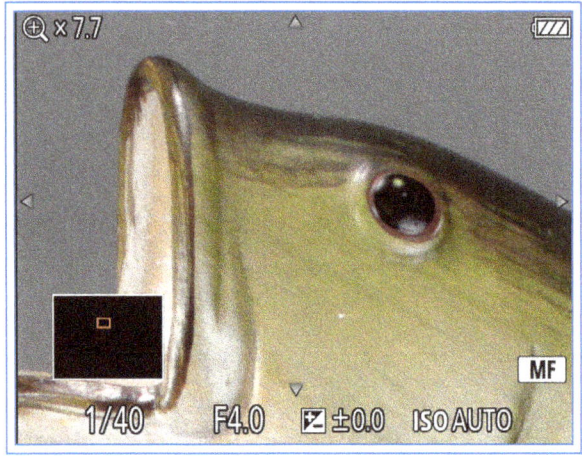

Figure 4-92. Focus Magnifier Frame at 7.7x Enlargement

An inset square will show the position of the Focus Magnifier frame. You can move the frame around the display while the display is enlarged and recall the frame to the center of the display by pressing the In-Camera Guide/Delete button. Press the Center button again, and the focus area will be magnified to 15.3 times normal. A final press will restore the display to normal size. Once you press the shutter button halfway, the magnifier frame will disappear. You can call it up again using this menu option. While the display is magnified, you can adjust the focus using the Control ring.

As noted above, Focus Magnifier acts in a similar way to MF Assist. As I discussed earlier in this chapter and will discuss in Chapter 7, when you turn on MF Assist with manual focus in effect, the focus area is enlarged to 7.7 times normal as soon as you start turning the Control ring to adjust the focus. Then, once the focus area is enlarged with that option, pressing the Center button will magnify the focus area to 15.3 times normal. You can toggle between the 7.7 and 15.3 magnifications using the Center button, and exit to the shooting screen by half-pressing the shutter button.

In other words, if the MF Assist menu option is active, the Center button acts to magnify the focus area once you have started to adjust focus in manual focus mode. With Focus Magnifier, pressing the Center button magnifies the display immediately, before you start focusing (if you are using manual focus or DMF). If you use the MF Assist option, the camera will enlarge the display as soon as you start turning the Control ring to adjust focus, and you will not be able to choose the location of the enlarged focus area until the display is already enlarged.

The Focus Magnifier feature is easier to use if you assign it to one of the control buttons. For example, you can use the Custom Key Settings option on screen 4 of the Custom menu to assign Focus Magnifier to the Left button. Then you can press that button to bring the enlargement frame up on the display at any time. You can quickly adjust the position of the frame, press the Center button once or twice to enlarge that area, and then evaluate the focus and take the picture.

You can set the length of time the Focus Magnifier frame remains on the display using the Focus Magnification Time item on screen 1 of the Custom menu, as discussed in Chapter 7. The time can be two seconds, five seconds, or No Limit.

As noted above, Focus Magnifier works differently for movies. When recording movies, this feature works with continuous AF, the only autofocus mode available for video recording, as well as for manual focus. (DMF is not available for video recording.) Also, the only magnification factor when shooting movies is 4.0x, rather than 7.7x and 15.3x, the factors when shooting still images. In order to turn on Focus Magnifier with continuous AF for movie recording, you must first set the Mode dial to the Movie position.

Screen 5 of the Shooting menu for the HX90V is shown in Figure 4-93.

Chapter 4: Shooting Menu | 81

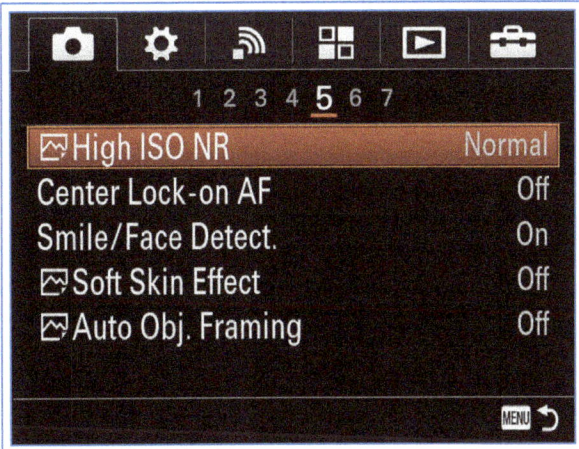

Figure 4-93. Screen 5 of HX90V Shooting Menu

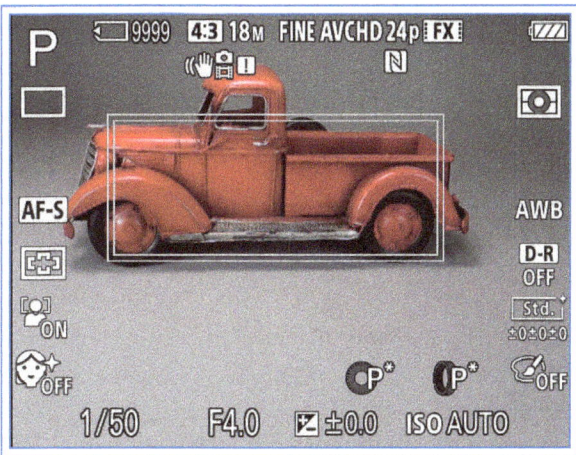

Figure 4-94. Double Frame for Center Lock-on AF

High ISO Noise Reduction

This option has three settings: Normal, Low, or Off; the default is Normal. This option removes noise caused by the use of a high ISO level. One problem with this sort of noise reduction is that it takes time to process your images after they are captured. You may want to set this option to Low or Off to minimize the delay before you can take another picture. This setting is not available in the Auto, Scene, or iSweep Panorama modes.

Center Lock-on AF

Center Lock-on AF is a special setting for tracking moving subjects when using autofocus. To use it, select this menu option and turn it on. The camera will display a message saying it will track the subject nearest to the screen center when you press the Center button. Then, from the shooting screen, locate the subject you want to focus on in the center of the screen and press the Center button. The camera will display a double-bordered frame that will move around the display and expand as needed to keep the subject inside the frame and in focus, as shown in Figure 4-94. When you are ready to take the picture, press the shutter button. To cancel the tracking, press the Center button. To start it again, press the Center button to reactivate the feature.

This option does not work with iSweep Panorama mode or with the Hand-held Twilight or Anti Motion Blur settings of Scene mode. It also does not work with digital zoom. In addition, it does not work unless the Center button is set to the Standard option using the Custom Key Settings option on the last screen of the Custom menu.

Smile/Face Detection

This option gives you access to two functions with fairly different features. There are four separate entries on the vertical menu that pops up when this menu item is selected, shown in Figure 4-95.

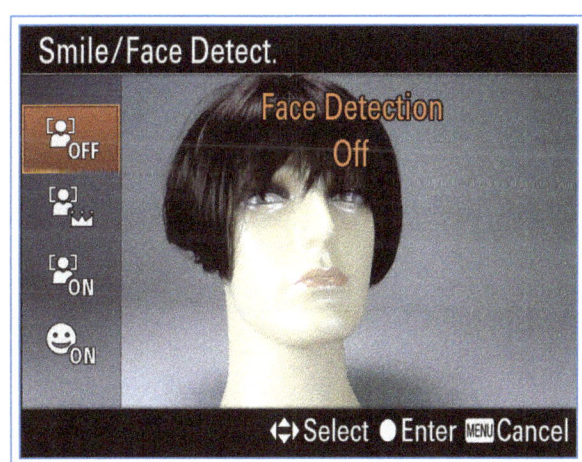

Figure 4-95. Smile/Face Detection Menu

You can select the top setting, Off, which leaves all options turned off, or you can select one of the other three, which operate as follows:

FACE DETECTION ON (REGISTERED FACES)

This option is designated on the menu screen by an icon of a person's head and a crown. When you select this choice, the camera searches for faces that you have previously registered using the Face Registration option on the Custom menu, as discussed in Chapter 7.

If the camera detects a registered face, it should consider that face to have priority, in which case it will place a white frame on the face and adjust the Focus

Area, Flash Mode, exposure compensation, white balance, and Red Eye Reduction values automatically to produce optimum exposure for that particular face. If there are multiple faces, some of which are registered, the camera should place a white frame over the one with the highest priority and purple frames over registered faces with lower priorities.

In daily shooting, I do not use this feature. It could be useful if you are taking pictures of children in a group setting and you want to make sure your own child is in focus and has his or her face properly exposed. I tested this option by registering one face and then aiming the camera at that face along with some unregistered faces. I found that the camera did a good job of distinguishing the registered face from the unregistered ones, though results undoubtedly will vary. This feature is certainly worth trying if it would be of use to you.

Face Detection On

This setting is similar to the previous one, except that it does not involve registered faces. As shown in Figure 4-96, the camera will detect any human faces, up to eight in total, and select one as the main face to concentrate its settings on.

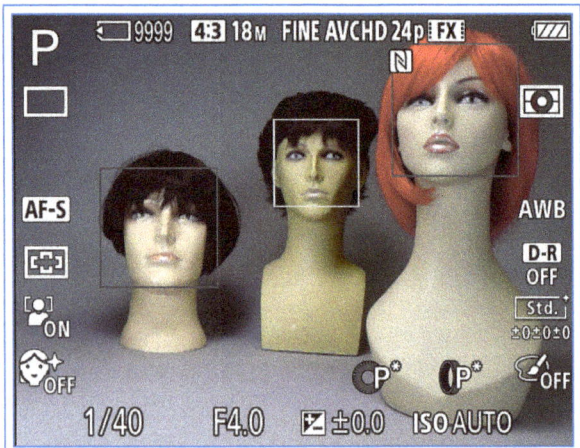

Figure 4-96. Face Detection In Use

Before you press the shutter button, the camera will display white or gray frames around any faces it finds. When you press the shutter button halfway to lock focus and exposure, the frame over the face the camera has selected as the main face will turn green. The camera may place multiple green frames if there are multiple faces at the same distance from the camera.

Smile Shutter

The final option for this menu item is the Smile Shutter, which is a sort of self-timer that is activated when the subject smiles.

After highlighting this option, use the Left and Right buttons to choose the level of smile that is needed to trigger the camera—Slight Smile, Normal Smile, or Big Smile. Then press the Center button to return to the shooting screen, and aim the camera at the subject or subjects. (You can, of course, put the camera on a tripod and aim it at yourself, if you want.)

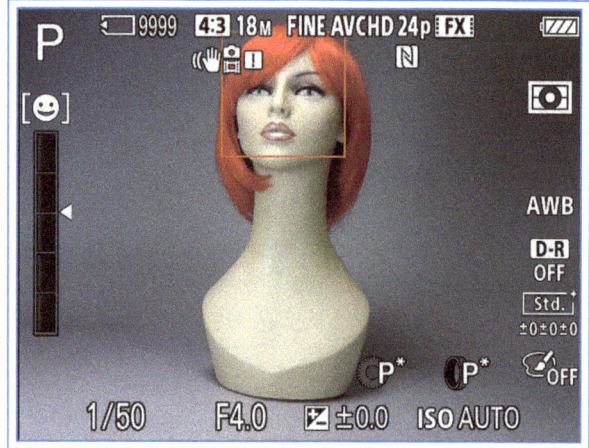

Figure 4-97. Smile Shutter Meter on Shooting Screen

As shown in Figure 4-97, the camera will show a meter on the left of the screen with a pointer to indicate how large a smile is needed to trigger a shot. As soon as the camera detects a big enough smile from any person, the shutter will fire. If a person smiles again, the camera will be triggered again, with no limit on the number of shots that can be taken. In effect, this feature acts as a limited kind of remote control with one specific function. I consider this option to be something of a novelty, which can be entertaining but is not necessary for everyday photography.

The Smile/Face Detection options are incompatible with certain settings, including iSweep Panorama mode, digital zoom, the Posterization setting for Picture Effect, the Focus Magnifier option (HX90V only), and the Night Scene, Landscape, and Sunset settings of Scene mode. In addition, the Smile Shutter is not compatible with any Picture Effect settings.

Chapter 4: Shooting Menu

Soft Skin Effect

This menu option softens skin tones in the faces of your subjects for still images. The option is dimmed and unavailable in some situations, such as when one of the continuous shooting options is selected. After you select it and turn it on, you can use the Right and Left buttons to set the level at Lo, Mid, or Hi, as shown in Figure 4-98. However, even if you turn the Soft Skin Effect option on, it will not produce any changes in your images unless you also have Face Detection turned on in the menu system and the camera has detected a face.

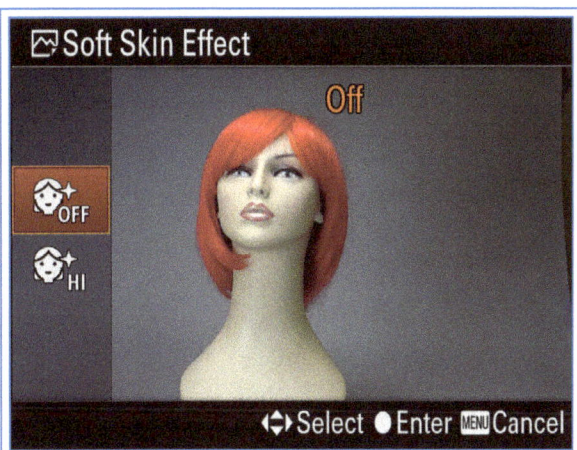

Figure 4-98. Soft Skin Effect Menu Options Screen

When it works, this setting reduces sharpness and contrast in areas that the camera perceives as skin tones. It can do a good job of smoothing out wrinkles. Figure 4-99 shows the results of a test I made. The image on the left was taken with the effect turned off; the image on the right had the setting at its Hi level.

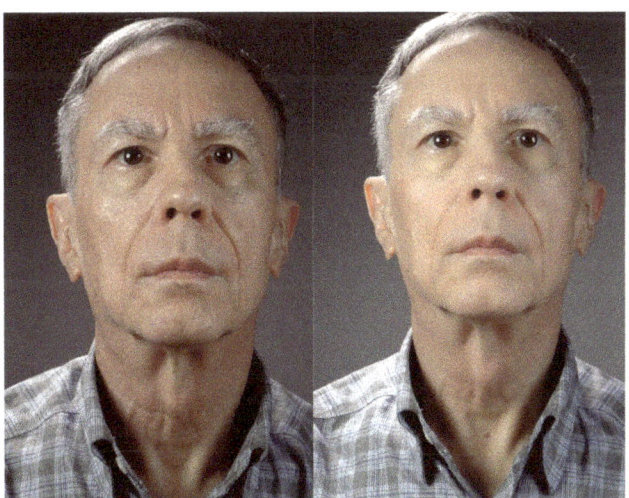

Figure 4-99. Soft Skin Composite Image

This can be a useful option for doing some basic retouching of your portraits in the camera.

Auto Object Framing

This menu option provides a somewhat unusual function: It rearranges the composition of your shot based on the camera's electronic judgment. To activate it, set it to Auto on the menu. Then, when you capture your image, the camera will display a large white frame around what it believes to be the subject if it finds that the image can benefit by being trimmed to fit the subject better. For this feature to work with faces, you need to have Face Detection turned on with the Smile/Face Detection menu option discussed above. Besides faces, Sony says that the feature will work with macro shots and objects tracked with Center Lock-on AF.

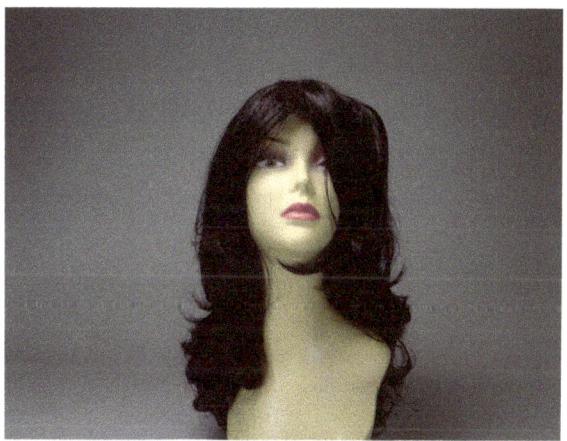

Figure 4-100. Auto Object Framing: Original Subject

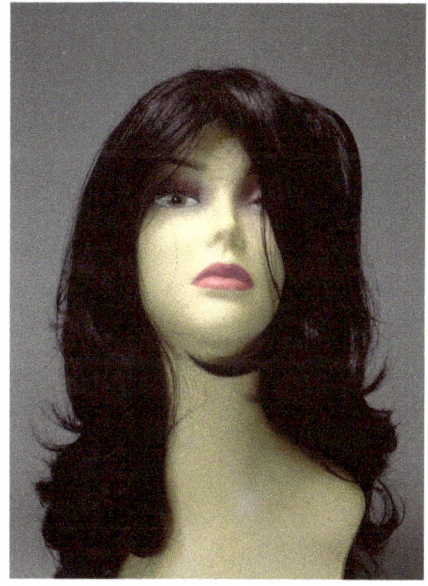

Figure 4-101. Auto Object Framing: After Adjustment

When you take a picture of the face or other subject, the camera may, if it finds it possible, crop the image and produce a new version of the image with the frame trimmed and resized to emphasize the subject in a more pleasing way. An example is shown in Figure 4-100 and Figure 4-101, which show the uncropped and cropped versions, respectively, of a mannequin head I photographed with Face Detection activated.

The camera's cropping looks appropriate, but I would rather do the cropping myself in Photoshop or just compose the image in this way to begin with.

The camera saves both versions, so there is no harm in using this feature. It could be useful if you are pressed for time or are unable to get into position to take the shot you want. If you need a more nicely cropped version of the image quickly for a slide show, perhaps, this could be a good way to fill that need.

This feature is available for selection only if the camera is using autofocus (or DMF, on the HX90V) and the lens is not zoomed beyond the optical zoom range.

Screen 6 of the Shooting menu for the HX90V is shown in Figure 4-102.

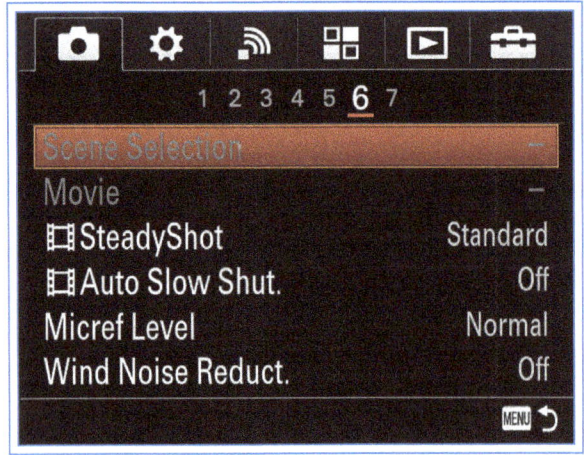

Figure 4-102. Screen 6 of HX90V Shooting Menu

Scene Selection

As discussed in Chapter 3, this option is used only when the camera is set to Scene mode; you use this menu item to select one of the settings in that shooting mode, including Portrait, Anti Motion Blur, Sunset, and others. You also can turn the Control wheel to change scene types from the shooting screen. In addition, the Scene Selection menu screen appears automatically when you turn the Mode dial to the SCN position and press the Center button, if the Mode Dial Guide option on screen 2 of the Setup menu is turned on.

(HX90V only) You also can use the Control ring to change scene types, as long as the Control Ring function is set to Standard through the Custom Key Settings option on the Custom menu and Focus Mode is not set to manual focus or DMF.

Movie

This menu item is available for selection only when the Mode dial is set to Movie mode (the position marked by a movie-film icon). This option lets you select one of the four available exposure settings for recording movies in that mode. I will discuss this option in Chapter 8.

SteadyShot (Movies)

This next option is for image stabilization, which can be adjusted through a menu option for movie-recording only, as indicated by the movie-film icon in front of its name. I will discuss this video-oriented SteadyShot option in Chapter 8. (These cameras have an optical stabilization system for still images that operates automatically; there is no menu option to control that feature.)

Auto Slow Shutter, Micref Level, and Wind Noise Reduction

I will discuss the Auto Slow Shutter, Micref Level, and Wind Noise Reduction menu options in Chapter 8, because they all are concerned with video recording.

Screen 7 of the Shooting menu on the HX90V is shown in Figure 4-103.

Chapter 4: Shooting Menu | 85

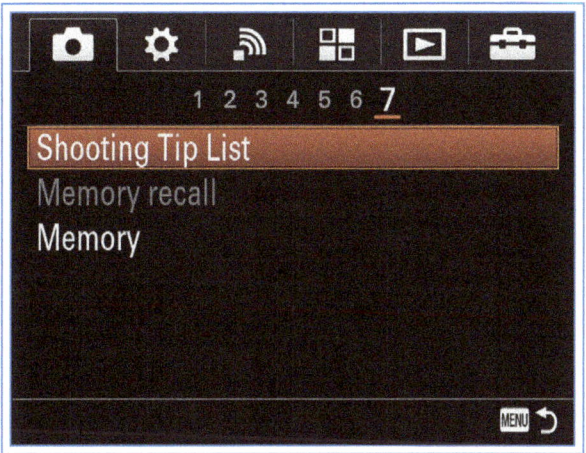

Figure 4-103. Screen 7 of HX90V Shooting Menu

Shooting Tip List

The Shooting Tip List option gives you access to a set of tips for photography in general. To use, it, select this option and then scroll through the list that appears on the screen, as shown in Figure 4-104, and select any topic that you wish to explore. This screen also can be summoned from the shooting screen by pressing the In-Camera Guide button, if it is assigned to the In-Camera Guide option using the Custom Key Settings item on the Custom menu.

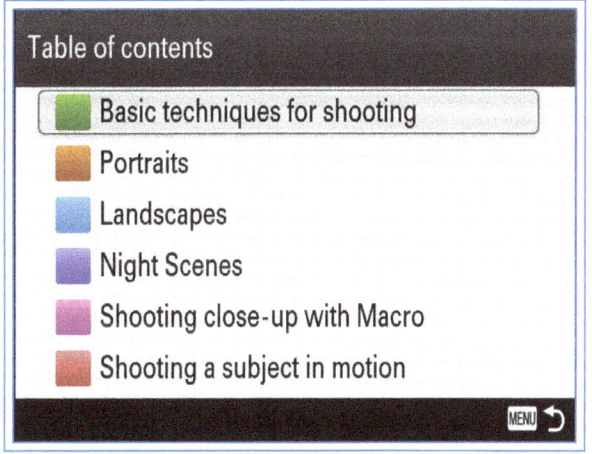

Figure 4-104. First Screen of Shooting Tip List

Memory Recall

The Memory Recall option is used only when the Mode dial is set to MR, for Memory Recall mode. Using this option, you can recall the shooting settings that you stored to one of the three slots for this mode, as discussed in Chapter 3.

When the Mode dial is first turned to the MR position, this option's main screen appears automatically on the camera's display with one of the three designations at the upper right highlighted, as shown in Figure 4-105.

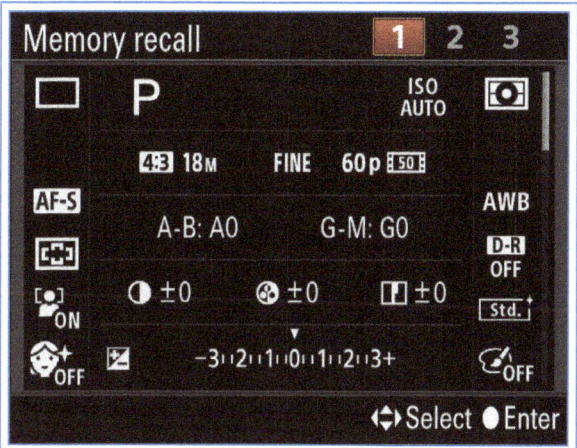

Figure 4-105. Memory Recall Screen

(If the Mode Dial Guide option is turned on through screen 2 of the Setup menu, the Mode Dial Guide screen will appear first; you then have to press the Center button to make this screen appear.)

If the camera is already set to Memory Recall mode and you want to change to one of the other memory registers, you can use the menu system to call up this option. Once the Memory Recall screen is displayed, either by turning the Mode dial to MR or by using this menu option, use the direction buttons or turn the Control wheel to select Register 1, 2, or 3 at the upper right of the screen. Then press the Center button, and the new set of shooting settings that were stored to that register will take effect.

Memory

The final option on the last screen of the Shooting menu, Memory, was discussed in Chapter 3 in connection with the Memory Recall shooting mode. Once you have set up the camera with the settings you want to store to a register of the Memory Recall shooting mode, you select the Memory menu option and choose one of the three numbered registers, as shown in Figure 4-106.

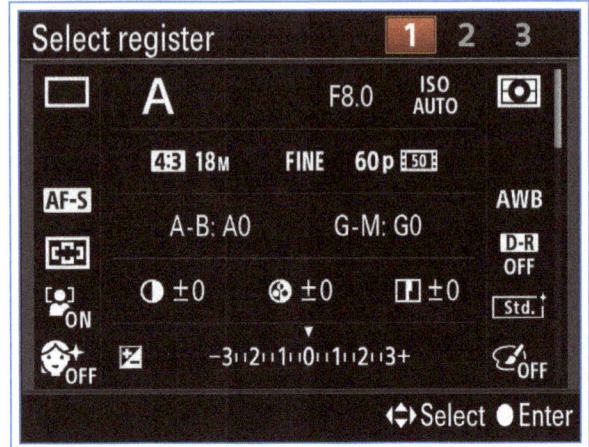

Figure 4-106. Memory Screen

Press the Center button, and all of the current settings will be stored to that register for the Memory Recall mode. You can recall those settings at any time by turning the Mode dial to the MR position (or selecting the Memory Recall menu option if the Mode dial is already at that position) and selecting Register 1, 2, or 3 from the camera's internal memory.

With either the Memory Recall or Memory option, you can scroll to additional screens using the Down button to see other settings currently in effect, such as ISO Auto Maximum and Minimum, Red Eye Reduction, High ISO NR, Center Lock-on AF, and several others.

Chapter 5: Physical Controls

The Sony HX80 and HX90V, like other compact cameras, do not have very many physical controls. They rely largely on the menus for changing settings. But these are high-quality compact cameras, and one aspect of that quality is that the controls can be configured to adjust many settings on the cameras. In this chapter, I'll discuss each of the physical controls and how they can be used to best advantage, starting with the controls on top of the camera, shown in Figure 5-1.

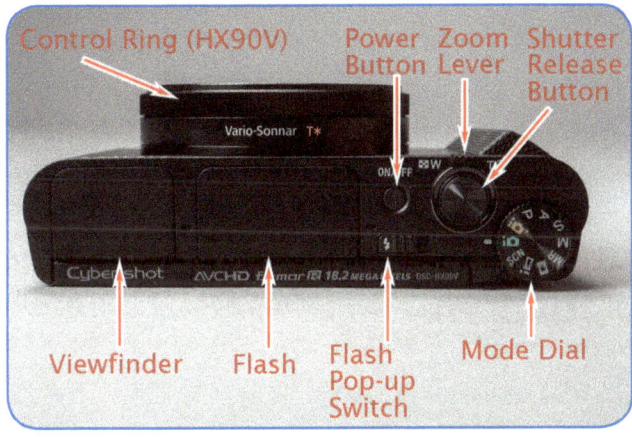

Figure 5-1. Controls on Top of Camera

I am using images of the HX90V camera for all of the following illustrations, because the bodies of the two camera models are sufficiently similar. I will note on the illustrations and in the text where the HX80 lacks a control that is present on the HX90V, such as the Control ring.

Mode Dial

The Mode dial has just one function—to select a shooting mode. I discussed the shooting modes in Chapter 3. To take a quick still picture, turn this dial to the green camera icon and fire away. To record a video sequence, turn the dial to that same position and press the red Movie button, just below the Mode dial at the top of the camera's back. It is important to remember that you can record a movie with the Mode dial set to any position. There is a movie-oriented mode on this dial, marked by a movie-film icon, but you do not have to select that icon to record movies.

Note, though, that the last screen of the Custom menu has an option called Movie Button for locking out the use of the Movie button unless the camera is in Movie mode. If the Mode dial is set to any position other than Movie, the Movie button will not start a movie recording if the Movie Button menu option is set to Movie Mode Only.

Shutter Release Button

When you press the shutter button halfway, the camera evaluates and locks focus and exposure if you're using standard settings, including single autofocus.

In Manual exposure mode, the camera still evaluates exposure when you press the shutter button, but it does not change the aperture or shutter speed settings you have made. If Auto ISO is in effect, the camera will adjust the ISO to achieve a normal exposure if possible.

Once you are satisfied with the settings, press the button all the way to take the picture. When the camera is set for continuous shooting, you hold this button down to cause the camera to fire repeatedly. You also can press this button halfway to exit to the live view from playback mode, menu screens, and help screens.

Zoom Lever

The zoom lever is a small ring with a short handle surrounding the shutter button. Its primary function is to vary the focal length of the lens between its wide-angle setting of 24mm and its telephoto setting of 720mm. If you have the camera set for Clear Image Zoom or Digital Zoom through the Zoom Setting item on the Custom menu, the lever will take the zoom to higher levels, as discussed in Chapter 7.

(HX90V only) You can also zoom using the Control ring, if you assign the zoom function to the Control ring using the Custom Key Settings option on the Custom menu. And, you can set the Control ring to use the Step Zoom function, which causes the lens to zoom in a predefined step each time you turn the ring. (That function is controlled by the Zoom Function on Ring option on screen 4 of the Custom menu.) Step Zoom does not work with the zoom lever, though. When you use the zoom lever, the lens zooms continuously, even if Step Zoom is turned on for the Control ring.

You can adjust the speed of zooming with the zoom lever using the Zoom Speed item on the Custom menu.

In playback mode, moving the zoom lever to the left produces an index screen, and moving the lever to the right enlarges the current image. Those operations are discussed in Chapter 6.

Power Button

This button is used to turn the camera on and off. You also can turn the camera's power on by pressing the Playback button, which places the camera into playback mode, or by popping up the EVF with the Finder switch.

Built-in Flash and Flash Pop-up Switch

The camera's built-in flash unit is normally retracted and hidden in the center area of the camera's top. If you want the flash to be available for use, you first have to pop it up using the flash pop-up switch, located directly behind the power button.

Once you have popped up the flash unit, if you want it to fire, you need to make an appropriate setting using the Flash Mode menu. You can find the Flash Mode option on the Shooting menu. You also can bring up that menu by pressing the Flash button, which is the Right button on the Control wheel, unless that button has been assigned to a different function using the Custom Key Settings option on the last screen of the Custom menu.

Once you have popped up the flash unit and selected a flash mode, the flash may fire when you press the shutter button, depending on the settings that are in effect and the lighting conditions.

If you want the flash to be stowed away again, you need to press it gently back down into the camera until it clicks into place. If you want to use "bounce flash," which causes the flash to be reflected by the ceiling or wall to reduce its intensity, you can pull the flash unit back carefully with your finger and hold the flash so that it is aiming upward while it fires. The flash will not bend back very far, though, so be careful not to press it back too strongly.

Electronic Viewfinder

One of the most interesting features of the Sony HX80 and HX90V is the retractable electronic viewfinder, or EVF. With this option, the camera can be used in bright conditions without having the LCD display washed out by sunlight. In addition, you can hold the camera up to your eye and keep it steady against your forehead while viewing a high-resolution image that includes the same information that is available with the LCD display.

To use the EVF, first pop it up by pressing down on the Finder switch on the left side of the camera. If the camera was not already powered on, popping up the viewfinder will turn the camera on.

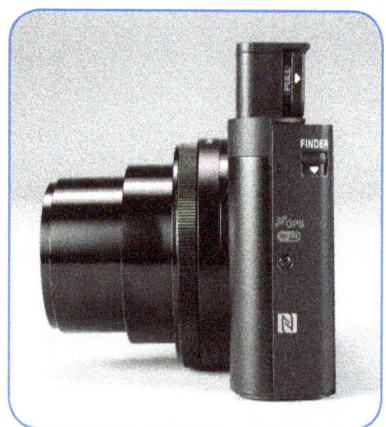

Figure 5-2. EVF Popped Up

Once the EVF has popped up, as shown in Figure 5-2, you need to grasp the sides of the eyepiece, without grabbing the upper lid of the viewfinder assembly, and gently pull the eyepiece out of the assembly, as shown in Figure 5-3.

Adjust the EVF for your vision using the diopter adjustment lever on top of the eyepiece, shown in Figure 5-4. How you use the EVF, of course, is a matter of personal preference. You can hold it up to either your left or right eye, depending on which feels more comfortable to you. If you wear glasses you may find it more comfortable to take them off and use the diopter adjustment lever to compensate.

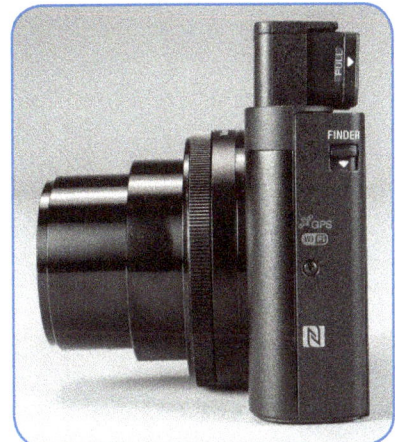

Figure 5-3. EVF Popped Up and Pulled Back

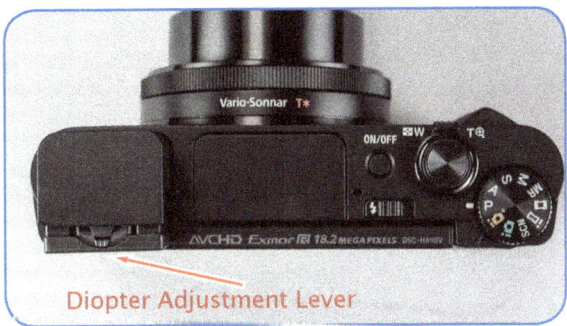

Figure 5-4. Diopter Adjustment Lever

By default, the camera switches automatically between the EVF and the LCD. That is, when the EVF is popped up and your head is against the EVF, the EVF is active and the LCD is turned off. When you move your head away from the EVF, the LCD screen becomes active and the EVF is turned off. If you want the EVF to be active whenever it is popped up, regardless of the position of your head, use the Finder/Monitor option on the Custom menu; set that option to Viewfinder to keep the EVF active at all times when it is popped up. (The eye sensor that detects the presence of your head near the screen is shown in Figure 5-7, later in this chapter.)

To adjust the brightness of the EVF, use the Viewfinder Brightness option on the Setup menu, as discussed in Chapter 7. The EVF does not function when the camera is being controlled by a smartphone.

The information displayed in the EVF is independent of what is displayed on the LCD screen. With one exception, you can set the EVF to display all of the same information that can be shown on the LCD, but you don't have to do that. (The one exception is the For Viewfinder display, which is available only on the LCD screen, as discussed in Chapter 7.)

To set the information displays for the LCD and EVF, use the Display Button option on the Custom menu to choose from the possible displays. Then, on the shooting screen, cycle from one display to another by pressing the Display button. I will discuss that menu option and the available information displays in Chapter 7.

When you have finished using the EVF, stow it inside the camera by pressing the eyepiece into the housing and then pushing the EVF down until it clicks into place. When you do that, the camera will turn off or stay powered on, depending on a menu setting. To determine what happens in that situation, go to the Function for VF Close option, the first item on screen 3 of the Setup menu. The choices are Power Off or Not Power Off. If you choose Power Off, the camera will turn off when you press the EVF down into the camera's body. If you choose Not Power Off, the camera will remain powered on when the EVF is stowed. I prefer to have the camera stay powered on, but it is good to have this choice available.

There are two items to discuss on the front of the camera, as seen in Figure 5-5.

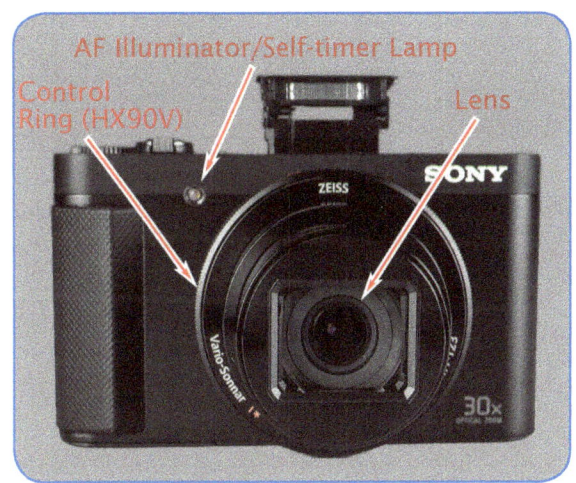

Figure 5-5. Items on Front of Camera

AF Illuminator/Self-Timer Lamp

The reddish light on the front of the camera to the upper left of the lens (as you face the camera) blinks to signal the operation of the self-timer, and it turns on in dark environments to assist with autofocusing. You can control its function for helping with autofocus through the AF Illuminator item on the Shooting menu, as discussed in Chapter 4. If you set that menu item to Auto, the lamp will light as needed for autofocus; if you set it to Off, the lamp will never light for that purpose, though it will still illuminate for the self-timer.

Control Ring (HX90V Only)

Whenever the HX90V is set to manual focus or DMF (direct manual focus) using the Focus Mode option on screen 3 of the Shooting menu, the Control ring adjusts focus. The ring also has other functions, depending on the settings you make.

To assign functions to the Control ring, use the Custom Key Settings option on screen 4 of the Custom menu. The first sub-option for this menu item is Control Ring, whose first screen of options is shown in Figure 5-6.

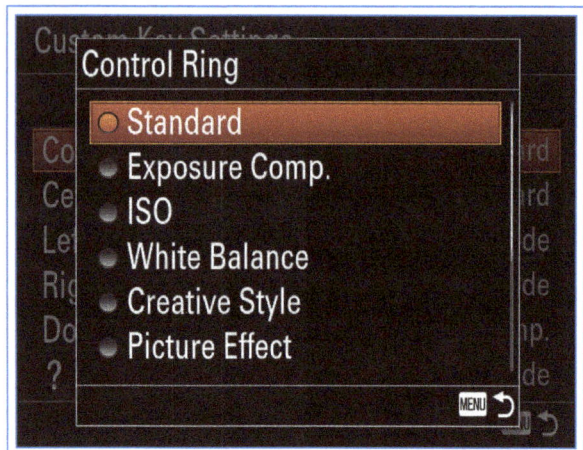

Figure 5-6. First Screen of Control Ring Menu Options

By default, the Control Ring item is set to Standard. When the Standard setting is in effect, the Control ring controls just one function in any given shooting mode; the function it controls depends on which shooting mode the camera is set to. For example, if the camera is set to the Aperture Priority mode, the Control ring controls aperture; in Shutter Priority mode, the ring controls shutter speed. In the Scene shooting mode, the ring controls selection of scene types. I usually leave the Control Ring menu item set to Standard because the functions the ring controls in the various shooting modes in that case are quite useful.

However, if you want to use the ring for one dedicated function no matter what shooting mode is in effect, you can use the Control Ring menu item to choose one of the following items that will stay assigned to the ring until you make another change: Exposure Compensation, ISO, White Balance, Creative Style, Picture Effect, Zoom, Shutter Speed, or Aperture. You also can choose Not Set, in which case turning the ring will have no effect (unless you activate a function, such as manual focus, that requires use of the ring).

A function assigned to the ring only works if the context permits it. For example, if you assign Aperture to the Control ring, the ring will control aperture if the camera is set to Aperture Priority or Manual exposure mode. In any other shooting mode, turning the ring will have no effect (except for adjusting manual focus) because aperture cannot be controlled manually in other modes. Also, when you are using the Photo Creativity option in Intelligent Auto or Superior Auto mode, any function assigned to the ring through the Custom menu will not operate, because that operation could conflict with the Photo Creativity settings. Table 5-1 lists the functions that are assigned to the Control ring with the Standard setting.

Table 5-1. CONTROL RING: STANDARD SETTING—
SHOOTING MODES VS. ASSIGNED FUNCTIONS

SHOOTING MODE	ASSIGNED FUNCTION
INTELLIGENT AUTO	ZOOM
SUPERIOR AUTO	ZOOM
PROGRAM	PROGRAM SHIFT
APERTURE PRIORITY	APERTURE
SHUTTER PRIORITY	SHUTTER SPEED
MANUAL EXPOSURE	APERTURE
SCENE	SCENE SELECTION
ISWEEP PANORAMA	PANORAMA DIRECTION
MEMORY RECALL	DEPENDS ON SAVED SETTING
MOVIE	DEPENDS ON MOVIE EXPOSURE MODE SETTING

The Control ring also is used in a few other situations regardless of how you have set its assigned function. When you press the Function button (discussed later in this chapter) in shooting mode, the camera activates a menu that shows several options—including items such as white balance, ISO, exposure compensation, etc.—depending on the settings you have chosen for that menu. Once you have pressed the Function button to display that menu, you can turn the Control ring (or the Control wheel) to select the value for the setting that is highlighted on the menu. The Control ring also is used to adjust settings using the Quick Navi system, which is also called up with the Function button.

When the camera is set to manual focus or DMF (direct manual focus), you use the Control ring to adjust focus. If the MF Assist option is turned on through screen 1 of the Custom menu, the display will be magnified to assist with focusing as soon as you start turning the Control ring. (With DMF, you have to half-press the shutter button while turning the Control ring to use MF Assist.) When the camera is set to either of those focus modes, you cannot use the Control ring for any other function.

The controls on the back of the cameras are seen in Figure 5-7.

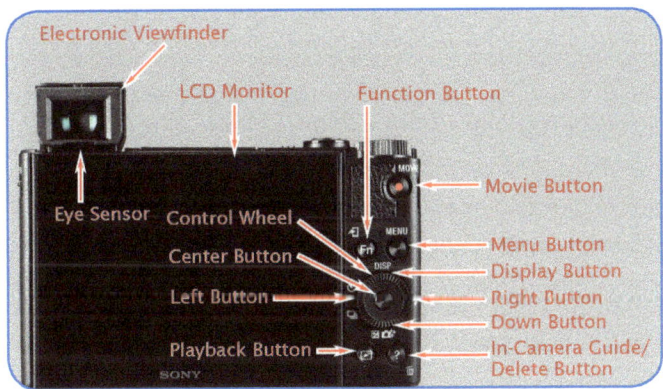

Figure 5-7. Controls on Back of Camera

Playback Button

This button to the lower left of the Control wheel, marked with a small triangle, is used to put the camera into playback mode, which allows you to view your recorded images and videos on the LCD screen or in the EVF. It also can be used instead of the power button to turn the camera on, placing the camera immediately into playback mode with the lens retracted. When the camera is in playback mode, you can press the shutter button halfway or press the Playback button again to switch the camera into shooting mode.

Movie Button

The red button at the upper right of the camera's back has just one function—to start and stop the recording of a movie sequence. As I noted in discussing the Mode dial earlier in this chapter, you can control how the Movie button operates. If you want to be able to start recording a movie in any shooting mode, go to the Custom menu and select the last option on the last screen, called Movie Button. If you set that menu option to Always (the default setting), then the Movie button will operate in any shooting mode. If you set the option to Movie Mode Only, then the Movie button will not start recording a movie unless the camera is set to Movie mode using the Mode dial. (Movie mode is the mode marked by a movie-film icon.)

This is a fairly important decision to make, and it depends on your preferences and likely uses of the camera. If you want to be able to start recording a video at any time without delay, leave the Movie Button option set to Always. The reason you might not want to do this is that it is easy to press the Movie button by mistake. I have done that often. When you press the button by mistake, you have to press it again to stop the recording, and wait for the camera to finish processing the movie before you can use any other controls. And, of course, the camera will have an unwanted file cluttering the memory card, until you delete it.

My preference is to limit use of the Movie button to when the camera is in Movie mode, but if I were going on a vacation and wanted to be able to start recording a movie in Intelligent Auto mode (or any other mode) without delay, I would enable the button for use in all modes.

There are differences in how the camera operates for video recording in different shooting modes. I will discuss movie making in detail in Chapter 8.

Menu Button

The Menu button, to the upper right of the Control wheel, is straightforward in its basic function. Press it to enter the menu system, and press it once more to return to whatever mode the camera was in previously (shooting mode or playback mode). The button also cancels out of sub-menus, taking you back to the previous menu screen. In playback mode, when an image has been enlarged using the zoom lever, you can press the Menu button (or the Center button) to return it to the normal-sized view.

Function Button

The button marked Fn, for Function, has different functions in shooting mode and playback mode.

SHOOTING MODE: FUNCTION MENU

When the camera is in shooting mode, the Function button helps you set up the camera according to your preferences. With the Function Menu Settings option on the last screen of the Custom menu (discussed in Chapter 7), you can assign up to 12 functions to the Function menu from more than 20 choices, including items such as ISO, Drive Mode, White Balance, Metering Mode, and Picture Effect. You also can choose Not Set, to leave a slot on the Function menu blank.

Scroll through the lines from Function Upper1 through Function Upper6 on the first sub-screen of this menu option and Function Lower1 through Function Lower6 on the second screen. On each line, press the Center button and then scroll through the numerous options to highlight the one you want, and press the Center button to confirm that selection.

Once you have assigned up to 12 options to this button, it is ready for action. To use an option, press the Function button when the camera is in shooting mode, and a menu will appear at the bottom of the display in two rows with six choices each, as shown in Figure 5-8.

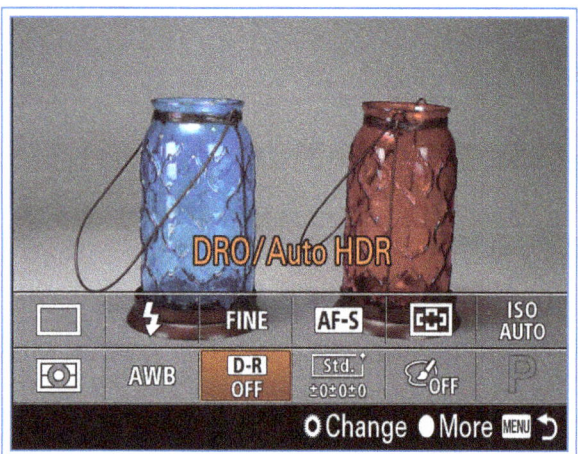

Figure 5-8. Function Menu on Shooting Screen

Use the four direction buttons to move to and highlight an option to adjust. Then turn either the Control wheel or the Control ring (HX90V only) to change the value of that option. For example, if you have moved the orange highlight block to the Quality item, turn the Control wheel or the Control ring (HX90V only) until the setting you want to make appears, as shown in Figure 5-9, where Fine is selected.

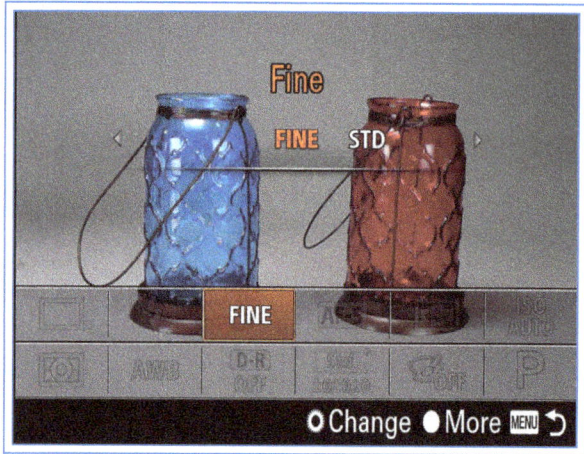

Figure 5-9. Fine Selected for Quality on Function Menu

Then, press the Function button to confirm the setting and exit from the Function menu screen. Or, if you want to make multiple settings from the Function menu options, after changing one setting you can press the Center button to go back to the Function menu and make more settings before you press the Function button to exit to the shooting screen.

If the setting you are adjusting needs to have a sub-option set, you can press the Center button to go directly to the screen for that setting. For example, suppose you want to set a sub-option for the Toy Camera Picture Effect. On the shooting screen press the Function button to bring up the Function menu, and scroll to the Picture Effect item. Then, instead of choosing a value with the Control wheel or Control ring (HX90V), press the Center button, and the camera will display a Picture Effect menu, as shown in Figure 5-10.

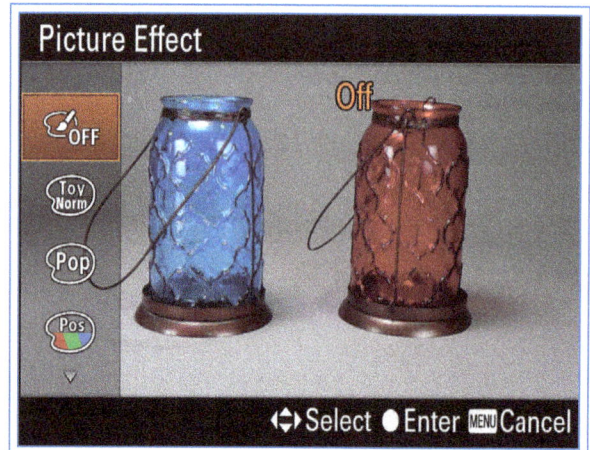

Figure 5-10. Picture Effect Menu from Function Menu

Chapter 5: Physical Controls | 93

On that screen, you can navigate to the Toy Camera option and select the sub-setting you want to select. When you have finished, press the Menu button to return to the Function menu. From there, you can press the Function button to return to the shooting screen.

There may be items on the Function menu whose icons are dimmed because the item is unavailable for selection in the current context. If you move the highlight to one of those items and then try to change the setting, the camera will display an error message.

Also, the selections I discussed above may not be available because they have not been assigned to the Function menu. If that is the case, you can use the Function Menu Settings menu option to assign them if you want to follow the examples.

I strongly recommend that you develop a group of 12 items to assign to the Function menu and make use of this speedy way to change important settings.

QUICK NAVI SYSTEM

In shooting mode, the Function button also gives you access to the Quick Navi system for changing settings rapidly. This system has similarities to the Function menu system I just discussed, but there are significant differences.

The Quick Navi system comes into play in only one situation—when you have called up the special display screen shown in Figure 5-11, which Sony calls the "For Viewfinder" display.

because this screen is designed for use when you are using the viewfinder to frame your composition, so you can see the live view through the viewfinder and see the details of your settings on this display, which appears only on the LCD screen.

The For Viewfinder display is summoned by pressing the Display button, but only if you have selected it for inclusion in the cycle of display screens.

You do that using the Display Button option on the Custom menu. From that option, select the sub-option for Monitor, then check the box for the For Viewfinder item on the next screen, as shown in Figure 5-12.

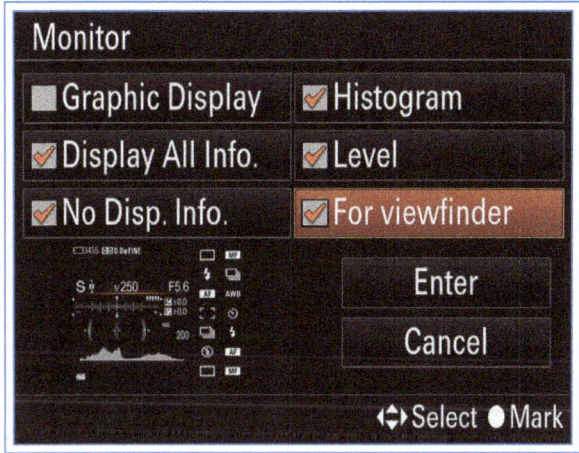

Figure 5-12. For Viewfinder Selected on Display Button Menu

As seen in Figure 5-11, the For Viewfinder screen displays a lot of information at the right, including Drive Mode, White Balance, Focus Area, DRO, Picture Effect, Creative Style, and several others.

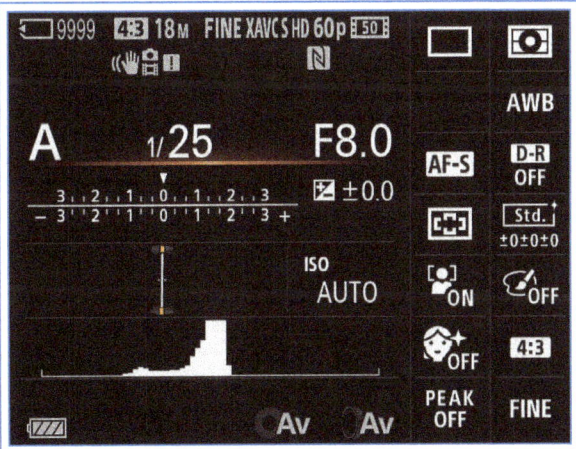

Figure 5-11. For Viewfinder Display Screen

This is the only shooting mode display that does not include the live view. It is called "For viewfinder"

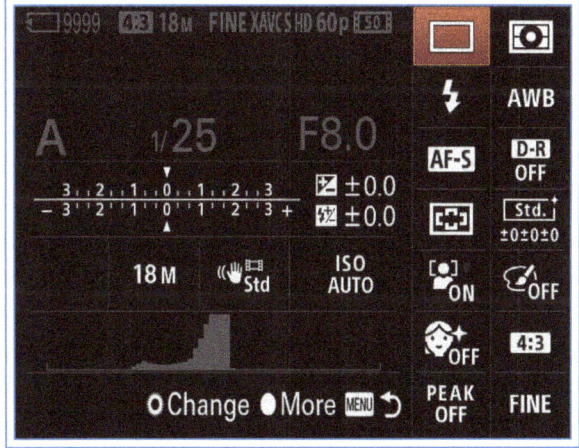

Figure 5-13. Quick Navi Screen

Normally, these items are displayed for information; you cannot adjust them. But, if you press the Function button, an orange highlight appears at the right, as shown in Figure 5-13, indicating that the Quick Navi system is in use.

Use the direction buttons to move through the settings. You can press the Left button to move the orange highlight to the left, to settings such as ISO, SteadyShot, and Image Size. When you have highlighted a setting to adjust, turn the Control wheel or the Control ring (HX90V only) to scroll through the available values and make the adjustment quickly.

When you use the Control wheel or Control ring (HX90V only) to adjust a setting, such as Picture Effect, a secondary window opens in the top part of the display, as shown in Figure 5-14, showing the options available for the setting.

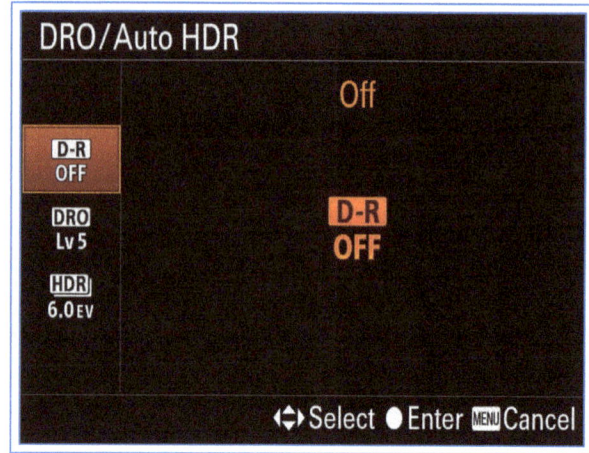

Figure 5-15. DRO Menu from Quick Navi System

On that screen, you can select HDR and set it to 6.0EV. Press the Center button to select this setting and exit to the For Viewfinder display.

You also can press the Center button when an option is highlighted, even if a sub-setting is not needed, if you prefer to use a menu screen to make the adjustment. For example, when Aspect Ratio is highlighted on the Quick Navi screen, you can press the Center button to call up a menu, rather than just turning the Control wheel or Control ring (HX90V only).

The Quick Navi system can streamline your ability to change settings once you get used to it. I recommend you devote some time to practicing with it, if speed is important to you.

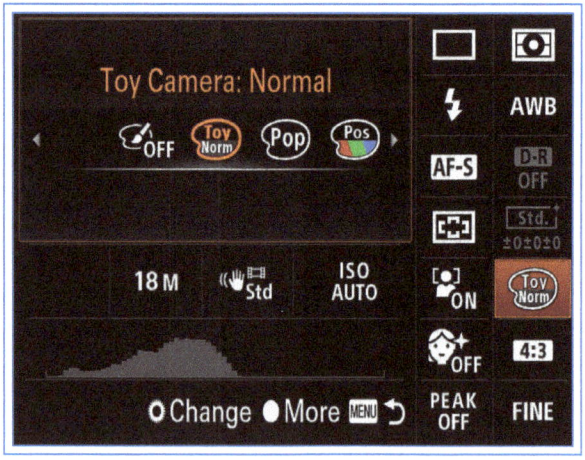

Figure 5-14. Secondary Window on Quick Navi Screen

After changing a setting, you can move to other settings using the direction buttons. Once you have made all of your changes, press the Function button again to exit to the static For Viewfinder display, which will now show the new settings in place.

If you select an option that requires a sub-setting, the steps are slightly different. For example, suppose you want to turn on HDR using the maximum setting of 6.0EV. From the Quick Navi screen, highlight the DRO option and, instead of turning the Control wheel or Control ring (HX90V only) to change the setting, press the Center button. You will be taken to a special menu screen for the DRO option, as shown in Figure 5-15.

Playback Mode: Send to Smartphone

When the camera is in playback mode, pressing the Function button activates the Send to Smartphone option, just as if you had chosen that menu option from the Wi-Fi menu. So, if you have taken a photo and want to transfer it to your phone for sharing with friends or posting to Facebook, you can press the Function button in playback mode and make the transfer quickly.

In-Camera Guide/Delete Button

The button marked with a question mark (?), to the right of the Playback button, is called the In-Camera Guide/Delete button. This button can be programmed to perform any one of numerous functions, or can be designated as Not Set. To make this choice, use the Custom Key Settings option on the last screen of the

Custom menu, and then select the ? Button sub-option. I will discuss that menu option in Chapter 7.

By default, this button is assigned the In-Camera Guide function. With that option, when the camera is displaying a menu you can press the button to display a brief help screen with guidance or tips about the menu option that is highlighted. The help screen varies depending on the context.

If the camera is displaying the main page of a menu screen with the highlight on a particular feature, pressing the ? button brings up a screen with a brief message explaining the use of that feature. For example, Figure 5-16 shows the message that is displayed when the Drive Mode item is highlighted on the Shooting menu.

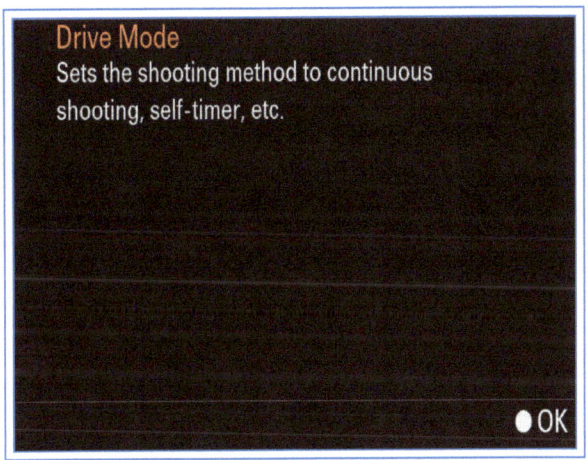

Figure 5-16. Help Screen for Drive Mode Menu Option

If you highlight a sub-option for a menu item and press the ? button, the camera will display a message with details about that option. For example, Figure 5-17 shows the help screen that was displayed when I pressed the ? button after highlighting the Continuous Shooting option for the Drive Mode item, with the Hi option selected for speed of shooting.

This help system is quite detailed; for example, it provides guidance even for different ISO settings, such as ISO 100, 400, and 1600, with tips about when to use each setting. The help function operates with all of the menu systems, including Custom, Playback, Setup, and the others, not just the Shooting menu. It also works with the Function menu and the Quick Navi system to give information about a highlighted option.

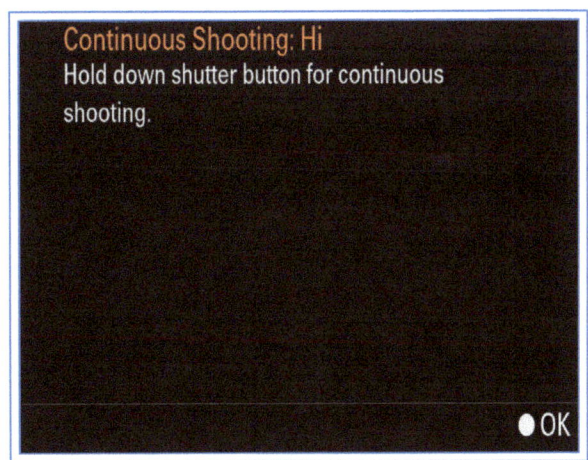

Figure 5-17. Help Screen for High-speed Continuous Shooting

The ? button has a special function when the camera is in the Intelligent Auto or Superior Auto mode, regardless of any function assigned to the button using the Custom Key Settings option. When you are using the Photo Creativity option in either of those modes and you have moved the indicator along the curved scale on the screen to change a setting (such as Brightness or Color), you can press the ? button to reset the option to its default value.

When the shooting screen is displayed, pressing the ? button calls up the Shooting Tip List, which you can scroll through to read various help screens about general photography topics.

When the camera is in playback mode, displaying a recorded image or movie (not a menu screen), this button becomes the Delete button, as indicated by the trash can icon to the lower right of the button. If you press it, the camera displays the message shown in Figure 5-18, prompting you to select Delete or Cancel.

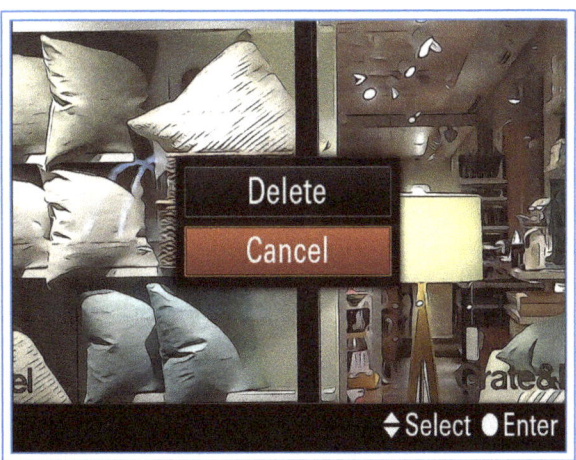

Figure 5-18. Message After Pressing Delete Button

If you highlight Delete and press the Center button, the camera will delete the image or video that was displayed. If you choose Cancel, the camera will return to the playback mode screen. This operation also works when an image is being displayed briefly with the Auto Review option, right after the image was captured.

How you program the ? button is, of course, a matter of personal preference. The In-Camera Guide option is quite useful, especially when you are first learning the operation of the camera. Once you are more confident with the camera's functions, you might want to use this button for an operation that is more useful when activated by a button than by digging through the menu system, such as Focus Area.

Control Wheel and Its Buttons

Several controls are within the perimeter of the Control wheel, the ridged wheel with icons around its outer edges. In the middle of the wheel is the Center button, a much-used control. The four edges of the wheel (up, down, left, and right) act as buttons. If you press the wheel's rim at any of those four points, you are, in effect, pressing a button. Each button has at least two functions—as a direction control along with one or more other specific assignments. When they act as direction controls, the buttons are used to navigate through menu options and other choices for controlling the camera's settings. The other main functions of the buttons are indicated by one or more icons at each button's position on the Control wheel. I will discuss all of these controls in turn.

Control Wheel

In many cases, to choose a menu item or a setting, you can turn this wheel. In some cases, you have the choice of using this wheel or pressing the direction buttons. One helpful feature of these cameras is that they place a round icon on the shooting screen representing the Control wheel when there is a value that can be adjusted at that point by the wheel. (If you don't see the icon, press the Display button until it appears.)

For example, in Figure 5-19, a screen shot from the HX80 camera, the icon, which looks like a gray ring lying flat on the screen in the lower right corner, is positioned next to the Av indicator, meaning the Control wheel can now control aperture. (On the HX90V, you might also see a more three-dimensional icon to the right of that one showing that the Control ring also can control aperture.)

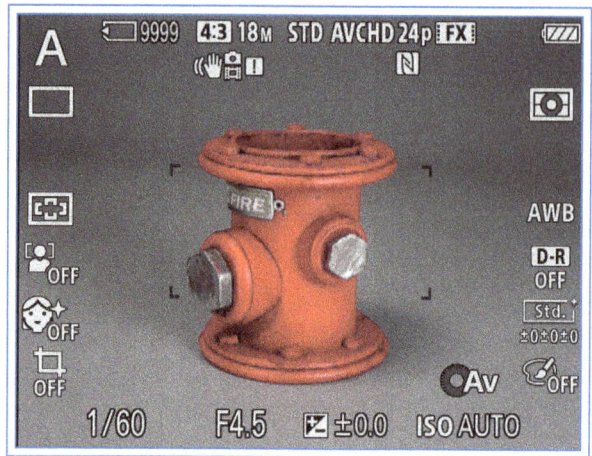

Figure 5-19. Icon on HX80 Showing Control Wheel Sets Aperture

In Aperture Priority mode, the Control wheel controls aperture, and in Shutter Priority mode it controls shutter speed. In Manual exposure mode, it controls both, by switching back and forth. When the camera is in Scene mode, you can turn the Control wheel to change the scene type, such as Portrait, Landscape, and the like. In iSweep Panorama mode, turning the wheel changes the direction of the panorama. In Program mode, it controls Program Shift.

The Control wheel has several other functions. When you are viewing a menu screen, you can navigate through the lists of options by turning the wheel. When you are adjusting items using the Function menu or Quick Navi system, you can change the value for the selected setting by turning the Control wheel. With the Flexible Spot setting for the Focus Area menu option, you can turn the Control wheel to adjust the size of the focus frame when the frame is activated for moving around the display.

(HX90V only) When you are using manual focus and you have the MF Assist or Focus Magnifier option turned on, you can turn the Control wheel to vary the area of the scene that is being magnified.

In playback mode, you can turn the Control wheel to navigate through images. Also, when a video is being played in the camera, you can turn the Control wheel to fast-forward or rewind, or, when the video is paused, to play it slowly, frame-by-frame, either forward or in reverse.

CENTER BUTTON

This button in the center of the Control wheel has many uses. On menu screens that have additional options, such as the Image Size screen, this button takes you to the next screen to view the other options. It also acts as a selection button when you choose certain options. For example, after you select Image Size from screen 1 of the Shooting menu and then navigate to your desired setting, you can press the Center button to confirm your selection and exit from the menu screen back to the shooting screen.

The Center button also has several other possible uses, depending on how it is set up. The last screen of the Custom menu (discussed in Chapter 7) has an item called Custom Key Settings, with a sub-option for setting the function of the Center button. Using that option, you can set the Center button to have its normal default functions by selecting the Standard option.

If you select the Standard option, then, if the Focus Area menu option is set to Flexible Spot or Expand Flexible Spot, pressing the Center button when the shooting screen is active brings up the screen for adjusting the location of the focus frame. If Center Lock-on AF is turned on with Focus Area set to Wide or Center, this button activates focus tracking.

(HX90V only) When the camera is set to manual focus and MF Assist or Focus Magnifier is turned on, pressing the Center button changes the magnification factor of the display.

If you prefer not to use the Standard option, you can use the Custom Key Settings option to set this button to carry out one of numerous other functions, or to be Not Set. I will discuss that menu option in Chapter 7.

In playback mode, you press the Center button to start playing a video whose first frame is displayed on the camera's screen. Once the video is playing, press the Center button to pause the playback and then to toggle between play and pause. When a panoramic image is displayed, press the Center button to make it scroll on the screen at a larger size using the full expanse of the display screen. When you have enlarged an image using the zoom lever, you can return it immediately to its normal size by pressing the Center button. When you are selecting images for deletion, protection, or printing using the appropriate Playback menu options, you use the Center button to mark or unmark an image for that purpose.

DIRECTION BUTTONS

Each of the four edges of the Control wheel is a button you can press to get access to a setting or operation. This is not immediately obvious, and sometimes it can be tricky to press in exactly the right spot, but these four buttons are important to your control of the camera. You use them to navigate through menus and screens for settings, whether moving left and right or up and down.

You also use these buttons in playback mode to move through your images and, when you have enlarged an image using the zoom lever, to scroll around within the magnified image.

In addition to navigation, the direction buttons are used for miscellaneous functions in connection with various settings. For example, when the camera is set to Manual exposure mode, you can press the Down button to toggle the action of the Control wheel between setting aperture and setting shutter speed. And, as with the Center button, the Right and Left buttons can be assigned to carry out other functions through the Custom Key Settings option on the last screen of the Custom menu, as discussed in Chapter 7.

Finally, each of the direction buttons has its own separate identity, as indicated by the one or two icons that appear near each of the buttons, as discussed below.

Up Button: Display

The Up button, marked "DISP," switches among information displays on the LCD screen and in the viewfinder, in both shooting and playback modes. As discussed in Chapter 7, you can change the contents of the shooting mode screens using the Display Button option on the Custom menu. The various display screens for playback mode are discussed in Chapter 6.

The Up button cannot be reassigned using the menu system; it is permanently assigned as the Display button.

Right Button: Flash Mode

When the camera is in shooting mode, pressing the Right button brings up a menu on the left of the display showing the options for setting the behavior of the flash unit. The options are Flash Off, Autoflash, Fill-flash, Slow Sync, and Rear Sync, although not all of them are available in any one shooting mode. This menu can also be summoned from the Shooting menu. I discussed the use of these settings in Chapter 4.

One important point is that you have to use the flash pop-up switch to pop up the flash before it can be used, no matter what option you have selected from the Flash Mode menu.

You can reassign the function of the Right button using the Custom Key Settings option on the last screen of the Custom menu. You can choose any one of numerous options, including Flash Mode, Focus Area, ISO, White Balance, Metering Mode, and others; I will discuss that menu option in Chapter 7.

Down Button: Photo Creativity/Exposure Compensation

The Down button has two icons directly below it, indicating that it has two different functions, depending on the shooting mode. In the Intelligent Auto and Superior Auto modes, pressing this button brings up the Photo Creativity option, which I discussed in Chapter 2. In the Program, Aperture Priority, Shutter Priority, Movie, and iSweep Panorama modes, this button controls exposure compensation, discussed below.

In Manual exposure mode, this button toggles the Control wheel's function between controlling aperture and controlling shutter speed. In that mode, you can use the Exposure Compensation item on the Shooting menu to adjust exposure compensation, or you can use the Custom Key Settings menu option to assign a control button or the Control ring (HX90V only) to adjust that setting. (Exposure compensation can be adjusted in Manual exposure mode only if ISO is set to Auto ISO.)

In Scene mode, the Down button has no function other than as a direction button. If you press it when the shooting screen is displayed in that shooting mode, you will see an error message.

Exposure Compensation

Here is an example of the use of exposure compensation to adjust for an unusual, or non-optimal, lighting situation. Figure 5-20 is a photo of a dark blue fabric ball in front of a bright white background, taken using the Program shooting mode with Metering Mode set to Multi.

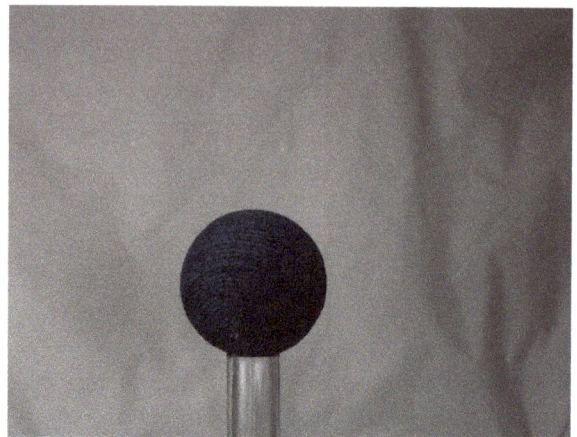

Figure 5-20. Exposure Compensation Example: Before Adjustment

The camera's metering system measured the light being reflected from the white background along with the light from the dark subject, and because of the bright background, the metering system reduced the exposure setting and underexposed the dark ball.

One solution to this problem is to use exposure compensation to increase the overall exposure of the image, so the subject will not be too dark. To accomplish this, press the camera's Down button to bring the exposure compensation scale up on the display, as shown in Figure 5-21.

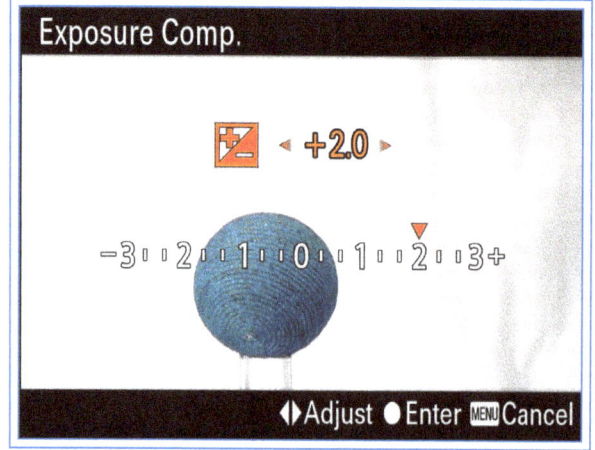

Figure 5-21. Exposure Compensation Adjustment Scale

Turn the Control wheel or press the Right button to move the orange triangle above the scale, so it points to a value to the right of the zero point.

As you do this, the numbers near the top of the display will change. With a negative value, the image would be darker than it otherwise would be; with a positive value, as shown here, it will be brighter. The camera's display will grow brighter or darker to indicate the effect of the adjustment.

In this case, with exposure compensation increased by 2.0 EV (exposure value) units, the blue ball becomes brighter along with the white background, and the photograph is no longer underexposed, as shown in the final image in Figure 5-22.

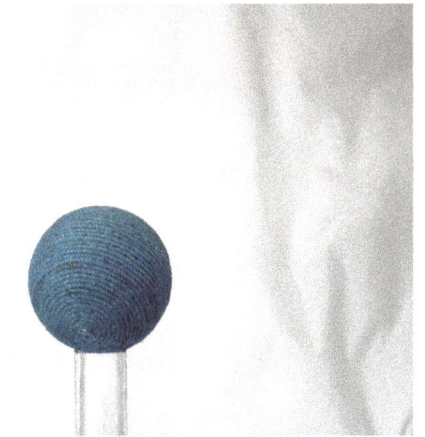

Figure 5-22. Exposure Compensation Example: After Adjustment

Some photographers follow the practice of generally leaving exposure compensation set at a particular amount, such as negative 0.7 EV. You might do this if you find your images generally are slightly overexposed or if you see that highlights are clipping in many cases. (You can tell if highlights are clipping by checking the histogram, as discussed in Chapter 6. If the histogram is bunched to the right, with no space between the data lines and the right side of the chart, highlights are clipping, or reaching the maximum value.) It is difficult to recover details from images whose highlights have clipped, so it can be a safety measure to underexpose images slightly to avoid that situation.

If you don't plan to leave a permanent exposure compensation setting in place, you should return the setting to the zero point when you are finished with it, so you won't inadvertently change the exposure of later images that don't need the adjustment. (The exposure compensation setting will remain in place even after the camera has been turned off and back on again.)

(HX90V only) If you use exposure compensation often, you can assign it to the Control ring using the Custom Key Settings menu option. Then you can turn the ring to adjust exposure compensation with a circular scale on the screen, as shown in Figure 5-23. (The ring will not adjust exposure compensation if the camera is set for manual focus or DMF, because the ring is used to adjust focus with those settings.)

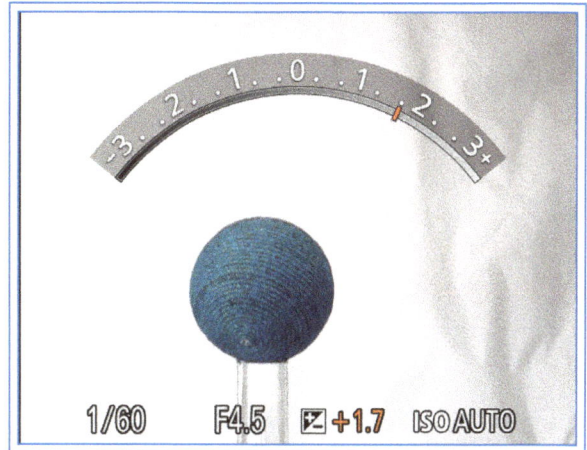

Figure 5-23. Display on HX90V When Control Ring Sets Exposure Compensation

There is one other duty performed by the Down button. In playback mode, when a movie is displayed as ready to play, you can press this button to move to a screen for adjusting the sound level for playback of movies, as shown in Figure 5-24.

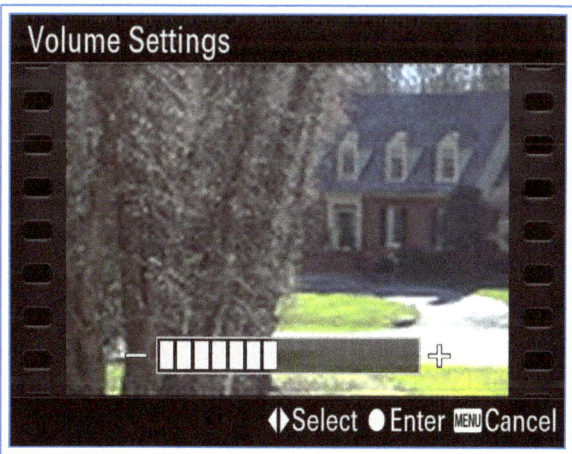

Figure 5-24. Volume Settings Screen from Down Button

This function also works when a still image is displayed, if the View Mode option on the Playback menu is set to a view that includes movies, such as Date View. When a movie is playing, you can press this button to get to the full panel of playback controls, as shown in Figure 5-25.

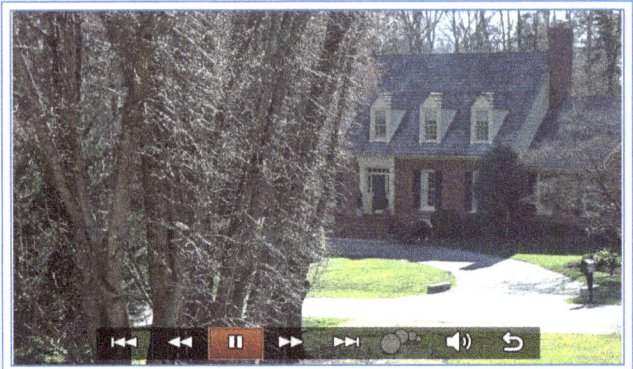

Figure 5-25. Full Panel of Movie Playback Controls

The Down button can be assigned to any one of several other options through the Custom Key Settings menu option on the last screen of the Custom menu.

Left Button: Self-Timer/Drive Mode

The Left button is labeled with the timer dial icon for the self-timer and the stack-of-frames icon for continuous shooting. When you press this button, the camera brings up the Drive Mode menu with its options for self-timer, continuous shooting, and several types of bracketing. I discussed these options in Chapter 4 in connection with the Drive Mode option on the Shooting menu.

You can reassign the function of the Left button using the Custom Key Settings option on the last screen of the Custom menu. You can choose any one of many options, as discussed in Chapter 7.

Tilting LCD Screen

The next item to be discussed is the tilting LCD screen. This screen, even without its tilting ability, is a notable feature of the camera. It has a diagonal span of three inches (7.5 cm) and provides a resolution of about 921,000 dots.

The screen can tilt to assist with various types of shots. First, it can rotate all the way over the top of the camera so the screen faces in the same direction as the lens, for use with self-portraits, as shown in Figure 5-26. If you turn on the self-portrait timer option on the Custom menu, then, when the screen is in this position, the camera will count down from three to one with large numbers on the screen, as shown in Figure 5-27. This orientation also is useful if you need to see yourself as you record a video blog.

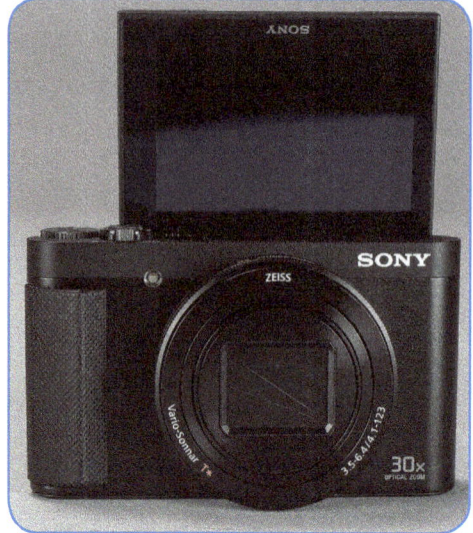

Figure 5-26. LCD Screen Rotated for Self-portraits

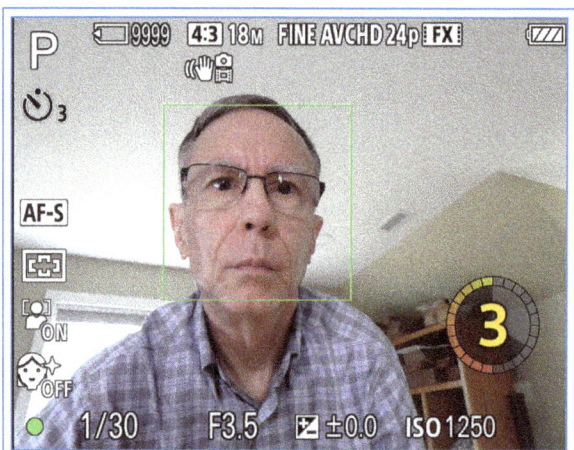

Figure 5-27. Countdown Screen for Self-portrait Timer

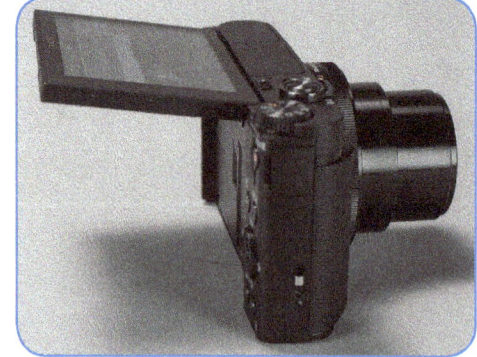

Figure 5-28. LCD Screen Positioned for Low-level Shots

If you need to take images from a vantage point near ground level, you can rotate the screen so it tilts upward toward your eye, as shown in Figure 5-28, and hold the camera down as far as you need to get a mole's-eye view of the world. It can be helpful to shoot upward like this when your subject is in an area with a busy, distracting background. You can hold the camera down low and shoot with the sky as your background to reduce or eliminate the distractions. This angle of the tilting display also is useful for street photography: You can fold the screen upward and look down at the camera while taking photos of people without drawing undue attention to yourself, particularly when the lens is zoomed in to a telephoto setting.

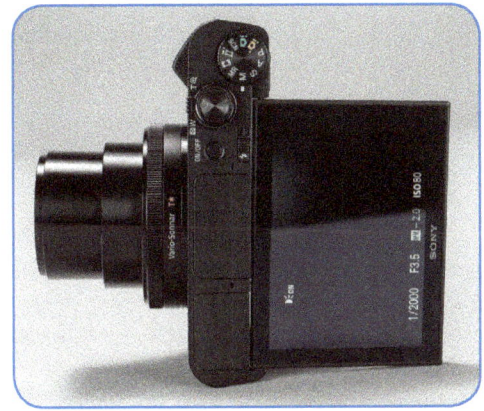

Figure 5-29. LCD Screen Positioned for Overhead Shots

Finally, you can tilt the LCD about halfway from the camera, as shown in Figure 5-29, and hold the camera upside-down above your head. With that position, you can hold the camera above your head and view the scene as if you were an arm's length taller or were standing on a small ladder. If you attach the camera to a monopod or other support and hold it up in the air, you can extend the height even farther and still view the LCD screen quite well. You can activate the self-timer before raising the camera up in the air to take the photo. You also can use a smartphone or tablet connected to the camera by Wi-Fi to trigger the camera by remote control while it is raised overhead, as discussed in Chapter 9, or you can use a wired remote control device, as discussed in Appendix A.

Ports and Other Items on Sides and Bottom of Camera

Figure 5-30 shows the right side of the camera with the protective flap over the Multi port opened. The Multi port is where you plug in the USB cable for charging the battery, powering the camera with an external power source, uploading images and videos to a computer, or connecting the camera directly to a printer to print images. You also can plug in other accessories that are compatible with this special terminal, including various models of wired remote controls, which I discuss in Appendix A.

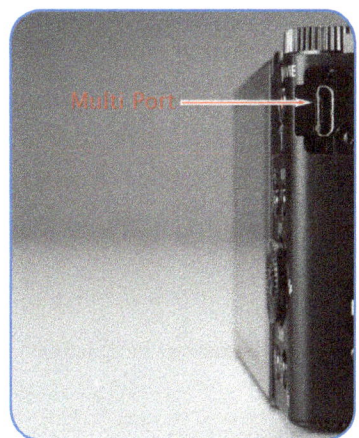

Figure 5-30. Multi Port on Right Side of Camera

The left side of the camera, shown in Figure 5-31, is where the Finder switch is located. Press down on this switch to release the electronic viewfinder so it will pop up. If the camera is turned off, popping up the viewfinder will turn the camera on. Pressing the viewfinder back into the camera's body will power the camera off or leave it powered on, depending on the setting of the Function for VF Close option on the Setup menu.

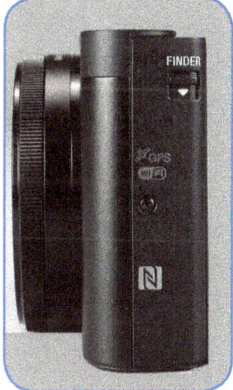

Figure 5-31. Items on Left Side of HX90V Camera

On the left side of the camera is a decorative letter N, which marks the NFC active area for the camera. This is where you touch the camera against the similar area on a compatible Android smartphone or tablet that uses the near field communication protocol. As discussed in Chapter 9, when the two devices are touched together at their NFC active areas, they should automatically connect through a Wi-Fi network. Once the connection is established, they can share images and the phone or tablet can control the camera in some ways. (The GPS logo in this image does not appear on the HX80 camera, which does not include GPS capability.)

The bottom of the camera is shown in Figure 5-32.

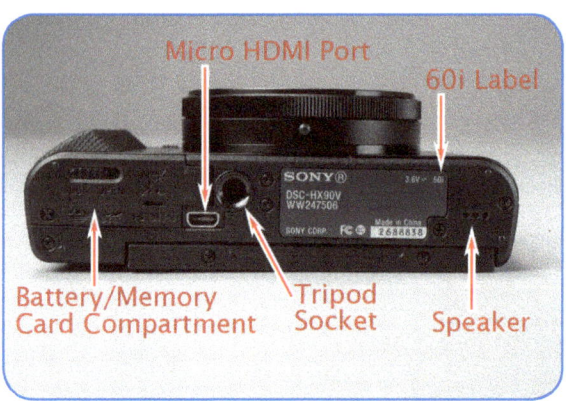

Figure 5-32. Items on Bottom of Camera

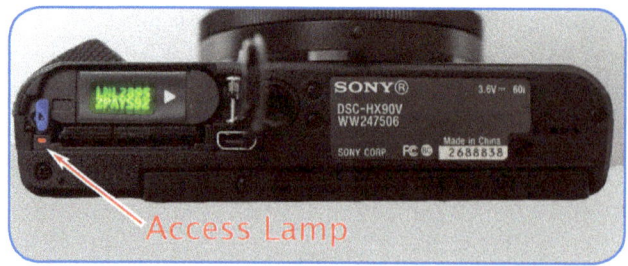

Figure 5-33. Red Access Lamp Inside Battery Compartment

Two important items here are the tripod socket and the battery/memory card compartment. There is an access lamp inside this compartment, as seen in Figure 5-33. The red access lamp lights when the camera is writing data to the memory card. When the lamp is lit, it's important not to remove the card or the battery from the compartment. Also on the bottom of the camera is the speaker, which emits the sound for movies played in the camera.

Another important item on the camera's bottom is the HDMI port, where you plug in an optional micro HDMI cable to connect the camera to an HDTV for viewing images and videos. You also can view the shooting display from the camera through this connection, so you can connect the camera to an HDTV to act as a monitor for your shooting of still images or videos. I will discuss that process in Chapter 9. You also can set the camera to output a "clean" HDMI signal, which can be routed through an HDMI cable to an external video recorder. I will discuss that process in Chapter 8.

Chapter 6: Playback and Printing

You may not spend a lot of time viewing images and videos in the camera, but it's still useful to know how the various playback functions work. You may need to examine an image closely in the camera to check focus, composition, and other aspects, or you may want to share images with friends and family. So it's worth looking at the playback functions of the HX80 and HX90V. I'll also discuss options for printing images in this chapter.

Normal Playback

First, you should be aware of the setting for Auto Review on the Custom menu. This setting determines whether and for how long the image stays on the screen for review when you take a new picture. If your major concern is to check images right after they are taken, this option is all you need to use. As discussed in Chapter 7, you can leave Auto Review turned off or set it to two, five, or 10 seconds.

To control how stored images and videos are viewed later on, you need to use the options available in playback mode. For normal review of images, press the Playback button, marked by a small triangle to the lower left of the Control wheel. Once you press that button, the camera is in playback mode, and you will see the most recent image or video saved to the memory card, depending on the View Mode setting on the Playback menu. To move back through older images and videos, press the Left button or turn the Control wheel to the left. To see more recent items, use the Right button or turn the wheel to the right. To speed through the items, hold down the Left or Right button.

Index View and Enlarging Images

In playback mode, you can press the zoom lever to view an index screen of images and videos or to enlarge a single image. When you are viewing an individual image or video, press the zoom lever once to the left, and you will see a screen showing either nine or 25 items, one of which is outlined by an orange frame, as shown in Figure 6-1. (You can choose whether this screen shows nine or 25 images using the Image Index option on the Playback menu, discussed later in this chapter.)

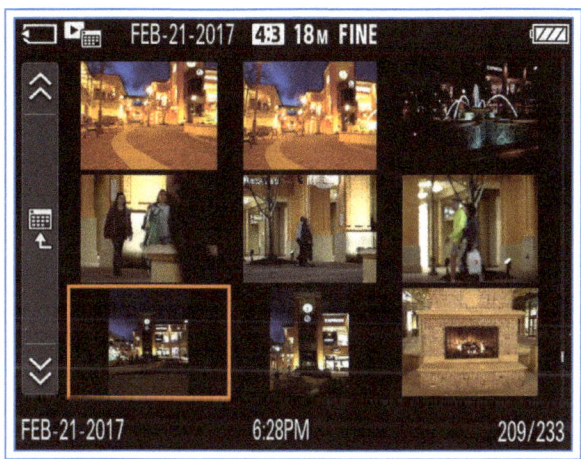

Figure 6-1. Index Screen with Nine Images

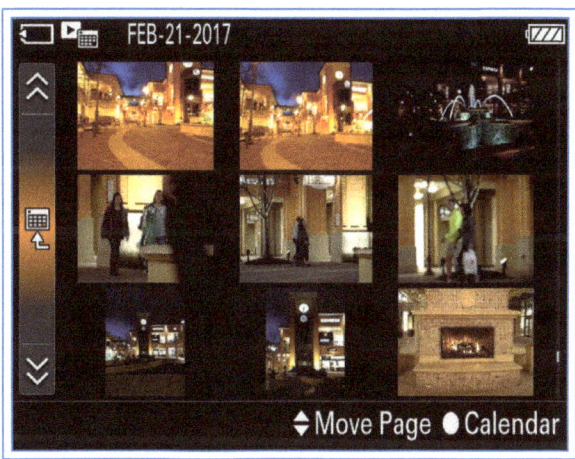

Figure 6-2. Navigation Strip Highlighted on Index Screen

You can press the Center button to view the outlined image or video, or you can move through the items on the index screen by pressing the four direction buttons or by turning the Control wheel. If you move the orange highlight to the far left of the display, as seen in Figure

6-2, you can use the Up and Down buttons to move through the images a screen at a time.

On the nine-image or 25-image index screen, one more press of the zoom lever to the left brings up another screen. For example, if View Mode, discussed later in this chapter, is set to Date View, this next screen will be a calendar display, as shown in Figure 6-3.

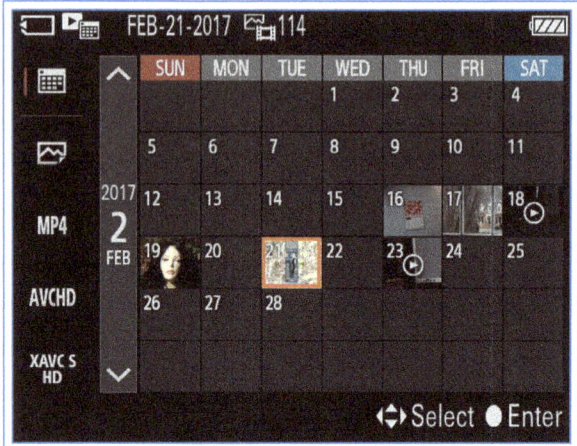

Figure 6-3. Calendar Index Screen

On that screen, you can move the orange frame to any date and press the Center button to bring up a view with all images and videos from that date. If you move the orange highlight to the narrow strip to the left of the calendar, as seen in Figure 6-4, you can move through the items by months with the Up and Down buttons.

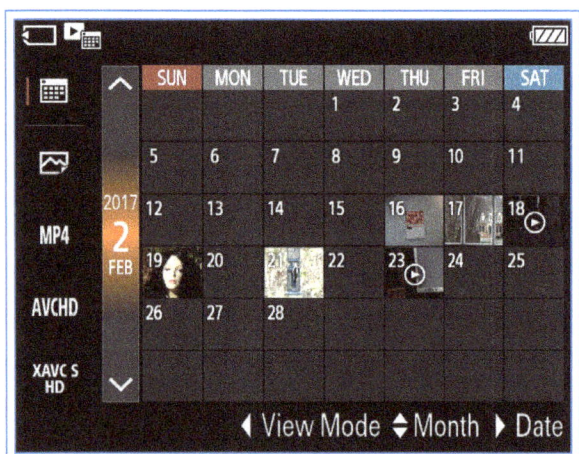

Figure 6-4. Navigation Strip Highlighted on Date View Screen

If you move the highlight to the far left of the screen, as in Figure 6-5, you can use the Up and Down buttons to move through the five icons, from which you can choose the date view, still-images view, MP4 videos view, AVCHD videos view, or XAVC S HD videos view. I will discuss those options later in this chapter, in connection with the View Mode option on the Playback menu.

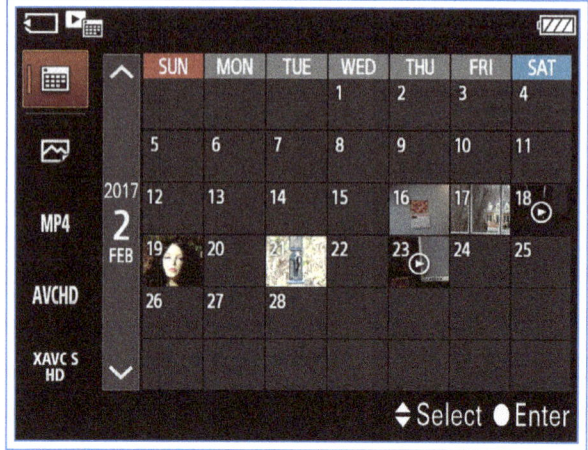

Figure 6-5. View Mode Selection Strip Highlighted

When you are viewing a single still image, one press of the zoom lever to the right enlarges the image. A display in the lower left corner of the image shows a thumbnail with an inset frame that represents the portion of the image that is filling the screen in enlarged view, as shown in Figure 6-6. This feature is useful for quickly checking the focus of the image.

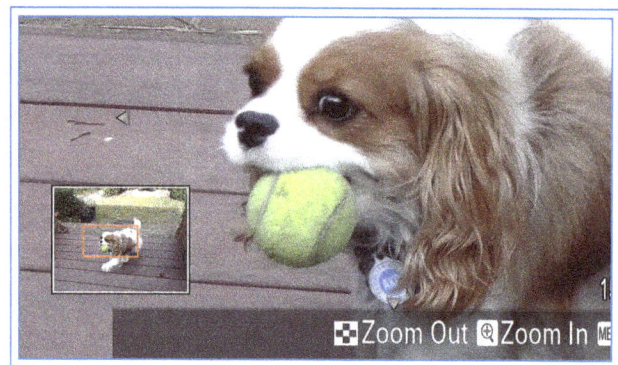

Figure 6-6. Enlarged Image

If you press the zoom lever to the right repeatedly, the image will be enlarged to increasing levels. While it is magnified, you can scroll in it with the four direction buttons; you will see the inset frame move around within the thumbnail image. To reduce the image size again, press the zoom lever to the left as many times as necessary or press the Center button or the Menu button to revert immediately to normal size. You can press the In-Camera Guide/Delete button to bring up the Delete screen for that image while it is enlarged. To move to other images while the display is magnified, turn the Control wheel.

Playback Screens

When you view an image in single-image mode, pressing the Display (Up) button repeatedly cycles through the three screens that are available: (1) full image with no added information; (2) full image with basic information, including date and time taken, image number, aspect ratio, aperture, shutter speed, ISO, and image size and quality, as shown in Figure 6-7; and (3) thumbnail image with detailed recording information, including exposure compensation, Picture Effect setting (if any), Metering Mode, DRO setting, shooting mode, white balance, and other data, plus a histogram, as shown in Figure 6-8.

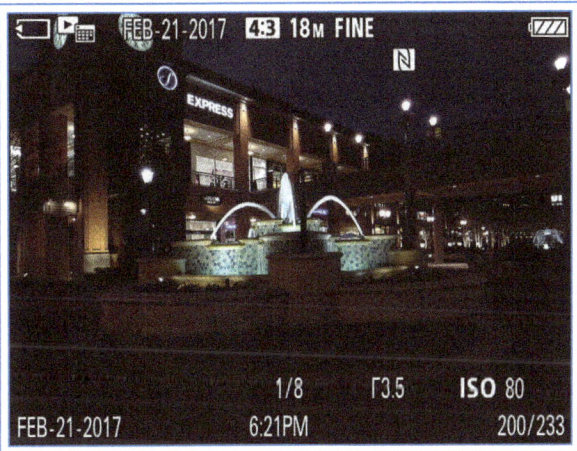

Figure 6-7. Playback Display with Basic Information

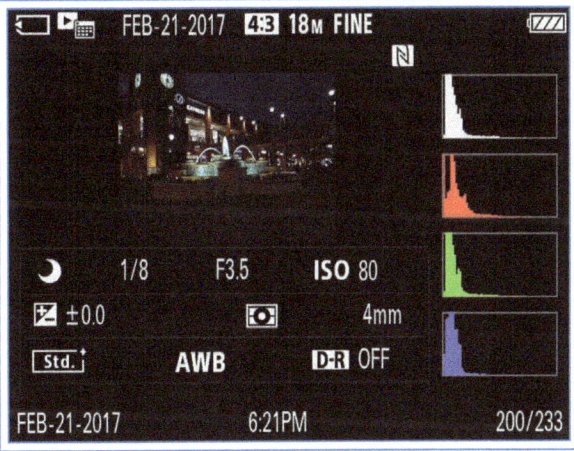

Figure 6-8. Playback Display with Detailed Information

A histogram is a graph showing the distribution of dark and bright areas in the image displayed on the screen. The darkest blacks are represented by peaks on the left and the brightest whites by peaks on the right, with continuous gradations in between. With these cameras, the histogram displayed in playback mode includes four boxes with information.

The top box provides information about the overall brightness of the image. The three lower boxes provide information about the brightness of the colors that make up the image: red, green, and blue. If a histogram has peaks bunched at the left, there are too many dark areas and few bright and white areas. If the graph runs into the left side of the chart, it means shadow areas are "clipped" so that details have been lost in the dark areas.

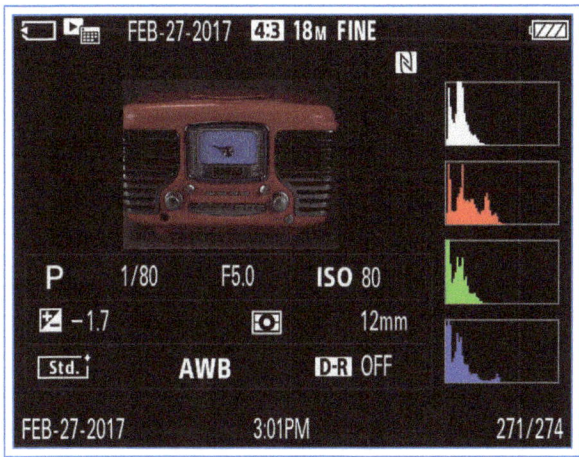

Figure 6-9. Histogram for Underexposed Image

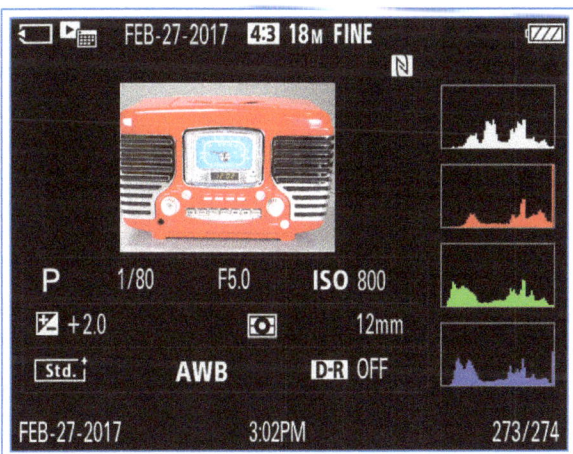

Figure 6-10. Histogram for Overexposed Image

The histogram in Figure 6-9 illustrates this degree of underexposure. A histogram with its high points bunched to the right means the opposite—too bright, as in Figure 6-10. When the graph runs into the right side of the chart, that means highlights are clipped and the image has lost details in bright areas.

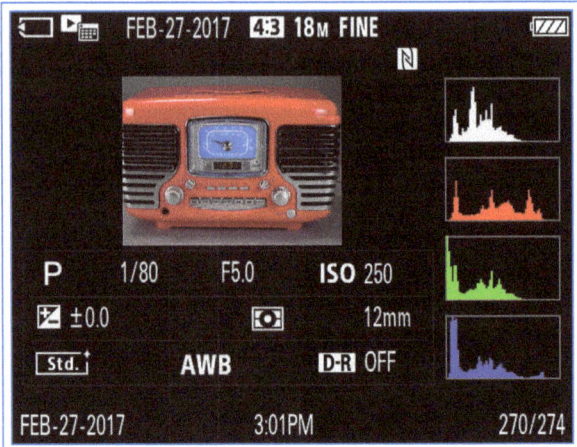

Figure 6-11. Histogram for Normally Exposed Image

A histogram that is "just right" has high points arranged more evenly in the middle of the chart. That pattern, as illustrated by Figure 6-11, indicates a good balance of light, dark, and medium tones.

When the playback histogram is displayed, areas containing highlights that are excessively bright will blink to show possible overexposure, indicating that you may need to take another shot with the exposure adjusted to correct that situation.

The histogram can give you helpful feedback about the exposure of images. Also, there may be instances in which it is appropriate to have a histogram skewed to the left or right for intentionally "low-key" (dark) or "high-key" (brightly lit) scenes.

To turn on the histogram for the live view in shooting mode, use the Display Button option on the Custom menu.

Deleting Images with the Delete Button

As I mentioned in Chapter 5, you can delete individual images by pressing the Delete button, also known as the In-Camera Guide button, which is marked with a question mark. If you press this button when a still image or a video is displayed, whether individually or highlighted on an index screen, the camera will display the Delete/Cancel box shown in Figure 6-12.

Highlight your choice and press the Center button to confirm. To delete multiple items, you need to use the Delete option on the Playback menu, discussed later in this chapter. You also can use the Delete button to delete an image when it is displayed immediately after it was taken, with the Auto Review option.

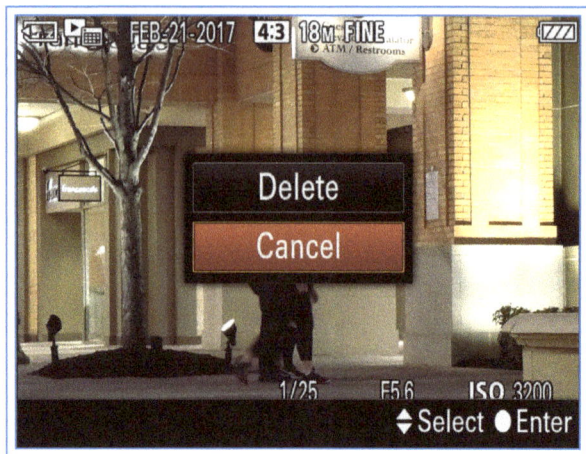

Figure 6-12. Message from Pressing Delete Button

Playback Menu

Other options for playback appear as items on the Playback menu, whose first screen on the HX90V is shown in Figure 6-13.

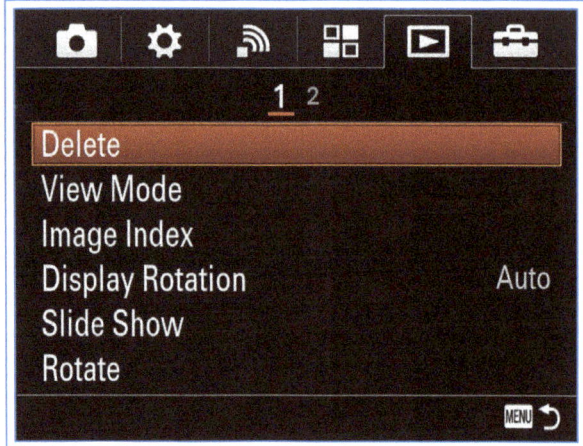

Figure 6-13. Screen 1 of HX90V Playback Menu

You get access to this menu by pressing the Menu button. The camera does not have to be in playback mode to get access to this menu, but, in playback mode, pressing the Menu button will take you directly to the Playback menu. Otherwise, you may need to navigate to this menu. You enter playback mode by pressing the Playback button when the camera is turned on in shooting mode. If the camera is turned off, you can turn it on in playback mode by pressing the Playback button instead of the power button.

Chapter 6: Playback and Printing | 107

Following is information about the items on the Playback menu:

Delete

Use this option to delete multiple images or videos in one operation. (If you just want to delete one or two images or videos, it's easier to display each item on the screen, then press the Delete button and confirm the erasure.) When you select the Delete command, the menu offers you various choices, as shown in Figure 6-14.

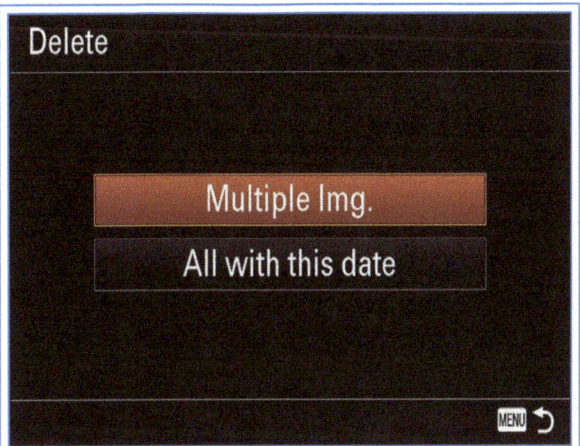

Figure 6-14. Delete Menu Options Screen

These choices may include Multiple Images, All in this Folder, or All with this Date, depending on the current setting for the View Mode option, discussed below. If the Delete command is dimmed and unavailable for selection, that means there are no items on the memory card that fall into the current View Mode category.

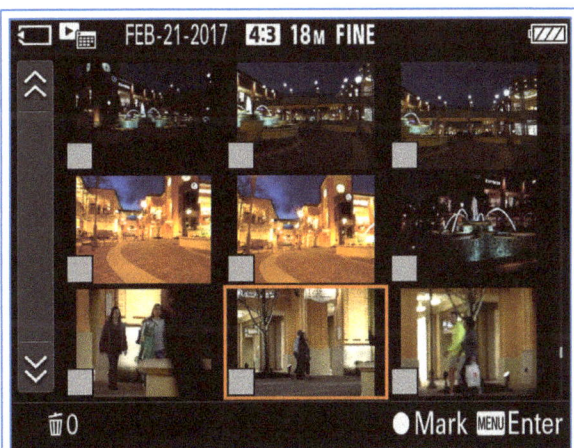

Figure 6-15. Multiple Images Selection Screen for Delete Option

If you choose Multiple Images, the camera will display images or videos with a check box at the left side, if any exist on the memory card, as shown in Figure 6-15.

The images and videos may be shown individually or on an index screen, depending on current settings. You can change between full-screen and index views using the zoom lever.

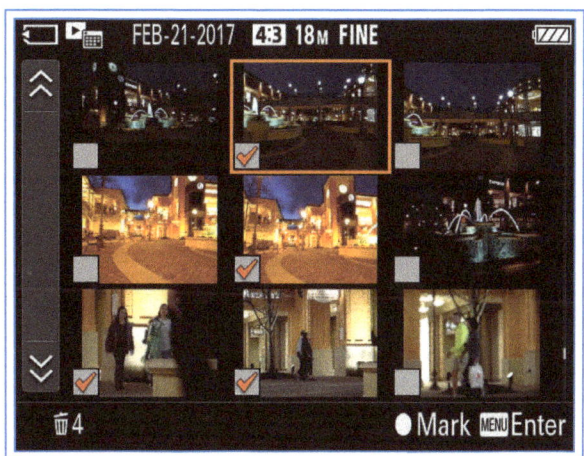

Figure 6-16. Images Marked for Deletion

Scroll through the images and videos with the Control wheel or the direction buttons. When you reach an image you want to delete, press the Center button to place a check mark in the check box on that image. Continue with this process until you have marked all images you want to delete, as shown in Figure 6-16. To unmark an image, press the Center button again.

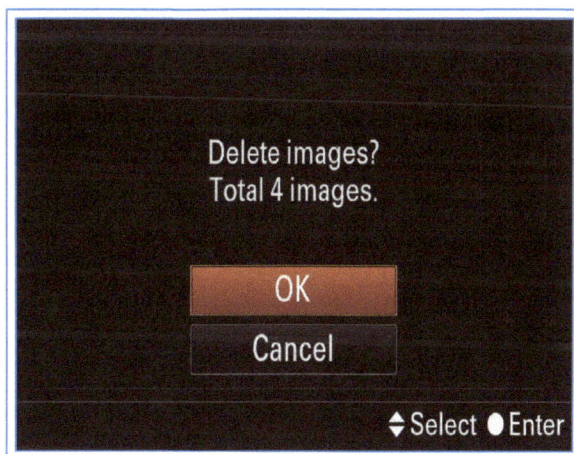

Figure 6-17. Delete Option Confirmation Screen

Then press the Menu button to move to the next screen, where the camera will prompt you to highlight OK or Cancel, as shown in Figure 6-17, and press the Center button to confirm. If you select OK, all of the marked images and videos will be deleted.

If, instead of Multiple Images, you choose All in Folder, the camera will display a screen asking you to confirm deletion of all files in the current folder. If you select All with this Date, you will have the opportunity to delete all images and videos from the selected date.

If any images have a key icon displayed at the top, those images are protected, and cannot be deleted using this option unless you first unprotect them, as discussed later in this chapter.

View Mode

This second option on the Playback menu lets you choose which images or videos are currently viewed in playback mode. The options are Date View, Folder View (Still), Folder View (MP4), AVCHD View, and XAVC S HD View, as shown in Figure 6-18.

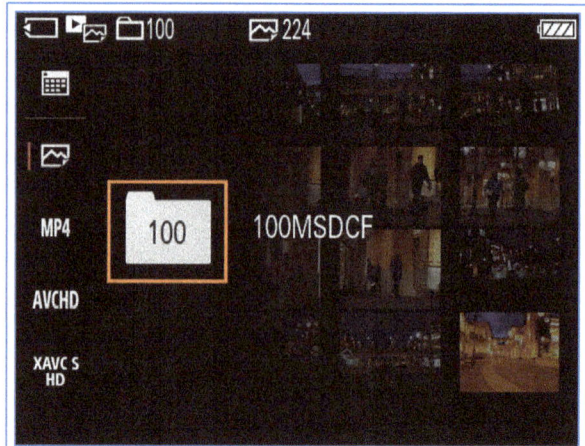

Figure 6-19. View Mode Set to Folder View (Still)

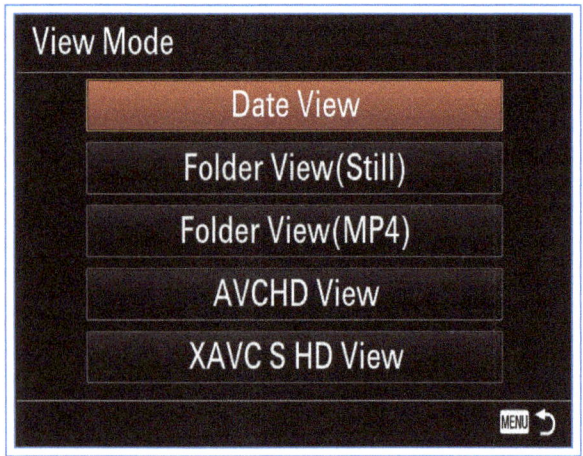

Figure 6-18. View Mode Menu Options Screen

If you select Date View, the camera will display the calendar screen shown earlier in Figure 6-3. You can navigate through that screen using the Control wheel or the direction buttons. Highlight a date and press the Center button; the camera will display all images and videos from that date. When the calendar screen is displayed, you can move to other months by highlighting the gray strip to the left of the calendar and using the Up and Down buttons.

If you select Folder View (Still), the camera will show a screen like that in Figure 6-19, which displays the folders available for selection.

Highlight the folder you want (there may be only one) and press the Center button; the camera will display all still images in that folder. You can navigate through the index screens for those images and select the image or images you want to view. If you select Folder View (MP4), the camera will display only the MP4 videos from the folder you select, if there are any such videos.

If you select AVCHD View, the camera will display a calendar screen with thumbnail images indicating which dates have AVCHD files associated with them. You can select any date with a thumbnail to display AVCHD videos from that date.

If you select XAVC S HD View, the camera will display a calendar showing the dates on which videos in that format were recorded.

My general preference is to use the Date View option, because then I can view both images and videos from a given date. However, if I want to locate a particular video, it can be quicker to choose one of the video views so I can limit my search to videos of a single format.

You can select a view option from an index screen without using the Playback menu. After moving the zoom lever to the left to call up the calendar display or folder display, move the highlight to the extreme left of the screen to the line of icons that represent the five view modes, as shown earlier in Figure 6-5, and select one of the modes from that display.

Image Index

This menu option, shown in Figure 6-20, gives you the choice of having the camera include either nine images or 25 images when it displays an index screen.

When you make this selection, the camera displays the index screen you chose, and it will display that screen whenever you call up the index screen using the zoom lever, as discussed earlier.

Whether you choose the nine-image screen or the 25-image screen depends on your preference and

Chapter 6: Playback and Printing | 109

other factors, including how many images and videos you have on your memory card and how easy it is to distinguish one from another by looking at the small thumbnail images.

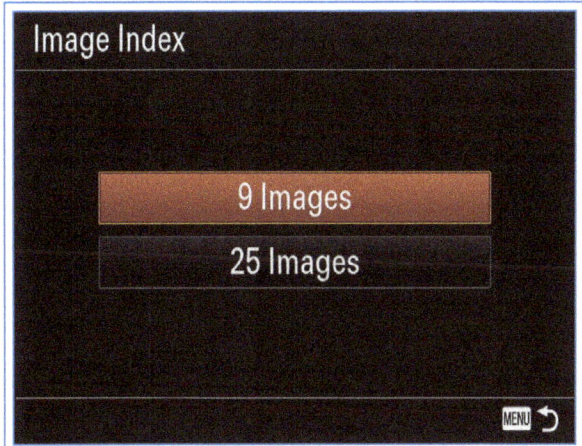

Figure 6-20. Image Index Menu Options Screen

The thumbnails on the nine-image screen are larger than those on the 25-image screen, and it may make sense to choose the nine-image screen unless you have so many images that it would be burdensome to scroll through them nine at a time.

Display Rotation

This next item on the Playback menu controls whether images shot with the camera held vertically appear that way when you play them back on the camera's screen. By default, this option is set to Auto, meaning images taken vertically are automatically rotated so that the vertical shot appears in portrait orientation on the horizontal display, as shown in Figure 6-21.

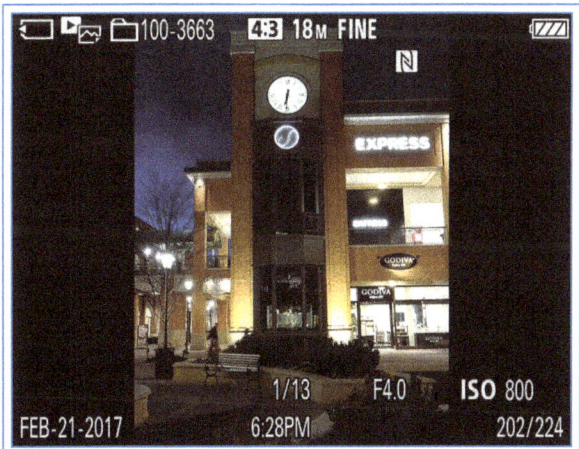

Figure 6-21. Vertical Image Rotated to Display Horizontally

With this setting, if you tilt the camera sideways so one side is up, a vertical image will rotate to fill the screen. In this way, you get the best of both worlds: Vertical images display in proper orientation (but smaller than normal) within the horizontal display, and, when you tilt the camera in playback mode, they display at full size.

If you change the setting to Manual, a vertical image will appear vertically on the horizontal screen, in the same way as shown in Figure 6-21. The difference with this setting from Auto is that, if you tilt the camera in playback mode, the image will not change its orientation.

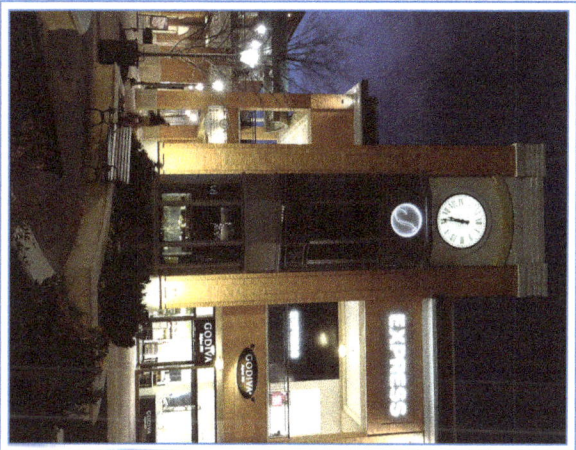

Figure 6-22. Vertical Image Displayed Without Rotation

If you set this option to Off, a vertical image will display horizontally on the display at full size, as shown in Figure 6-22, so you would have to tilt the camera in playback mode to see it in its proper orientation. With all of these settings, you can use the Rotate option on the Playback menu, discussed later in this chapter, to rotate an image manually to a different orientation.

Slide Show

This feature sets the camera to automatically play still images and videos in sequence at an interval you specify. This option will be dimmed and unavailable if the View Mode option on the Playback menu is set to Folder View (MP4), AVCHD View, or XAVC S HD View. If that is the case, use the View Mode menu option to select either Date View or Folder View (Still). If you select Date View, the Slide Show option will display all of your movies, in all four formats, along with your still images. Each movie will play in full before the show advances to the next item, unless you interrupt it with one of the controls. If you select Folder View (Still), the

Slide Show option will display only the still images from the folder you selected.

When you select the Slide Show option and press the Center button, the next screen has two options you can set: Repeat and Interval, as seen in Figure 6-23. If Repeat is turned on, the show will keep repeating; otherwise, it will play only once.

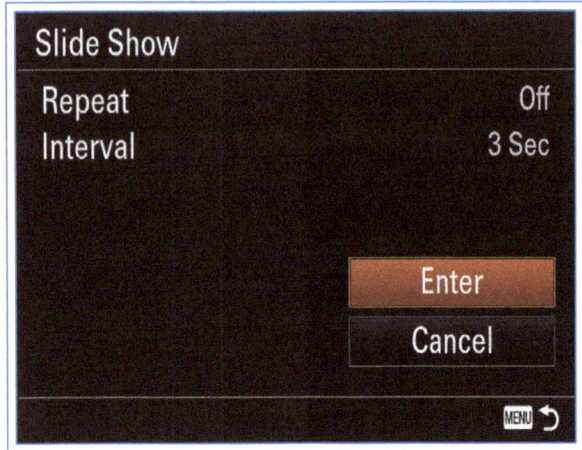

Figure 6-23. Slide Show Menu Options Screen

The camera will not power off automatically in this mode, so be sure to stop the show when you are done with it. The Interval setting, which controls how long each still image stays on the screen, can be set to one, three, five, 10, or 30 seconds. (The Interval setting does not apply to movies, each of which plays to its end.)

Once the options are set, navigate to the Enter box at the bottom of the screen using the Control wheel or the Down button, and press the Center button to start the show. You can move forward or backward through images (and videos, if included) with the Right and Left buttons. Hold the buttons down to fast-forward or fast-reverse through the images and videos.

You can stop the show by pressing the Menu button or the Playback button. There is no way to pause the show and resume it. When a movie is playing as part of the show, you can control its volume by pressing the Down button and then adjusting the sound with the Left and Right buttons or the Control wheel. Each movie plays fully before the next movie or image is displayed, but you can skip to the next movie or image using the Right button.

The Slide Show option does not provide settings such as transitions, effects, or music. You cannot select which images to play; this option just lets you play all of your still images from the selected folder, if you are using Folder View, or all still images and videos starting from the selected date, if you are using Date View.

ROTATE

The Rotate option is a way to rotate a still image manually. Select this menu item, and you will see a screen like that in Figure 6-24, prompting you to press the Center button to rotate the image.

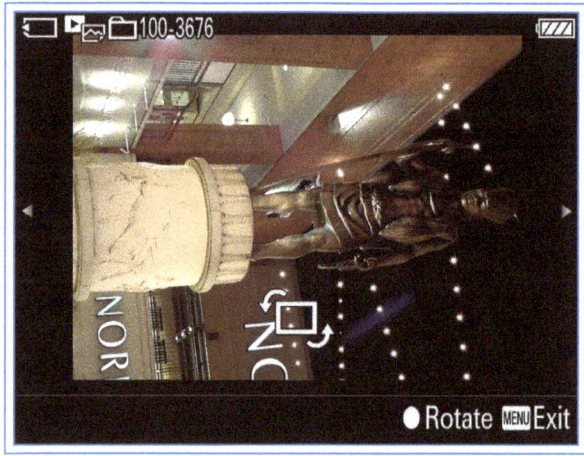

Figure 6-24. Rotate Menu Options Screen

Each time you press the button, the image will rotate 90 degrees counter-clockwise. You can use this option for images taken vertically, when Display Rotation, discussed above, is turned off. This option does not work for videos, only still images.

The second screen of the Playback menu is shown in Figure 6-25.

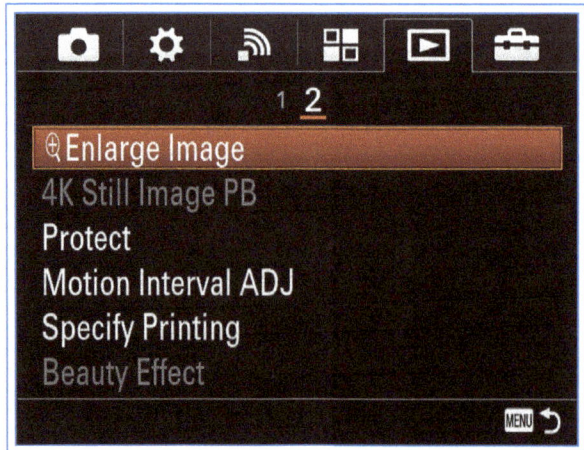

Figure 6-25. Screen 2 of HX90V Playback Menu

ENLARGE IMAGE

This option performs the same magnification for still images that you can do with the zoom lever, as discussed earlier in this chapter. When you select this option, the enlarged image will appear on the screen; you can use the zoom lever to change the enlargement factor.

4K STILL IMAGE PLAYBACK

This menu item is dimmed and cannot be selected unless the camera is connected to a TV set or monitor that supports 4K resolution. The standard known as 4K is a relatively recent option for HDTVs. The 4K stands for 4,000, meaning each frame has a horizontal resolution of about 4,000 pixels. A standard HD (high-definition) TV set outputs frames with a horizontal resolution of 1920 pixels and a vertical resolution of 1080 pixels. A 4K TV frame has a horizontal resolution of 3840 (two times 1920) and a vertical resolution of 2160 (two times 1080). The overall resolution of the 4K TV image is about 8 megapixels, while the resolution of full HDTV is about 2 megapixels, so a 4K picture has 4 times the resolution of full HDTV.

The idea behind this menu option is that, in order to view the images from your camera on a TV set at the highest possible quality, you can take advantage of a technology that offers 8 MP of resolution rather than the 2 MP that is offered by standard HDTV sets. So, if you have a 4K TV available, you can connect your camera using an optional HDMI cable and enjoy your still images at the highest possible resolution.

PROTECT

With the Protect feature, you can "lock" selected images or videos so they cannot be erased with the normal erase functions, including using the Delete button and using the Delete option on the Playback menu, discussed above. However, if you format the memory card using the Format command, all data on the card will be erased, including protected images.

To protect images or videos using this menu item, the procedure is similar to the one for deleting images, discussed above. When you select this option, the camera will display a screen similar to that shown earlier in Figure 6-14 for the Delete option, with choices to select multiple images; all from the same date or folder as the current image; or to cancel protection for all images with this date or from this folder. (The current View Mode setting will determine whether the choices are for the current date or the current folder.)

If you select Multiple Images, the camera will present you with either index screens or individual images. As with the Delete option, you can scroll through your images and mark any image's check box for protection by pressing the Center button. When you have finished marking images, press the Menu button and the camera will display a confirmation screen. If you select OK to confirm, the marked images and videos will be protected. Any item that is protected will have a key icon in the upper right corner to the left of the battery icon, as shown in Figure 6-26.

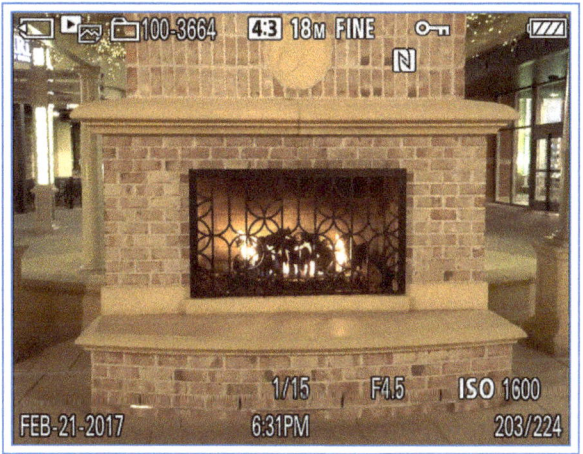

Figure 6-26. Protected Image with Key Icon

The key icon will be visible when the image is viewed with the detailed information screen or the basic information screen, but it will not appear in the image-only view.

To unprotect multiple images or videos in one operation, select the appropriate Cancel option from the Protect item on the Playback menu. That option will prompt you to Cancel All with this Date or to Cancel All in this Folder, depending on the View Mode setting.

MOTION INTERVAL ADJUSTMENT

This menu option gives you a way to adjust the length of time the camera uses for the interval between frames when it creates the Motion Shot effect in playing back a movie. The adjustment screen for this option is shown in Figure 6-27.

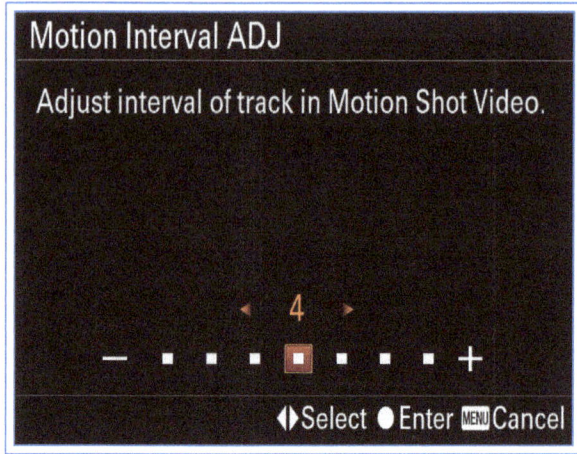

Figure 6-27. Motion Interval Adjustment Screen

The default value is four; you can set the interval to any value from one to seven. The higher the number, the greater the spacing between images in the motion shot. I will discuss this option in Chapter 8, where I discuss movie playback features.

Specify Printing

This option lets you use the DPOF (Digital Print Order Format) function, a printing protocol built into the camera. The DPOF system lets you mark various images on your memory card to be added to a print list, which can then be sent to your own inkjet or laser printer. Or, you can take the memory card to a commercial printing company to print out the selected images.

To add images to the DPOF print list, select the Specify Printing option from the Playback menu. On the next screen, shown in Figure 6-28, choose the option for Multiple Images.

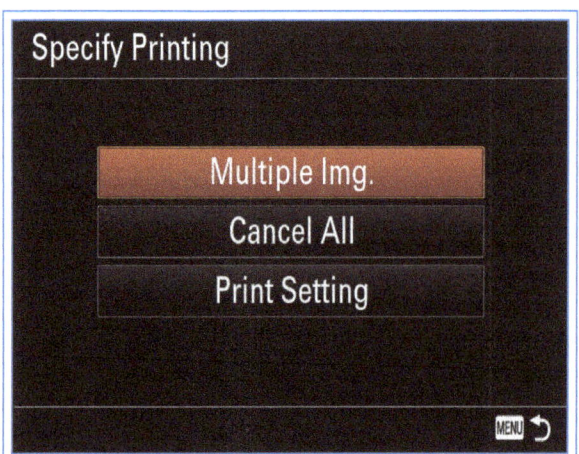

Figure 6-28. Specify Printing Menu Options Screen

The camera will display the first image with a check box at the left or an index screen with an orange frame around the currently selected image and a check box in the lower left corner of each image thumbnail, as with the Delete and Protect functions discussed earlier. You can choose to display individual images or index screens using the zoom lever. There will be a small printer icon in the lower left with a zero beside it at first, meaning no copies of any images have been set for printing yet. Use the Control wheel or direction buttons to move through the images.

When an image you want to print is displayed, press the Center button to mark it for printing or to unmark it. You can then keep browsing through images and adding them to (or removing them from) the print list. As you add images to the list, the counter in the lower left corner will show the total number of images selected for printing.

When you have finished selecting images to be printed, press the Menu button to move to a screen where you can confirm your choices by selecting OK. You also can turn the Date Imprint option on or off to specify whether or not the pictures will be printed with the dates they were taken. To do this, go to the first screen of the Specify Printing menu option and select Print Setting.

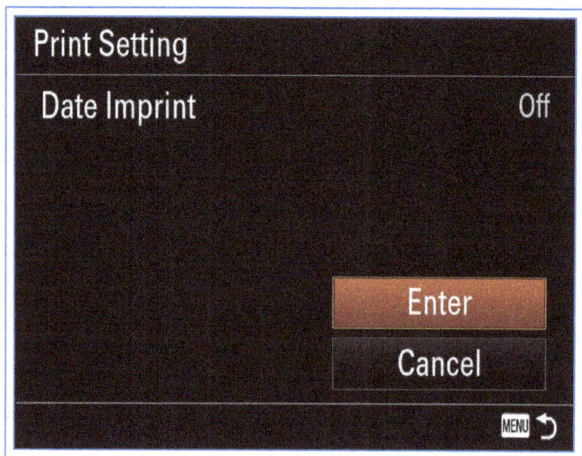

Figure 6-29. Print Setting Menu Options Screen

On the next screen, shown in Figure 6-29, you can turn on Date Imprint, to have the date printed on each image. You can take the memory card with the DPOF list to a service that prints photos using this system, or you can connect the camera to a Pictbridge-compatible printer to print the images. To cancel a Specify Printing order, go to the Specify Printing menu item and select the Cancel All option.

Beauty Effect

This last option on the Playback menu gives you a set of tools for retouching photographs of faces that you have previously taken. To use this feature, navigate to a still image of a face in playback mode and select this option from the Playback menu. The camera will display the image with an orange frame or a white frame around any face it detects. If the camera does not detect a face, it will display an error message. If it detects multiple faces, use the Left and Right buttons to select the one you want to retouch; the selected face will be marked with the orange frame.

After selecting the chosen face, press the Center button to move to the next screen, shown in Figure 6-30.

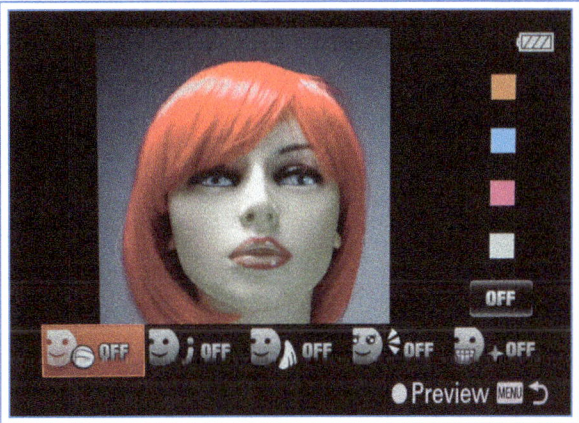

Figure 6-30. Beauty Effect Adjustments Screen

On this screen, the camera displays five controls, from left to right: Skin Toning, Skin Smoothing, Shine Removal, Eye Widening, and Teeth Whitening. Highlight an adjustment you want to make using the Left and Right buttons, and adjust each of these settings using the Up and Down buttons or the Control wheel.

When they are all adjusted as you want, press the Center button to generate a preview. The camera will display Before and After images on a screen like that shown in Figure 6-31.

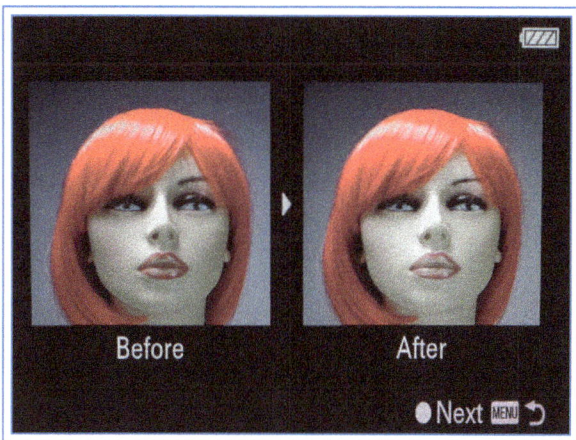

Figure 6-31. Beauty Effect Preview Screen

If you are satisfied, press the Center button, and select OK to confirm on the next screen. Then, if you need to adjust another face in the same image, select that image again and make adjustments for the next face.

Chapter 7: Custom and Setup Menus

In earlier chapters, I discussed the options available in the Shooting and Playback menu systems. The Sony HX80 and HX90V have two other menu systems—Custom and Setup—that help you set up the camera and customize its operation. In this chapter, I will discuss the options on those menus. I'll discuss menu options for movie recording in Chapter 8 and I'll discuss the Wi-Fi and Application menus in Chapter 9.

Custom Menu

The Custom menu, whose first screen on the HX90V is shown in Figure 7-1, gives you control over items that affect the ways you use the camera to take pictures and videos, but that do not change photographic settings such as white balance, ISO, focus modes, and matters of that nature.

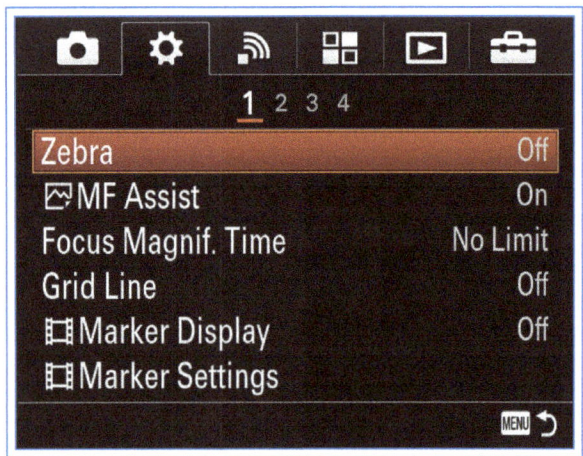

Figure 7-1. Screen 1 of HX90V Custom Menu

With this menu, the items to be adjusted are more in the categories of control and display options that help you use the major settings. Details about the options on the four screens of this menu follow. (The Custom menu has only three screens on the HX80, because that camera model does not include manual focus or a Control ring, so some menu items relating to those options are not present in the menu system.)

Zebra

This first Custom menu option gives you a tool for gauging the exposure of an image or video in shooting mode. When you turn this menu option on, you can select a value from 70 to 100 IRE in five-unit increments, or 100+ for values greater than 100. The IRE units are a measure of relative brightness or exposure, with 0 representing black and 100 representing white. Figure 7-2 shows the screen for selecting values up to 90.

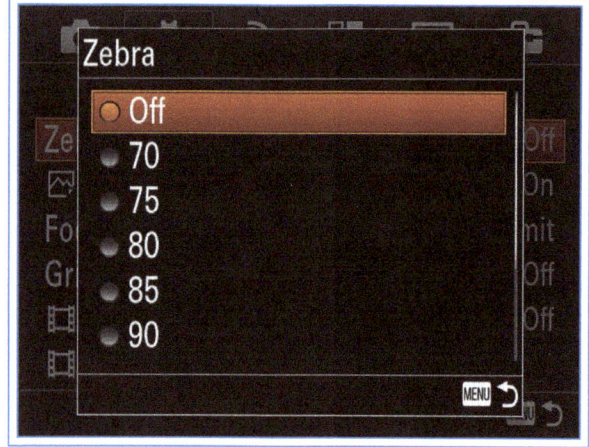

Figure 7-2. First Screen of Zebra Menu Option

When you turn this option on to any level, you very likely will see, in some parts of the display, the black-and-white "zebra" stripes that give this feature its name.

Zebra stripes originally were created as a feature for professional video cameras, so the videographer could see whether the scene would be properly exposed. This tool often is used in the context of taping an interview, when proper exposure of a human face is the main concern.

There are various approaches to using these stripes. Some videographers like to set the zebra function to 90 IRE and adjust the exposure so the stripes barely appear in the brightest parts of the image. Another recommendation is to set the option to 75 IRE for a scene with Caucasian skin, and expose so that the stripes barely appear in the area of the skin.

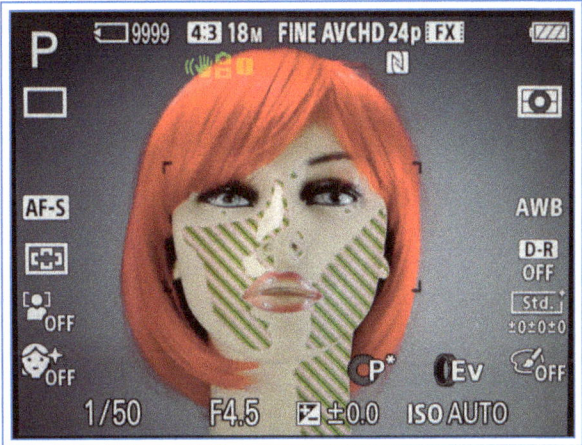

Figure 7-3. Zebra Set to IRE 75

In Figure 7-3 I set IRE to 75 and exposed to have the stripes appear clearly on the mannequin's face and neck.

As the brightness of the lighting increases for a subject, there may be no stripes at first, then they will gradually appear until they cover the subject, then they will seem to disappear, because the exposure is so bright that the subject is surrounded by an outline of "marching ants" rather than having stripes in its interior. The goal is to set the camera's exposure so the stripes are maximized on the subject at the chosen numerical level.

Zebra is a feature to consider, especially for video recording, but the HX80 and HX90V have an excellent metering system, including both live and playback histograms, so you can manage without this option if you don't want to deal with its learning curve.

MF Assist (HX90V Only)

The MF Assist option is for use with still images when manual focus or DMF is in effect. With MF Assist turned on in manual focus mode, the camera enlarges the image as soon as you start turning the Control ring to adjust focus, as shown in Figure 7-4. This feature helps show whether a particular area is in sharp focus. If you turn this option off, you can use another focusing aid, such as Focus Magnifier, discussed in Chapter 4, or Peaking Level, discussed later in this chapter. Or, you can use this option and Peaking at the same time, to provide even more assistance.

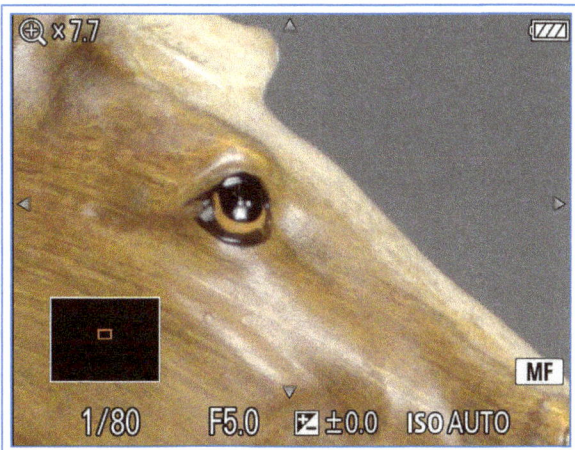

Figure 7-4. MF Assist In Use

When DMF is in effect, you have to keep the shutter button pressed halfway down while turning the Control ring to use the MF Assist enlargement feature.

I find MF Assist helpful, especially because I can set the camera to leave the enlarged screen in place indefinitely using the Focus Magnification Time option, discussed below. However, the Focus Magnifier option also is helpful, and may be preferable in one way because you can move the orange magnifier frame to the position you choose on the display before you press the Center button to magnify that area.

In some cases, if a subject does not have edges or other features to focus on, enlarging the view may not be very helpful. In those situations, Peaking Level may be more useful. Or, you may find that using Peaking Level in conjunction with MF Assist is the most useful approach of all. You should experiment with the various options to find what works best for you.

Focus Magnification Time (HX90V Only)

This option controls how long the display stays magnified with the MF Assist option, discussed above, or the Focus Magnifier option, discussed in Chapter 4. The choices are two or five seconds or No Limit, as seen in Figure 7-5. The default is two seconds.

If you select No Limit, the image will stay magnified until you press the shutter button all the way to take the picture or press it halfway to dismiss the enlarged view. My preference is to use No Limit so I can take my time to adjust manual focus precisely.

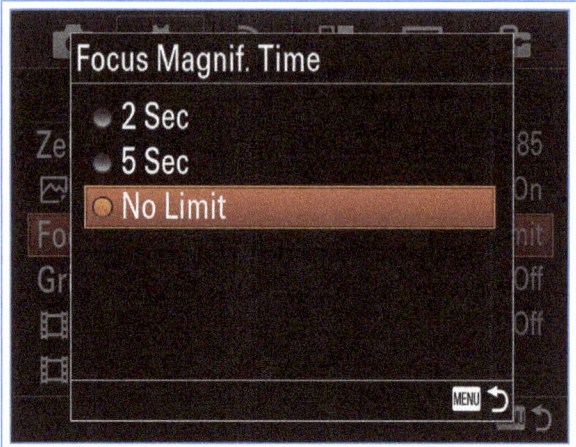

Figure 7-5. Focus Magnification Time Menu Options Screen

Note, though, that with the No Limit option, whenever you turn the Control ring to adjust focus when using MF Assist, the image will be enlarged, and it will not revert to the normal-sized view until you press the shutter button halfway. If you want to be able to keep adjusting focus with a view of the unenlarged subject, it may be preferable to select one of the options with a time limit or use the Focus Magnifier option.

GRID LINE

With this option, you can select one of four settings for a grid to be superimposed on the shooting screen. By default, there is no grid. If you choose one of the grid options, the lines will appear in your chosen configuration whenever the camera is showing the live view in shooting mode, whether the detailed display screen is selected or not. Of course, the grid does not appear when the For Viewfinder display, with its black screen full of shooting information, is displayed. The four options are seen in Figure 7-6.

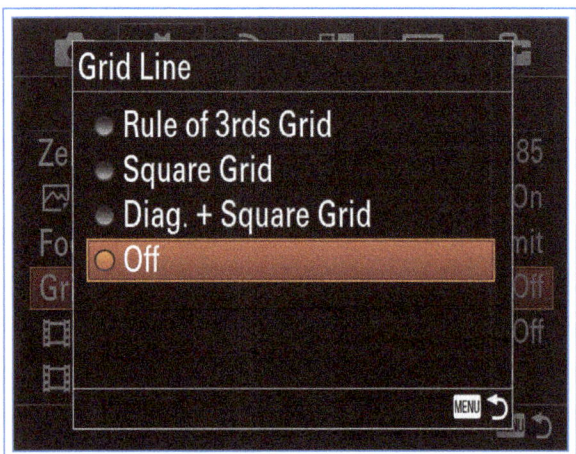

Figure 7-6. Grid Line Menu Options Screen

Following are descriptions of these choices, other than Off, which leaves the screen with no grid.

Rule of Thirds Grid

This arrangement of two vertical and two horizontal lines divides the screen into nine blocks, as seen in Figure 7-7.

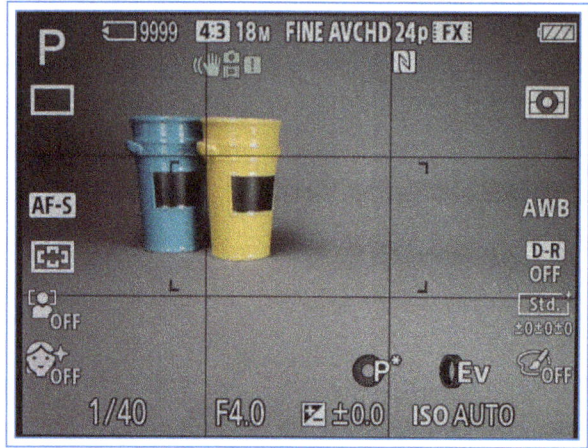

Figure 7-7. Rule of Thirds Grid In Use

This grid reflects a rule of composition that calls for locating an important subject at an intersection of these lines, which will place the subject one-third of the way from the edge of the image. This arrangement can add interest and asymmetry to an image.

Square Grid

With this option, five vertical and three horizontal lines divide the display into 24 blocks, as seen in Figure 7-8.

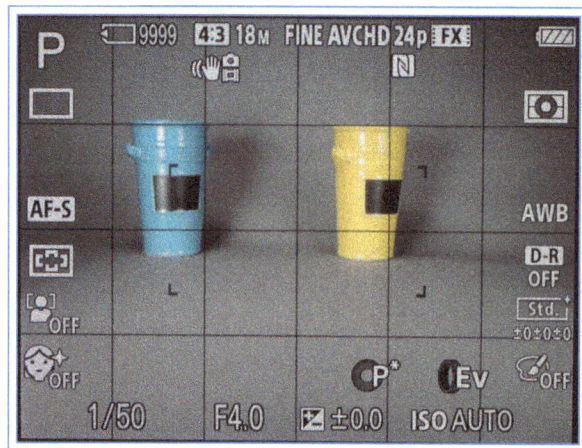

Figure 7-8. Square Grid In Use

In this way, you can still use the Rule of Thirds, but you have more lines available for lining up items, such as the edge of a building, that need to be straight.

Chapter 7: Custom and Setup Menus | 117

Diagonal Plus Square Grid

The last option has a grid of four blocks in each direction and adds two diagonal lines, as shown in Figure 7-9.

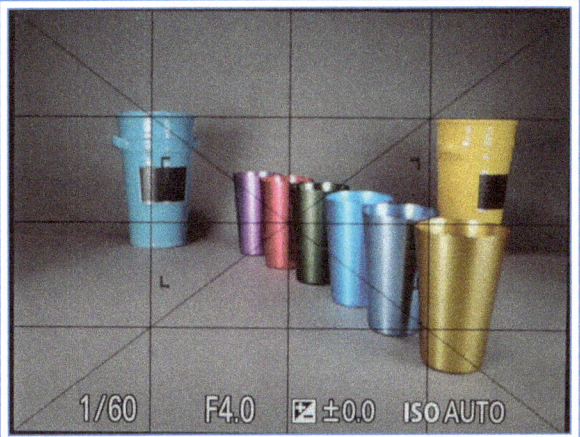

Figure 7-9. Diagonal Plus Square Grid In Use

The idea is that placing a subject or, more likely, a string of subjects along one of the diagonals can add interest to the image by drawing the viewer's eye into the image along the diagonal line.

MARKER DISPLAY

This option, which can be turned either on or off, controls whether or not various informative guidelines, called "markers," are displayed on the camera's screen for movie recording. There are four special markers available, which outline the aspect ratio and other areas on the screen. Any or all of them can be selected for use with the Marker Settings menu option, directly below this one on the Custom menu. If you turn Marker Display on, then, any of the four markers that you have selected will be displayed on the shooting screen while a movie is being recorded in any mode. The markers also will be displayed while the Mode dial is set to the Movie mode position, even before recording starts.

If this option is turned on, the selected markers will display on the camera's display screen, but they will not be recorded with the movie.

MARKER SETTINGS

This menu option works together with the Marker Display option, discussed above. This option lets you activate any or all of the four available markers— Center, Aspect, Safety Zone, and Guideframe, as shown in Figure 7-10.

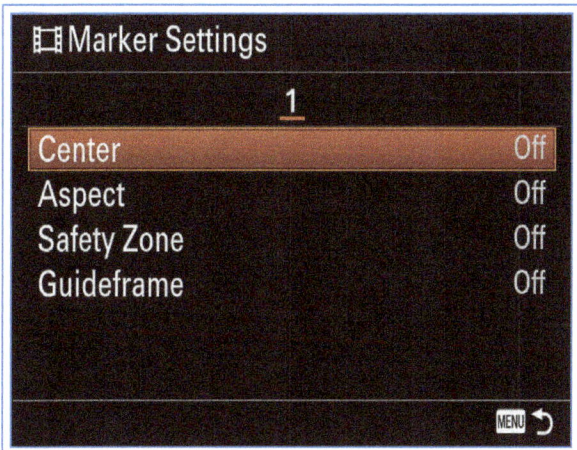

Figure 7-10. Marker Settings Menu Options Screen

If you turn on the Center marker, it places a cross in the center of the display, as illustrated in Figure 7-11. If you are shooting video in a busy or hectic environment, this marker may help you keep the main subject centered in the display so you don't cut it off.

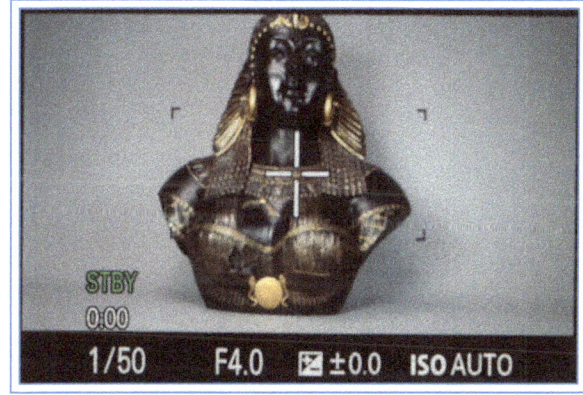

Figure 7-11. Center Marker In Use

The Aspect marker can be off or set to any one of seven ratios: 4:3, 13:9, 14:9, 15:9, 1.66:1, 1.85:1, or 2.35:1. Figure 7-12 shows the display with the 2.35:1 setting.

This setting places vertical white lines at the sides of the frame or horizontal white lines at the top and bottom of the frame, to outline the shape of the movie frame for the chosen aspect ratio. These lines are useful if you plan to alter the aspect ratio of your footage in post-production, to show what parts of the image will be cut off and help you frame your shots accordingly.

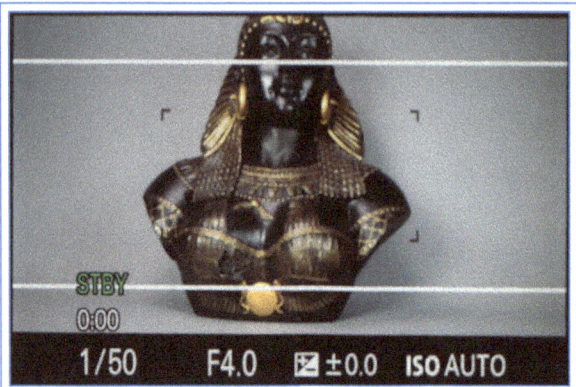

Figure 7-12. Aspect Marker 2.35:1 In Use

The Safety Zone marker can be off or set to 80% or 90%. The guidelines outline either 80% or 90% of the area of the display. The purpose of these lines is to provide a margin for safety, because the average consumer television set may not display the entire broadcast signal provided to it.

If you set these lines to mark a safety zone, you can make sure that your important subjects are included in the area that definitely will be displayed on most television sets. Figure 7-13 shows the display with the 80% safety zone marker activated.

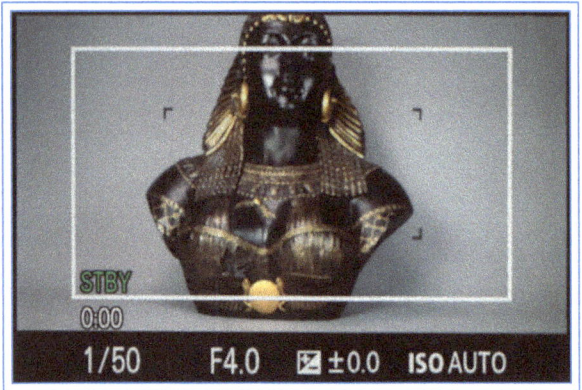

Figure 7-13. Safety Zone 80% Marker In Use

Finally, the Guideframe option, if turned on, displays a grid that is similar to the Rule of Thirds grid available with the Grid Line option, discussed earlier in this chapter. That option uses thin, black lines, which may be hard to see when you are shooting video under difficult conditions. The bold, white lines of the Guideframe setting should be more useful for video shooting. You cannot use both options at the same time; Grid Line is not available when Marker Display is turned on. Figure 7-14 shows the Guideframe option in use.

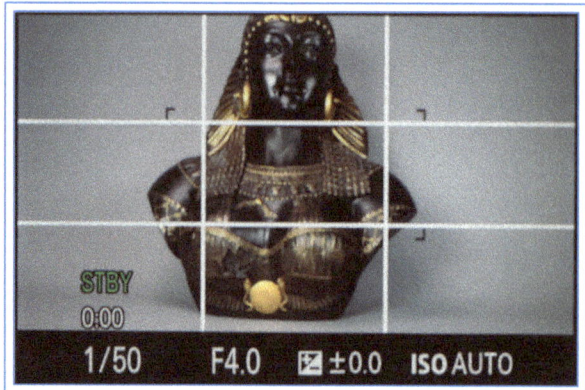

Figure 7-14. Guideframe Marker In Use

Screen 2 of the Custom menu on the HX90V is shown in Figure 7-15.

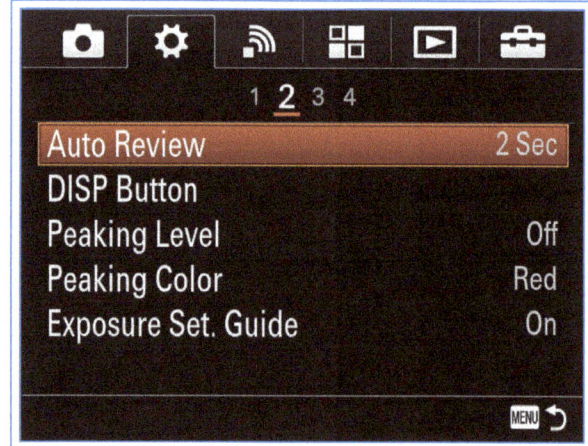

Figure 7-15. Screen 2 of HX90V Custom Menu

Auto Review

With the Auto Review option, shown in Figure 7-16, you can set the length of time that a still image appears on the display screen immediately after you capture it.

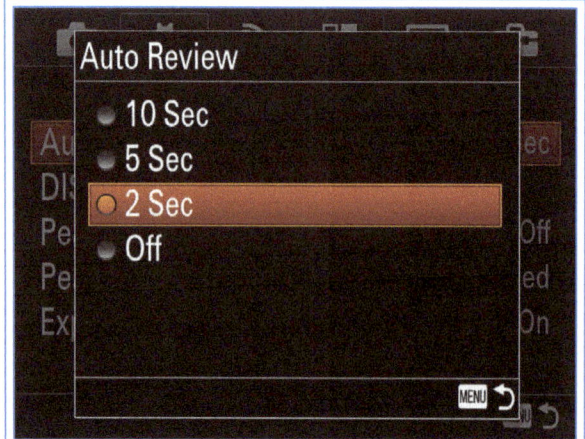

Figure 7-16. Auto Review Menu Options Screen

Chapter 7: Custom and Setup Menus | 119

The default is two seconds, but you can set the time to five or 10 seconds, or you can turn the function off. If you turn it off, the camera will return to shooting mode as soon as it has saved a new image to the memory card. When this option is in use, you can always return to the live view by pressing the shutter button halfway. The Auto Review option does not apply to movies; the camera does not display the beginning frame of a movie that was just recorded until you press the Playback button.

While a new image is displayed, you can use functions of playback mode such as enlarging the image, displaying index screens, or moving to other images. If you start one of these actions before the camera has reverted to shooting mode, the camera will stay in playback mode. You also can delete an image using the Delete button while it is displayed with this option.

Display Button

This option lets you choose what screens appear in shooting mode as you repeatedly press the Display button. There are sub-options that let you select the screens for the monitor (LCD) and the electronic viewfinder, as seen in Figure 7-17.

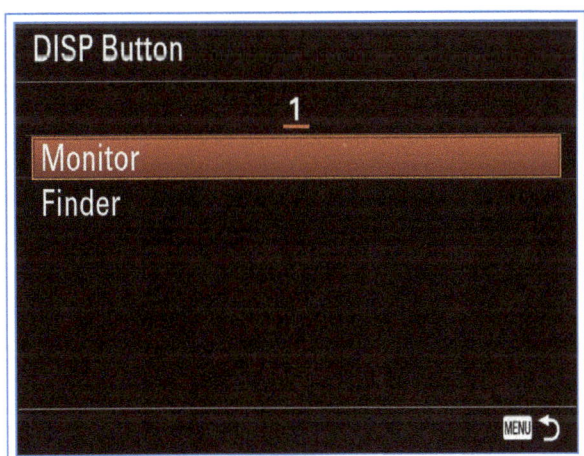

Figure 7-17. Display Button Menu Options Screen

You can make different choices of display screens for the LCD monitor and the viewfinder, so pressing the Display button when you are using the monitor may bring up a different set of screens than when you are using the viewfinder.

After you decide to choose display screens for the monitor or the viewfinder, you will see a screen like that shown in Figure 7-18. This screen shows the six display screens you can select for the monitor. The selection screen for the viewfinder is identical to the one in Figure 7-18, except that the sixth choice, For Viewfinder, is not available as a choice to appear in the viewfinder. That display screen is designed to appear on the monitor to provide shooting information when you are viewing the live view through the viewfinder.

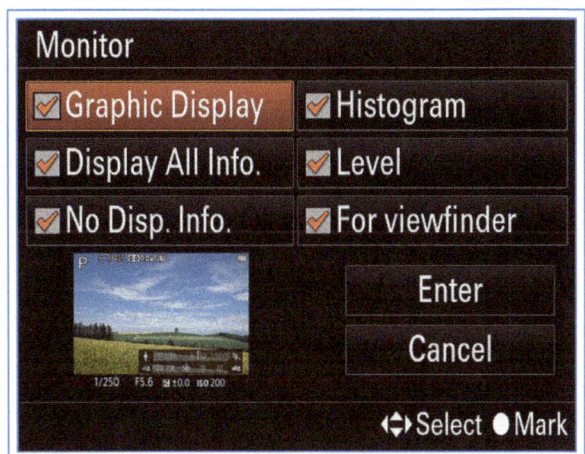

Figure 7-18. Options for Monitor Display Screens

Five of the six display screens available for the monitor are shown in Figure 7-19 through Figure 7-23. The screen displaying just the image with very little information is not shown here.

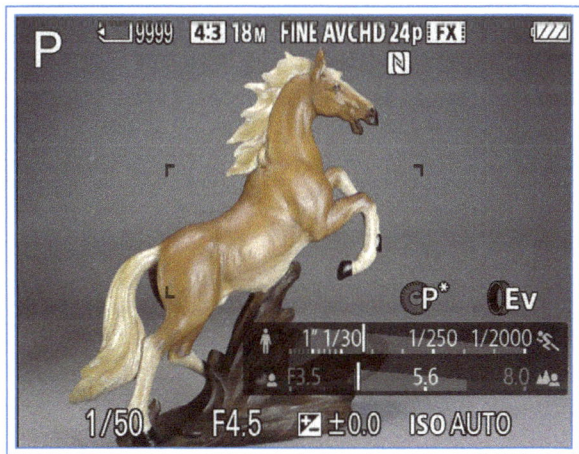

Figure 7-19. Graphic Display Screen

Figure 7-19 shows the screen with the Graphic Display in the lower right corner. That display illustrates the use of faster shutter speeds to stop action and wider apertures to blur backgrounds. I find it distracting and not especially helpful, but if it is useful to you, by all means select it.

I find the Display All Information screen, shown in Figure 7-20, to be cluttered, but it has useful information.

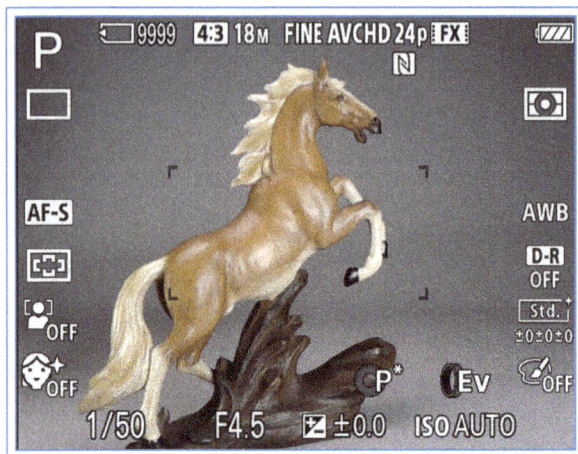

Figure 7-20. Display All Information Screen

You can always move away from this screen by pressing the Display button (if there is at least one other display screen available), and I like to have it available for times when I need to see what settings are in effect. If you don't have this screen available, you won't be able to see icons that indicate the status of certain features, such as the DRO option.

The third option, displaying minimal information, isn't shown here. That display is helpful for focusing and composing your shot, and I always include it in the cycle of display screens. If the camera is using autofocus (as the HX80 always does), the focus frame is displayed on this screen. Also, the SteadyShot warning icon will flash if the camera is set to Auto, Program, or Aperture Priority mode, if the camera needs to set a slow shutter speed. The icon alerts you that you may need to use flash or a tripod, or to change a setting such as ISO to avoid motion blur from camera shake.

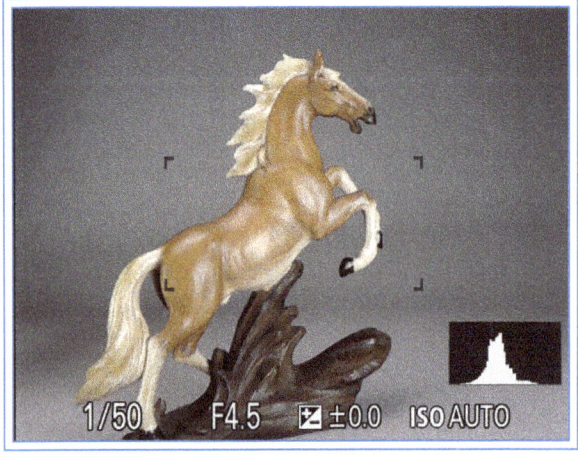

Figure 7-21. Histogram Display Screen

The next option, in Figure 7-21, is the histogram screen.

This shooting mode histogram, unlike the one displayed in playback mode, shows only basic exposure information with no color data. However, it helps you decide whether your image will be well exposed, letting you adjust exposure compensation and other settings as appropriate while watching the live histogram on the screen. If you can make the histogram display look like a triangular mountain centered in the box, you are likely to have a good result.

You should try to keep the body of the histogram away from the right and left edges of the graph, in most cases. If the white area of the histogram runs into the left edge, that means shadow areas are clipping and details in those areas are being lost. If it hits the right edge, you are losing details in highlights. If you have to choose, it is best to keep the graph away from the right edge, because it is harder to recover details from clipped highlights than from clipped shadows.

The fifth available display screen, shown in Figure 7-22, shows the level, which is a useful tool for leveling the camera both side-to-side and front-to-back.

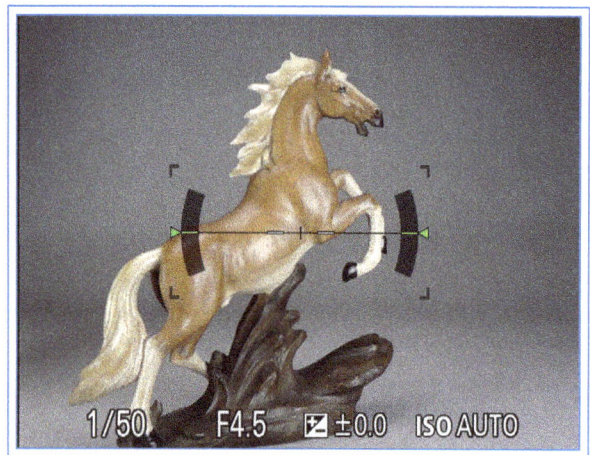

Figure 7-22. Level Display Screen

Watch the small orange lines on the screen; when the outer two ones have turned green, the camera is level side-to-side; when the inner two lines are green, the camera is level front-to-back.

The sixth choice, shown in Figure 7-23, which is available only for the monitor, is called For Viewfinder. This option is the only one that does not include the live view. Instead, it displays a black screen with detailed information about the camera's settings, so you can check your settings after (or before) you look at the live view in the viewfinder. In addition, as I discussed

Chapter 7: Custom and Setup Menus | 121

in Chapter 5, this screen is the basis for the Quick Navi system.

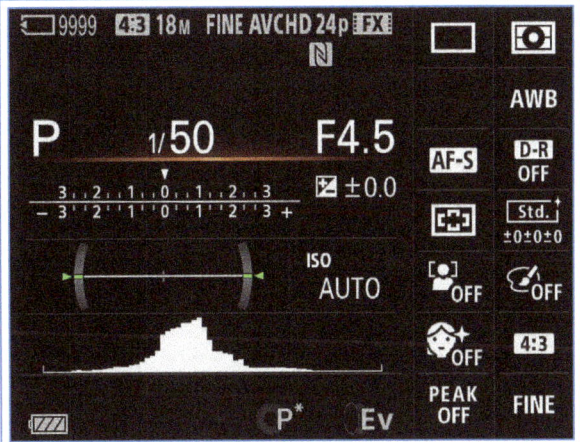

Figure 7-23. For Viewfinder Display Screen

When you press the Function button, the settings on the screen become active. You can navigate through the settings using the direction buttons and adjust them using the Control wheel or the Control ring (HX90V only). The For Viewfinder screen does not appear while recording a movie or when the camera is in Movie mode.

Once you select the Display Button option and choose whether to select screens for the monitor or viewfinder, you can scroll through the six (monitor) or five (viewfinder) choices using the Control wheel or the direction buttons. When a screen you want to have displayed is highlighted, press the Center button to put an orange check mark in the box to the left of the screen's label, as seen in Figure 7-18.

You can also press that button to unmark a box. The camera will let you un-check all six of the items (or all five for the viewfinder), but if you do that, you will see an error message as you try to exit the menu screen. You have to check at least one box so that some screen will display when the camera is in shooting mode.

After you select the screens you want to have displayed for the monitor and for the viewfinder, highlight the Enter block and press the Center button. Then, when the camera is in shooting mode, those screens will be displayed; cycle through them by pressing the Display button. If you have selected only one screen, pressing that button will have no effect in shooting mode when the live view is displayed.

Even if you select only the screen with practically no information, the LCD always displays shutter speed, aperture, exposure compensation, and ISO at the bottom of the image. With the viewfinder, the camera always displays those values at the bottom and displays Aspect Ratio, Image Size, Quality, File Format, and a few other values in a strip at the top of the screen.

PEAKING LEVEL (HX90V ONLY)

The Peaking Level option, whose menu screen is shown in Figure 7-24, controls the HX90V's use of the Peaking display to assist with manual focus.

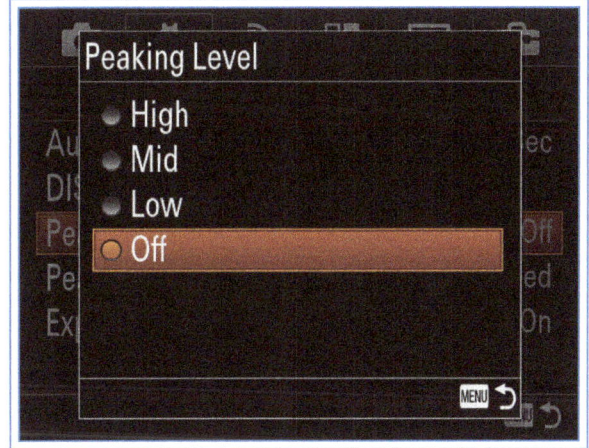

Figure 7-24. Peaking Level Menu Options Screen

By default, this option is turned off. You can turn the feature on with a level of Low, Mid, or High. When it is on and you are using manual focus or DMF (direct manual focus), the camera places an outline of pixels with the selected intensity around any areas of the image that have edges the camera can distinguish. As focus becomes sharper, the pixels become thicker. Figure 7-25 illustrates this feature with a composite image in which Peaking Level was turned off for the left image and set to Mid for the right image.

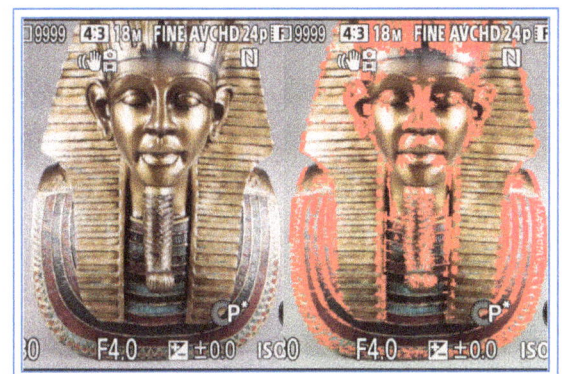

Figure 7-25. Peaking Composite Image

The idea is that these pixels provide a clearer indication that focus is sharp than just relying on your judgment of sharpness. When I first used a camera with this feature, I found it distracting and not as useful as options such as MF Assist and Focus Magnifier that enlarge the screen for a clearer view when using manual focus. However, after further experience, I have come to appreciate the usefulness of the Peaking feature for some situations. For example, taking photographs of subjects that do not have sharp edges to focus on can be easier when the camera places colored pixels in areas of sharp focus.

Some photographers set Creative Style to Black and White while focusing so the Peaking color will stand out, and some like to set Peaking Level to Low so the color is not overwhelming, letting them see when the color just starts to appear. Some like to turn on MF Assist to enlarge the screen when using Peaking. You should experiment to find what approach works best for you.

For an excellent demonstration of how Peaking works, see this YouTube video posted by a participant in the Sony Cyber-shot Talk forum at dpreview.com at http://youtu.be/jMAlMQev7Kw.

Note that Peaking also works with DMF, even if you are using the autofocus function of that setting.

PEAKING COLOR (HX90V ONLY)

This option lets you choose red, yellow, or white for the color of the pixels that the Peaking Level feature places around the edges of in-focus areas of the image. The default color is white. The Peaking Level feature is likely to be most useful when the color you choose for the effect contrasts with the main colors in your subject.

EXPOSURE SETTINGS GUIDE

The next option on the Custom menu, when turned on, places one or two moving scales at the bottom of the screen to show the settings for aperture, shutter speed, or both, when you adjust those settings using the Control wheel. (When you adjust any of the above values using the Control ring, the HX90V always displays a circular scale in the top half of the screen.)

The display varies according to the shooting mode. In Program mode, two scales display aperture and shutter speed when you activate Program Shift using the Control wheel. In Shutter Priority mode, a single scale displays shutter speed as you adjust it. In Aperture Priority mode, a single scale shows the aperture as you adjust it. In Manual mode, the display varies according to which value is currently being adjusted by the Control wheel. Figure 7-26 shows the display when shutter speed is being adjusted. I find this display distracting, so I leave it turned off, but it might be useful to see this display to let you know what value is being set, in some circumstances.

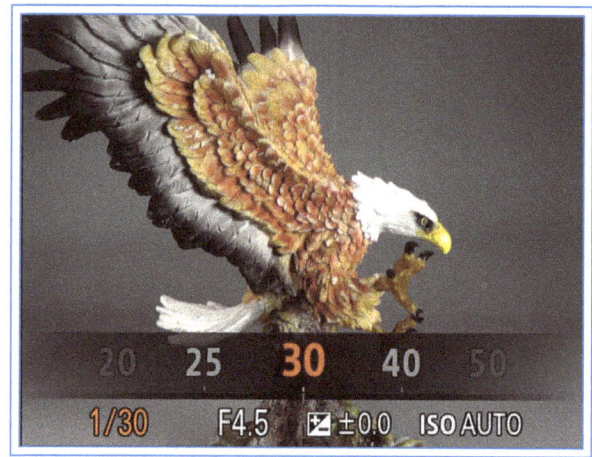

Figure 7-26. Exposure Settings Guide Display for Shutter Speed

Screen 3 of the Custom menu on the HX90V is shown in Figure 7-27.

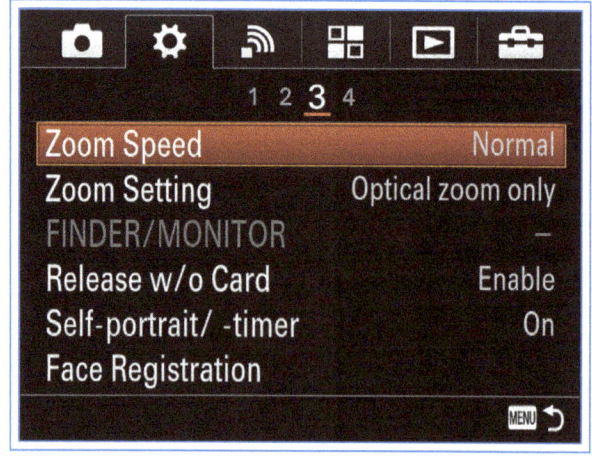

Figure 7-27. Screen 3 of HX90V Custom Menu

ZOOM SPEED

This option, which can be set to Normal or Fast, controls how quickly the lens zooms in or out when you move the zoom lever. It also controls the speed of zooming the lens when you are using an optional wired remote control, as discussed in Appendix A. The setting for this item depends on your preference. You may prefer the smoother zooming of the Normal setting, especially if you like to find an intermediate focal length for your shots. But, if you like to change focal lengths quickly to zoom all the way in or out, the Fast setting will save some time.

(HX90V only) If you want to increase the speed of zooming using the Control ring, use the Zoom Function on Ring option on screen 4 of the Custom menu, discussed later in this chapter, and set the value to Quick instead of Standard.

Zoom Setting

The Zoom Setting option provides two ways to give the camera extra zoom range, using features called Clear Image Zoom and Digital Zoom. To explain these features in context, I will discuss all three zoom methods that the camera offers—optical zoom, Clear Image Zoom, and Digital Zoom. I will also discuss a fourth feature that is related to these, called Smart Zoom.

Optical zoom is the camera's "natural" zoom capability—moving the lens elements so they magnify the image, just as binoculars do. You can call optical zoom a "real" zoom because it increases the information that the lens gathers. The optical zoom of the HX80 and HX90V operates within a range from 24mm at the wide-angle setting to the fully zoomed-in telephoto setting of 720mm.

To complicate matters a bit, the actual optical zoom range of the camera's lens is 4.1mm to 123mm; you can see those numbers engraved on the lens housing. You also see the actual zoom range numbers on the detailed screen in playback mode. But the numbers that are normally used to describe the zoom range of a compact camera's lens are the "35mm-equivalent" figures, which translate the actual zoom range into what the range would be if this were a lens on a camera that uses 35mm film. This translation is done because many photographers are familiar with the zoom ranges and focal lengths of lenses for traditional 35mm cameras, on which a 50mm lens is considered "normal." I use the 35mm-equivalent figures throughout this book.

The Digital Zoom feature of these cameras magnifies the image electronically without any special processing to improve the quality. This type of zoom does not really increase the information gathered by the lens; rather, it just increases the apparent size of the image by enlarging the pixels within the area captured by the lens. On some cameras, the amount of digital zoom can be very large, such as 100 times normal, but such a large figure can be considered as a marketing ploy to lure customers, rather than a feature of real value to the photographer.

The other option on the Zoom Setting menu, Clear Image Zoom, is a special type of digital zoom developed by Sony. With this feature, the camera does not just magnify the area of the image; rather, the camera analyzes the image and adds pixels through interpolation. This system produces a smoother, more realistic enlargement than the Digital Zoom feature. With Clear Image Zoom, the camera achieves greater quality than with Digital Zoom, though not as much as with the "pure" optical zoom.

Finally, there is another way the camera can use a zoom range greater than normal optical zoom with no loss of image quality. The standard range of 24mm to 720mm is available when Image Size is set to Large. However, if Image Size is set to Medium, Small, or VGA, the camera needs only a portion of the pixels on the image sensor to create the image at the reduced size. It can use the "extra" pixels to enlarge the view of the scene. This process, which Sony calls Smart Zoom, is similar to what you can do using software such as Photoshop. If the image size does not need to be Large, you can crop out some pixels from the center (or other area) of the image and enlarge that area, thereby retaining the same overall image size with a magnified view of the scene.

With Smart Zoom, if you set Image Size to M, S, or VGA, the camera can zoom to a greater range than with Image Size set to L and still keep the full quality of the optical zoom. You will end up with lower-resolution images, but that may not be a problem if you are going to post them on a website or share them via e-mail.

In short, optical zoom provides the best quality for magnifying the scene; Clear Image Zoom gives excellent quality; and Digital Zoom produces magnification with reduced image quality. Smart Zoom gives you greater zoom range with no image deterioration, but at the expense of resolution.

Here is how to use these settings. I will assume for the first part of this discussion that you are leaving

Image Size set to L, because that is the best setting for excellent results in printing and editing your images.

When you select the Zoom Setting menu option and press the Center button, the camera displays the screen shown in Figure 7-28, giving you the choice of Optical Zoom Only; On: Clear Image Zoom; or On: Digital Zoom. If you turn on Digital Zoom, Clear Image Zoom will automatically be activated also. Optical Zoom is always available, no matter what settings are used.

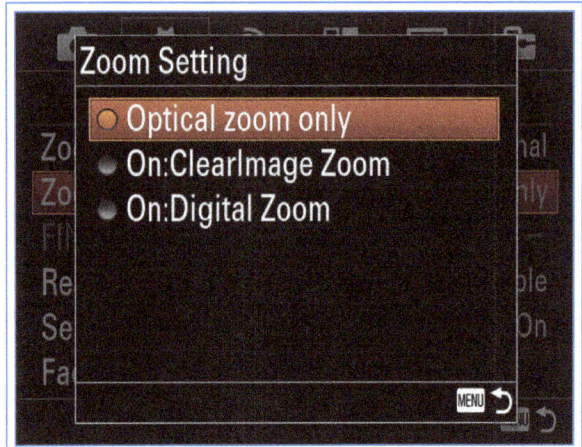

Figure 7-28. Zoom Setting Menu Options Screen

If you turn on only Clear Image Zoom, you will have greater zoom range than normal, as discussed above, with minimal quality loss. If you also turn on Digital Zoom, you will get even greater zoom range, but quality will suffer as the lens is zoomed past the Clear Image Zoom range. When these various settings are in effect, you will see different indications on the camera's display.

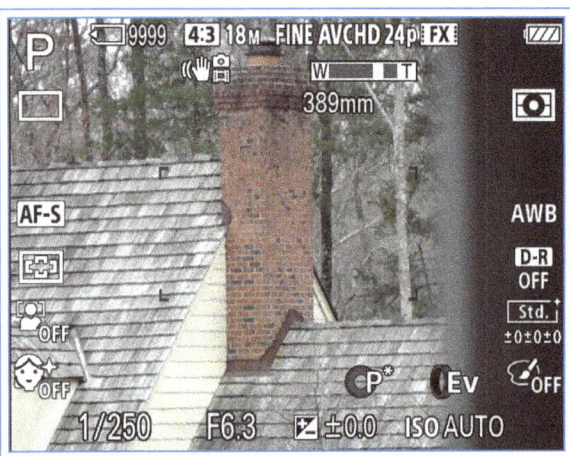

Figure 7-29. Zoom Scale for Optical Zoom Only

In Figure 7-29, Image Size is set to L and both Clear Image Zoom and Digital Zoom are turned off. The zoom scale at the top of the screen goes only as far as 720mm. (The zoom is set to 389mm on this screen.)

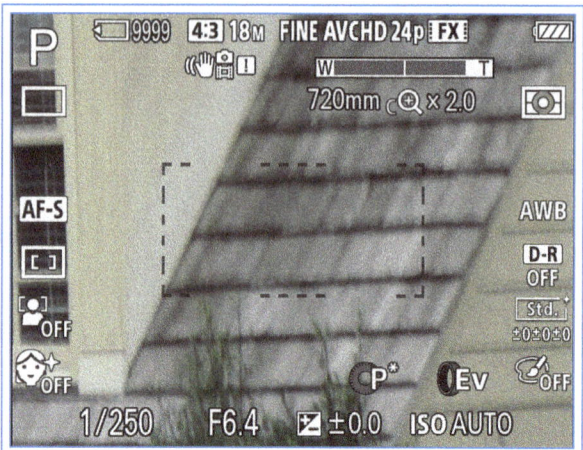

Figure 7-30. Zoom Scale for Clear Image Zoom

In Figure 7-30, Clear Image Zoom is turned on. The zoom indicator shows the lens can zoom to 2.0 times the normal range. There is a small vertical line in the center of the zoom scale showing where the zoom changes from optical-only to expanded (Clear Image Zoom or Digital Zoom, depending on the settings). The magnifying glass icon with the "C" beneath the scale means Clear Image Zoom is turned on.

Once the lens zooms past the optical zoom range, the sound of the zoom mechanism stops, so you can tell by listening when the camera has entered the range of Clear Image Zoom and Digital Zoom.

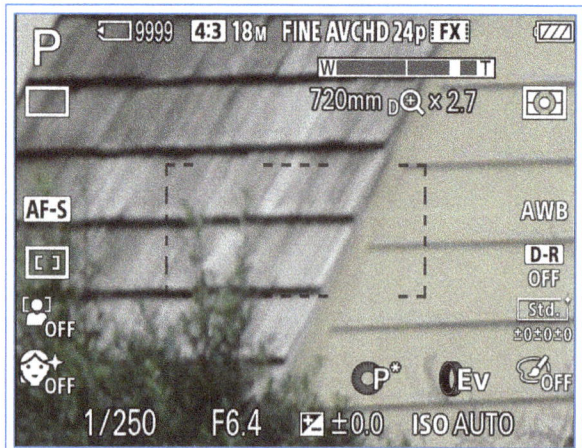

Figure 7-31. Zoom Scale for Digital Zoom

In Figure 7-31, both Clear Image Zoom and Digital Zoom are turned on, and the zoom indicator can go up to four times normal magnification. The magnifying glass icon beneath the scale has a "D" beside it, indicating that Digital Zoom is now in effect.

Chapter 7: Custom and Setup Menus

With an Image Size setting smaller than Large, the zoom indicator will use a letter S to show that the camera is using Smart Zoom, as the zoom range extends beyond the standard optical zoom range. In Figure 7-32, with Image Size set to Small, the lens is zoomed in to 1.2 times the optical range, and the zoom indicator displays an S to indicate that Smart Zoom is in effect. With smaller image sizes, the ranges of Clear Image Zoom and Digital Zoom also are expanded.

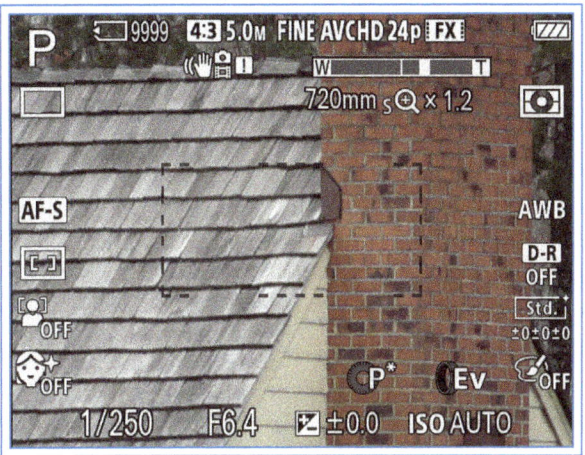

Figure 7-32. Zoom Scale for Smart Zoom

For example, as shown in Figure 7-33, with Image Size set to Small and Digital Zoom turned on, the lens can be zoomed in to 7.6 times the normal optical range. (In this example, it is zoomed to 4 times normal, but with more capacity available to zoom further on the scale.)

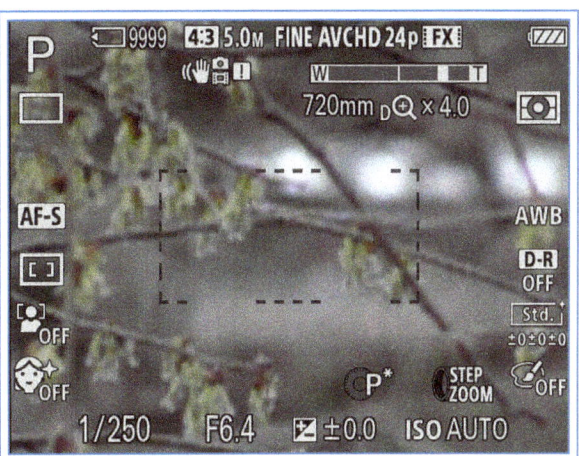

Figure 7-33. Zoom Scale for Digital Zoom and Smart Zoom

Table 7-1 shows the zoom ranges available with Image Size set to Large, Medium, and Small, with settings of optical zoom, Clear Image Zoom, and Digital Zoom. In all cases, Aspect Ratio is 4:3; with some other Aspect Ratio settings, results would be different.

Table 7-1. MAXIMUM ZOOM RANGE AT VARIOUS IMAGE SIZES

	LARGE	MEDIUM	SMALL	VGA
OPTICAL ZOOM (WITH NO DETERIORATION)	720MM	960MM	1344MM	5500MM
CLEAR IMAGE ZOOM (WITH MINIMAL DETERIORATION)	1440MM	1920MM	2712MM	11000MM
DIGITAL ZOOM (WITH SIGNIFICANT DETERIORATION)	2880MM	3864MM	5424MM	11000MM

To summarize the situation with zoom, when Image Size is set to Large, you can zoom up to 720mm with no deterioration using optical zoom; you can zoom to about 1440mm with minimal deterioration using Clear Image Zoom; and you can zoom to about 2880mm using Digital Zoom but with significant deterioration. The values are greater for smaller Image Size settings, but with lower resolution in the images.

My preference is to limit the camera to optical zoom and avoid any deterioration. However, many photographers have found that Clear Image Zoom yields surprisingly good results, and it is worth using when you cannot get close to your subject. I do not like to use Digital Zoom to take a picture. However, it can be useful to zoom in to meter a specific area of a distant subject, or to check the composition of your shot before zooming back out and taking the shot using Clear Image Zoom or optical zoom.

Clear Image Zoom and Digital Zoom are not available when the Smile Shutter or face detection is in use, or in iSweep Panorama mode. Smart Zoom is not available when recording movies.

Whenever the lens is zoomed into the range of Clear Image Zoom or Digital Zoom, the Focus Area option is disabled and the camera uses a broad focus frame, which is represented by the dotted area seen in Figure 7-34. Any Metering Mode setting other than Multi is set to Multi when non-optical zoom is in use, but only while the lens is actually zoomed past the optical zoom range. It reverts back to the previous setting if the lens is zoomed back within the optical zoom range.

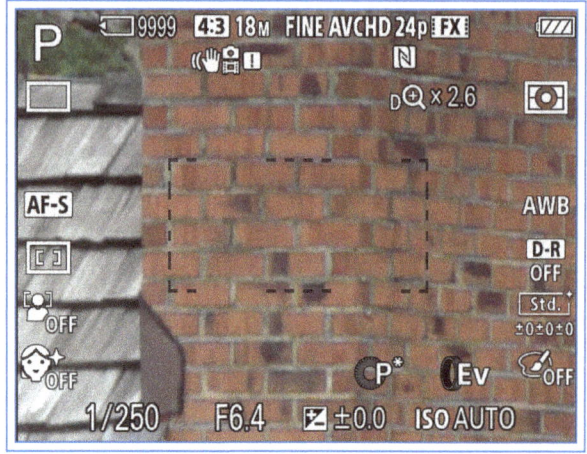

Figure 7-34. Large, Dotted Focus Frame for Non-optical Zoom

Finder/Monitor

This next option on the Custom menu, shown in Figure 7-35, lets you choose whether to view menus and shooting and playback displays on the camera's LCD screen or in the viewfinder. The viewfinder can provide the same information as the LCD screen (depending on menu settings), but its display is viewed inside an eye-level window that is shaded from daylight, giving you a clear view of the shooting, playback, and menu screens.

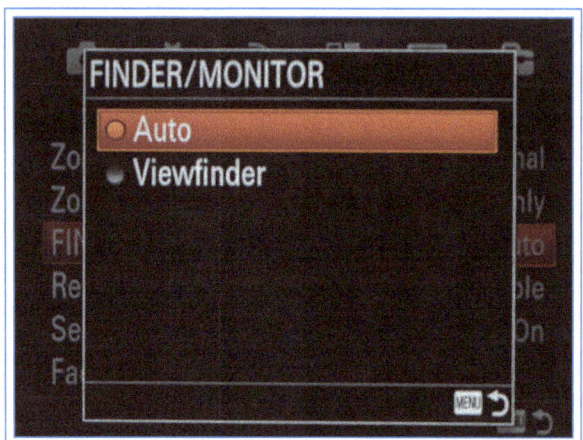

Figure 7-35. Finder/Monitor Menu Options Screen

By default, this option is set to Auto, which means the camera switches the view to the viewfinder automatically when you move your head near the camera, if the viewfinder has been popped up. The camera turns on the viewfinder display and blacks out the LCD. (There is a small eye sensor below the viewfinder window that detects the presence of an object nearby.)

If you prefer to use the viewfinder at all times, set this option to Viewfinder. With that setting, the camera will turn off the LCD and will leave the viewfinder active at all times while it is popped up.

To put this another way, with the Auto setting the camera will activate the LCD screen when you are not using the viewfinder; with the Viewfinder setting, the camera will never activate the LCD screen, unless you retract the viewfinder. When you retract the viewfinder, the camera will always use the LCD screen.

My preference is to use the Auto setting because I find it convenient to view the image on the LCD unless conditions are quite bright. If you prefer to use the viewfinder, you may want to use the Viewfinder setting so the camera will never turn off the viewfinder until you press it back down into the camera.

Release without Card

This option can be set to either Enable or Disable. If it is set to Enable, you can operate the camera's shutter release button even if there is no memory card inserted in the camera. In that case, the camera will display a NO CARD warning message, but it will let you operate the shutter and an image will be saved temporarily. This setting is useful if the camera is on display in a retail store, so customers can operate the controls and see how a saved image would look, without having to have an expensive memory card left in the camera. As I noted in Chapter 1, there is no easy way to save an image taken when this setting is active, although in an emergency you may be able to send the image through the HDMI port to a video capture device.

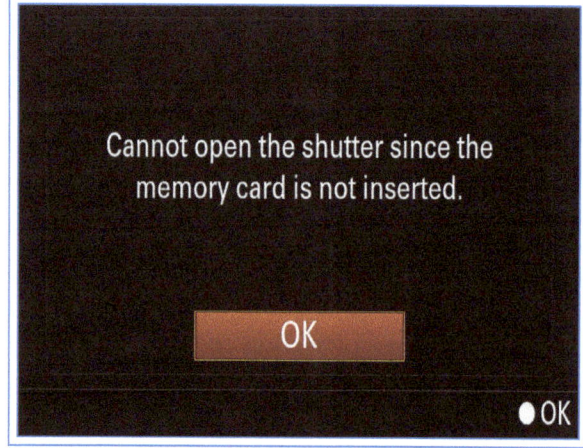

Figure 7-36. Warning Message: Shutter Cannot Operate without Card

If you select Disable, the NO CARD warning still appears. In addition, if you try to press the shutter

Chapter 7: Custom and Setup Menus | 127

button, the camera will display a warning message advising that the shutter cannot be operated with no memory card inserted, as shown in Figure 7-36. This setting is the safest, because it protects against operating the camera when there is no card inserted to save images or videos.

Self-portrait Timer

This option can be turned either on or off. If it is turned on, then, when you flip the LCD screen up and around so it faces forward, the camera will display a large three-step countdown timer when you press the shutter button, so you can get ready for a self-portrait. The timer screen is shown in Figure 7-37. It includes a three-second self-timer icon in the upper left corner. If this menu option is turned off, you can still take a self-portrait, but without the on-screen timer.

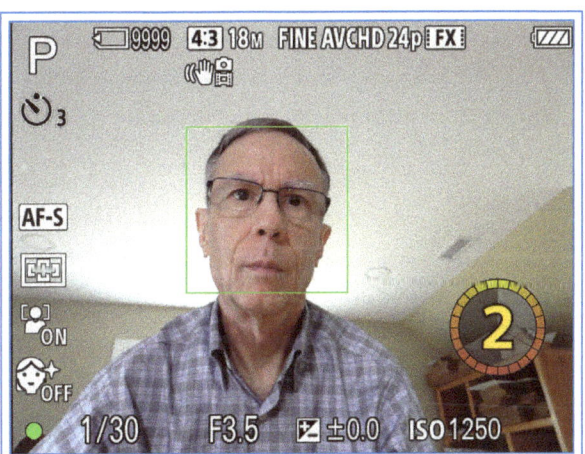

Figure 7-37. Countdown Screen for Self-portrait Timer

When you use this option, the camera locks focus when you press the shutter button to start the timer, and, if your position changes during the countdown, the focus may be incorrect.

To avoid this problem, you can turn off this option and take the picture with no delay. Another approach is to use the Smart Remote Embedded app to control the camera, as discussed in Chapter 9, or a wired remote control as discussed in Appendix A. Or, you can just make sure your face does not change its distance from the camera after you press the shutter button to start the self-portrait timer.

Face Registration

This next option lets you register human faces so the camera can give those faces priority for face detection. You can register up to eight faces and assign each one a rank from one to eight, with one being the highest. Then, when you set the Shooting menu option for Smile/Face Detection to On (Registered Faces), the camera will try to detect the registered faces first in the order you have assigned them. This feature can be useful if, for example, you take pictures at school functions and you want to make sure the camera focuses on your own children.

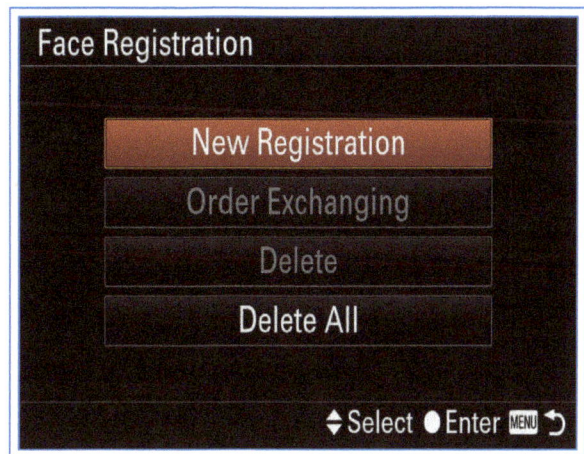

Figure 7-38. Face Registration Menu Options Screen

To use this menu option, select it and on the next screen, shown in Figure 7-38, select New Registration. Press the Center button, and the camera will place a square frame on the screen.

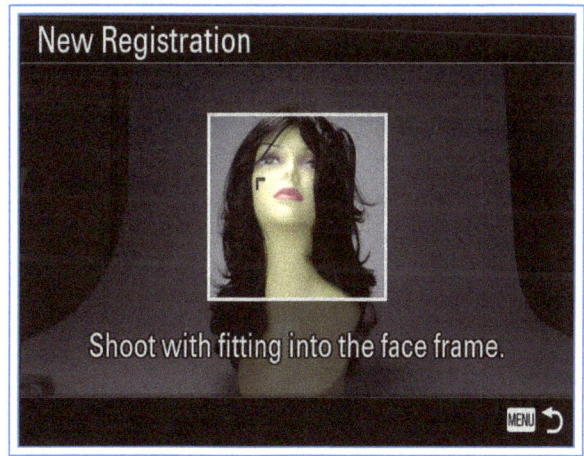

Figure 7-39. Screen to Register New Face

Compose a shot with the face to be registered inside that frame, as shown in Figure 7-39, and press the shutter button to take a picture of that face.

If the process works, the camera will display that face with the message "Register face?" Highlight the Enter bar on that screen and press the Center button to complete the registration process. Later, you can use the Order Exchanging option to change the priorities of the registered faces, and you can delete registered faces individually or all at once using other menu options.

Screen 4 of the Custom menu on the HX90V is shown in Figure 7-40.

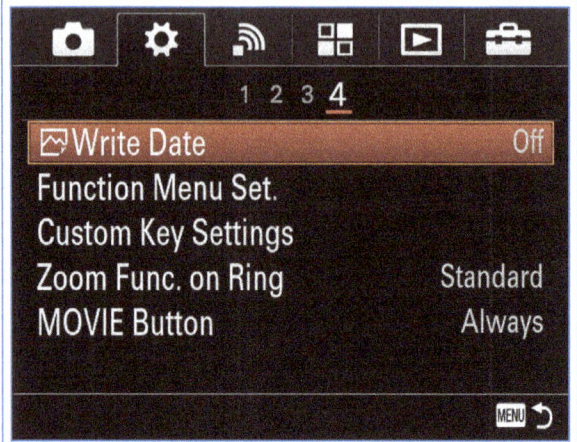

Figure 7-40. Screen 4 of HX90V Custom Menu

Write Date

This next setting on the Custom menu embeds the date in the lower right corner of your still images, as shown in Figure 7-41. This embedding is permanent, so the information cannot be deleted other than through cropping or other editing procedures. Use this option only if you want the date recorded permanently on your images, perhaps for a scientific research project.

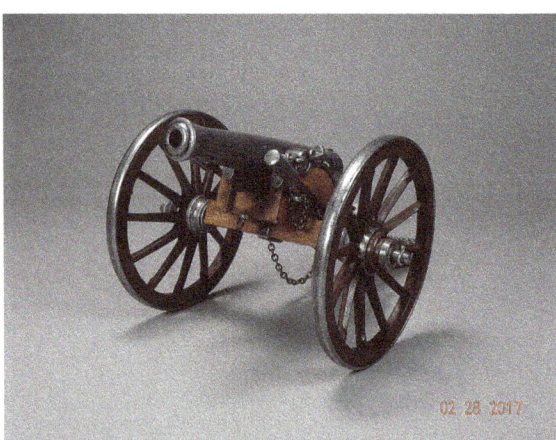

Figure 7-41. Write Date Option In Use

Be careful that you do not leave this setting turned on when you don't want the date imprinted on your images; the camera does not put any indication on the display screen that this setting is in effect. This option is not available with panoramas, bracketing, continuous shooting, or in Movie mode.

Function Menu Settings

When you press the Function button in shooting mode, the camera displays up to 12 options in blocks at the bottom of the display, as shown in Figure 7-42.

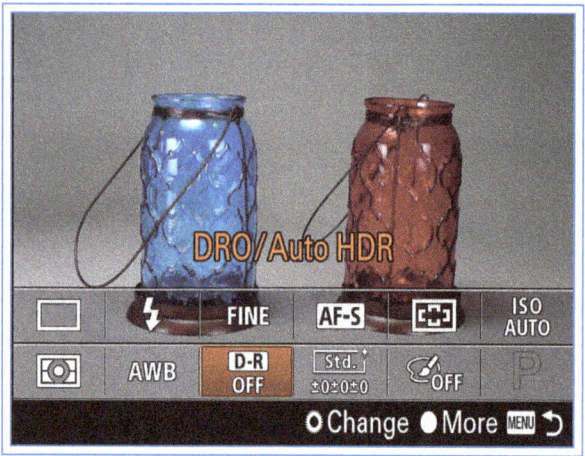

Figure 7-42. Function Menu In Use on Shooting Screen

You move through those options with the direction buttons. Adjust the main settings with the Control wheel or the Control ring (HX90V only). To make secondary settings, press the Center button to go to a menu screen for the option being adjusted.

Use the Function Menu Settings menu item to assign options to the Function menu. When you select this option, the camera initially shows the screen in Figure 7-43, listing the assignments for the upper six blocks of the Function menu.

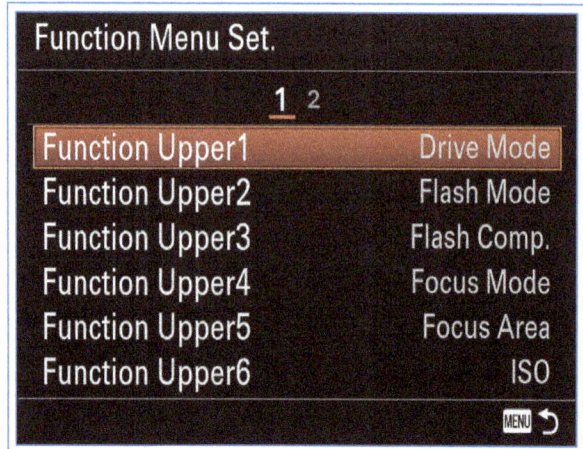

Figure 7-43. First Screen of Function Menu Settings Item

On screen 2 of the menu item, you can make assignments for the lower six blocks. When you press the Center button on any one of these 12 lines, you will see a screen like that in Figure 7-44, listing the options that can be assigned to that block.

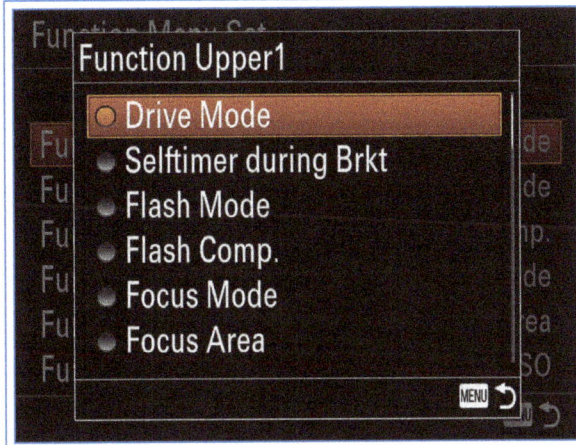

Figure 7-44. List of Options for a Function Menu Slot

For each menu block, the possible assignments are:

- Drive Mode
- Self-timer During Bracketing
- Flash Mode
- Flash Compensation
- Focus Mode (HX90V only)
- Focus Area
- Exposure Compensation
- ISO
- Metering Mode
- White Balance
- DRO/Auto HDR
- Creative Style
- Shoot Mode
- Picture Effect
- Center Lock-on AF
- Smile/Face Detection
- Soft Skin Effect
- Auto Object Framing
- Image Size
- Aspect Ratio
- Quality
- SteadyShot (Movies)
- Zebra
- Grid Line
- Marker Display
- Peaking Level (HX90V only)
- Peaking Color (HX90V only)
- Not Set

Press the Center button when the option you want to assign to a given block is displayed, and the camera will place an orange dot on that line to indicate that that feature is assigned to that block.

I recommend assigning a function to each of the 12 blocks and experiment to find the best setup. Remember that you can use the Control ring (HX90V only) and the Center, Left, Right, Down, and In-Camera Guide buttons for your most important settings, such as, perhaps, ISO, Flash Mode, Drive Mode, and Exposure Compensation, so you can reserve these 12 blocks for other options.

CUSTOM KEY SETTINGS

I described this menu option in Chapter 5, in discussing physical controls that can have settings assigned to them. Now I will discuss the settings that can be assigned to these controls.

When you select the Custom Key Settings option, you will see the screen shown in Figure 7-45. (This screen on the HX80 will not include the line for Control ring, because that model does not have a Control ring.)

Navigate to the line for a control and press the Center Button. You will see a screen listing all the options that can be assigned to that control. In most cases, these assignments are self-explanatory. When you assign a function, such as ISO, to a button, pressing the button calls up the menu screen for the option, which lets you adjust it as if you had selected it from the Shooting menu.

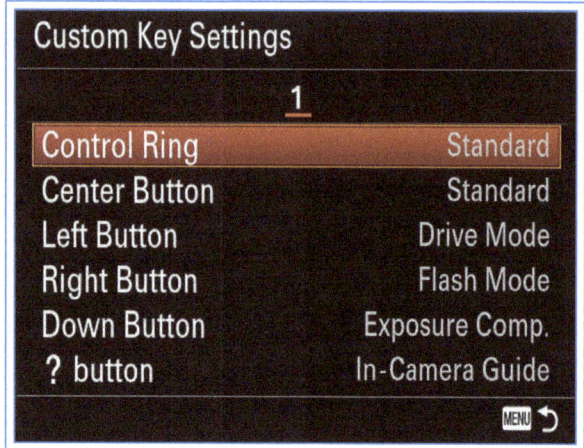

Figure 7-45. Custom Key Settings Menu Options Screen (HX90V)

However, there are differences for some controls, and there are some items that can be assigned through this option that are not available through any menu. I will discuss these details below.

Control Ring (HX90V Only)

The first control on the Custom Key Settings menu screen is the Control ring. This control is a special case, because, of course, it is not a button but a ring. The options that can be assigned to the ring are Standard, Exposure Compensation, ISO, White Balance, Creative Style, Picture Effect, Zoom, Shutter Speed, Aperture, or Not Set, the first six of which are shown in Figure 7-46. You have to scroll down to see the remaining options.

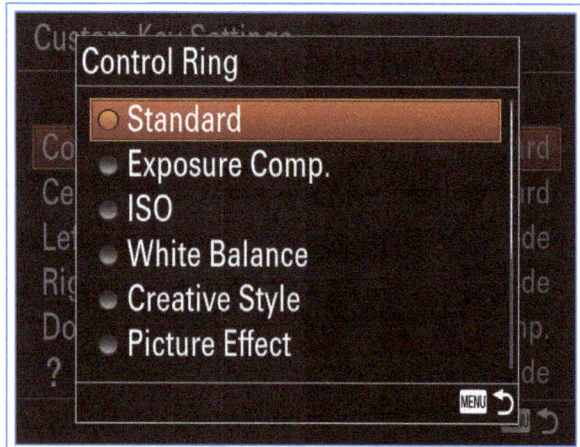

Figure 7-46. List of Options for Control Ring

This feature is powerful because, when you assign a setting such as ISO to this ring, you can use the ring to adjust the setting instantly. For example, if you choose ISO, then, when the camera is in shooting mode, all you have to do is turn the Control ring and the ISO setting will change. You can then immediately press the shutter button to take a picture with the new setting.

However, you cannot get access to all aspects of these settings by turning the ring. For example, if you assign ISO to the ring, you can select a numerical ISO value or Auto ISO, but you cannot set the minimum and maximum settings for Auto ISO, and you cannot select a value for the Multi Frame Noise Reduction setting.

Similarly, if you assign white balance to the Control ring, you can select a white balance setting, including Custom or Color Temperature, but you cannot set a new Custom White Balance or choose a new Color Temperature setting, and you cannot fine-tune the white balance using the color axes. For those options, you need to use the White Balance menu option. Likewise, with Creative Style assigned to the ring, you cannot adjust the contrast, sharpness, and saturation parameters of a selected setting.

However, with Picture Effect, you can select any of the settings or sub-settings, because the Control ring will cycle through all of the options, including, for example, the sub-settings for Toy Camera, which are Normal, Cool, Warm, Green, and Magenta.

When the Control ring has been assigned to a function, the camera puts an icon representing the ring in the bottom right of the screen next to an icon or label indicating the setting currently assigned to the ring. For example, Figure 7-47 shows the screen as it appears when ISO has been assigned to the Control ring.

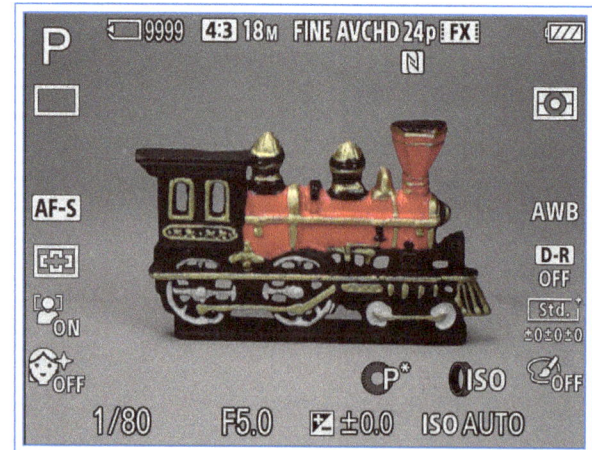

Figure 7-47. Icon on Shooting Screen When Control Ring Sets ISO

Chapter 7: Custom and Setup Menus

By default, the Control ring's function is set to Standard. In that case, the ring controls various functions in the various shooting modes, as shown in Table 7-2.

Table 7-2. Control Ring: Standard Setting— Shooting Modes vs. Assigned Functions

Shooting Mode	Assigned Function
Intelligent Auto	Zoom
Superior Auto	Zoom
Program	Program Shift
Aperture Priority	Aperture
Shutter Priority	Shutter Speed
Manual Exposure	Aperture
Scene	Scene Selection
iSweep Panorama	Direction
Movie	Depends on Movie exposure mode setting
Memory Recall	Depends on saved setting

Or you can choose the final option, Not Set, in which case the ring will control only manual focus from the shooting screen. (It also will select items with the Function menu and Quick Navi system.) In my opinion, the Standard option is the most useful, but you might prefer to use the Control ring for one specific purpose, such as controlling exposure compensation, ISO, or zoom for all shooting modes.

Center Button

If you select Center Button from the Custom Key Settings menu screen, the camera will display a screen like that shown in Figure 7-48, which lists the first six of the many options that can be assigned to the Center button.

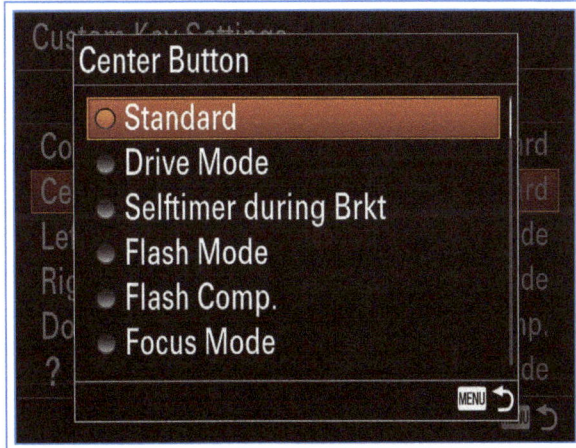

Figure 7-48. List of Options for Center Button

The complete list, which is much longer than a single screen, includes all of the following choices, any one of which can be assigned to this button:

- Standard
- Drive Mode
- Self-timer During Bracketing
- Flash Mode
- Flash Compensation
- Focus Mode (HX90V only)
- Focus Area
- Exposure Compensation
- ISO
- Metering Mode
- White Balance
- DRO/Auto HDR
- Creative Style
- Picture Effect
- Smile/Face Detection
- Soft Skin Effect
- Auto Object Framing
- SteadyShot (Movies)
- Image Size
- Aspect Ratio
- Quality
- In-Camera Guide
- Memory
- Center Lock-on AF
- Focus Magnifier (HX90V only)
- Movie [duplicates function of red Movie button]
- Zebra
- Grid Line

- Marker Display Selection
- Peaking Level (HX90V only)
- Peaking Color (HX90V only)
- Send to Smartphone
- Download Application
- Application List
- Monitor Brightness
- Not Set

Scroll through the list and press the Center button to make your selection. The dot next to the chosen option will turn orange to mark the choice.

Most of these options are self-explanatory because, when a button has an option assigned, pressing the button will simply call up the menu screen for that option, if the option is available in the current shooting mode. For example, when the Left button is assigned to Drive Mode, when you press the button, the camera displays the Drive Mode menu, just as if you had used the Menu button to get access to that option. (In some cases the screen looks different from the menu screen called up with the Menu button, but the regular menu options are available in every case.) I will not discuss those options here; see Chapter 4 for discussion of the Shooting menu, Chapter 7 for discussion of the Custom and Setup menus, and Chapter 9 for discussion of the Wi-Fi and Application menus.

The In-Camera Guide option is not available from a menu, but it is the default setting for the In-Camera Guide button; I discussed it in Chapter 5. When this function is assigned, you can press the button when a menu option is highlighted to bring up a help screen with information about that option.

When Marker Display Select is assigned to a button, the button switches between the options for the Marker Display menu item without first calling up a menu screen.

There are a few other selections for the Center button (and the other control buttons) that do not call up a menu screen. Instead, they perform a function that is not available from a menu option. I will discuss those selections below.

Standard

I discussed this option in Chapter 5, where I discussed the physical controls, because this option is assigned by default to the Center button. It cannot be assigned to any other button or control. When the Center button is assigned to the Standard option, it has two functions when pressed while the shooting screen is displayed. First, if Focus Area is set to Flexible Spot or Expand Flexible Spot, pressing the Center button makes the focus frame movable, allowing you to re-position it on the display. Second, if Center Lock-on AF is turned on with single AF in effect and Focus Area set to Wide or Center, pressing the assigned button initiates tracking of the subject in the center of the display.

MOVIE

The MOVIE setting does not call up a menu option, and it is not equivalent to the similarly named Movie option on the Shooting menu. Instead, when you assign a button to this setting, the button takes on the same role as the camera's red Movie button. This option gives you another way to start and stop the recording of a video. If you set the Movie Button menu option to Movie Mode Only, this button will start recording a video only if the Mode dial is set to Movie mode.

Download Application

When you select Download Application for the Custom Key Settings option for the Center button, the camera will display a screen showing the applications that have been downloaded to the camera from Sony's website for camera apps, as discussed in Chapter 9. Scroll through these applications and press the Center button to select the application you want. Then, when you press the assigned button in Shooting mode, the camera will launch the application you selected when you assigned the button to this function.

Not Set

The last option that can be assigned to the Center button is called Not Set. If you choose this option, then the button will not be assigned any special function. You may want to select this option if you will be using a limited number of settings and don't want to risk activating a different setting by pressing the button accidentally.

Chapter 7: Custom and Setup Menus | 133

Left Button

The choices of assignments for the Left button are the same as for the Center button, except that the Standard option is not available.

Right Button

The Right button has the same options available for assignment as the Left button.

Down Button

The Down button has the same options available for assignment as the Left button.

In-Camera Guide Button

This button also can be assigned any of the same options as the Left button.

ZOOM FUNCTION ON RING (HX90V ONLY)

This first item on the last screen of the Custom menu determines the way the Control ring operates when you are using it to zoom the lens in and out. As I discussed earlier in this chapter, when its function is set to Standard, the Control ring controls zoom in the two Auto modes. In any other shooting mode, you have to set the Control ring's function to Zoom to enable it to zoom the lens. You set the ring's function using the Custom Key Settings menu option, discussed above.

When the ring is set to control zoom, you can use the Zoom Function on Ring menu option to choose between Standard, Quick, and Step for the way the zoom operates, as shown in Figure 7-49.

With Standard, when the Control ring is used to zoom the lens, it does so continuously, just as the zoom lever does. That is, as you turn the ring, the lens zooms through all focal lengths that are available.

With optical zoom, that means it will zoom from the 24mm wide-angle setting to the 720mm telephoto setting in continuous increments. With Clear Image Zoom and Digital Zoom, the zoom levels increase beyond the 720mm point.

If you choose Quick, the Control ring still zooms continuously, but at a faster rate. You might choose this option if you often need to zoom the lens all the way in or all the way out and are not so concerned with setting intermediate focal lengths or making precise adjustments. (There is a similar setting called Fast for the zoom lever, under the Zoom Speed option on screen 4 of the Custom menu.)

If you set this menu option to Step, then the Control ring zooms the lens only to certain preset values: 24mm, 28mm, 35mm, 50mm, 70mm, 85mm, 100mm, 135mm, 200mm, 300mm, 400mm, 500mm, 600mm, and 720mm. When you nudge the ring toward the wide-angle or telephoto side, the zoom will move to the next preset focal length. You should give the ring a quick nudge and then release it; if you keep turning it, it will move past the next value and go on to the one after that.

There are some limitations with the Step Zoom function on the HX90V. First, if you set the camera for manual focus or DMF using the Focus Mode menu option, the Control ring will control manual focus and will not zoom the lens.

Next, the Step Zoom feature works only for the Control ring; the zoom lever will always zoom the lens continuously. Also, the Step Zoom feature does not work when shooting movies.

Finally, if you turn on Clear Image Zoom or Digital Zoom using the Zoom Setting option on screen 4 of the Custom menu, or use Smart Zoom, the Step Zoom feature will not include specific increments for the zoom range beyond the optical limit of 70mm. Instead, as shown in Figure 7-50, where Smart Zoom is in use, the camera displays the range of preset increments along with an area at the right side of the scale extending from the 720mm mark to a magnifying glass

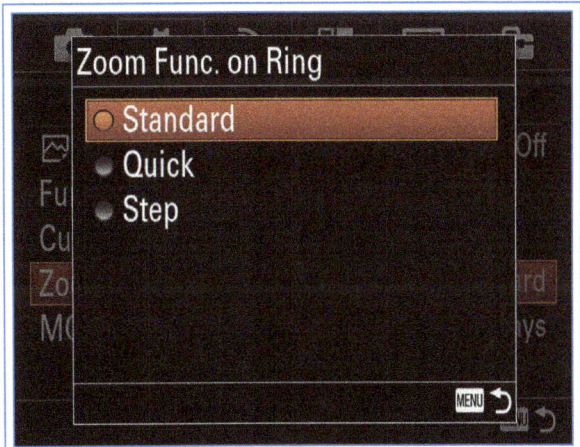

Figure 7-49. Zoom Function on Ring Menu Options Screen

icon at the far right, showing a general area of extended zoom range.

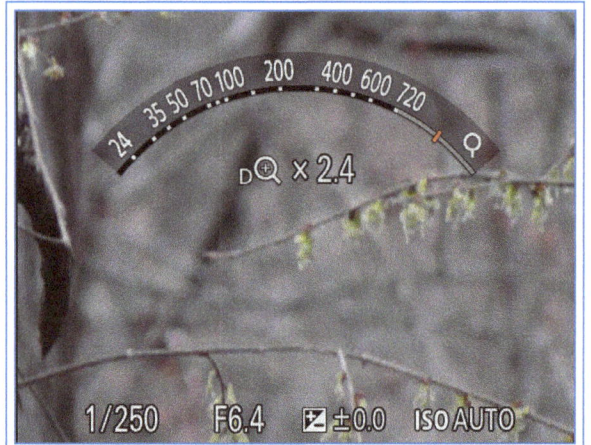

Figure 7-50. Zoom Scale for Step Zoom with Non-optical Zoom

Step zoom is a valuable feature in some situations. For example, if you want to set a specific focal length for a shot, using Step Zoom is an excellent way to make sure you have the lens zoomed to the exact focal length you want.

You might want to choose a focal length of 35mm or 200mm, for example, to compare shots from the HX90V against shots from another camera using that same setting.

Movie Button

This option, shown in Figure 7-51, lets you lock out the operation of the red Movie button to avoid accidentally starting a video recording. The two choices are Always and Movie Mode Only.

If you want to be able to start recording a video at any time without delay, you should leave the Movie Button option set to Always. With that setting, you can start recording a movie by pressing this button, no matter what shooting mode is set on the Mode dial. This is a convenient system, because you can start shooting a video at a moment's notice without having to turn the Mode dial to the Movie position. If you choose Movie Mode only, the Movie button will not operate unless the Mode dial is at the Movie mode position.

If you have used the Custom Key Settings option on the Custom menu to assign one of the control buttons to the MOVIE function, so it acts as another Movie button, the setting of the Movie Button menu option will also affect the operation of that button. If the menu option is set to Movie Mode Only, that other button will not start a movie recording unless the Mode dial is at the Movie position.

As I discussed in Chapter 5 in the section on the Movie button, the main reason to choose the Movie Mode Only option is if you are afraid you may press the Movie button by mistake. I have pressed it by mistake several times myself, so, unless I am on a trip when I may want to record movies quickly, I leave this menu option set to Movie Mode Only, to avoid having to stop and delete unwanted recordings.

Setup Menu

The next menu to be discussed is the Setup menu, marked by the toolbox icon. Its first screen on the HX90V is shown in Figure 7-52.

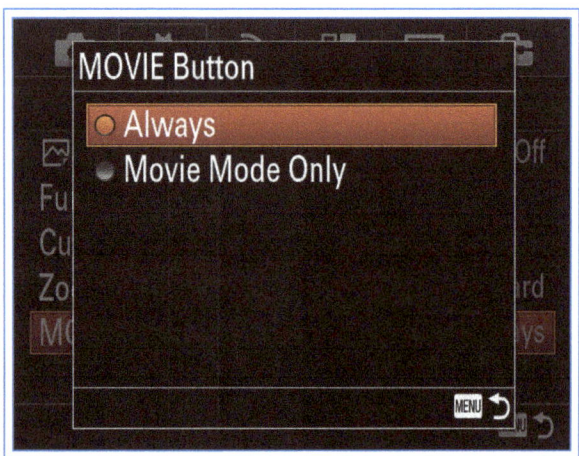

Figure 7-51. Movie Button Menu Options Screen

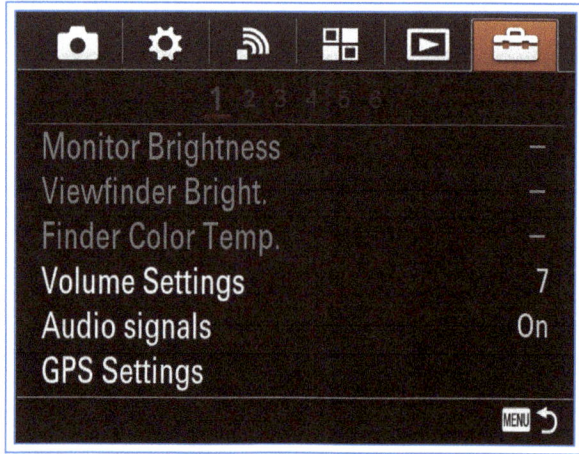

Figure 7-52. Screen 1 of HX90V Setup Menu

Chapter 7: Custom and Setup Menus | 135

This menu has options for matters like USB connections, display brightness, audio options, file numbering, formatting a memory card, video settings, and others. I will discuss each menu item below.

Monitor Brightness

When you select the Monitor Brightness menu option, you will see the brightness scale shown in Figure 7-53. Using the controls on that screen, you can adjust brightness to one or two units above or below normal. Press the Left or Right button to make the adjustment.

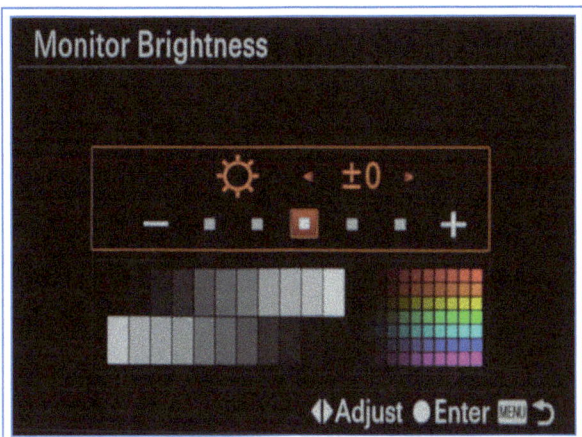

Figure 7-53. Monitor Brightness Adjustment Scale

If your battery is running low and you don't have a spare, you may want to set the monitor to its minimum brightness to conserve power. Conversely, you can increase brightness if you're finding it difficult to compose the image on the screen.

Viewfinder Brightness

This second option on the Setup menu for the HX80 and HX90V is similar to Monitor Brightness, except that you have to look into the viewfinder to make adjustments. You can set the brightness to Auto or Manual, as shown in Figure 7-54. With Auto, the camera adjusts the brightness based on a reading of ambient light from a light sensor. If you select Manual, you can make the same adjustment using a brightness scale as discussed above for the Monitor Brightness option.

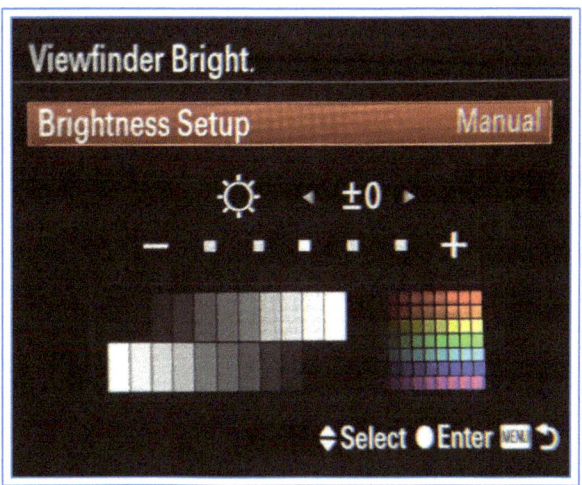

Figure 7-54. Viewfinder Brightness Adjustment Scale

Finder Color Temperature

This option, whose adjustment screen is shown in Figure 7-55, lets you adjust the color temperature of the view through the viewfinder.

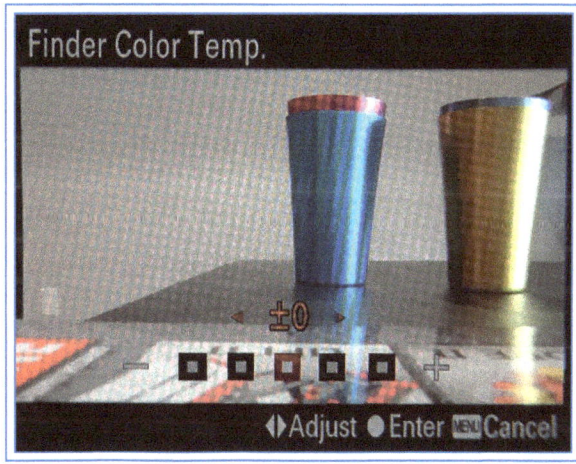

Figure 7-55. Finder Color Temperature Adjustment Screen

As with Viewfinder Brightness, you have to look into the viewfinder to make adjustments. You can use the camera's controls to lower the color temperature by one or two units, which will make the view appear slightly more reddish, or "warmer," or you can raise it by one or two units to make it more bluish, or "cooler." I have not found a reason to take advantage of this adjustment, but it is easy to use and it may be helpful to you.

Volume Settings

This option, whose settings screen is shown in Figure 7-56, lets you set the volume for playback of movies at a level from zero to 15. The default level is seven. You can also set this level when a movie is playing by pressing the Down button to get access to the detailed controls, which include a volume setting option.

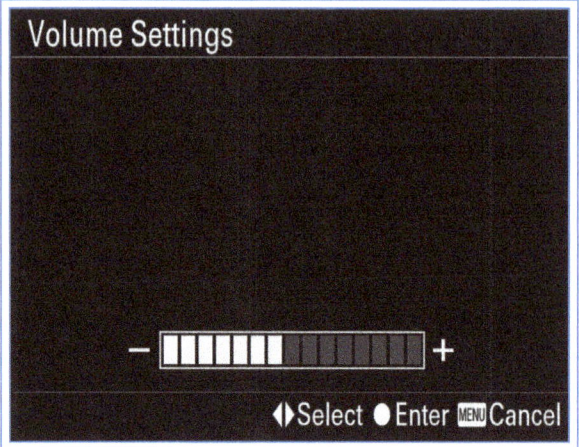

Figure 7-56. Volume Settings Screen

When a movie is on the screen in playback mode before playback starts, pressing the Down button calls up the volume adjustment screen immediately. Pressing that button when a still image is displayed in playback mode also calls up the volume screen, if View Mode is set to Date View, which includes videos as well as stills.

AUDIO SIGNALS

This option's main screen is shown in Figure 7-57.

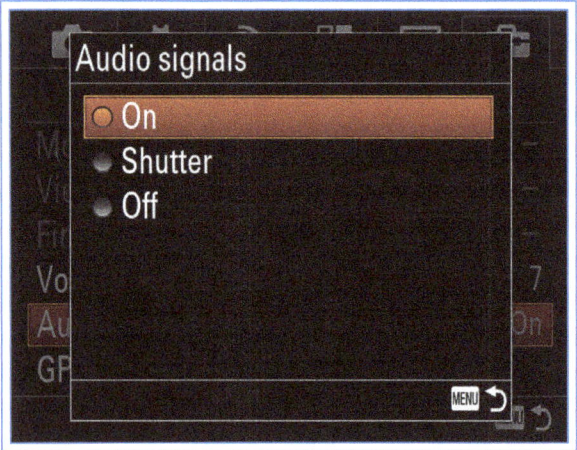

Figure 7-57. Audio Signals Menu Options Screen

This menu item lets you choose whether or not to activate the various sounds the camera makes when an operation takes place, such as pressing the shutter button, confirming focus, or pressing a control button.

By default, the sounds are turned on, but it can be helpful to silence them during a religious ceremony, or when you are doing street photography and want to avoid alerting your subjects. There is a separate entry for Shutter, so you can leave the shutter sound turned on while silencing sounds such as focus beeps if you want.

GPS SETTINGS (HX90V ONLY)

This menu option, whose main screen on the HX90V is shown in Figure 7-58, gives access to six sub-options for managing the operation of the HX90V camera's built-in global positioning system (GPS) capabilities. The six sub-options are discussed below.

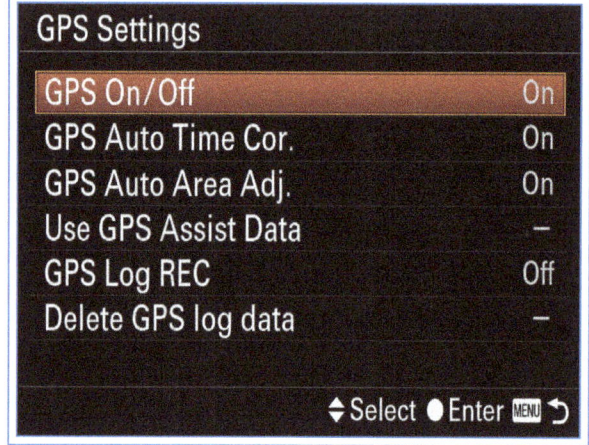

Figure 7-58. GPS Settings Menu Options Screen

GPS On/Off

This first sub-option can be used to enable or disable the camera's GPS capability. It is useful to be able to turn off GPS when you are in a country that does not permit the use of GPS devices or if you are not interested in using the GPS functions. When you have enabled the GPS capability, images you capture while it is turned on will have a small GPS satellite icon in the upper right corner when displayed in PlayMemories Home, as shown in Figure 7-59.

In addition, those images will include location information, which can be displayed in any program that displays EXIF data. For example, Figure 7-60 shows the metadata information as displayed in Adobe Bridge CC for an image I captured with the HX90V with GPS activated.

Chapter 7: Custom and Setup Menus | 137

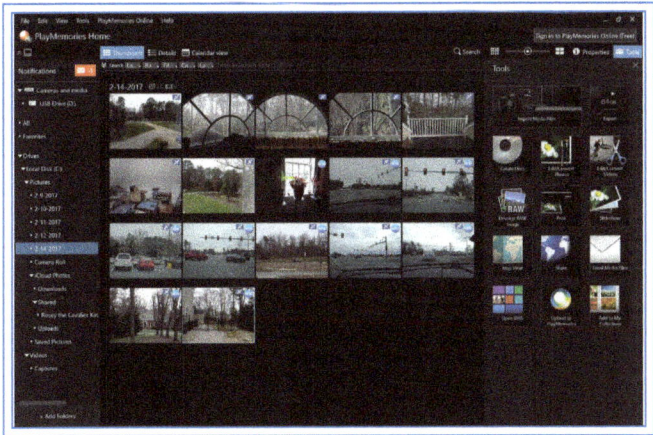

Figure 7-59. GPS Icons on Thumbnails in PlayMemories Home

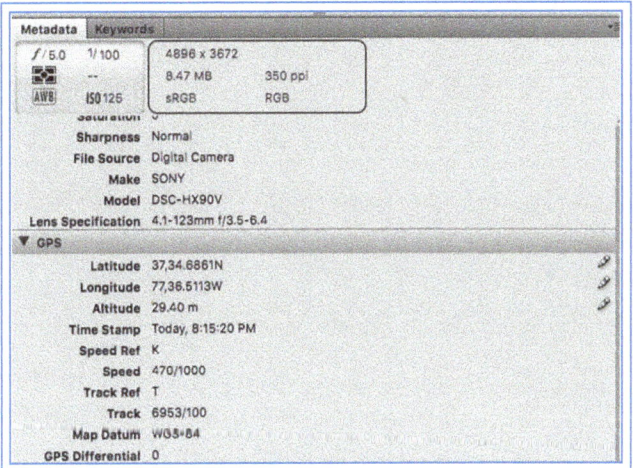

Figure 7-60. GPS Information Displayed for Image in Adobe Bridge

GPS Auto Time Correction

If you turn this next sub-option on, the camera will acquire the current time information from GPS satellites when GPS is turned on and the camera is able to receive signals from the satellites. You may want to have this option turned on in order to get accurate time information while on a trip.

GPS Area Adjustment

This sub-option can be turned on to let the camera receive location data from the GPS system, in order to make the time information match the time for the current location.

Use GPS Assist Data

This next sub-option gives you a way to download updated GPS assist data. This data, which is useful for a period of about 30 days, helps the camera determine its location more quickly when receiving information from the GPS satellites. It is not necessary to download or use this data, but it may speed up the camera's GPS operations. If you use the GPS options frequently, it is worth following the simple steps outlined below to update the data.

To do this, first, make sure you have the latest version of Sony's PlayMemories Home software installed. You can download it for Windows or Mac computers at www.sony.net/pm. Then, take the memory card from your camera and insert it into a card reader connected to your computer. Start the PlayMemories Home software, and select the option called GPS Support Tool, which should be found as an icon in the Tools area of the program.

When you select that icon, the program should display a dialog box indicating that it has found the memory card attached to the computer. Select the Update Now option, and the software will download the GPS assist data and write it to the card. Then eject the card from the computer and insert it into the camera. Now, when you select the Use GPS Assist Data menu option, the camera will display a screen like that in Figure 7-61, stating that the assist data is in use, and giving the dates for which it will remain valid.

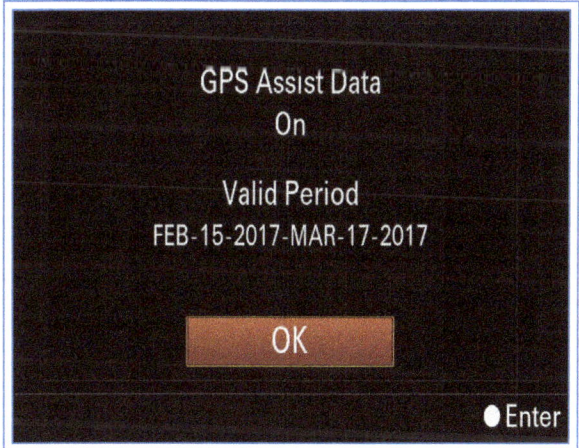

Figure 7-61. GPS Assist Data Screen

GPS Log Recording

This next sub-option lets you activate the camera's ability to record a log of its locations using its GPS function. In order to turn on this feature, you first have to make sure the GPS On/Off sub-option is set to On. Then, set GPS Log Recording to On. From that point, for about the next 24 hours, the camera will record its positions as determined through the GPS functionality. Of course, for this feature to work, the camera must be in a series of locations where it can receive GPS signals. So, if the camera is indoors or otherwise in an area shielded from the satellite signals, it will not receive location information.

When you want to end recording of the current log, turn the GPS Log Recording sub-option to Off. The camera will then save the completed log to the memory card.

When you have finished recording the log, remove the memory card from the camera, insert it into a card reader connected to your computer, and start the PlayMemories Home software. Then, import the images that were taken while the log was being recorded. When the images are imported into PlayMemories Home, select the Map View option from the Tools area. You can then view the images with their locations on the map, and you can select the Track option to view the GPS track. Figure 7-62 is a screen shot from the computer where I uploaded several images that I took with the GPS log activated. The thick red line shows the route I traveled.

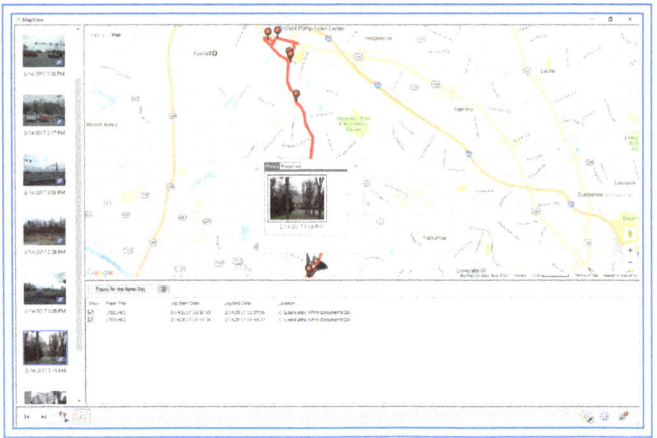

Figure 7-62. PlayMemories Home Screen Showing GPS Route

I was not able to get the Map View function to work on the Macintosh version of the PlayMemories Home software, but it worked well on a computer running Windows 10.

Screen 2 of the Setup menu on the HX90V is shown in Figure 7-63.

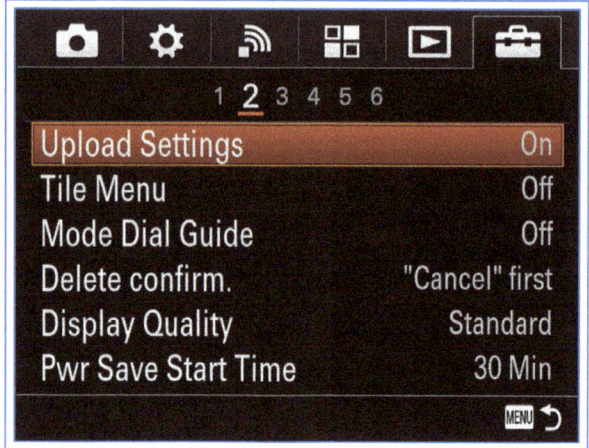

Figure 7-63. Screen 2 of HX90V Setup Menu

Upload Settings

This first item on the second screen of the Setup menu on the HX90V, as seen in Figure 7-63, appears only when an Eye-Fi card is in the camera. If no Eye-Fi card is present, this menu option does not display at all, leaving a blank space at the bottom of this menu screen. On the HX80 also, this option appears at the top of screen 2 when an Eye-Fi card is present.

As discussed in Chapter 1, an Eye-Fi card is a memory card with a transmitter to send images to a computer over a Wi-Fi network. This menu item has only two settings—On or Off. You might want to use the Off setting if you are on an airplane where you may be required to turn off radio transmitters. Or, if you know you will not be using the Eye-Fi uploading capability for a while, you can turn this menu option off to save some battery power.

Of course, these cameras have built-in Wi-Fi capability, which makes it less likely you will use an Eye-Fi card.

Tile Menu

If you turn this option on, the camera displays a screen with six tiles representing the various menu systems, as shown in Figure 7-64, when you press the Menu button.

This screen gives you a graphic representation of which menu is which, and it lets you get quick access to the menu of your choice. You navigate through the six blocks using the direction buttons or the Control wheel. I prefer to leave this option turned off, because, without it, pressing the Menu button takes me directly to the last menu option I was using. From there, I can navigate quickly to any other menu system. But for those who are new to this camera or who like having a large display to show the menu choices clearly, the Tile Menu option may be worth using.

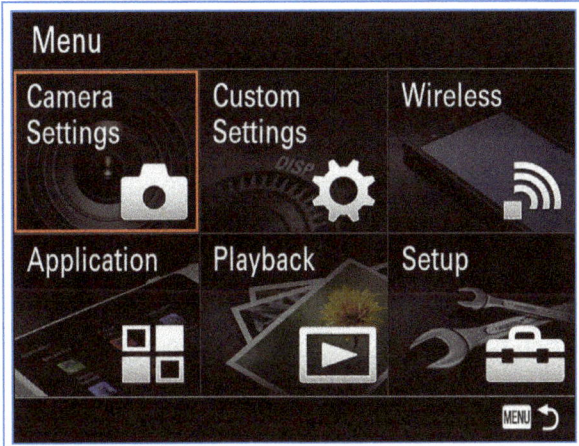

Figure 7-64. Tile Menu Option In Use

MODE DIAL GUIDE

This menu item lets you turn on or off the Mode Dial Guide, a display that appears when you turn the Mode dial to select a shooting mode, as shown in Figure 7-65.

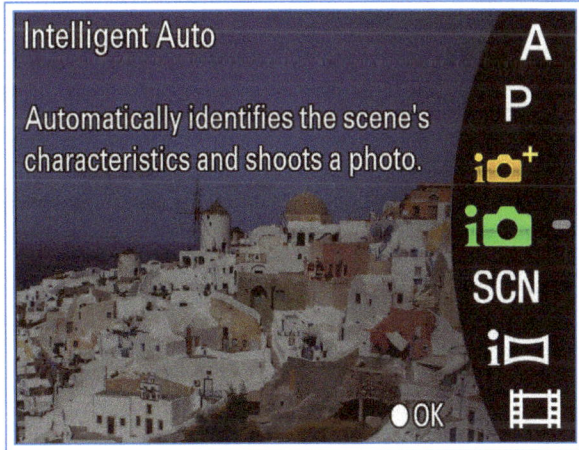

Figure 7-65. Mode Dial Guide In Use

This guide is helpful when you first start using the camera, but it can be annoying if you don't need the reminders, and you have to press the Center button or Menu button, or press the shutter button halfway, to dismiss the screen. I leave this option turned off to speed up my shooting.

DELETE CONFIRMATION

This menu item has two possible settings, as shown in Figure 7-66: "Delete" First or "Cancel" First.

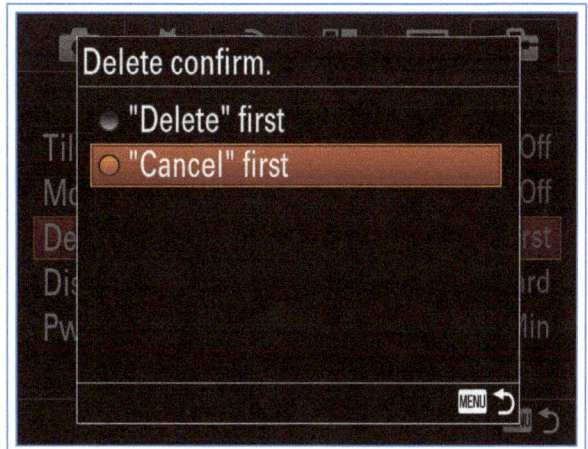

Figure 7-66. Delete Confirmation Menu Options Screen

This option lets you fine-tune how the camera operates for deleting images. Whenever you press the Delete button to delete an image in playback mode, the camera displays a confirmation screen, as shown in Figure 7-67, with two choices: Delete or Cancel.

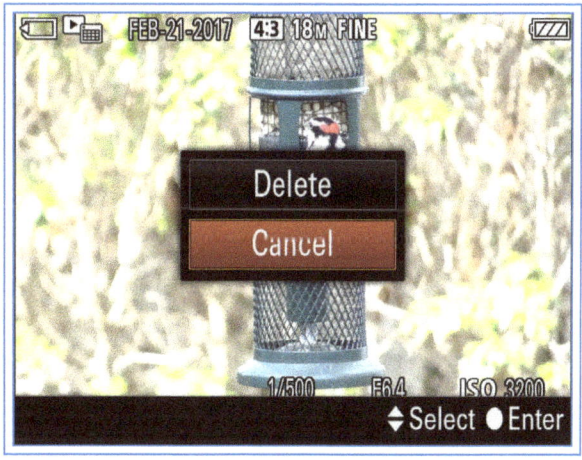

Figure 7-67. Confirmation Screen from Pressing Delete Button

One of those choices will be highlighted when the screen appears; you can then press the Center button to accept that choice and the operation will be done. You also can use the Control wheel or the Up or Down button to highlight the other option before you press the Center button to carry out your choice.

Which setting you choose for this menu item depends on how careful you want to be to guard against the accidental deletion of an image. If you like to move quickly in deleting images, choose "Delete" First. Then, as soon as the confirmation screen appears, the "Delete" option will be highlighted and you can press the Center button to carry out the deletion. If you prefer to have some assurance of avoiding an accidental deletion, choose "Cancel" First, so that, if you press the Center button too quickly when the confirmation screen appears, you will only cancel the operation, rather than deleting an image.

Unless you use the Delete button often and need to save time, I recommend you leave this menu item set at the "Cancel" First setting to be safe.

Display Quality

This menu item lets you choose Standard or High for the quality of the display. According to Sony, with the High setting the camera displays the live view on the LCD screen or in the viewfinder at a higher resolution than with the Standard setting, at the expense of additional drain on the battery.

I have tried several experiments with these settings, viewing small print in a catalog using both the viewfinder and the LCD display with both Display Quality settings, and I have not found a noticeable difference. There may be situations in which this option has a more noticeable impact on the display, but my recommendation is to leave it at Standard to conserve battery life.

Power Save Start Time

This option lets you set the interval before the camera turns off automatically to save power, when no controls have been operated for a specified length of time. The default time is two minutes; with this option you can also choose one, five, or 30 minutes, as shown in Figure 7-68. After the designated time, the camera does not just go into a "sleep" mode, it powers off. You have to turn it back on by pressing the power button, the Playback button, or the Finder switch.

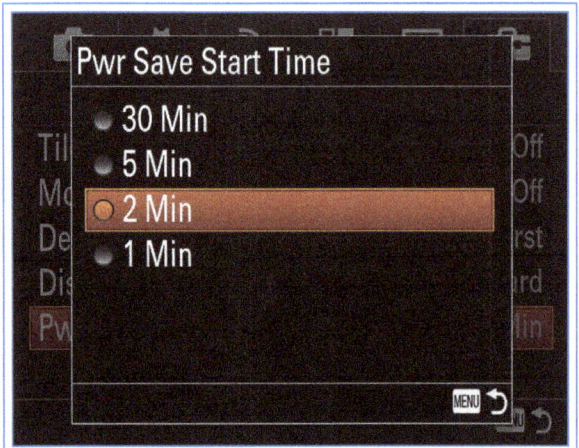

Figure 7-68. Power Save Start Time Menu Options Screen

You cannot turn the power-saving function off. However, the camera will not power off automatically when you are recording movies, when a slide show is playing, when the camera is connected to a computer to upload images, or when the camera is being powered through the Multi port.

The setting you use depends on your preferences. I am usually well aware of the camera's status, and I like to use the maximum 30-minute period for this option so the camera does not power down just when I am about to use it again. I always have extra batteries available and I'm not too concerned if I have to replace the battery. If you are out in the field and running low on battery power, you might want to choose a shorter time for this option, to conserve battery life.

NTSC/PAL Selector (Cameras Sold in Europe and Other PAL Areas Only)

This menu option, which is not shown in an illustration in this book, controls which television system the camera uses for recording videos—NTSC or PAL. The NTSC system is used in the United States and other parts of North America, as well as Japan, South Korea, and some other countries. The PAL system is used in many parts of Asia, Africa, and Europe. This menu option is included only with cameras that are sold for the areas, such as Europe, where the PAL system is in use. Those cameras have the indication "50i" on the label on the bottom of the camera. Other cameras, such as those sold in the United States, have the label "60i" on the bottom, and do not include this menu option. Therefore, it does not appear on my camera, and I have no illustration that includes it.

If your camera does have this option, you can use it to switch between the NTSC system and the PAL system.

For purposes of using the HX80 or HX90V camera, the difference between the two systems is that the NTSC system primarily uses multiples of 30 for frame rates (such as 30, 60, or 120 frames per second), while the PAL system uses multiples of 25 (such as 25, 50, or 100 frames per second). You will see these differences in the options for the Record Setting item on screen 2 of the Shooting menu. If you choose NTSC, the options will be mostly in multiples of 30, although there will be some entries for 24 fps, another NTSC standard. If you choose PAL, the options will be in multiples of 25.

In general, you should use the setting that is standard for the area where you will be using the camera.

It is important to choose this setting before you start recording files on your memory card. Once you have started using a card under one of these systems, you cannot change to the other system without re-formatting the memory card. When you select this menu option, you will see a message warning that you will have to re-format the card to continue. In addition, if you switch a 50i (PAL) camera, it will always display the message "Running on NTSC" whenever the camera is turned on.

The options on screen 3 of the Setup menu on the HX90V are shown in Figure 7-69.

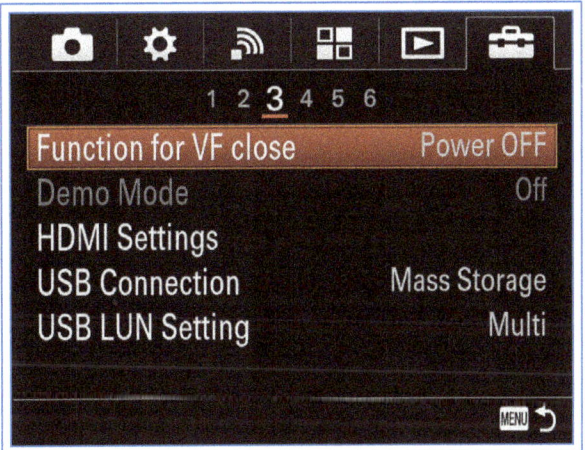

Figure 7-69. Screen 3 of HX90V Setup Menu

FUNCTION FOR VF CLOSE

This first option on screen 3 of the Setup menu on the HX80 and HX90V controls what happens when you push the viewfinder back down into the camera. The choices are Power Off or Not Power Off. If you choose Power Off, the camera will turn off when you stow the viewfinder back in its housing. If you choose Not Power Off, the camera will stay powered on.

I prefer the Not Power Off option so I can keep shooting or using playback functions after the viewfinder has been retracted. But, if you use the viewfinder primarily, you may like the convenience of turning the camera off by pressing the viewfinder back into its slot. (Lifting the viewfinder into place with the Finder switch always turns the camera on, regardless of the setting for this menu option.)

DEMO MODE

The Demo Mode menu item automatically plays a movie if the camera has not had any controls operated for about one minute. This feature is designed for use by retail stores, so they can leave the camera turned on with a continuous demonstration on its screen. But you can use it for your own purposes, if you want to create a movie that demonstrates the camera's features for friends, for example, or if you just like the idea of having the camera play a movie when it's not otherwise occupied.

For this feature to be available for selection on the menu screen, the camera has to be powered by an AC adapter or other USB power source through the Multi port. Otherwise, this line on the menu will be dimmed. The AC adapter that comes with the HX90V, model number AC-UB10C in the United States, will not work for this purpose. For that camera, you need to obtain an adapter such as Sony's AC-UD10, AC-UD11, or a third-party power source such as the Mophie PowerStation XL, which is discussed in Appendix A. However, the adapter that comes with the HX80—AC-UUD12—does work for this purpose.

When this option is turned on and the camera is in shooting mode, after one minute of inactivity the camera will enter Demo Mode. At that point, the camera will automatically play a movie, which you have to provide. It cannot be just any movie. The movie the camera will play in Demo Mode must be recorded in the AVCHD format, it must be protected using the Protect option on the Playback menu, and it must be the oldest AVCHD movie on the memory card.

So, if you have a reason to use this option, you may want to use a fresh memory card and record a single AVCHD movie on the card, and then use the Protect function to protect it. When the movie plays, it plays audio as well as video, and it will keep repeating in a loop. To exit from Demo Mode, you can press the Center button or just turn the camera off.

HDMI SETTINGS

The HDMI Settings menu option has four sub-options, as shown in Figure 7-70.

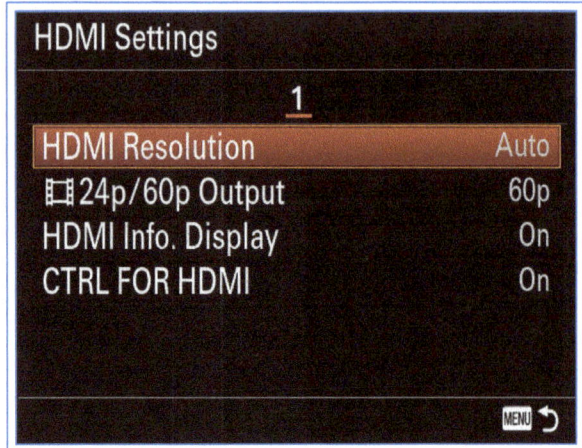

Figure 7-70. HDMI Settings Menu Options Screen

HDMI Resolution

The HDMI Resolution option can be set to Auto, 1080p, or 1080i. This setting controls how the camera displays images and videos on an HDTV in playback mode. Ordinarily, the Auto setting will work best; the camera will set itself for the optimum display according to the resolution of the HDTV it is connected to. If you experience difficulties with that connection, you may be able to improve the image on the HDTV's screen by trying one of the other settings.

24p/60p Output

This menu option is labeled with a movie-film icon, meaning it is for use only in connection with video functions. This option, which is available only for cameras using the NTSC system, has a very specific use. It is applicable when you have recorded video using one of the Record Setting formats that include the 24p or 60p frame rate. It also applies only if you have set the HDMI Resolution item, under HDMI Settings on the Setup menu, to 1080p.

If the above conditions are met, that means you have some video footage recorded at 24 or 60 frames per second. As I will discuss in Chapter 8, the 24p setting is slower than the standard NTSC setting of 30 frames per second, and produces what some people consider to be a more "cinematic" look for the footage.

When you send your 24p video footage out through an HDMI cable to an HDTV set, you may prefer to send it in a way that looks more like standard TV video, using the 60p setting. Or, you may prefer to send your 60p footage in a way that looks more like 24p footage. That is the function of this menu option. If all of the conditions described above are met, you can select 24p or 60p for the 24p/60p Output option, whichever you prefer.

This option also may be of use when you are sending 24p video footage out through the HDMI cable to an external video recorder, if 60p footage is a better option for use by the recorder.

HDMI Information Display

This feature controls the behavior of the camera when you connect it to an HDTV set or other external device using an optional micro HDMI cable. However, unlike the HDMI Resolution option discussed above, which controls what happens when the camera is in playback mode, playing your images and videos on an HDTV set, this menu option controls what happens in shooting mode when the HDMI connection is active.

If this menu option is set to On, which is the default setting, then, when the camera is connected to an HDTV or external recorder in shooting mode, the screen of the external device displays exactly what you would see on the camera's display in that mode if the camera were not connected to the device, including icons and figures showing camera settings.

With the On setting, the HDTV acts as a large, external monitor for the camera, and the screen of the camera itself is blank. I use this setting a great deal myself, because this is how I capture screen shots for this book. Once the camera is connected, I can capture all of the information and settings that appear on the shooting screens and menu screens of the camera, with a few exceptions for special settings that are not output through the HDMI port, such as the Zebra stripes.

If this menu option is set to Off, then, when the camera is connected to an HDTV or other external device in shooting mode, the external device's screen displays only the image that is being viewed by the camera, with no shooting information displayed at all. If you press the Display button, nothing will happen on the external screen; the view will not switch to another display with more information on it. However, at the same time, the camera's screen continues to display all of the shooting information it normally would, including the image and whatever information is chosen by presses of the Display button.

You might use the Off setting when you want to display images from the camera's shooting mode on a large HDTV screen, possibly at a wedding or other gathering, and not have the images cluttered or marred by any shooting information at all. For example, I have seen occasions where a camera is used to focus on an unsuspecting person in the audience, and that person's image suddenly appears on the large screen for everyone to see.

Also, this option is useful for video production when you need to output a "clean" video signal that does not include any shooting information from the camera. That signal can be sent through an HDMI cable to a video recorder for recording to another medium, or for display on a large monitor being viewed by the production team. For example, you can record video directly from the camera to a computer by outputting the clean HDMI signal to a device such as the Intensity Pro by Blackmagic Design. There are similar devices available from companies such as AverMedia, Hauppage, and Elgato. You also can send the clean signal to an external video recorder such as the Atomos Shogun. However, the audio signal is not sent through the HDMI cable in shooting mode, so you would have to record the audio separately, using the video recorder.

With the On setting, you can press the Display button to show a screen with very minimal shooting information, but that screen still shows the basic information of aperture, shutter speed, exposure compensation, and ISO value at the very bottom of the screen, and shows the shooting mode in the upper left corner. If you don't want even that minimal level of information to interfere with the video display, choose the Off setting.

This setting does not change the behavior of the camera for playback of images and video; its only effect is on the display of information in shooting mode through an HDMI connection.

CTRL for HDMI

This sub-option is of use only when you have connected the camera to an HDTV and you want to control the camera with the TV's remote control, which is possible in some situations. If you want to do that, set this option to On and follow the instructions for the TV and its remote control. This option is intended to be used when you connect the camera to a Sony Bravia model HDTV.

USB Connection

This option sets the technical standard that the camera uses for connecting to a computer using the USB cable. This menu item has three choices, as shown in Figure 7-71: Auto, Mass Storage, and MTP, which stands for Media Transfer Protocol.

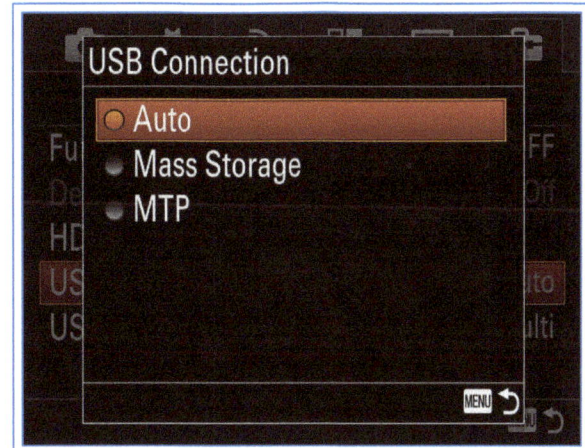

Figure 7-71. USB Connection Menu Options Screen

You ordinarily should select Auto, and the camera should detect which standard is used by the computer you are connecting the camera to. If the camera does not automatically select a standard and start transferring images, you can try one of the other settings to see if it works better than the Auto setting. You may find it necessary to use the MTP option when connecting your camera to the computer to download apps from the playmemoriescameraapps.com site.

USB LUN Setting

This is an option that should not often be needed. LUN stands for logical unit number. This item has two possible settings—Multi or Single. Ordinarily, it should be set to Multi, the default. In particular, it should be set to Multi when the camera is connected to a Windows-based computer and you are using Sony's PlayMemories Home software to manage your images. If you encounter a problem with a USB connection to a computer, you can try the Single setting to see if it solves the problem.

Screen 4 of the Setup menu on the HX90V is shown in Figure 7-72.

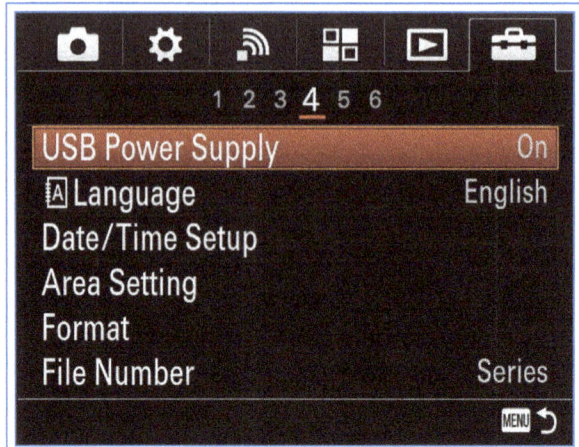

Figure 7-72. Screen 4 of HX90V Setup Menu

USB Power Supply

The USB Power Supply option, which can be turned either on or off, controls whether or not the camera's battery will be charged or the camera will be powered through the USB cable when the camera is connected by its USB cable to a computer.

If you use the AC adapter provided with the camera or an external USB battery, as discussed in Appendix A, to provide power to the camera, you do not need to have this menu option turned on. When the USB cable is connected to an external power supply, power will be provided to the camera even with this option turned off.

Turning this option on gives you another avenue for keeping the camera's battery charged. The only problem is that if your computer is running on its battery, then that battery will be discharged more rapidly than usual. If you are plugging the camera into a computer that is plugged into a wall power outlet, there should be no problem in using this option.

As I will discuss in Appendix A, I recommend that you get an external battery charger and at least one extra battery for the camera, because even if you can charge the battery in the camera using the USB cable, you don't have the ability to insert a fully charged battery into the camera when the first battery is exhausted.

I recommend leaving this option at its default setting of On, unless you will be connecting the camera to a battery-powered computer or other device and you don't want to run down the battery on that device.

Language

This option gives you the choice of language for the display of commands and information on the camera's LCD screen and in the viewfinder. Once you have selected this menu item, scroll through the language choices using the Control wheel or the direction buttons and press the Center button when your chosen language is highlighted.

Date/Time Setup

I discussed this item in Chapter 1. When the camera is new or has not been used for a long time, it will prompt you to set the date and time and will display this menu option. If you want to call up these settings on your own, you can do so at any time.

When you press the Center button on this menu line, you will see a screen like that in Figure 7-73, with the choice of adjusting Daylight Savings Time (On or Off), Date/Time, or Date Format.

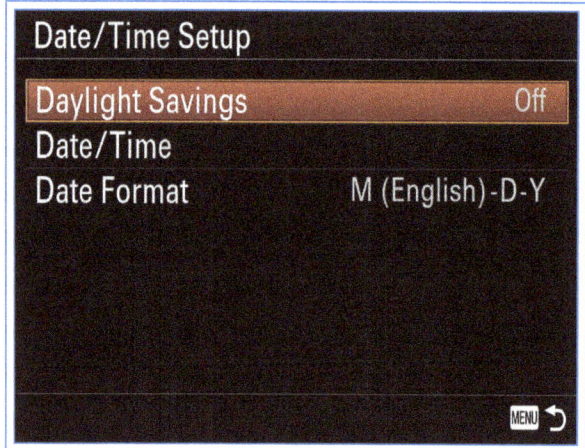

Figure 7-73. Date/Time Setup Main Options Screen

To adjust Date/Time, select that option and press the Center button. The camera will display a screen like that shown in Figure 7-74.

Scroll through the options for setting month, day, year, and time by turning the Control wheel or pressing the Left and Right buttons. As you reach each item, adjust its value by using the Up and Down buttons. When all of the settings are correct, press the Center button to confirm them and exit from this screen.

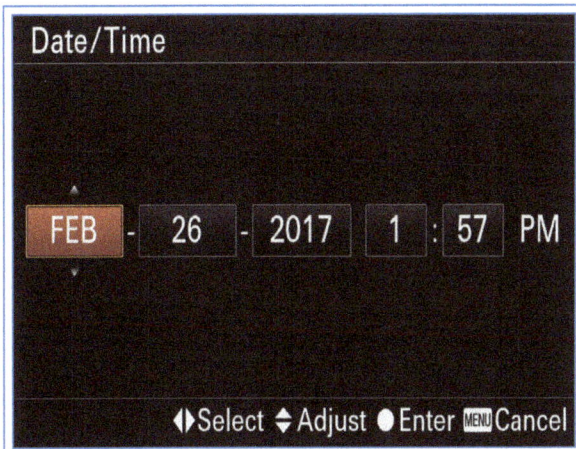

Figure 7-74. Screen for Setting Date and Time

From the first menu screen, you can also turn Daylight Savings Time on or off depending on the time of year, and you can choose a date format according to your preference.

Area Setting

The next option on the Setup menu, Area Setting, lets you select a location so you can adjust the date and time for a different time zone when you are traveling. When you highlight this item and press the Center button, the camera displays the map shown in Figure 7-75.

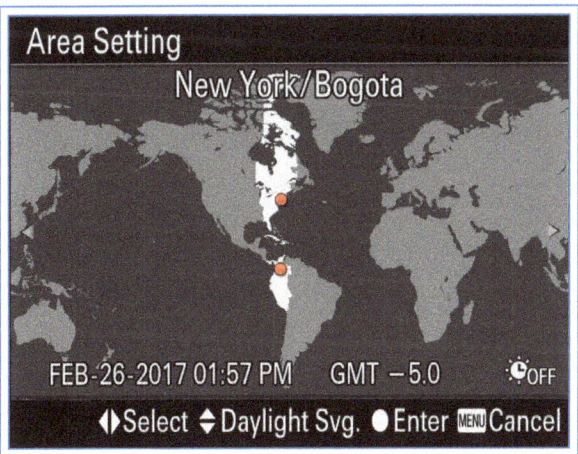

Figure 7-75. Area Setting Map Screen

Turn the Control wheel or press the Left and Right buttons to move the light-colored highlight over the map until it covers the area of the location you want to set. If you want to adjust the setting for Daylight Savings Time, press the Up or Down button to make the adjustment. Then press the Center button and the date and time will be adjusted for that location until you change the location again using this menu item.

Format

This next option on the Setup menu is used to prepare a new memory card to store images and videos with the correct data format. This command also is useful when you want to wipe all the data off a card that has become full or you have copied a card's images to your computer or other storage device. Choose this process only when you want or need to completely wipe all of the data from a memory card. When you select the Format option, as shown in Figure 7-76, the camera will warn you that all data currently on the card will be deleted if you proceed.

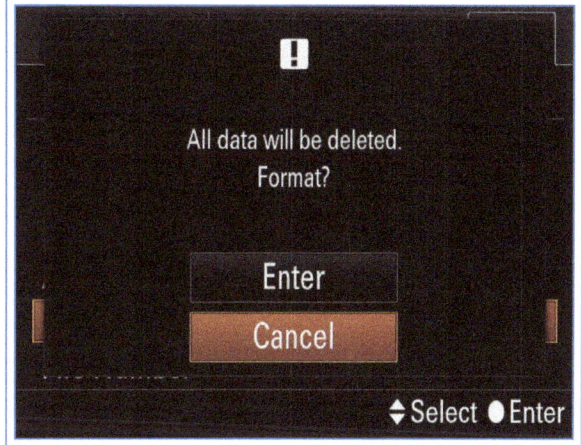

Figure 7-76. Format Confirmation Screen

If you reply by highlighting Enter and pressing the Center button to confirm, the camera will format the card that is in the camera, and the result will be a card that is empty and properly formatted to store new images and videos.

With this procedure, the camera will erase all files, including those that have been protected from accidental erasure with the Protect function on the Playback menu. It's a good idea to periodically save your images and videos to your computer or other storage device and then re-format your card to make sure it is properly set up for recording new images and videos. It's also a good idea to use the Format command on any new memory card when you first insert it into the camera. Even though it likely will work without that procedure, it's best to make sure the card is set up with Sony's method of formatting for the camera.

File Number

This option controls how the camera assigns file numbers to images and MP4 movies. The choices are Series or Reset, as seen in Figure 7-77.

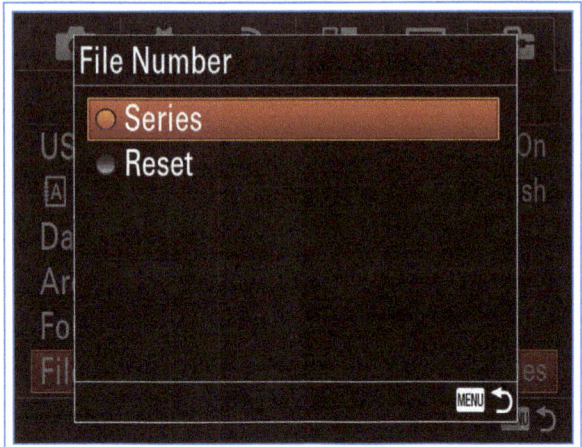

Figure 7-77. File Number Menu Options Screen

With Series, the camera continues numbering where it left off, even when the camera creates a new folder for images or you put a new memory card in the camera. For example, if you have 112 images on your first memory card, the last image likely will be numbered 100-0112: 100 for the folder number (the first folder number available) and 0112 for the image number. If you then switch to a new memory card with no images on it, the first image on that card will be numbered 100-0113 because the numbering scheme continues in the same sequence. If you choose Reset instead, the first image on the new card will be numbered 100-0001 because the camera resets the numbering to the first number.

Screen 5 of the Setup menu on the HX90V is shown in Figure 7-78.

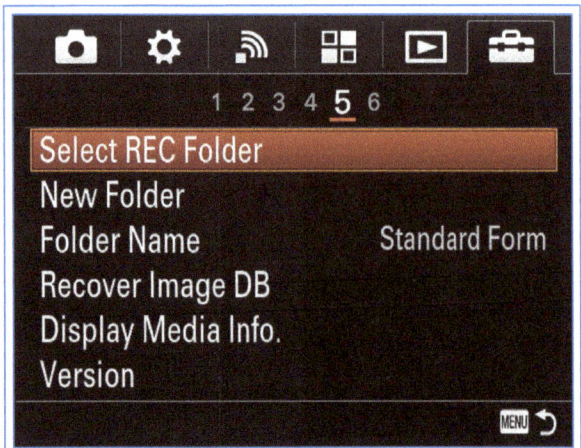

Figure 7-78. Screen 5 of HX90V Setup Menu

Select REC Folder

When you select this menu item, the camera displays an orange bar with the name of the current folder, as shown in Figure 7-79.

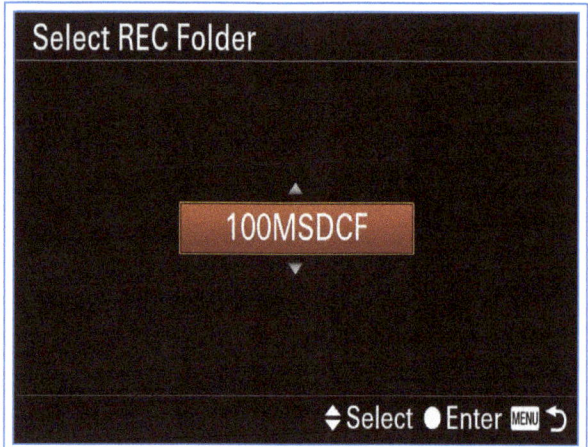

Figure 7-79. Select REC Folder Screen

You can use the Up and Down buttons or turn the Control wheel to choose another folder on the memory card if one exists, so you can store future images in that folder. For example, if you take some photos for business and some for pleasure, you could create a new folder for business shots (see the next menu item, below). The camera would then use that folder. Afterward, you could use the Select REC Folder option to select the folder where your personal images are stored and take more images that will be stored there. This option is not available if you use Date Form for the Folder Name option, discussed later in this section. This option also selects the folder number for storing MP4 videos, though that folder is different from the one for still images.

New Folder

This next item lets you create a new folder on your memory card for storing images. After you highlight this item on the menu screen and press the Center button, you will see a message announcing that a new folder has been created, as shown in Figure 7-80. The camera will store new images in that folder until you select another folder with the Select REC Folder option, discussed above, or create another folder using this option.

Chapter 7: Custom and Setup Menus | 147

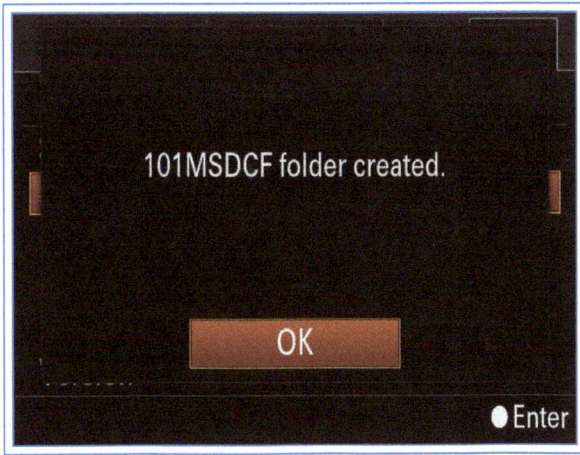

Figure 7-80. New Folder Confirmation Message

The camera will create a new folder for storing MP4 videos at the same time. The camera also will create a new folder once a folder contains 4,000 images. Folders for still images are created within the DCIM folder, and folders for MP4 videos are created within the MP_ROOT folder. (AVCHD videos and XAVC S videos are stored in different folders that are not affected by this command.)

I find this option useful for organizing images. When I go on a trip to take photos at a particular location, I often create a new folder to store the photos from that trip so I can easily find them and upload them to my computer when I return.

Folder Name

This option gives you a choice of two methods for naming folders that store still images on your memory card, as seen in Figure 7-81: Standard Form or Date Form.

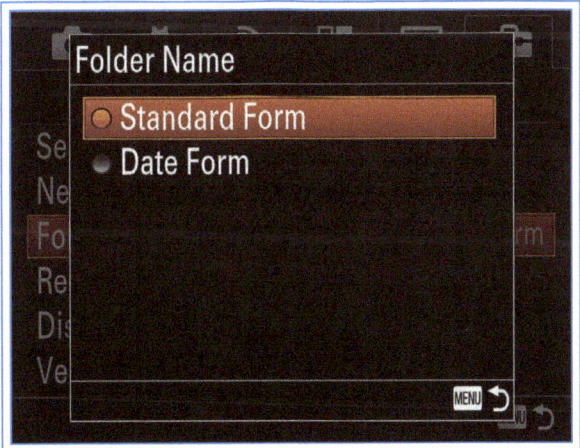

Figure 7-81. Folder Name Menu Options Screen

Standard Form uses the folder number, such as 100, 101, or higher, followed by the letters MSDCF. An example is 100MSDCF. If you choose Date Form, folder names will have the same 100 or higher number followed by the date, in a form such as 10070223 for a folder created on February 23, 2017, using only one digit to designate the year.

I find the date format confusing and hard to read, and I am used to the MSDCF format. If you use the date format, you will end up having a folder for every date on which you record still images. You may prefer having your image folders organized in that way so you can quickly locate images from a particular date. I prefer having fewer folders and organizing the images using software on my computer according to my own preferences.

Recover Image Database

This menu item activates the Recover Image Database function. If you select this option and press the Center button to confirm it on the next screen, as shown in Figure 7-82, the camera runs a check to test the integrity of the file system on the memory card.

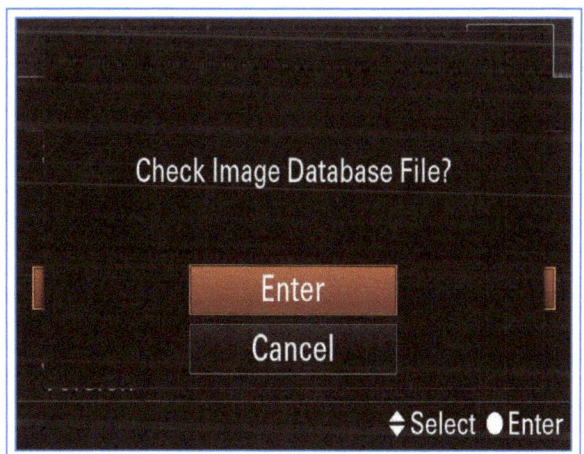

Figure 7-82. Recover Image Database Confirmation Message

I have never used this menu option, but if the camera is having difficulty reading the images on a card, using this option might recover the data.

Display Media Information

The next item on this menu screen gives you another way to see how much storage space is remaining on the memory card that is currently in the camera.

When you select Display Media Information and press the Center button, the camera displays a screen like that in Figure 7-83, with information about the number of still images or the hours and minutes of video that can be recorded using current settings.

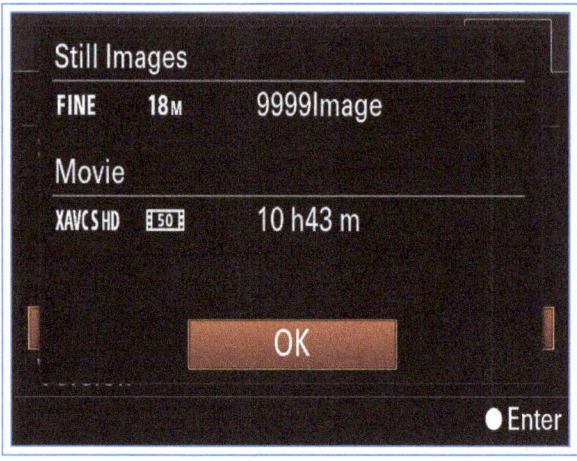

Figure 7-83. Display Media Information Screen

It is nice to have this option available, although the number of images that can be recorded is also displayed on the detailed shooting screen, and the number of minutes of video that can be recorded is displayed on the video recording screen once a recording has been started. The available storage time for video files is displayed before a recording starts, if the Mode dial is set to the Movie position.

VERSION

This menu option displays the current version of the firmware installed in your camera. The Sony Cyber-shot DSC-HX90V and the DSC-HX80, like other digital cameras, are programmed at the factory with firmware, which is a set of computer instructions electronically implanted in the camera. These instructions control all aspects of the camera's operation, including the menu system, functioning of the controls, and in-camera processing of your images. The reason you may want to check to see what version is installed is that, in many cases, the manufacturer will release an updated version of the firmware that may fix problems or bugs in the system, provide minor enhancements, or, in some cases, even provide major improvements, such as adding new shooting modes or menu options.

To determine the firmware version installed in your camera, highlight this menu option and press the Center button, and the camera will display the version number, as shown in Figure 7-84.

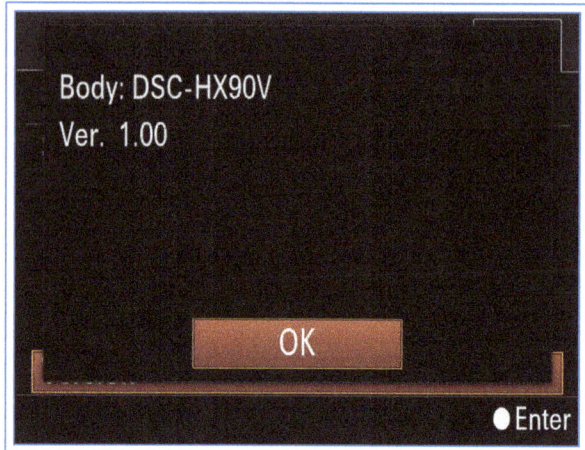

Figure 7-84. Version Screen

To see if firmware upgrades have been released, visit Sony's support website at http://esupport.sony.com. Find the link for Drivers and Software, then the link for Cyber-shot Cameras, and then a link to any updated version for your camera model. The site will provide instructions for downloading and installing the new firmware.

Screen 6 of the Setup menu on the HX90V is shown in Figure 7-85.

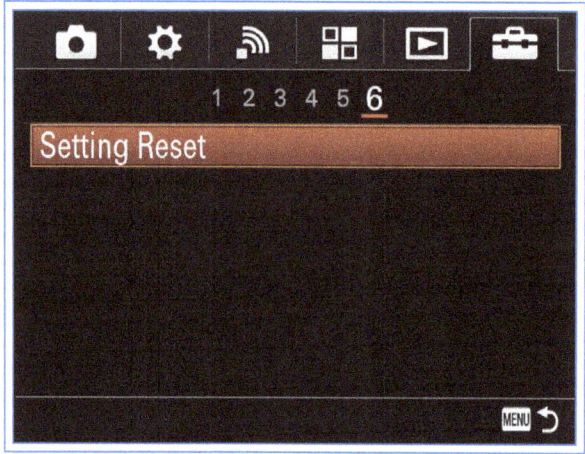

Figure 7-85. Screen 6 of HX90V Setup Menu

SETTING RESET

This final option on the Setup menu is useful when you want to reset some or all of the camera's settings to their original (default) values. This action can be helpful if you have been playing around with different settings and you find that something is not working as expected.

With this item, the camera presents you with two sub-options: Camera Settings Reset and Initialize, as shown in Figure 7-86.

If you choose Camera Settings Reset, only the settings that directly affect the shooting of images and videos are reset. If you select Initialize, all settings, including items such as Audio Signals and Monitor Brightness, are reset to their factory values.

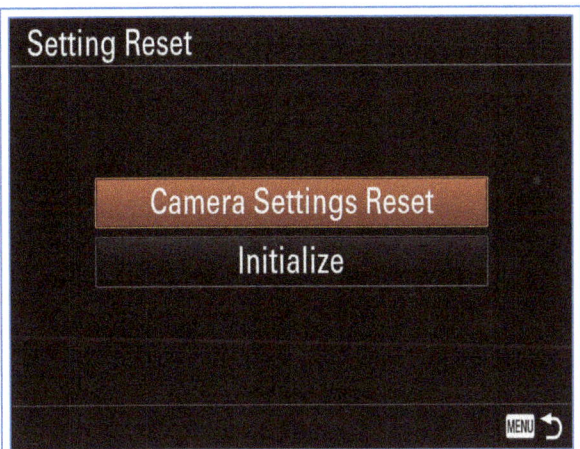

Figure 7-86. Setting Reset Menu Options Screen

Chapter 8: Motion Pictures

Movie-Making Overview

In one sense, the basics of making movies with the HX80 and HX90V can be stated in four words: "Press the red button." (That is, the red Movie button at the upper right corner of the camera's back.) In most situations, you can press and release that button while aiming at your subject, and you will get good results. You do not need to worry about special settings, particularly if you set the camera to one of the more automatic modes, such as Intelligent Auto or Scene. (You can record a movie with the Mode dial at any position, as discussed later in this chapter.)

To stop recording, press the red button again. If you prefer not to run the risk of recording unwanted movies by pressing the Movie button accidentally, you can change the button's operation so it activates movie recording only when the camera is in Movie mode, as discussed in Chapter 7.

If you're mainly a still photographer with little interest in movie making, you don't need to read further. Be aware that the red button exists, and if an interesting event starts to happen, you can turn the Mode dial to the green camera icon for Intelligent Auto mode, press the Movie button, and capture footage to post on YouTube or elsewhere with a minimum of effort. But for users who want to explore these cameras' motion picture capabilities more thoroughly, there is additional information to discuss.

First, there is a requirement that may decide what memory card you get for your camera. To record movies in the highest-quality XAVC S HD format, you have to use a memory card with a capacity of at least 64 GB and a speed of at least Class 10 or UHS Speed Class 1. If you do not use a card with those specifications, the camera will display an error message and will not record video using that format.

I have used the SanDisk Extreme PRO 64 GB SDXC card, rated in UHS Speed Class 1, the Lexar Professional 128 GB SDXC card, also rated in that speed class, as well as the SanDisk Extreme 256 GB SDXC card and the SanDisk Extreme PRO 512 GB SDXC card, both of which are rated in UHS Speed Class 3, for recording the highest-level formats with no problems, but there are other choices available. The cards listed above are shown in Figure 8-1.

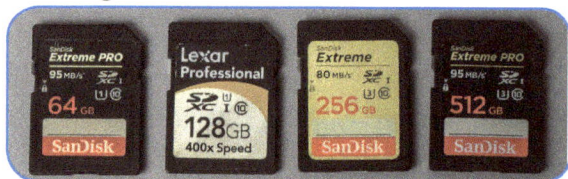

Figure 8-1. SD Cards Rated for XAVC S HD Video Format

Also, it's important to note that these camera, like most cameras in their class, have built-in limitations that prevent them from recording any sequence longer than about 29 minutes (20 minutes for the MP4 format using the 1920 x 1080 60p 28M Record Setting option). You can, of course, record multiple sequences adding up to any length, depending on the amount of storage space available on your memory cards.

If you plan to record a large amount of HD video, you should get a high-capacity and high-speed card. A 64 GB card can hold about two hours and 35 minutes of the highest quality of XAVC S HD video, five hours of the highest quality of AVCHD video, or about 22 hours of the lowest quality of MP4 HD video. (I will discuss these video formats later in this chapter.)

Details of Movie Settings

As I noted above, the one step that is a necessity for recording a movie with the HX80 or the HX90V is to press the Movie button. However, there are numerous settings that affect the way the camera records a movie when that button is pressed.

I will discuss four categories of settings: (1) movie-related selections you make on the Shooting menu; (2) the position of the Mode dial; (3) other selections you make on the Shooting menu and other menus; and (4) settings you make with the camera's physical controls.

Movie-Related Shooting Menu Options

First, the movie-related options on the Shooting menu control the format and other important settings for movies you record. I discussed this menu in Chapter 4, but I did not provide details about all of the movie-oriented options in that chapter.

As noted above, you can press the Movie button to start a video recording at any time and in any shooting mode, as long as the Movie Button option on the last screen of the Custom menu is set to Always. Because of this ability to shoot movies in any shooting mode, you can always change the settings for movie recording using the Shooting menu, no matter what shooting mode the camera is set to. I will discuss each item on the Shooting menu that has an effect on your shooting of videos.

At this point, I will discuss the Shooting menu options that apply only to movies; later in this chapter, I will discuss options on this menu and other menus that affect movies as well as still images, such as White Balance, ISO, Picture Effect, and others.

File Format

The first item on screen 2 of the Shooting menu, File Format, gives you a choice of the three available movie recording formats—XAVC S HD, AVCHD, and MP4, as shown in Figure 8-2.

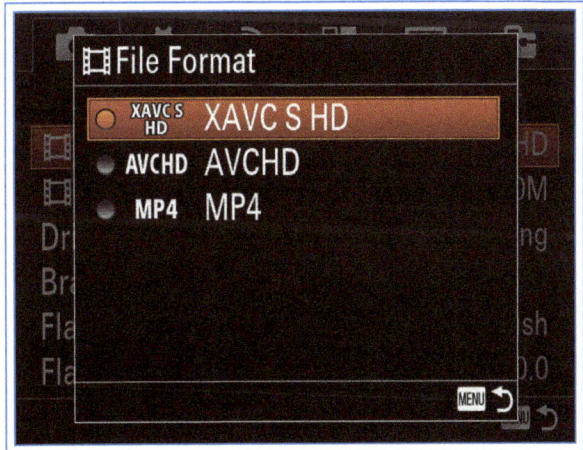

Figure 8-2. File Format Menu Options Screen

This setting determines the format the camera will use for movies when you press the Movie button. The characteristics of the formats are discussed below.

XAVC S HD

This first option for File Format uses the high-quality XAVC S format, and records using a high-definition (HD) resolution of 1920 x 1080 pixels, sometimes known as Full HD. This option will give you excellent quality. However, as noted earlier, you have to use a memory card with a capacity of at least 64 GB and a speed of at least Class 10 or UHS Speed Class 1, when recording video with this format.

AVCHD

If you don't want to purchase the high-speed memory card required for the XAVC S format, but you still want high quality for your movies, you can choose AVCHD. This format, developed jointly by Sony and Panasonic, has become increasingly common in advanced digital cameras. It provides excellent quality, and movies recorded in this format on the HX90V can be used to create Blu-ray discs.

MP4

If you want to record movies with excellent video quality but in a format that is easier to edit with a computer than the first three options and easy to share on the Internet or by email, you can choose MP4. The MP4 format is compatible with Apple Computer's QuickTime software, and the files can be edited with various software programs, including QuickTime, iMovie, Windows Movie Maker, and many others.

Record Setting

The Record Setting item on the Movie menu is another quality-related option for recording video. (The accent is on the second syllable of "Record.") The choices for this item are different depending on whether you choose XAVC S HD, AVCHD, or MP4 for File Format. I will discuss these options assuming you have your camera set for NTSC, the video standard used in the United States. If your camera was purchased in a region that uses the PAL system, and you have not switched the camera to the NTSC system using the NTSC/PAL Selector menu option, the choices for Record Setting will include numbers such as 50p and 25p instead of 60p, 30p, and 24p.

XAVC S HD

If you choose XAVC S HD, the three choices for Record Setting are 60p 50M, 30p 50M, and 24p 50M, as shown in Figure 8-3.

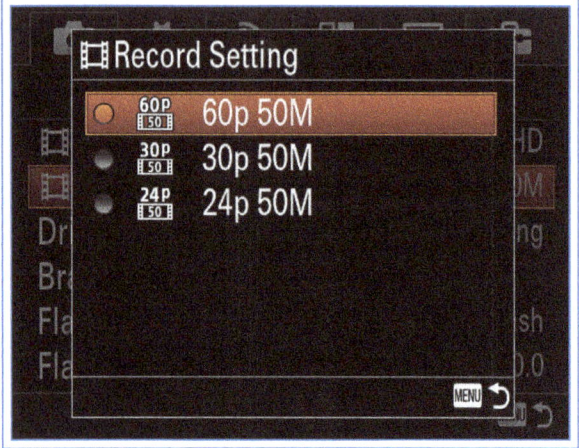

Figure 8-3. Record Setting Options for XAVC S HD Format

For these choices, the letter "p" is for progressive, which means the camera records 60, 30, or 24 full video frames per second. (The other option, used with some AVCHD formats, as discussed below, is designated by the letter "i," standing for interlaced. With those options, such as 60i, the camera records 60 fields, or half-frames, per second, which yields lower quality and fewer possibilities for editing.) The standard speed for recording video in the United States is about 30 frames per second, and using the 30p setting will yield excellent quality.

If you use the 60p option, the camera will record at two times normal speed, and so will record twice as much video information as with the 30p choice. If you use that higher speed, you can produce a slow-motion version of your footage at high quality. This possibility exists because the 60p footage is recorded with twice the number of full frames as 30p footage, so the quality of the video does not suffer if it is played back at one-half of the normal speed. If you think you may want to slow down your footage significantly for playback, you should choose the 60p setting.

Video recorded with the 60p setting will play back at normal speed in the camera. To play it back in slow motion, you can use a program such as iMovie for the Mac or Movie Maker for Windows. Just set the playback speed to a factor of 0.5x to play the footage at the slower speed.

If you select 24p, your video will be recorded and played back at 24 fps. The 24p rate is considered by some people to be more "cinematic" than the 30p format. This may be because 24 fps is a standard speed for movie cameras that shoot with film. My preference is to use the 30p option, but if you find that 24p suits your purposes better, you have that option with these cameras.

The 50M designation means that these formats record video with a bit rate up to a maximum of 50 megabits per second, which is a high rate that yields excellent quality.

All of these options are recorded in full HD, meaning the pixel count for each video frame is 1920 x 1080.

AVCHD

When AVCHD is selected for File Format, the five choices for Record Setting are 60i 24M(FX), 60i 17M(FH), 60p 28M(PS), 24p 24M(FX), and 24p 17M(FH), as seen in Figure 8-4.

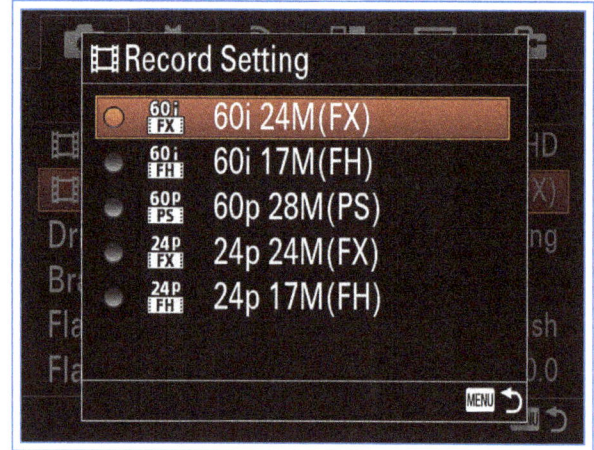

Figure 8-4. Record Setting Options for AVCHD Format

60i and 60p Video Formats

Three of these settings use 60 fields or frames per second. As noted above, the letter "i" or "p" stands for interlaced or progressive. With interlaced video, the camera records 60 fields per second; a field is equal to one-half of a frame, and the two halves are interlaced to form 30 full frames. The video frame rate of about 30 frames per second (fps) is the standard video playback rate in the United States.

If the letter is "p," for progressive, the camera records 60 full frames per second, which yields higher quality than interlaced video. The 60 frames are later translated into 30 frames for playback at the standard rate of 30 fps. However, as with the XAVC S HD format, if your video-editing software has this capability, you can play back 60p footage in slow motion at one-half the normal speed and still maintain full HD quality.

The 28M, 24M, or 17M designation states the "bit rate," or volume, of video information that is recorded—either 28, 24, or 17 megabits per second. The higher-numbered settings provide greater quality at the cost of using more storage capacity on the memory card and requiring greater computer resources to edit.

The final designations, FH, FX, and PS, are proprietary labels used by Sony for these various qualities of video. They have no particular meanings; they are just labels for various levels of video quality—PS is the highest, then FX, and then FH.

Choose 60p 28M if you want the highest quality (including slow-motion capability), 60i 24M for excellent quality, or 60i 17M for excellent quality that takes up fewer resources.

24p Video Formats

As with the XAVC S HD options discussed above, the 24p formats are available if you want a more "cinematic" look for your footage. (If your camera uses the PAL system, it will offer 25p formats instead of 24p.)

MP4

If, instead of XAVC S HD or AVCHD, you choose MP4 for File Format, you have three choices for Record Setting: 1920 x 1080 60p 28M, 1920 x 1080 30p 16M, and 1280 x 720 30p 6M, as shown in Figure 8-5.

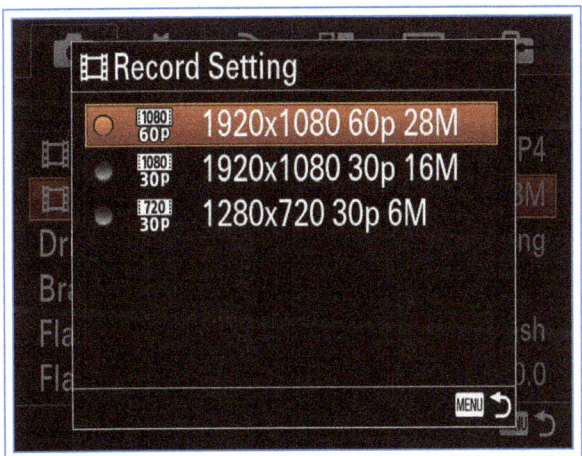

Figure 8-5. Record Settings Options for MP4 Format

The first two settings provide full HD resolution with the same pixel count as XAVC S HD or AVCHD. The third setting, 1280 x 720, has a lower resolution, but is still HD. As you can see from the bit rate values for these settings, 28M, 16M, and 6M, the bit rates are lower than those of the highest-quality AVCHD or XAVC S HD settings. Therefore, the quality is not as great, but the MP4 formats take up less storage space than AVCHD or XAVC S HD and, as noted above, are easier to manipulate with a computer and to send by e-mail.

If you choose the MP4 file format, I recommend you select the 1920 x 1080 60p 28M option to get maximum quality from this setting, unless you are recording a video of household possessions for an inventory or shooting another subject that does not require such high quality. However, you should recall that because of a four GB limitation on file size, the HX80 and HX90V can record only 20 minutes of MP4 video at a time in this high-quality HD format. So, if you need to record for a time longer than that in one sequence, you should choose the 1920 x 1080 30p 16M setting, which will still yield excellent quality and record for 29 minutes at a time.

MOVIE (EXPOSURE MODE)

This item on the Shooting menu can be selected only when the camera's Mode dial is set to Movie mode, as shown in Figure 8-6. In other shooting modes, this menu option cannot be selected.

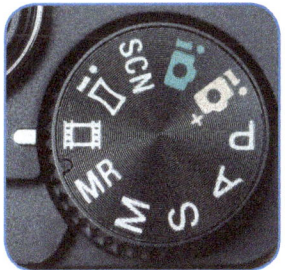

Figure 8-6. Mode Dial at Movie

When the camera is in Movie mode, the Movie option on the menu lets you select an exposure mode for shooting movies. If you have the Mode Dial Guide option turned on through screen 2 of the Setup menu, you won't need to use the Movie option when you first select the Movie mode. When you turn the Mode dial to the Movie position and then press the Center button, the screen with choices for the Movie item will appear automatically. If the Mode Dial Guide option is not active or if the Mode dial is already set to Movie mode, you get to this screen by selecting Movie from the Shooting menu.

With the Mode dial set to Movie mode, navigate to screen 6 of the Shooting menu, select the second item, Movie, and a screen will appear with four options: Program Auto, Aperture Priority, Shutter Priority, and Manual Exposure, as shown in Figure 8-7. Move through these choices by turning the Control wheel or by pressing the Up and Down buttons.

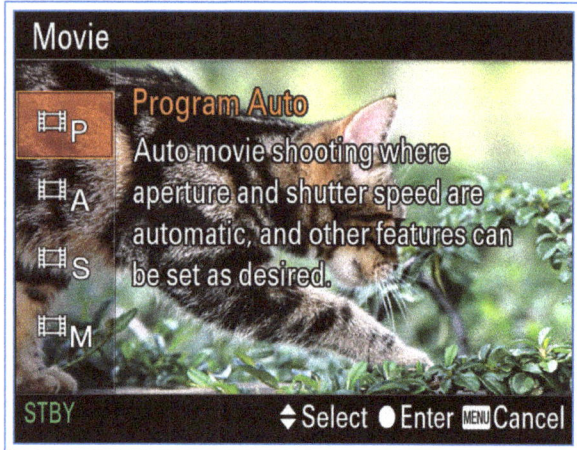

Figure 8-7. Movie Menu Options Screen

You also can call up this screen of options by assigning Shoot Mode to the Function menu using the Function Menu Settings option on the last screen of the Custom menu. If you do that, then, with the Mode dial set to Movie, you can press the Function button to activate the Function menu, scroll to the Shoot Mode item, and select your choice of Movie exposure mode. (The Shoot Mode item will be labeled Movie in the Function menu when the Mode dial is at the Movie position.)

Following are details about the behavior of these cameras when shooting movies with each of the Movie menu option settings.

Program Auto

With the Program Auto setting, which is highlighted in Figure 8-7, the camera sets aperture and shutter speed according to its metering, and it uses settings from the Shooting menu that carry over to video recording, including ISO, Metering Mode, White Balance, DRO, and Face Detection.

In this mode, the camera can set the aperture anywhere from f/3.5 to f/6.4, depending on the focal length, and it can use a shutter speed as fast as 1/12800 second,

much faster than the maximum for still photos. (Sony evidently determined not to let the camera use the smallest aperture setting of f/8.0 with this shooting mode.) The camera will normally not use a shutter speed slower than 1/30 second, 1/50 second, or 1/60 second, depending on the settings for File Format and Record Setting. It can use a slightly slower speed in most cases if you turn on the Auto Slow Shutter option, discussed later in this chapter.

Aperture Priority

With the Aperture Priority setting, shown in Figure 8-8, you can set the aperture, just as in the similar mode for still images, and the camera will set the shutter speed based on its metering.

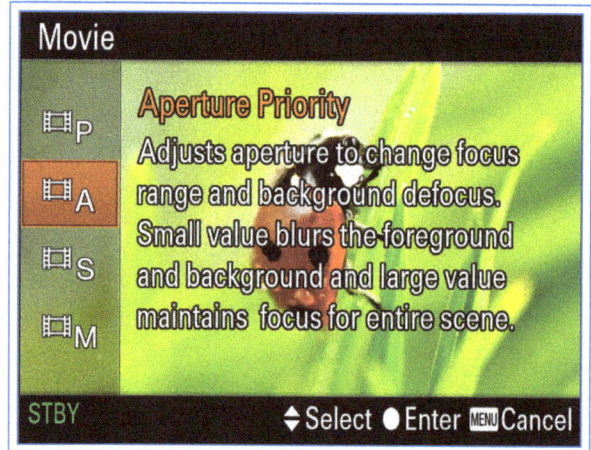

Figure 8-8. Aperture Priority Setting for Movie Mode

You can set the aperture anywhere from f/3.5 to the most narrow f/8.0, depending on the focal length setting of the lens. As with the Program Auto exposure mode for movies, discussed above, the camera will not use shutter speeds slower than those listed for that mode, unless you turn on the Auto Slow Shutter option.

With this setting, you can adjust the aperture during a video recording. This may not be something you need to do often, but it can be useful in some situations.

For example, you may be recording at a garden show, and at some point you may want to open the aperture wide to blur the background as you focus on a small plant. Afterward, you may want to close the aperture down to a narrow value to achieve a broad depth of field to keep a large area in focus.

Also, you can use aperture control to do a fadeout. For example, in indoor lighting you may start with aperture at f/3.5 and ISO at 200, with Auto Slow Shutter off. Press the Movie button to start recording. When you're ready, turn the Control wheel or Control ring (HX90V only, and only if Control ring is set to control aperture) to f/8.0. The scene should fade to black. In brighter light, you may need to reduce ISO to its minimum setting of 80.

Shutter Priority

With the Shutter Priority mode for movies, shown in Figure 8-9, you set the shutter speed and the camera will set the aperture.

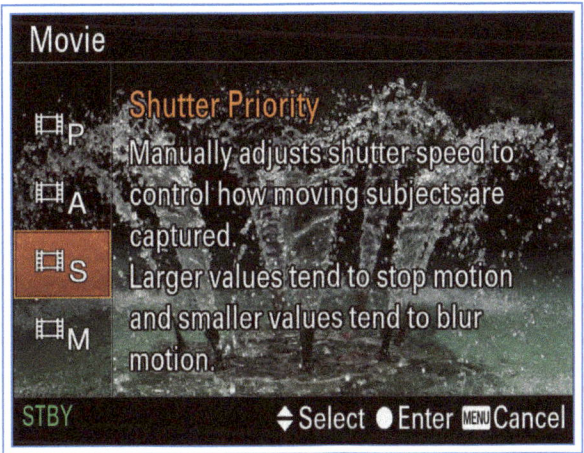

Figure 8-9. Shutter Priority Setting for Movie Mode

Unlike the situation with the Aperture Priority exposure mode for movies, in which the camera normally will not set the shutter speed slower than 1/30 second (or a higher value for some formats), you are able to set the shutter speed as slow as 1/4 second in this mode in most cases, even if Auto Slow Shutter is turned off. You can select a shutter speed from 1/4 second all the way to the maximum shutter speed for movies, which is 1/12800 second.

Of course, to expose your video normally at a shutter speed of 1/12800 second, you must have bright lighting, a high ISO setting, or both. Using a fast shutter speed for video can yield a crisper appearance, especially when there is considerable movement, as when shooting sports or other fast-moving events. In addition, having these very fast shutter speeds gives the camera flexibility for achieving a normal exposure when recording video in bright conditions.

With slower shutter speeds, particularly below the normal video speed of 1/30 second (equivalent to 30 fps), footage can become blurry with the appearance of smearing, especially with panning motions. If you are shooting a scene in which you want to have a drifting, dreamy appearance that looks like motion underwater, this option may be appropriate. You will not be able to achieve good lip sync at the slower shutter speeds, so this technique would not work well for realistic recordings of people talking or singing.

One interesting point is that you can preview this effect on the camera's display even before you press the Movie button to start recording. If you have the shutter speed set to 1/4 second in Movie mode, you will see any action on the screen looking blurry and jerky as if it had already been recorded with this slow shutter speed.

With the Shutter Priority exposure mode for movies, you also can achieve a fadeout effect, as with Aperture Priority mode, discussed above. Just turn the Control wheel or Control ring (HX90V only) smoothly to increase the shutter speed to its fastest speed of 1/12800 second, and the scene may go black, depending on the lighting conditions. You may need to set the ISO to 80 to achieve full darkness.

Manual Exposure

The last setting for the Movie menu item, shown in Figure 8-10, gives you more complete control over the exposure of your videos.

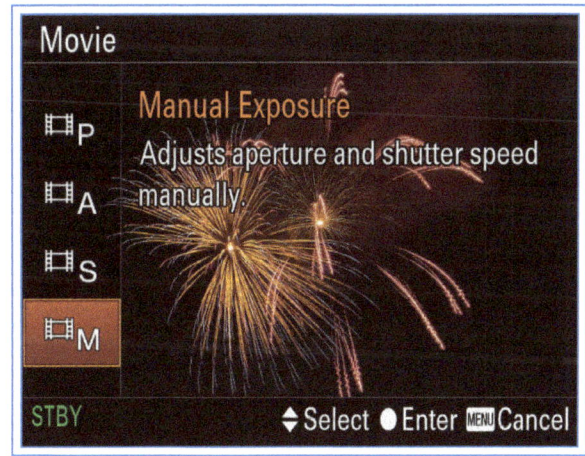

Figure 8-10. Manual Exposure Setting for Movie Mode

As with Manual exposure mode for stills, you can adjust both the aperture and the shutter speed to achieve your desired effect. With video shooting, you can adjust the aperture from f/3.5 to f/8.0, depending on the focal length set for the lens, and you can adjust the shutter speed from 1/12800 second to 1/4 second. Using these settings, you can create effects such as fades to and from black as well as similar fades to and from white.

For example, if you begin a recording in normal indoor lighting using settings of 1/60 second at f/3.5 with ISO set to 800, you can start recording the scene, and, when you want to fade out, start turning the Control wheel slowly to the right, increasing the shutter speed smoothly until it reaches 1/12800 second. (You may have to press the Down button to let the Control wheel control shutter speed.) Depending on how bright the lighting is, the result may be complete blackness. Of course, you can reverse this process to fade in from black.

If you want to fade to white, here is one possible scenario. Suppose you are recording video with shutter speed set to 1/400 second and aperture set to f/3.5 at ISO 3200. When you want to start a fade to white, make sure the Control wheel is setting shutter speed, and turn the Control wheel smoothly to the left until the shutter speed decreases all the way to 1/4 second. In fairly normal lighting conditions, as in my office as I write this, the result will be a fade to a bright white screen.

There are, of course, other uses for Manual Exposure mode when recording videos, such as shooting "day for night" footage, in which you underexpose the scene by using a fast shutter speed, narrow aperture, or both, to turn day into night for creative purposes. Also, you might want to use Manual Exposure mode when you are recording a scene in which the lighting may change, but you do not want the exposure settings to change. In other words, you may want some areas to remain dark and some to be unusually bright, rather than have the camera automatically adjust the exposure. In some cases, having a constant exposure setting can be preferable to having the scene's brightness change as the metering system adjusts the exposure.

Note that you can set ISO to Auto ISO with the Manual Exposure setting if you want. With the Auto ISO setting, you can maintain a constant aperture and shutter speed, but the camera will adjust exposure using the ISO setting to the extent that it can. You might want to use that setup if you need to maintain a narrow aperture to have a broad depth of field.

STEADYSHOT (MOVIES)

The SteadyShot item on the Shooting menu, highlighted in Figure 8-11, is labeled with a movie-film icon, meaning it applies only for recording movies.

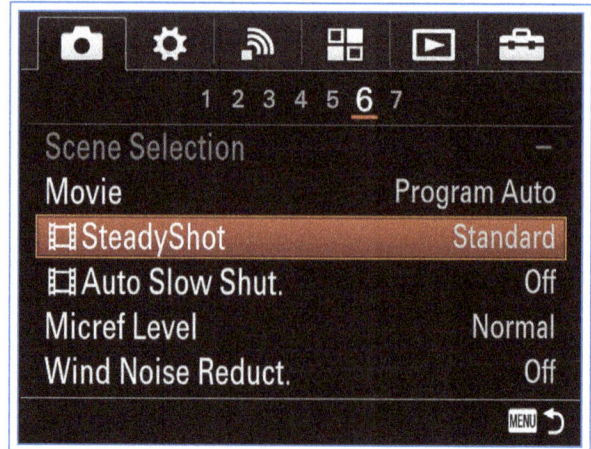

Figure 8-11. SteadyShot (Movies) Item Highlighted on Menu

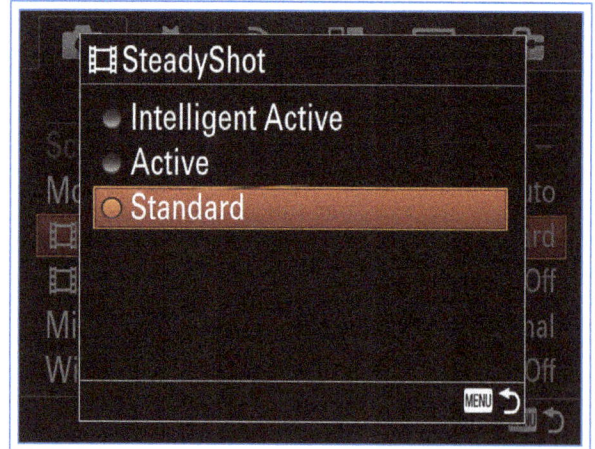

Figure 8-12. SteadyShot (Movies) Menu Options Screen

As shown in Figure 8-12, the SteadyShot (Movies) setting offers three options: Standard, Active, and Intelligent Active. If you select Standard, the camera uses an internal stabilization system that compensates for mild motions of the camera. If you select Active or Intelligent Active, the camera uses an additional stabilizing system that can compensate for unwanted camera movement to a greater extent.

With the Intelligent Active setting, the camera crops the video frame noticeably in order to process the stabilization, resulting in a reduced angle of view.

Figures 8-13 through 8-15 illustrate the cropping that results with the various settings of SteadyShot (Movies), using the same scene in each case. In Figure 8-13, SteadyShot (Movies) was set to Standard; in Figure 8-14 to Active; and in Figure 8-15 to Intelligent Active.

Chapter 8: Motion Pictures | 157

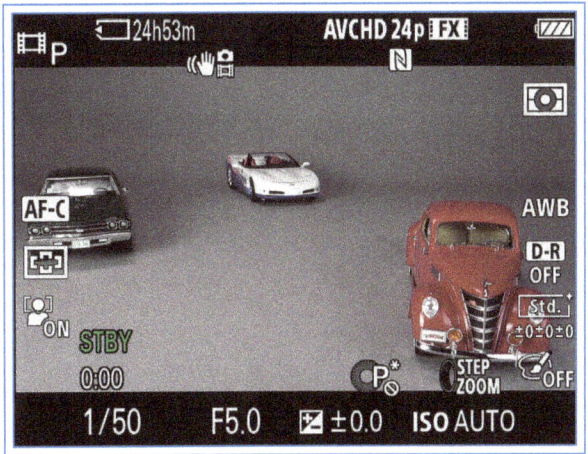

Figure 8-13. Framing Example: SteadyShot (Movies) Standard

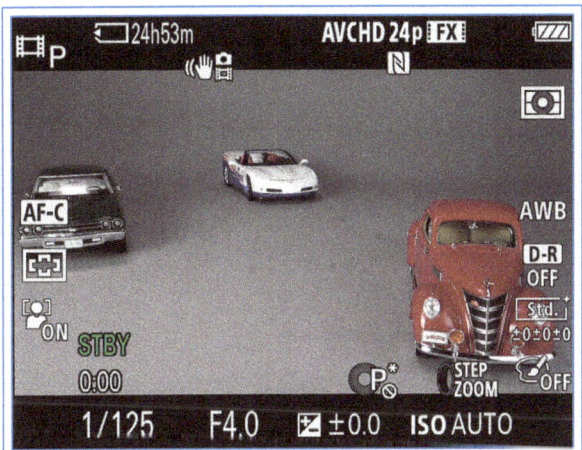

Figure 8-14. Framing Example: SteadyShot (Movies) Active

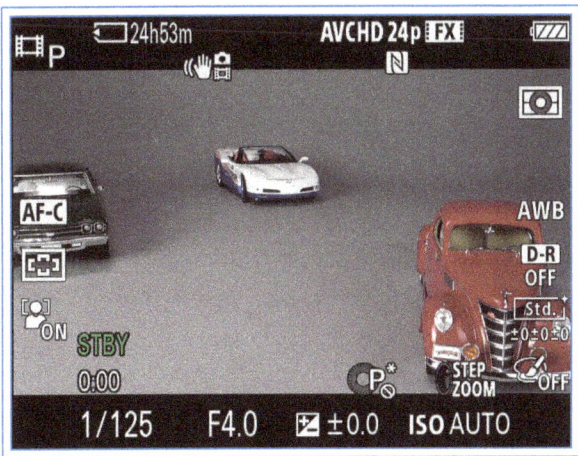

Figure 8-15. Framing Example: SteadyShot (Movies) Intelligent Active

As you can see, the Standard and Active settings do not crop the frame, but the Intelligent Active setting crops pixels from all four sides of the frame. I recommend using Standard or Active in most cases to avoid the cropping that comes from using the Intelligent Active setting. If you need to shoot movies when there is a great likelihood of camera movement, though, the Intelligent Active setting can be useful. It can be especially helpful if you need to hand-hold the camera as you walk.

AUTO SLOW SHUTTER

This next item on the Shooting menu can be turned either on or off, as shown in Figure 8-16. When this option is turned on and the camera is recording a movie using automatic exposure, it will automatically use a slower shutter speed than normal if the lighting is too dim to achieve a proper exposure otherwise.

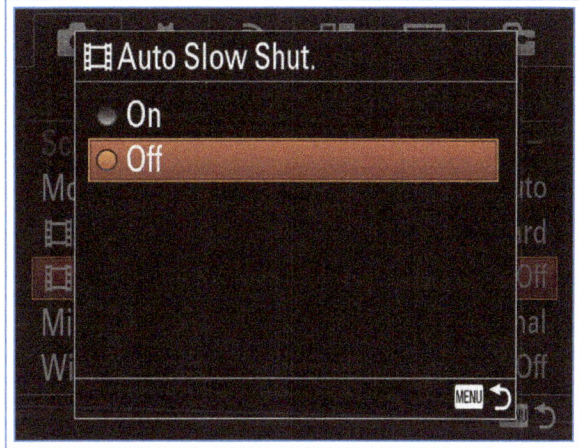

Figure 8-16. Auto Slow Shutter Menu Options Screen

The details of this option depend on the setting for Record Setting on screen 2 of the Shooting menu. (The File Format setting does not matter; the rules stated here apply for all File Format settings.)

If Record Setting is at a 60p or 60i setting, the camera normally will not use a shutter speed slower than 1/60 second. (This makes sense, because, in order to record 60 fields or frames per second with good quality, a shutter speed of 1/60 second is needed.) If Auto Slow Shutter is on, the camera can use a shutter speed as slow as 1/30 second.

If Record Setting is at one of the 30p settings, the camera ordinarily will use a shutter speed no slower than 1/30 second, but it will go down to 1/15 second with Auto Slow Shutter turned on.

If Record Setting is at one of the 24p settings, the camera ordinarily will use a shutter speed no slower than 1/50 second, but it will go down to 1/25 second with Auto Slow Shutter turned on.

Rather confusingly, the camera will let you turn on Auto Slow Shutter when the Mode dial is set to Movie and the Movie exposure mode is set to Shutter Priority or Manual Exposure. However, the setting you make for shutter speed will stay in place and the Auto Slow Shutter option will have no effect, even when the menu item is turned on. The same situation is true when the Mode dial is set to the Shutter Priority or Manual exposure mode for stills. You can shoot video in those modes while adjusting the shutter speed and you can turn on Auto Slow Shutter, but that setting will have no effect; the shutter speed you set will take priority.

In addition, for the Auto Slow Shutter option to work, ISO must be set to Auto ISO.

The use of an unusually slow shutter speed can produce a slurred or blurry appearance because the shutter speed may not be fast enough to keep up with the motion in the scene. But, if you are recording in a dark area, this option can help you achieve properly exposed footage, so it is worth considering in that situation.

Micref Level

The next movie-related option is Micref Level, the fifth item on screen 6 of the Shooting menu.

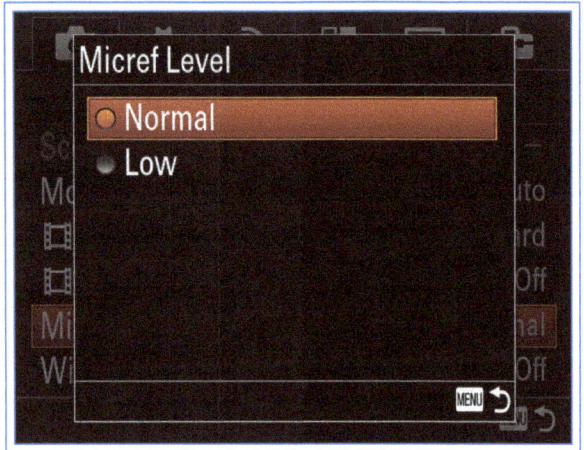

Figure 8-17. Micref Level Menu Options Screen

This option, whose screen is shown in Figure 8-17, can be set to Normal or Low.

This setting controls how the camera records audio for movies using its built-in stereo microphone. With Normal, the default setting, the camera uses an automatic gain control to boost the level of quiet sounds to an audible volume. However, it also boosts the level of ambient sounds from sources such as heating or air conditioning equipment. You might want to use this setting if you are recording a speech or a small, relatively quiet event, so the camera will not miss any important sounds.

The Low setting would be more appropriate when you are recording an event such as a concert, and you want to let the sound level vary according to the sound levels of the music without any artificial boosting or limiting.

Wind Noise Reduction

This option, if turned on, activates an electronic filter designed to reduce the volume of sounds in the low frequencies of wind noise. I recommend not activating this feature unless the wind is quite strong, because it limits the sounds that are recorded. With video (or audio) editing software, you can remove sounds in the frequencies that may cause problems for the sound track, but using the camera's built-in wind noise filter may permanently remove or alter some wanted sounds.

Effects of Mode Dial Position on Recording Movies

The second factor that affects video recording is the position of the Mode dial. As I discussed above, you can shoot movies with the dial in any position (if the Movie Button menu option is set that way), and you can get access to many movie-related menu items no matter what position the dial is in. However, as I noted above, the shooting mode does make some difference for your movie options.

First, the position you select on the Mode dial determines whether you can adjust the aperture and/or shutter speed for your movies. If the dial is set to the Intelligent Auto, Superior Auto, Scene, Program, or iSweep Panorama mode, the camera will set both aperture and shutter speed automatically. However, if the dial is set to the Aperture Priority, Shutter Priority, or Manual exposure position, you will be able to adjust the aperture, shutter speed, or both aperture and shutter speed, just as you can when shooting still images. The range of available shutter speeds is different for movies than for still images, but you can make these adjustments at any time.

You also can adjust aperture and/or shutter speed when the Mode dial is set to the Movie position and you select one of the more advanced exposure modes using the Movie item on the Shooting menu. For example, if you select Manual Exposure for the Movie menu item with the Mode dial at the Movie position, you can adjust both aperture and shutter speed for your movies, in the same way as if the Mode dial were set to the M position.

Because of the ability to adjust aperture and/or shutter speed while recording movies in the advanced still-shooting modes, you might wonder why you would ever use the Movie position on the dial—why not just set the dial to A, S, or M if you want to adjust aperture and/or shutter speed while recording a movie, or to P if you want the camera to set the aperture and shutter speed automatically?

The answer is that several options or settings are available only when the Mode dial is at the Movie position. For one thing, you will see how the video recording will be framed before you press the Movie button to start recording. If the Mode dial is at one of the still-oriented positions such as Auto, Scene, or one of the PASM modes, the display will show the live view according to the current setting for Aspect Ratio on screen 1 of the Shooting menu. If that setting is 3:2, 4:3, or 1:1, it will not correspond to the framing of the video, which will be recorded in a widescreen format, until you press the Movie button to start recording. (If Aspect Ratio is set to 16:9, the display will show approximately how the video framing will look before you press the Movie button.)

When the Mode dial is at the Movie position, the camera adjusts the live view to show how the video will look before you press the Movie button, so you will know before you start the recording how to set up the shot to include all of the needed background and foreground elements.

In addition, when the Mode dial is at the Movie position, you can take advantage of the Movie Button menu option on the Custom menu to restrict video recording to that one shooting mode. In this way, you can make it impossible to start a recording accidentally by pressing the Movie button when the Mode dial is set to a still-oriented mode such as Auto, Scene, or one of the PASM modes. If that setting is turned on, you will need to turn the Mode dial to the Movie position in order to record a video.

Moreover, the Marker Display option on the Custom menu can be selected in any shooting mode, but any marker you have selected for display will not appear in still-oriented modes until you actually start recording. When the Mode dial is at the Movie position, you will see the marker on the display before the recording starts, so you can set up your composition ahead of time.

Also, the camera's shooting mode has an effect on what options are available on the Shooting menu and with the control buttons, as discussed in following sections of this chapter. For example, if the Mode dial is set to either Auto setting, iSweep Panorama, or Scene, the Shooting menu options are limited. If the Mode dial is set to Program, Aperture Priority, Shutter Priority, or Manual exposure, the options are greater. This point is important for video shooting because, as discussed below, several important Shooting menu options carry over to movie recording.

If the camera is set to Program mode (P on the Mode dial), you can make several settings that will control the recording of videos while the Mode dial is in that position. The camera will set the aperture and shutter speed automatically, as it does with still-image shooting. You can use exposure compensation to vary the exposure, but only within the range of plus or minus 2.0 EV, instead of the 3.0-EV positive or negative range for still shooting.

If the camera is set to Aperture Priority mode (A on the Mode dial), you will have the same Shooting menu options as in Program mode, and you can also set the aperture. The camera will set the shutter speed automatically, but the range of available shutter speeds will be somewhat different than for still images. That range is partly determined by the Record Setting option selected and the setting of the Auto Slow Shutter menu option, as discussed earlier in this chapter.

If the camera is set to Shutter Priority mode (S on the mode dial), you will have the same Shooting menu options as in Program mode, and you can also set the shutter speed. In this case, you can set the shutter speed anywhere from 1/4 second (the camera's slowest setting for movies) to 1/12800 second (the camera's fastest setting for movies), regardless of the Record Setting or Auto Slow Shutter settings.

If the camera is set to Manual exposure mode (M on the mode dial), you will have the same Shooting menu options as before and you can set both shutter speed and aperture, with the same range for shutter speed settings noted above for Shutter Priority mode.

If the camera is set to iSweep Panorama mode, it will act largely as if it were set to Movie mode with the Program Auto exposure mode selected. If it is set to Scene mode, it will shoot movies as if it were set to Intelligent Auto mode, in which limited menu options are available. It will not recognize any specific scene settings, such as Portrait, Advanced Sports Shooting, or Sunset.

There is a lot of information involved in outlining the differences in the HX80 and HX90V's behavior for video recording in different shooting modes, so I am including below a table that lays out the more important differences, for reference.

Table 8-1. Behavior of Camera When Recording Movies in Various Shooting Modes

SHOOTING MODE:	AUTO	SCENE	PANORAMA	MOVIE	M	S	A	P
ADJUST APERTURE DURING VIDEO RECORDING	No	No	No	YES, DEPENDING ON MOVIE MENU OPTION SETTING	YES	No	YES	No
ADJUST SHUTTER SPEED DURING VIDEO RECORDING	No	No	No	YES, DEPENDING ON MOVIE MENU OPTION SETTING	YES	YES	No	No
SEE VIDEO FRAMING BEFORE RECORDING STARTS	No	No	No	YES	No	No	No	No
SEE MARKER DISPLAY ITEMS BEFORE RECORDING STARTS	No	No	No	YES	No	No	No	No
CAN RECORD VIDEO IF MOVIE BUTTON MENU OPTION IS SET TO MOVIE MODE ONLY	No	No	No	YES	No	No	No	No

Effects of Other Shooting Menu Settings on Recording Movies

There are other Shooting menu options that have an effect on movie recording, beyond the options discussed above that are applicable only to movie recording, including File Format, Record Setting, Auto Slow Shutter, and the others discussed earlier in this chapter.

One of the main reasons the shooting mode is important for movies is that, just as with still photography, some menu options are not available in some shooting modes. For example, in an advanced still-shooting mode such as Aperture Priority or Program, video recording will be affected by such settings as Focus Mode (HX90V only), Focus Area, Exposure Compensation, ISO, Metering Mode, White Balance, DRO, Creative Style, Picture Effect, Focus Magnifier (HX90V only), Center Lock-on AF, and Face Detection, among others.

In some cases, you can adjust these settings while the video is being recorded. You cannot get access to the Shooting menu by pressing the Menu button; you have to use a control button or the Control ring (HX90V only) to call up the item to adjust. Of course, you have to have that setting assigned to the button or ring ahead of time.

For example, you can adjust ISO while recording a video, but only if ISO is assigned to the Control ring (HX90V only) or one of the control buttons using the Custom Key Settings menu option on the Custom menu, or to the Function menu. Table 8-2 shows which of these settings can be adjusted while a video recording is in progress.

Table 8-2. SHOOTING MENU ITEMS THAT AFFECT MOVIES, AND ITEMS THAT CAN BE ADJUSTED DURING VIDEO RECORDING

SHOOTING MENU ITEM	CAN ADJUST DURING VIDEO RECORDING
FILE FORMAT	No
RECORD SETTING	No
FOCUS MODE (HX90V ONLY)	YES
FOCUS AREA	NO (DOES NOT AFFECT MOVIE RECORDING)
EXPOSURE COMPENSATION	YES
ISO	YES
METERING MODE	No
WHITE BALANCE	No
DRO/AUTO HDR	No
CREATIVE STYLE	No
PICTURE EFFECT	No

FOCUS MAGNIFIER (HX90V ONLY)	YES
CENTER LOCK-ON AF	YES
SMILE/FACE DETECTION	NO
MOVIE (SHOOT MODE)	NO
STEADYSHOT (MOVIES)	NO
AUTO SLOW SHUTTER	NO
MICREF LEVEL	NO
WIND NOISE REDUCTION	NO

There are built-in limitations with some of these settings. Focus Mode, available only on the HX90V, can be set to continuous autofocus or manual focus only. Focus Area does not affect movie recording at all; it is automatically set to Wide once a recording starts. Exposure compensation can be adjusted to plus or minus 2.0 EV only, rather than the 3.0 EV range for still images. You cannot set ISO to Multi Frame Noise Reduction, which would cause the camera to take multiple shots. With Picture Effect, you can use some of the sub-settings, but you cannot use Soft Focus, HDR Painting, Rich-tone Monochrome, Miniature, Watercolor, or Illustration. (As noted on the table, you cannot get access to the Picture Effect settings during video recording.)

There are some other options on the Shooting menu that have no effect for recording movies. Some of these settings are clearly incompatible with shooting movies, such as Drive Mode, Flash Mode, and Auto Object Framing. Some are less obvious, including AF Illuminator and Scene Selection.

There are two other points to make about using Shooting menu settings for movies. First, you have a great deal of flexibility in choosing settings for your movies, even when the camera is not set to the Movie position on the Mode dial. You can set up the camera with the ISO, Metering Mode, White Balance, Creative Style, Picture Effect (to some extent), or other settings of your choice, and then press the Movie button to record using those settings. In this way, you could, for example, record a black-and-white movie in a dark environment using a high ISO setting. Or, you could record a movie that is monochrome except for a broad selection of red objects, using the Partial Color-Red effect from the Picture Effect option, with the red color expanded using the color axis adjustments of the White Balance setting. (Note that you can't use Creative Style and Picture Effect settings at the same time.)

Second, you have to be careful to check the settings that are in effect for still photos before you press the Movie button. For example, if you have been shooting stills using the Posterization setting from the Picture Effect menu option and then suddenly see an event that you want to record on video, if you press the Movie button, the movie will be recorded using the Posterization effect, making the resulting footage practically impossible to use as a clear record of the events. Of course, you may notice this problem as you record the video, but it takes time to stop the recording, change the menu setting to turn off the Picture Effect option, and then press the Movie button again, and you may have missed a crucial part of the action by the time you start recording again.

One way to lessen the risk of recording video with unwanted Shooting menu options is to switch the Mode dial to the Intelligent Auto position before pressing the Movie button. That action will cause the camera to use more automatic settings and will disable the Creative Style and Picture Effect options altogether. (Of course, you have to have the Movie Button item on the Custom menu set to Always for this approach to work.)

Effects of Physical Controls When Recording Movies

The next settings that carry over to some extent from still-shooting to video recording are those set by the physical controls. In this case, as with Shooting menu items, there are differences depending on the position of the Mode dial. I will not try to describe every possible combination of shooting mode and physical control, but I will discuss some settings to be aware of.

First, you can use the exposure compensation button while recording movies when the Mode dial is set to the P, A, S, M, Movie, or Sweep Panorama setting. Exposure compensation is not available during video recording in the Auto or Scene modes. The range of exposure compensation for movies is plus or minus 2.0 EV, rather than the plus or minus 3.0 EV for still images. If you set exposure compensation to a value greater than 2.0 (plus or minus), the camera will set it back to 2.0 after you press the red Movie button to start shooting a movie.

Second, the Function button operates normally. For example, if the Mode dial is set to P for Program mode, then, after you press the Movie button to start recording a movie, you can press the Function button and the Function menu will appear on the screen. This menu will let you control only those items that can be controlled under current conditions, as seen in Figure 8-18.

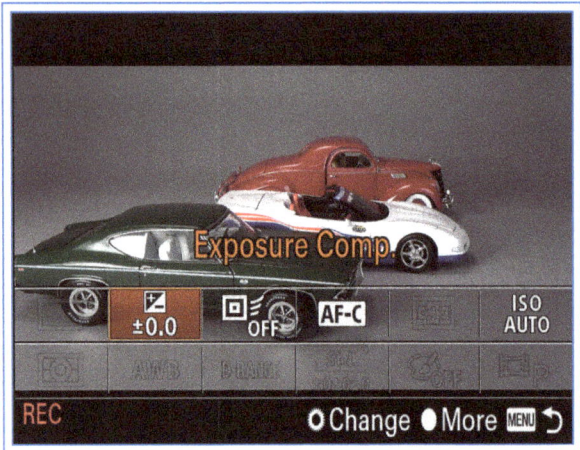

Figure 8-18. Function Menu During Movie Recording

If you start recording a movie while the Mode dial is set to a mode such as Intelligent Auto in which most options on the Function menu are not available, the camera will display the menu, but few items can be selected, as shown in Figure 8-19.

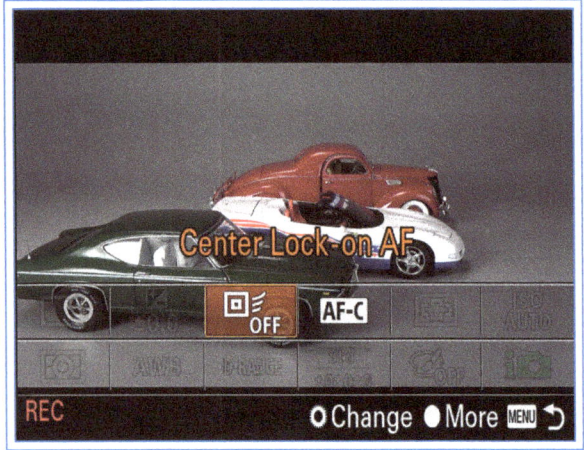

Figure 8-19. Function Menu During Video Recording - Intelligent Auto Mode

Third, if you assign the Center, Left, Right, Down, or In-Camera Guide button or the Control ring (HX90V only) to carry out a particular operation using the Custom Key Settings option on the Custom menu, you can use that control to perform the operation while recording a movie if the action is compatible with movie recording in the current shooting mode.

(HX90V only) For the Control ring, the functions that can be assigned and controlled during video recording are exposure compensation, ISO, zoom, shutter speed, and aperture. Although White Balance, Creative Style, or Picture Effect can be assigned to the ring and controlled before the recording starts, those listed above are the only items that can be controlled by the ring during the recording.

In addition, there are numerous options that can be assigned to a control button that will function during video recording, if the current context permits that control. For example, if the Left button is set to control ISO and you are shooting a movie with the Mode dial set to P, pressing the Left button will bring up the ISO menu and you can select a value while the movie is recording. If the Mode dial is set to Intelligent Auto, though, pressing the button will have no effect during recording, because ISO cannot be adjusted in that shooting mode.

If the Center button is assigned its Standard setting through the Custom Key Settings menu option and Center Lock-on AF is turned on through the Shooting menu, you can press the Center button during video recording to activate tracking focus. Of course, with the HX90V, to use tracking focus, the camera has to have an autofocus mode selected using the Focus Mode menu option. (The HX80 always uses autofocus.)

Following is a list of functions that can be assigned to one of the control buttons and that can be controlled during video recording by pressing the button:

- Standard
- Self-timer During Bracketing
- Focus Mode (HX90V only)
- Exposure Compensation
- ISO
- Center Lock-on AF
- Focus Magnifier (HX90V only)
- Movie (acting as red Movie button)
- Zebra
- Grid Line
- Marker Display Selection

- Peaking Level (HX90V only)
- Peaking Color (HX90V only)

The Self-timer During Bracketing option is not useful for video recording, but Sony for some reason has made that item available for use with an assigned button during movie recording, so I have included it on the list.

Some more notes about physical controls: Program Shift does not function during video recording. If you turn the Control wheel (or Control ring on the HX90V when it is set to Standard) while the camera is set to Program mode, the exposure settings will not change while the camera is recording a movie. The Photo Creativity feature, described in Chapter 2, does not work during movie recording. Also, of course, a function assigned to a control will not operate unless the context permits. For example, Peaking Level and Peaking Color will work only if manual focus is in use, and Marker Display Selection will work only if one or more of the Marker Settings options have been turned on.

Summary of Options for Recording Movies

As I have discussed, there is some complication in trying to explain all of the relationships among the controls and settings of the HX80 and HX90V for recording movies. To cut through that complication, I will provide a summary of your options for recording movies with the HX80 and HX90V.

To record a video clip with standard settings, set the Mode dial to the Intelligent Auto or Scene position and press the Movie button. With the HX80, the camera will adjust exposure and focus automatically. With the HX90V, the camera will adjust exposure automatically, and you can use either continuous autofocus (set in this mode using the AF-S setting for Focus Mode) or manual focus (MF setting).

In those shooting modes, you cannot adjust many shooting options, such as ISO, White Balance, DRO, Creative Style, or Picture Effect. You can use options such as Center Lock-on AF, Face Detection, and SteadyShot (Movies). You can choose File Format and Record Settings options to control the video quality.

For more control over video shooting, set the Mode dial to the P, A, S, or M position. Then you can control several additional Shooting menu options, including ISO, White Balance, Metering Mode, Creative Style, and Picture Effect, among others. With the HX90V, you can choose autofocus or manual focus in the same way as for the more automatic shooting modes. With either camera model, you can adjust aperture, shutter speed, or both, or let the camera set them, depending on which shooting mode you select.

For maximum control over movie recording, set the Mode dial to the movie-film icon for Movie mode. Then select an option for the movie exposure mode from the Movie item on the Shooting menu. To control aperture, choose Aperture Priority; to control shutter speed, choose Shutter Priority; to control both aperture and shutter speed, choose Manual Exposure. Other options can be selected from the Shooting menu.

Control buttons operate during movie recording if the context permits, as discussed earlier. There are many possibilities for assigning settings to them. If you want a good set of functions tailored for video recording, use the list in Table 8-3 to start, and adjust it for your own needs:

Table 8-3. SUGGESTED CONTROL ASSIGNMENTS FOR MOVIE RECORDING

CONTROL	FUNCTION
CONTROL RING (HX90V)	ISO
CENTER BUTTON	STANDARD
LEFT BUTTON	FOCUS MODE (HX90V)/CENTER LOCK-ON AF
RIGHT BUTTON	FOCUS MAGNIFIER (HX90V)/MARKER DISPLAY SEL.
DOWN BUTTON	EXPOSURE COMPENSATION
IN-CAMERA GUIDE BUTTON	ZEBRA

If you want the HX80 or HX90V to be ready to record good, standard video footage at a moment's notice without having to remember a lot of settings, I recommend that you set up one of the three registers of the Memory Recall shooting mode with a solid set of movie-recording settings. Table 8-4 lists one set of settings to consider. (Settings not listed here can be set however you like.)

Table 8-4. SUGGESTED SHOOTING MENU SETTINGS FOR RECORDING MOVIES IN MOVIE MODE

FILE FORMAT	AVCHD
RECORD SETTING	60P 28M (PS)
FOCUS MODE (HX90V ONLY)	AF-C
ISO	ISO AUTO
METERING MODE	MULTI

Table 8-4. Suggested Shooting Menu Settings for Recording Movies in Movie Mode

White Balance	Auto White Balance
DRO/Auto HDR	Auto
Creative Style	Standard
Picture Effect	Off
Center Lock-on AF	On
Smile/Face Detection	On
Movie	Program Auto
SteadyShot (Movies)	Standard
Auto Slow Shutter	Off
Micref Level	Normal
Wind Noise Reduction	Off

Other Settings and Controls for Movies

There are several other points to be made about recording videos that don't concern the Shooting menu. Here are brief notes about these issues.

(HX90V only) The Step Zoom function is not available for video recording, even if the Zoom Function on Ring option is set to Step on the last screen of the Custom menu. The zoom operates continuously for movies. (Actually, if Zoom Function on Ring is set to Step, the camera will display the Step Zoom scale, but the zoom will operate continuously during video recording despite the presence of the scale on the screen.)

The Display button operates normally to change the information that is viewed during video recording. The screens that are displayed are controlled by the Display Button option on the Custom menu. However, the For Viewfinder screen does not appear for video shooting, even if it was selected through that menu option.

In playback mode, when the first frame of a movie is displayed before playback has started, the Display button operates normally for movies. The screen with space for a histogram will display, but the spaces for histogram and other information will be blank.

(HX90V only) The MF Assist option on screen 1 of the Custom menu does not operate for video recording, so the camera will not magnify the display when you turn the Control ring to adjust manual focus. However, you can assign the Focus Magnifier function to one of the control buttons and use that capability to enlarge the screen when using manual focus. After you press the assigned control button to put the orange frame on the display, press the Center button to enlarge the area within the frame to 4.0 times normal. (This is less than the 7.7x and 15.3x enlargement factors for still shooting.) Then turn the Control ring to adjust the focus. Half-press the shutter button to dismiss the Focus Magnifier frame.

Movie Playback

As with still images, you can transfer movies to a computer for editing and playback or play them back from the camera, either on the camera's display or on a TV connected to the camera.

If you want to play your movies in the camera, there is one basic point to be mindful of. As I discussed in Chapter 6, the View Mode option on screen 1 of the Playback menu controls what images or videos you will see in playback mode. If you don't see the video you are looking for, check to make sure this menu option is set to display all files from a certain date (Date View), Folder View (MP4), AVCHD View, or XAVC S HD View.

Once you have selected the proper mode to view your video, navigate to that file by pressing the direction buttons or turning the Control wheel. When the first frame of the selected video is displayed on the screen, you will see a playback triangle inside a circle, as shown in Figure 8-20. In the lower right corner of the screen will be a Play prompt with a white circle icon indicating that you can press the Center button to play the video. (If you don't see that prompt, press the Display button one or more times until it appears.)

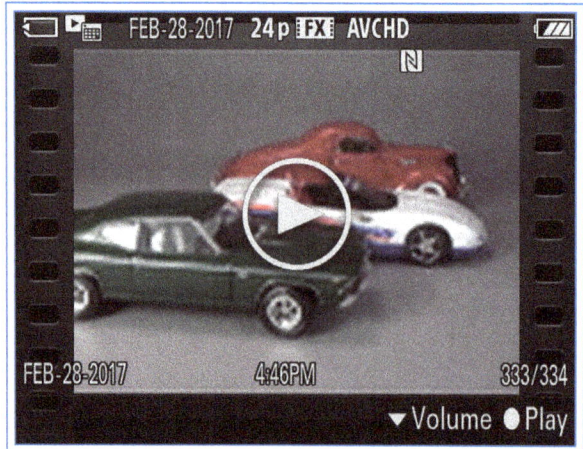

Figure 8-20. Movie Ready to Play in Camera

After you press the Center button to start playback, you will see more icons at the bottom of the screen, as in Figure 8-21. From the left, these icons indicate: Rewind/Fast Forward; Pause; Open Control Panel; and Exit.

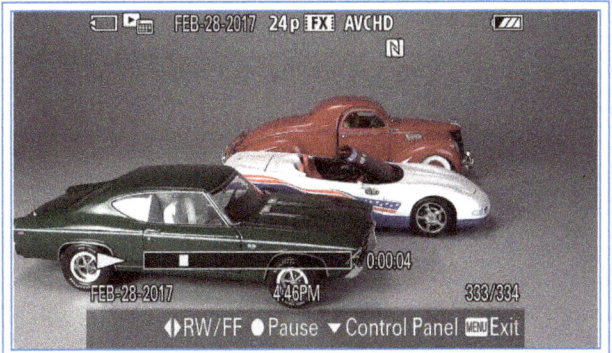

Figure 8-21. Initial Movie Playback Controls

From this screen, you can press the Left or Right button repeatedly to play the movie rapidly forward or backward; multiple presses increase the speed up to four times.

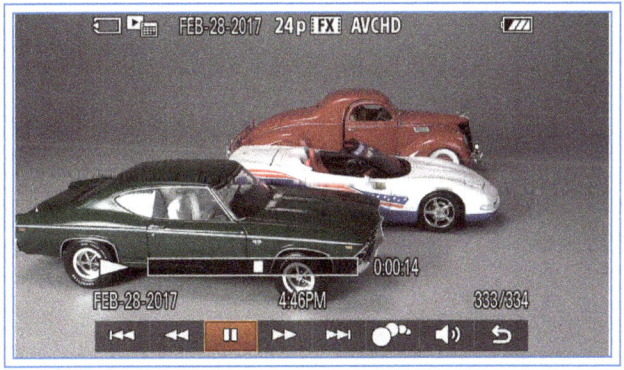

Figure 8-22. Detailed Movie Playback Controls While Playing

While the video is playing, if you press the Down button, you will see a new line of controls at the bottom of the screen, as seen in Figure 8-22.

When the movie is playing, these icons indicate, from left to right: Previous Movie; Fast Reverse; Pause; Fast Forward; Next Movie; Motion Shot; Volume; and Close Control Panel.

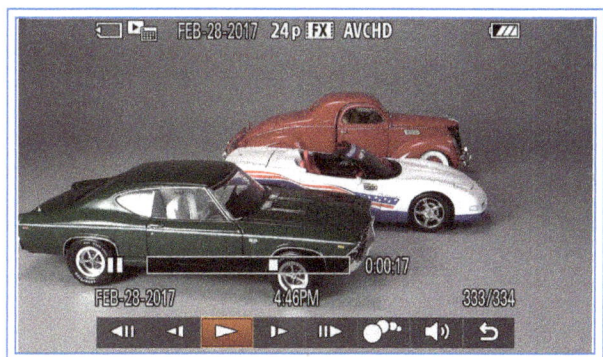

Figure 8-23. Detailed Movie Playback Controls While Paused

When the movie is paused, the icons change, as in Figure 8-23. Those icons indicate, from left to right: Previous Frame; Reverse Slow; Normal Playback; Forward Slow; Next Frame; Motion Shot; Volume; and Close Control Panel.

In either case, move through the icons with the Left and Right buttons, and press the Center button to select the function for that icon.

When a movie is playing, you can fast-forward or fast-reverse through a video at increasing speeds by turning the Control wheel right or left or by pressing the Right or Left button.

MOTION SHOT FEATURE

The icon on the movie playback control panel that is a series of shrinking circles represents the Motion Shot feature. With this option, you can slow down the playback of a movie and display a motion sequence as a series of multiple exposures on the camera's screen, or on a TV screen if you have the camera connected to one.

This feature works only with AVCHD and MP4 movies, not with movies recorded in the XAVC S HD format. To use the feature, let the movie play up to the point where you want to start the effect. For example, suppose you recorded some children playing basketball. You could play the movie up to the point where a child shoots the ball toward the basket. At that point, or just before it, use the Right button to scroll to the Motion Shot icon, highlight it, and press the Center button to select it.

The camera will then play back the video as a series of multiple exposures tracing the path of the object in motion. For example, Figure 8-24 shows how this feature processed a video sequence of a basketball shot.

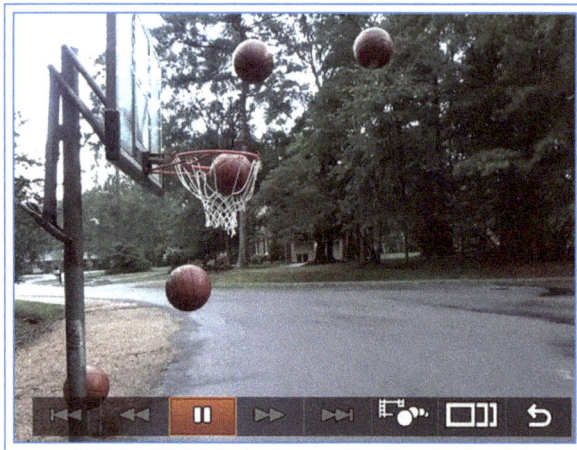

Figure 8-24. Motion Shot Example

If the images of the moving object overlap too closely on your first attempt, you can make an adjustment using the Motion Interval Adjustment option. On the video control panel, once you have selected the Motion Shot icon, the line of icons will change, as shown at the bottom of Figure 8-25. The Motion Shot icon will change to an icon for exiting the Motion Shot mode, which looks like a smaller version of the Motion Shot icon.

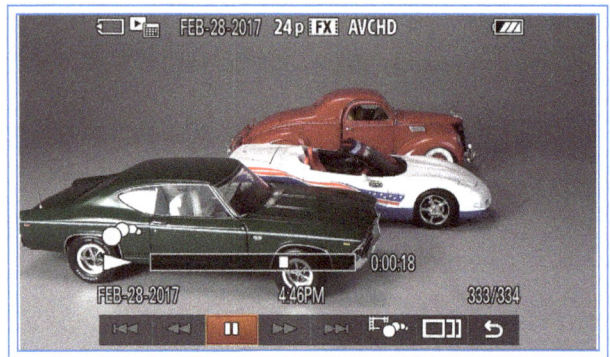

Figure 8-25. Movie Playback Icons After Selecting Motion Shot

The icon to the right of that one, which looks like a set of rectangular frames, lets you adjust the interval between the images. Select that icon and adjust the scale to a lower number to place the images closer together and to a higher number to place them farther apart. You also can adjust the interval using the Motion Interval Adjustment option on screen 2 of the Playback menu.

You cannot save the results of your work with the Motion Shot feature unless you connect the camera to a video capture device using an HDMI cable, as I did for Figure 8-24. I view this feature as an interesting novelty that lets you examine the path of an object in motion in some detail. It might be helpful for checking your golf swing or for adding interest to a video demonstration.

Editing Movies

The HX80 and HX90V cameras cannot edit movies in the camera. (At least, not with the options that come with the camera. It may be that an application will be developed for in-camera movie editing in the future.) If you want to do any editing, you will have to do it with a computer. For Windows, you can use software such as Windows Movie Maker. If you are using a Mac, you can use iMovie or any other movie editing software that can deal with MP4 and AVCHD files, and with XAVC S HD files, if you record movies using that formats. I use Adobe Premiere Pro CC on my Mac, and it handles all of these file types well.

You also can use the PlayMemories Home software that is available for free from Sony for use with these cameras. To install PlayMemories Home on your computer, you need to download the software from the internet. at http://www.sony.net/pm. This software is updated with new features periodically, so be sure to keep checking the website for updates.

One issue you may encounter when first starting to edit movie files from these cameras is finding the files. When you insert a memory card into a card reader, the still images are easy to find; on my computer, the SD card shows up as No Name or Untitled; then, beneath that level, there is a folder called DCIM; inside it are folders with names such as 100MSDCF, which contain the still images. (If you use the Folder Name option on the Setup menu to select Date Form, the folder names will be based on dates the images were taken; an example is 10070215 for images taken on February 15, 2017.)

The movie files are a bit trickier to find. The XAVC S HD files that you need to find and import into your software for editing have an .mp4 extension, but they are not the same as the more ordinary .mp4 files. Here is the path to a sample XAVC S HD file: Untitled\Private\M4ROOT\CLIP\C0007.MP4.

Here is the path to an AVCHD movie file: Untitled\Private\AVCHD\BDMV\Stream\0006.MTS. These files can be difficult to find on a Macintosh, because the Finder may not immediately show the contents of the AVCHD folder. You may have to right-click on the AVCHD item in the Finder and select Show Package Contents in order to view the BDMV folder. You may have to repeat that process to see the contents of the BDMV folder.

Here is the path to an ordinary MP4 movie file: Untitled\MP_ROOT\100ANV01\MAH00180.MP4.

You can avoid the complications of finding the movie files on a memory card by connecting the camera to your computer using the USB cable. Most video-editing software should detect the camera and import the movie files automatically, ready for you to edit them.

Also, with the HX80 and HX90V, you can transfer your files to your computer using the Wi-Fi capabilities that are built into the camera, as discussed in Chapter 9.

Chapter 9: Wi-Fi, Applications, and Other Topics

Connections Using Wi-Fi and NFC

The HX80 and HX90V can connect to computers, smartphones, and tablets using a Wi-Fi network. As noted in Chapter 1, you can transfer images and videos wirelessly using an Eye-Fi card or other memory card that includes Wi-Fi connectivity, but having Wi-Fi circuitry built into the camera gives you features that are not available with a card. Also, with some devices, the HX80 and HX90V can use NFC technology to establish a Wi-Fi connection without going through the steps that are ordinarily required. In this section, I will describe these features and give examples of how you can use them.

First, here is one note to remember when using any of the camera's Wi-Fi features: The Wi-Fi menu has an option called Airplane Mode near the bottom of its first screen. If that option is turned on, no Wi-Fi features will work. Make sure that menu setting is turned off when setting out to use the Wi-Fi options.

Sending Images to a Computer

Although you can edit and print images and edit videos to some extent using a smartphone or tablet, the easiest way to work with them is to transfer them to a computer. The traditional ways to do this are to connect the camera to the computer with the camera's USB cable or to use a memory card reader. However, there are two methods you can use to transfer your images and videos to a computer over a wireless network, eliminating the need to use a USB connection or a card reader.

First, as discussed in Chapter 1, you can use an Eye-Fi card or a similar memory card with the capability to transfer your files wirelessly to the computer. This system works well, but it requires the purchase and use of this special type of memory card.

The other approach for wireless transfer is to use the Wi-Fi capability built into the camera. Once you have the camera and computer set up to communicate over a wireless network, you can use the Send to Computer menu option to transfer images and videos from the camera's memory card over that network, regardless of what type of memory card is installed. Here are the steps to set up the camera and computer:

1. Install Sony PlayMemories Home software on the computer. The software can be downloaded for Windows-based or Macintosh computers at http://www.sony.net/pm/.

2. Run the software you downloaded in Step 1. Follow the program's prompts to connect the camera to the computer using the camera's USB cable, and select the option to designate this computer to receive images from the camera. (That step needs to be done only once, unless you later switch to a different computer.)

3. On a Macintosh, after starting PlayMemories Home, from the PlayMemories Home menu at the top of the screen, select Preferences, then Wireless Auto Import, and follow the prompts, including connecting the camera to the computer using its USB cable. Set the USB Connection item on the camera's Setup menu to Auto. After the software displays a message saying the computer has been set to receive images from camera wirelessly, eject the camera from the computer and disconnect the USB cable.

4. On a computer using Windows, start by turning on the camera and connecting it to the computer with the USB cable. Then start PlayMemories Home. At the left side of the program's screen, select the name of the camera, then select the option to the right for Wi-Fi Import Settings, and follow the

Chapter 9: Wi-Fi, Applications, and Other Topics | 169

prompts to set this camera as the one to receive files by Wi-Fi. When this process is complete, disconnect the camera from the computer.

5. When you are ready to transfer files, make sure the camera is within range of a wireless access point, also known as a Wi-Fi router. Normally, this will be a private, secured network at your home or office.

6. If the router has a button labeled WPS (Wi-Fi–protected setup), use that button to connect the camera to the network. Select the WPS Push option on the second screen of the Wi-Fi menu, and the camera will display the screen in Figure 9-1.

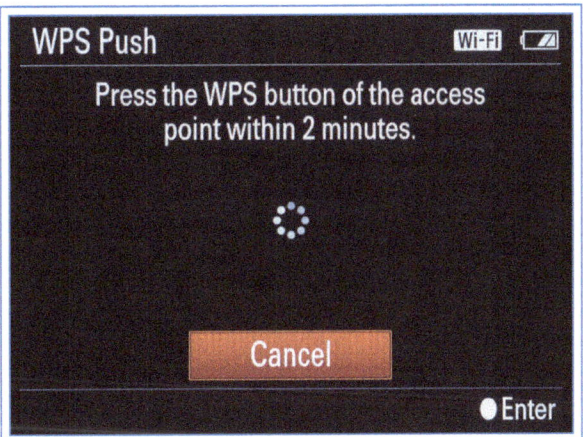

Figure 9-1. Camera Screen After Selecting WPS Push

7. Within two minutes, press the WPS button on the router. Figure 9-2 shows an example of that sort of button.

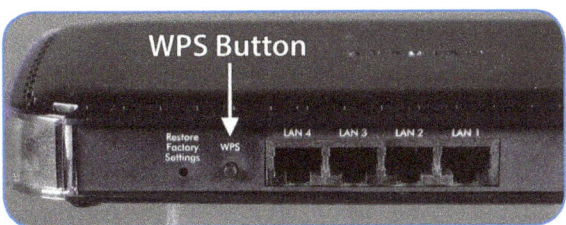

Figure 9-2. WPS Button on Router

8. If the setup is successful, the camera will display a message saying the access point has been registered. Proceed to Step 12.

–or–

If the router does not have a WPS button, or if pushing the button does not work, go to Step 9.

9. Locate the name of the network and its password. (This information may be on a label on the router or modem.)

10. Select the Access Point Settings option on the second screen of the Wi-Fi menu, as shown in Figure 9-3.

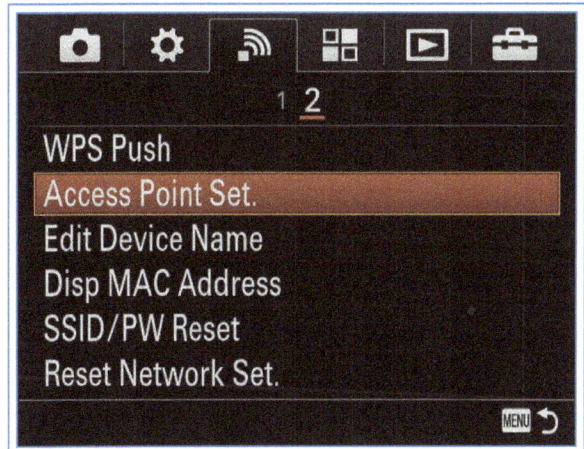

Figure 9-3. Access Point Settings Highlighted on Wi-Fi Menu

11. If the name of your network appears on the camera's screen, as shown in Figure 9-4 enter the network's password, as shown in Figure 9-5 The camera will display a virtual keyboard to let you enter the necessary characters.

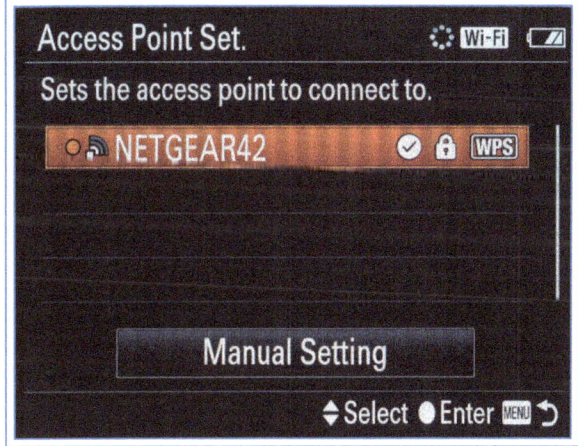

Figure 9-4. Network Name on Camera Screen

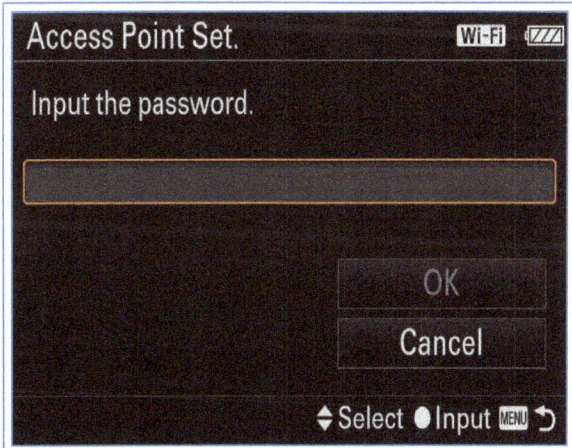

Figure 9-5. Screen to Enter Network Password

–or–

If the access point does not appear on the camera's screen, enter its SSID (network ID), using the Manual Setting option on the menu screen, as shown in Figure 9-6, and then enter the network's password, as shown in Figure 9-5.

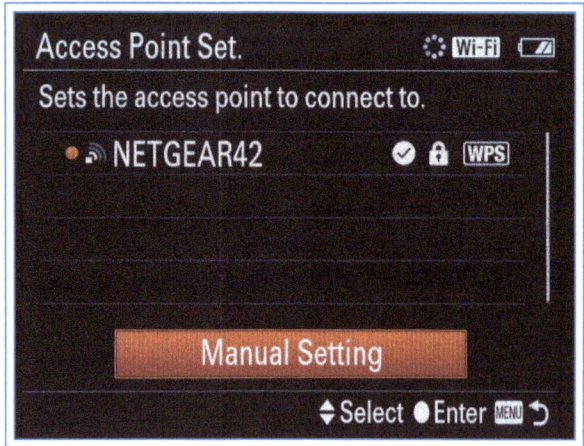

Figure 9-6. Manual Setting Option Highlighted on Menu

12. On the Wi-Fi menu select Send to Computer, as shown in Figure 9-7.

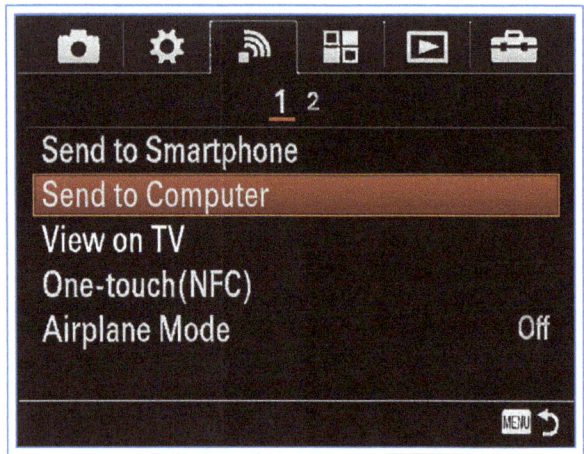

Figure 9-7. Send to Computer Highlighted on Menu

13. The camera will display a screen like that in Figure 9-8, reporting the name of the computer it is connecting to.

14. Depending on what computer you are using, the computer may display an Importing dialog box. The images and videos will be uploaded to the appropriate folder on your computer. You can designate that folder using the software installed in Step 1. On my Macintosh, the default folder is the Pictures folder; the computer places the images and videos in a sub-folder bearing the date

of the transfer. The process also worked well with a Windows-based computer using Windows 10.

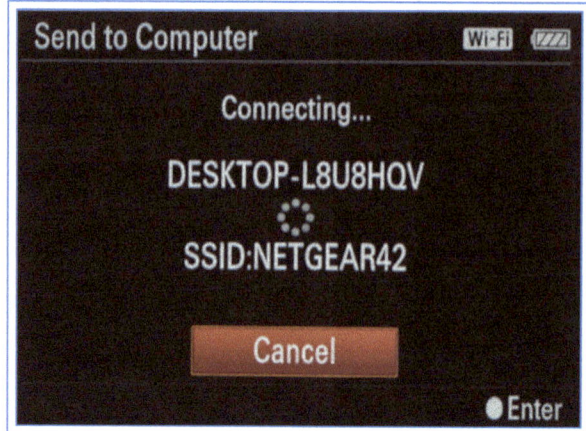

Figure 9-8. Camera Screen Showing Computer Connection

15. The camera will only transfer images and videos that have not previously been transferred wirelessly to the computer, but there is no way to select which of those items will be transferred. The transfer may take a long time, especially if the transfer includes AVCHD and XAVC S videos. In fact, Sony does not recommend transferring XAVC S videos using the Send to Computer option. I ran a test using a 30-second video recorded with the XAVC S HD format. The camera did manage to send the file to my computer, within a few minutes.

16. Once the transfer is complete, the computer will display a message to that effect, and the camera may turn off.

I have not found this option to be as useful as transferring images and videos using a card reader or a USB cable, because of the time it takes for the transfer. However, if you have only a few items to transfer, it can be convenient to have this option available.

Sending Images to a Smartphone

If you don't need to print your images or do heavy editing, you may want to transfer them to a smartphone or tablet so you can send them to social networks, display them on the larger screen of your tablet, or otherwise share and enjoy them.

You can transfer your images and MP4 videos (not XAVC S HD or AVCHD videos) wirelessly from the HX80 or HX90V to a smartphone or tablet that uses either the iOS (iPhone and iPad) or Android operating system. These two systems have different capabilities.

Chapter 9: Wi-Fi, Applications, and Other Topics | 171

With iOS devices, you have to use the camera's menu system to connect. With many Android devices, you can use NFC technology, which establishes a Wi-Fi connection automatically when the camera is touched against the smartphone or tablet.

Here are the steps for connecting using the menu system, using an iPhone as an illustration:

1. Install Sony's PlayMemories Mobile app on the phone; it can be downloaded from the App Store for the iPhone or from Google Play for Android devices. Figure 9-9 shows the app's icon on an iPhone.

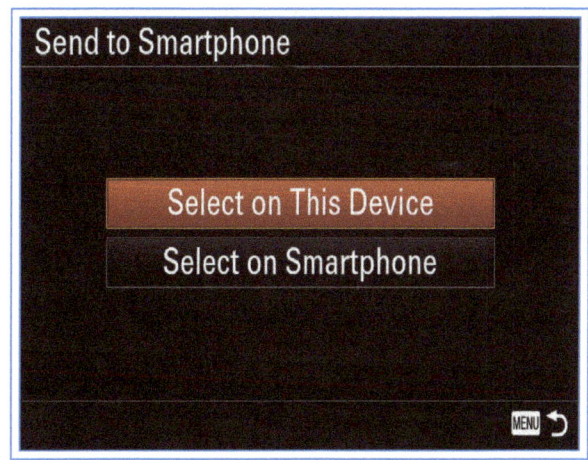

Figure 9-10. Select on This Device Highlighted on Camera

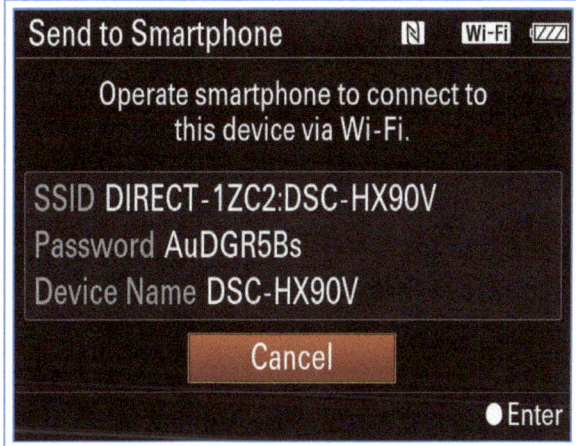

Figure 9-11. Network Name and Password on Camera Screen

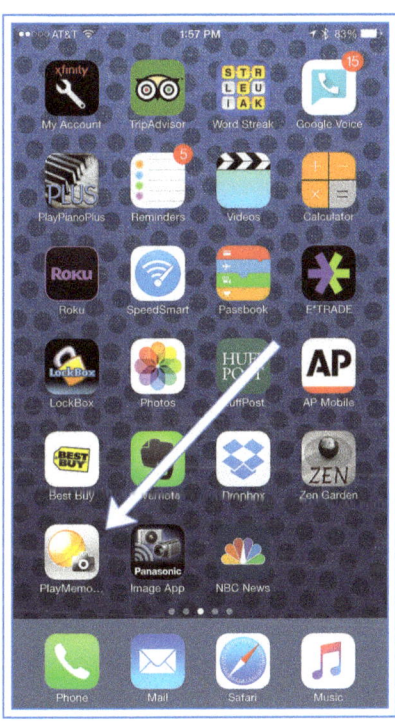

Figure 9-9. PlayMemories Mobile App on iPhone

2. Put the camera into playback mode and select an image or MP4 video to be transferred to the phone.

3. On the camera's Wi-Fi menu, select Send to Smartphone, and from that option choose Select on This Device, as shown in Figure 9-10. On the next screen, you can choose to transfer This Image, All Images (or All Movie (MP4)) on Date, or Multiple Images.

4. On the next screen, as shown in Figure 9-11, the camera will display the SSID (name) of the Wi-Fi network it is generating, along with a password.

5. On the phone, go to the Settings app, select Wi-Fi, and select the network displayed on the camera's screen, as shown in Figure 9-12. The first time you connect to that network, you will have to enter the password displayed on the camera's screen. After that initial connection, you can connect to that network without entering the password.

6. The camera will then display a message saying "Connecting." At this point, start the PlayMemories Mobile app on the iPhone.

7. The phone will display a message saying it is copying the images or videos from the camera, and will confirm the copying with a screen like that in Figure 9-13. The images or videos will appear in the Camera Roll area on an iPhone.

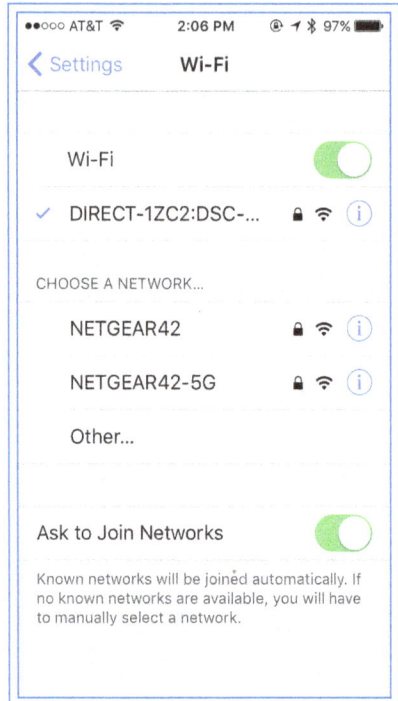

Figure 9-12. Camera's Network Selected on iPhone

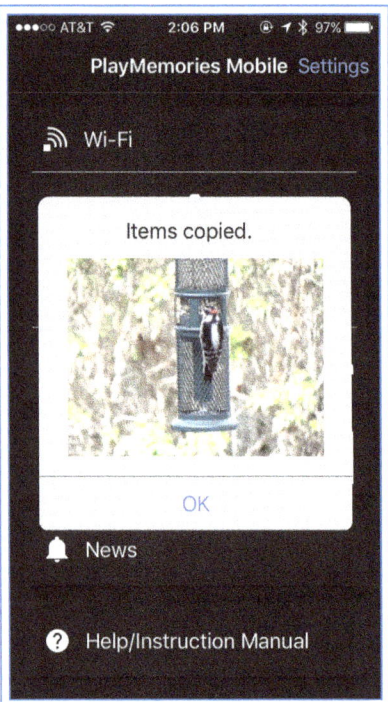

Figure 9-13. Copying Confirmation Screen

CONNECTING WITH NFC

If you are using an Android phone or tablet that has NFC capability built in, the steps for connecting that device to the HX80 or HX90V are simpler. I tested the procedure using a Samsung Galaxy S6 smartphone, but the same process should work with many Android devices that have NFC included. Here are the steps:

1. On the Android device, go to the Google Play Store and find and install the PlayMemories Mobile app, as shown in Figure 9-14.

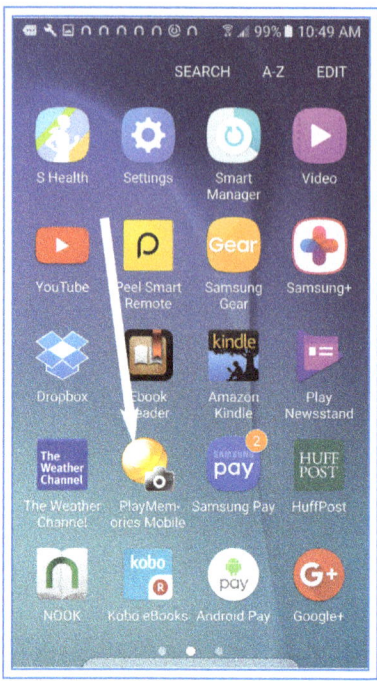

Figure 9-14. PlayMemories Mobile App on Samsung Phone

2. On the Android device, go to the Settings app, and under the NFC and Payment item, make sure NFC is turned on and Android Beam is turned on, as shown in Figure 9-15.

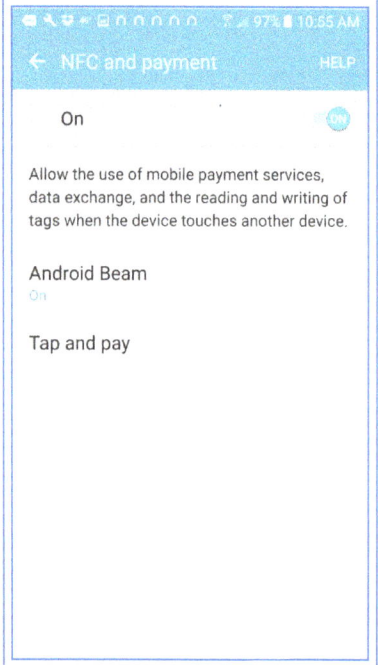

Figure 9-15. NFC Activated on Samsung Phone

3. Put the camera into playback mode and display an image you want to send to the Android device.

4. Find the NFC icon on the left side of the camera, which looks like a fancy "N," as shown in Figure 9-16.

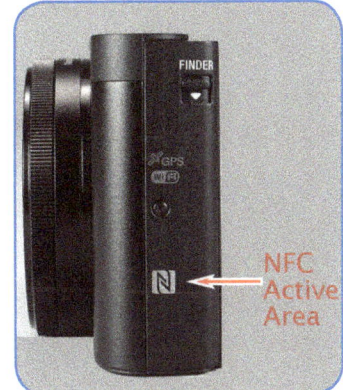

Figure 9-16. NFC Area on Side of Camera

5. While both devices are active, touch the N on the camera to the NFC area on the Android device. (On the Galaxy S6, this area is on the back, as shown in Figure 9-17.) Be sure the two areas touch; you cannot have the two NFC spots separated by more than about a millimeter, if that.

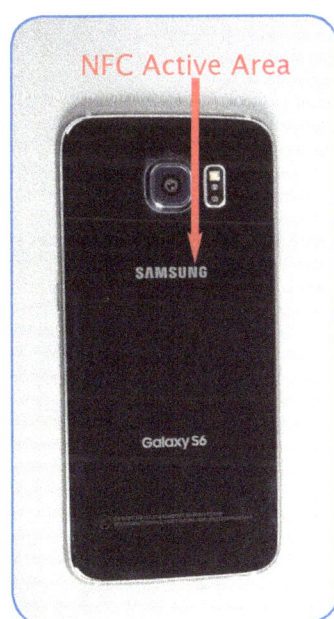

Figure 9-17. NFC Area on Samsung Galaxy S6

6. Hold the devices together, and within a couple of seconds you may hear a sound, depending on settings, and the camera will transfer the image to the Android device; you should see a display saying the transfer is complete, as in Figure 9-18.

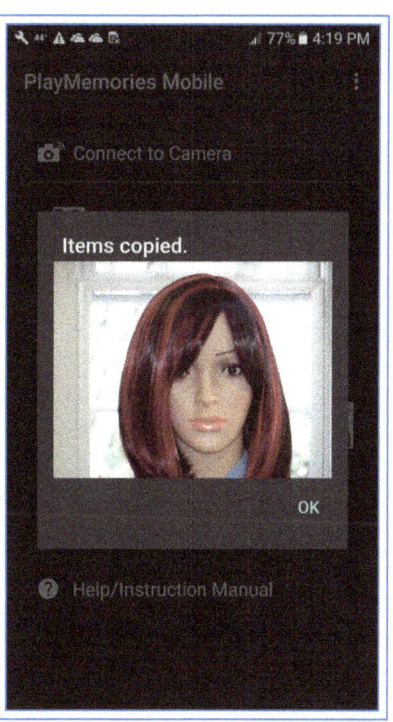

Figure 9-18. Transfer Confirmation Message on Samsung Phone

7. The image will appear in the Google Photos app on the Android device.

8. If you want to transfer multiple images, select that option from the camera's menu before touching the camera to the Android device to start the transfer.

9. By default, when you transfer images to a smartphone or tablet, the maximum image size will be 2.0 MP. If the image originally was larger than that, it will be reduced to that size. You can change this setting to send the images at their original size or at the smaller VGA size, if you want. To do that on your device, find the settings for the PlayMemories Mobile app. On an iPhone, go to Settings, then scroll to find PlayMemories Mobile. On an Android device, open PlayMemories Mobile, then tap the Settings icon.

Using a Smartphone or Tablet as a Remote Control

You can use a smartphone or tablet as a remote control to operate the HX80 or HX90V from a distance of up to about 33 feet (10 meters), as long as the devices are in sight of each other. Here are the steps with an iPhone:

1. Go to the camera's Application menu, marked by an icon with white and black blocks. Highlight the first item, Application List. Press the Center button

to display the list of applications, or apps, currently loaded into the camera.

2. Use the direction buttons or the Control wheel to highlight the app called Smart Remote Embedded or Smart Remote Control, as shown in Figure 9-19.

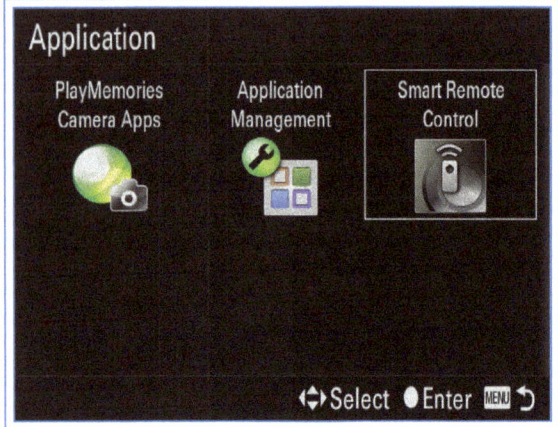

Figure 9-19. Smart Remote App Icon Highlighted on Menu

If you have downloaded an updated version of this app, it will be called Smart Remote Control instead of Smart Remote Embedded. I strongly recommend that you download the updated version, which has considerably more functionality than the basic Smart Remote Embedded app.

3. Start the app by pressing the Center button, and the camera will display a screen with information for its Wi-Fi network, including a scannable QR Code in a square on the right, as shown in Figure 9-20.

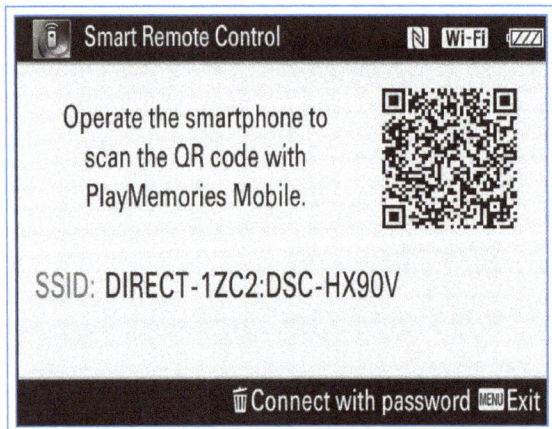

Figure 9-20. Network Name and QR Code on Camera Screen

4. On the phone, open the PlayMemories Mobile app, select the option for scanning the camera's QR code, and aim the phone's camera at that code. Then follow the prompts, which may include confirming an installation profile on the phone. If you prefer, you can press the Delete button on the camera to go to a screen similar to Figure 9-11, for connecting using the network ID and password instead of the QR Code.

5. Set up the camera on a tripod or just place it where you want it, aiming at your intended subject.

6. Open the PlayMemories Mobile app on the iPhone if it is not already open.

7. The camera will display a screen like that shown in Figure 9-21, with an icon in the upper left corner showing that the camera can now be controlled from the phone.

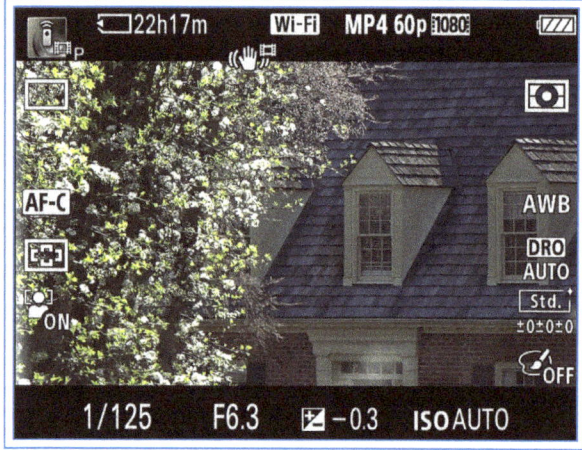

Figure 9-21. Camera's Screen During Remote Control by App

8. The phone will display a screen like that in Figure 9-22, with the view from the camera's lens and several control icons.

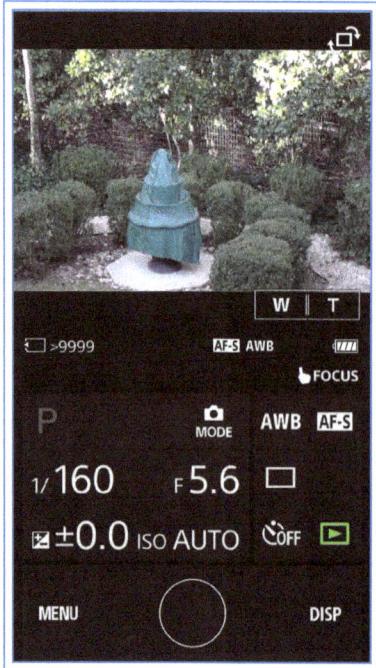

Figure 9-22. Smart Remote Control Screen on iPhone

9. Using these controls, you can zoom the lens and control exposure compensation. You can press the Menu label at the lower left of the screen to get access to settings for the self-timer, image review, and save options, as shown in Figure 9-23. You also can adjust several menu options using the camera's controls. For example, you can use the Mode dial to change the shooting mode and you can use the Creative Style menu option.

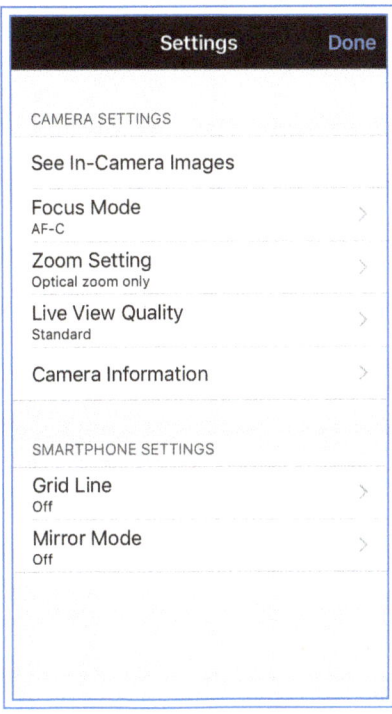

Figure 9-23. Settings Menu Items in Smart Remote App

10. If you download the updated Smart Remote Control version of the app, which is illustrated in Figure 9-22, you can focus by touching the screen with your finger. You also can use the settings panel to turn on the Touch Shutter function, which lets you trigger the shutter as the focus is set, when you touch the phone's screen with your finger. (If you use the original Smart Remote Embedded app, the available options will be somewhat different than those described and illustrated here.)

11. With the updated app, you can record a movie by turning the camera's Mode dial to the Movie position. At that point, the camera icon on the app's screen will change to a round red icon, as shown in Figure 9-24. Press that icon to start or stop video recording. You also can control ISO, exposure compensation, aperture, and shutter speed, depending on the shooting mode on the camera's Mode dial.

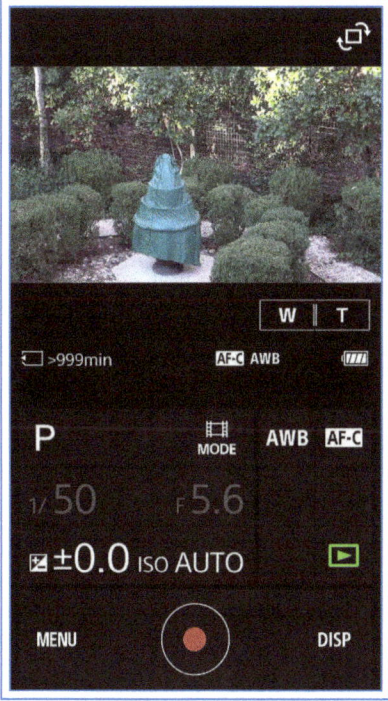

Figure 9-24. Remote App Set for Recording Video

12. By default, images saved to the phone will be resized down to 2.0 MP unless they already were that small or smaller. Movies will be saved only to the camera; they cannot be displayed on the phone.

13. When you have set up the shot as you want it, press the camera icon on the iPhone app to take the picture or the red icon to start the video recording.

14. If you are using an Android device with NFC capability, you should be able to connect to the camera by touching the device to the camera, as discussed above in connection with transferring images. To do this, though, you may first have to register the Smart Remote Embedded (or Smart Remote Control) app using the One-touch (NFC) menu option on screen 1 of the camera's Wi-Fi menu. (This app may be registered by default.)

15. Once the connection has been made, you can separate the devices to the standard remote-control distance of up to about 33 feet (10 meters). If you have difficulty making an NFC connection, start the PlayMemories Mobile App on the Android device before touching the camera to that device. The camera can then be controlled using the PlayMemories Mobile app on the Android device, as noted in the numbered steps above.

The features of the remote control app are likely to change as Sony updates this and other apps; you can download updated versions at www.playmemoriescameraapps.com.

You can use the remote-control setup if you want to place your camera on a tripod in an area where birds or other wildlife may appear, so you can control the camera from a distance without disturbing the animals. (The wireless remote will work through glass if you are indoors behind a window.)

Also, you can try pole aerial photography, which involves attaching the camera to a painter's pole or other pole about 10 to 16 feet (three to five meters) long, as shown in Figure 9-25, to get shots from a higher vantage point than would otherwise be possible. See polepixie.com for information about equipment for making this sort of attachment.

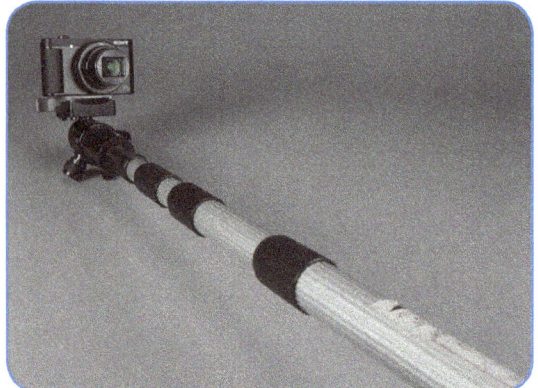

Figure 9-25. Sony HX90V Camera Attached to Pole

I took the image shown in Figure 9-26 using this pole, which allowed me to get a shot from about 10 feet (three meters) outside an upstairs window that would not have been possible otherwise.

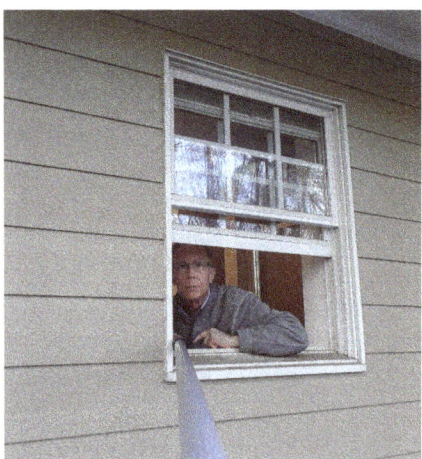

Figure 9-26. Image Taken from Pole Using Remote App

With this system, I could see exactly where the camera was being aimed. It was somewhat tricky holding the pole steady while using the iPhone, but if you have another person to help, this setup can be useful for higher-angle photos of properties being sold, viewing above crowds, and other applications. Being able to control the camera remotely also might be useful in other situations in which you want to have the camera set up unattended, such as when you want to capture images in a classroom or other group setting without calling attention to the camera.

Wi-Fi Menu

I have discussed some of the options on the Wi-Fi menu, whose first screen on the HX90V is shown in Figure 9-27, but there are several other options to discuss.

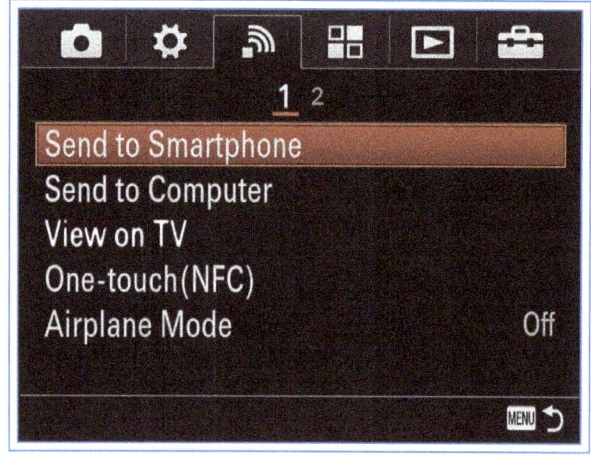

Figure 9-27. Screen 1 of HX90V Wi-Fi Menu

Following is information about each of the items on this menu.

Send to Smartphone

This first Wi-Fi menu option lets you transfer images or MP4 videos wirelessly from the camera to a smartphone or tablet. I discussed the steps for using this option earlier in this chapter.

Send to Computer

This next option lets you send images and movies directly from the HX80 or HX90V to a computer via a Wi-Fi network. I discussed this process earlier in this chapter.

View on TV

This option sets up the camera to transmit still images (not movies) wirelessly to a Wi-Fi–enabled TV, such as a Sony Bravia TV. The procedure will vary with the TV set you are using. Once the connection is established, you can browse through the images using the controls on the camera or the remote control of the TV if the TV is compatible with this setup.

This is a useful option once it is working properly, but I found it hard to set up. I eventually got it to work using WD TV Live, a media player made by Western Digital. I connected that device to an HDTV using an HDMI cable, and configured the device to connect to my home network. Then I connected a laptop computer running Windows 10 to the same network. I also downloaded a program called Serviio from http://serviio.org and configured this system to work as a DLNA streaming media server on my network. (DLNA stands for Digital Living Network Alliance; see www.dlna.org.)

Once everything was working together, I selected the View on TV menu option and the camera displayed the screen shown in Figure 9-28 as it connected to the WD TV Live device. Then the camera began sending still images to the TV through the wireless network.

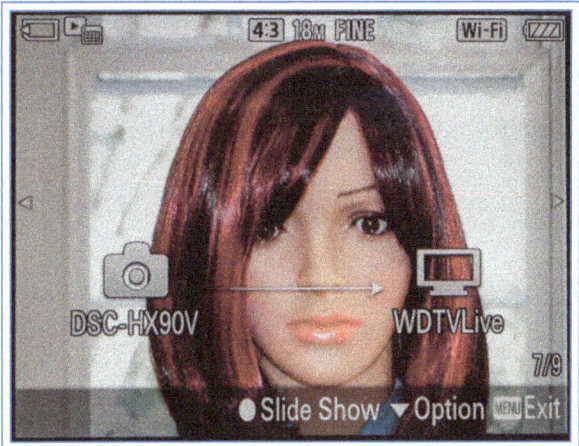

Figure 9-29. Camera Screen While Sending Images to TV

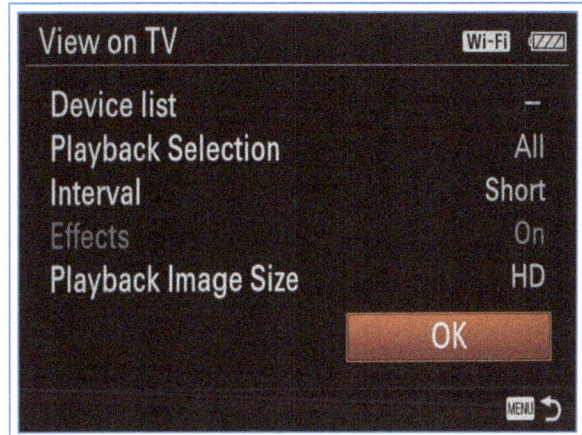

Figure 9-30. Additional Menu Options for View on TV

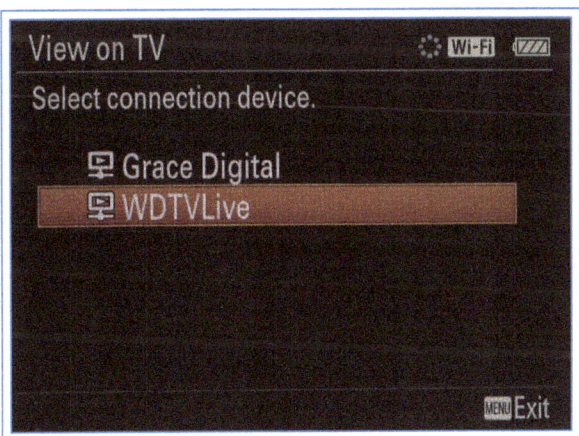

Figure 9-28. Camera Screen After Finding WD TV Live

The camera displayed the screen shown in Figure 9-29, with a few control icons at the bottom. Once this screen appeared, I pressed the Center button to pause the transmission, and pressed the Down button to display the screen shown in Figure 9-30, with additional options, including 4K display mode, found under the Playback Image Size option.

If you don't mind some possible technical complications, this option may be great for you. Otherwise, I recommend that you view your images on a TV using an HDMI cable, a USB flash drive, or some other direct connection.

One-touch (NFC)

The HX90V has built-in near field communication (NFC) functionality, which means it can establish a wireless connection just by touching a smartphone or tablet that also has NFC built in. As of this writing, many Android phones and tablets have this feature, but Apple devices, such as iPhones and iPads, do not.

To use the NFC feature to start a camera app, you first have to use this menu option to register that app. Then, with the smartphone or tablet turned on and the camera in shooting mode, touch the N mark on the left side of the camera to the NFC area on the smartphone or tablet. The two devices should immediately start to establish a connection, and the application you registered using this menu option should launch. For example, you might want to register the Smart Remote Embedded application or another application that you have downloaded from Sony's site. (According to Sony, the Smart Remote Embedded app is registered by default, so you may not need to register it yourself.)

You don't have to use this menu option before using the camera to connect to a phone or tablet to transfer images.

Airplane Mode

This option is a quick way to disable all of the camera's functions related to Wi-Fi, including Eye-Fi card activity and the camera's own internal Wi-Fi network. As indicated by its name, this option is useful when you are on an airplane and you are required to disable electronic devices. In addition, this setting can save battery power, so it may be worthwhile to activate it when you are on an outing with the camera and you won't need to use any Wi-Fi capabilities for a period of time.

If you are trying to use any of the camera's built-in Wi-Fi functions such as Send to Smartphone or Send to Computer and notice that the menu options are dimmed, it may be because this option is turned on. Just turn it back off and the Wi-Fi options should be available again.

The second and final screen of the Wi-Fi menu is shown in Figure 9-31.

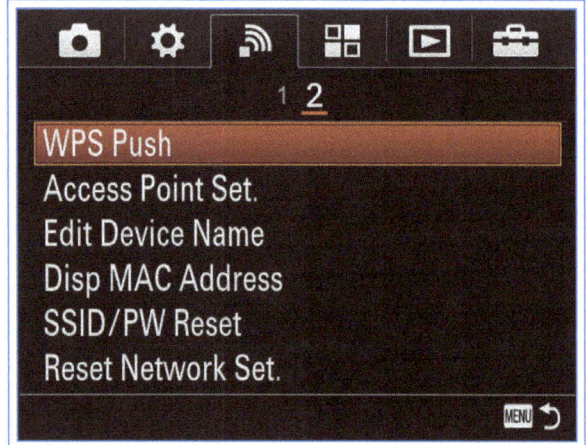

Figure 9-31. Screen 2 of HX90V Wi-Fi Menu

WPS Push

The WPS Push option gives you an easy way to set up your camera to connect to a computer over a Wi-Fi network. Ordinarily, to connect to a wireless network using the camera's menu system, you have to use the Access Point Settings option and then enter the network password into the camera to establish the connection. The WPS Push option gives you a shortcut if the wireless access point or wireless router you are connecting to has a WPS button. That option, if it is present, is likely to be a small button on the back or top of the router, and it is likely to have the WPS label next to it or on it. For example, one router I connect to has the button shown earlier in Figure 9-2.

If the router has a WPS button, you will not have to make manual settings or enter a password. All you have to do is select the WPS Push menu option on the HX80 or HX90V, and then, within two minutes, press the WPS button on the router. If the operation is successful, the camera's display screen will show that the connection has been established, as shown in Figure 9-32.

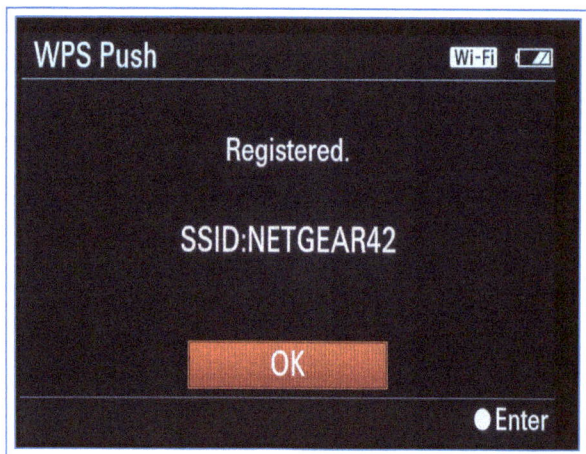

Figure 9-32. Camera Screen After Successful WPS Push

Once that connection has been made, you will be able to connect your camera to a computer on that network to transfer images using the Send to Computer option.

If the connection does not succeed using WPS Push, you will need to use the Access Point Settings option, the next item on screen 2 of the Wi-Fi menu.

Access Point Settings

This option is for connecting the camera to a router if WPS Push, discussed above, is not available or does not work. I discussed the use of this option earlier in this chapter, in connection with sending images and videos to a computer wirelessly.

Chapter 9: Wi-Fi, Applications, and Other Topics | 179

EDIT DEVICE NAME

This next option, shown in Figure 9-33, lets you change the name of your camera as it is displayed on the network. The default name is DSC-HX80 or DSC-HX90V, and I have found no reason to change it, especially because doing so would require me to use the camera's laborious data-entry system. This option could be useful, though, if you are in an environment where other cameras of the same model are present and you need to distinguish one camera from another by using different names.

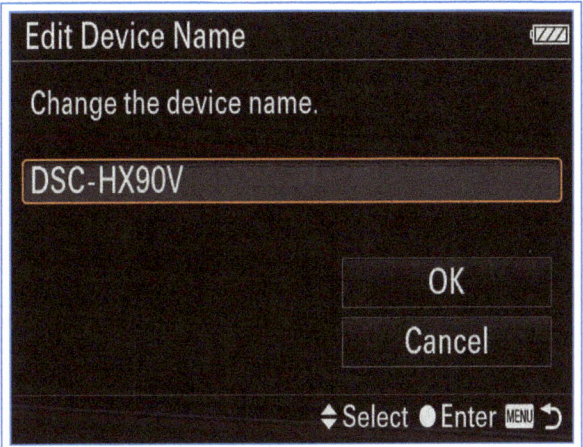

Figure 9-33. Edit Device Name Screen

DISPLAY MAC ADDRESS

If you select this menu option, the camera will display a screen like that seen in Figure 9-34, which provides the MAC address of your camera. MAC stands for media access control.

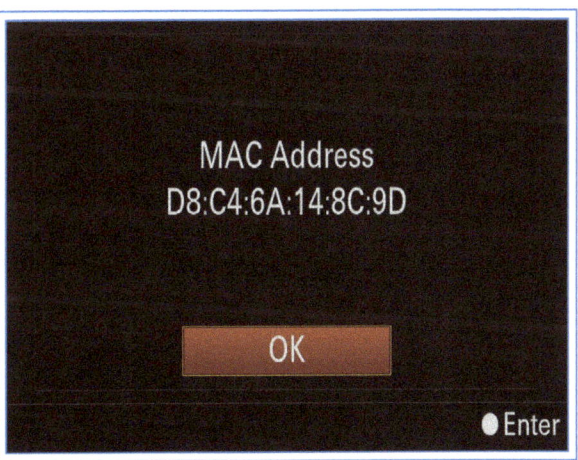

Figure 9-34. Display MAC Address Screen

The MAC address is a string of characters that identifies a physical device that can connect to a network. In some cases, a router can be configured to reject or accept devices with specified MAC addresses. If you are having difficulty connecting your camera to your Wi-Fi router using the options discussed above, you can try configuring your router to recognize the MAC address of your camera, as reported by this menu item. I have not had to use this option, but it is good to have it available in case it is needed.

SSID/PW RESET

When you connect your HX80 or HX90V to a smartphone or tablet, either to transfer images or to control the camera remotely from the other device, the camera generates its own Wi-Fi network internally. With this option, whose main screen is shown in Figure 9-35, you can force the camera to change the SSID (name) and password of its own wireless network.

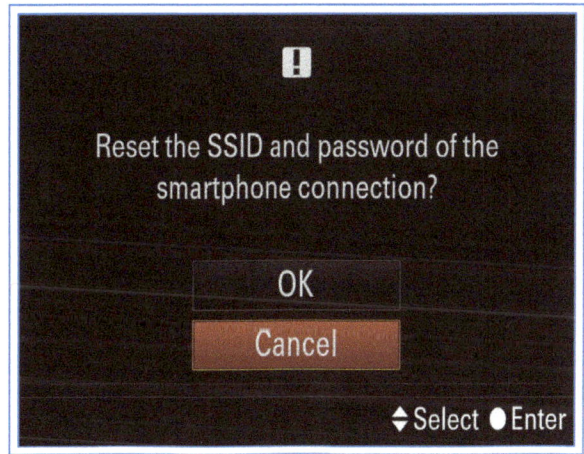

Figure 9-35. SSID/PW Reset Menu Options Screen

You might want to do this if, for example, you have attended a conference where you allowed other people to connect their smartphones to your camera, and now you want to reset the camera's network ID so they will no longer have access to the camera's network.

RESET NETWORK SETTINGS

This final item on the Wi-Fi menu lets you reset all of the camera's Wi-Fi network settings, not just the SSID and password. This option is useful if you are having problems and need to get a fresh start with the wireless functions, if you are switching to a new wireless network where you use the camera, or if you are selling the camera and want to erase these settings.

Applications and Application Menu

The one menu system I have not yet discussed in any detail is the Application menu, represented by an icon with white and black blocks, to the right of the Wi-Fi menu's icon. This menu system opens the door to expansions of the camera's features through applications, or apps, that you can download from a Sony website. I will give a brief introduction to this capability, though there undoubtedly will be changes to the website and the available options as time goes by.

The apps available from Sony are similar to apps for smartphones and tablets. Each app provides a separate function or set of functions, and is represented by a name and an icon. The apps are found on the HX80 or HX90V by going to the Application menu and selecting the first item, Application List, shown in Figure 9-36.

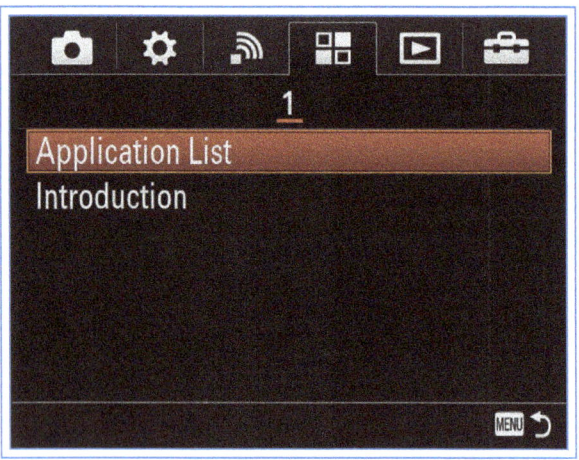

Figure 9-36. Application Menu Screen

When you highlight that item and press the Center button, you will see a screen like that in Figure 9-37, with icons for all apps currently loaded in the camera. If you highlight any of those icons and press the Center button, you will activate that app.

Although it is likely that the set of initial apps will change over time, when my camera was new it came with just one actual camera app installed—Smart Remote Embedded, which lets you use a smartphone or tablet to control the camera. (The camera included two other apps that involve downloading and management of camera apps.) Sony has updated that app to add new features in a version called Smart Remote Control, whose icon is shown in Figure 9-37, and I won't be surprised if it is updated further in the future.

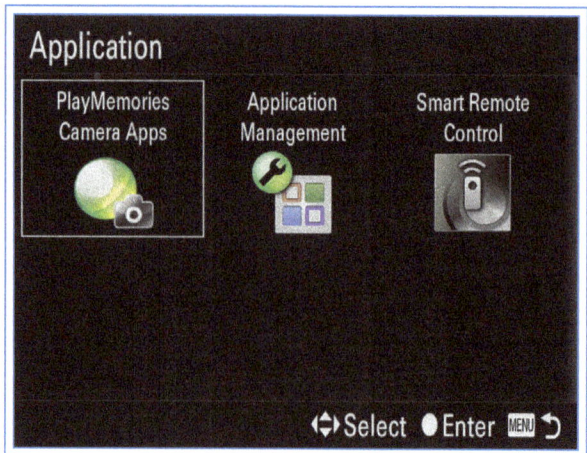

Figure 9-37. Application List Menu Screen

Besides the app that came pre-installed, Sony has, as of this writing, made available only a few other apps for the HX80 and HX90V, although many other apps are available for other Sony cameras. The only apps listed as compatible with the HX80 and HX90V, all of which are free, are Smart Remote Control, My Best Portrait, and Sync to Smartphone. In order to install and use any of these apps, you first have to go to Sony's site at www.playmemoriescameraapps.com and create an account. Then you can obtain information about the apps and download them by connecting your camera to the computer using the camera's USB cable. You may have to set USB Connection to MTP on the Setup menu to get these steps accomplished.

Once the account is set up and you have your camera registered with a Wi-Fi access point, you can also download an app directly to your camera. To manage installed apps and view how much storage space has been used, you use the administrative app called Application Management, whose icon is shown in Figure 9-37.

To download an app directly from the camera, use the PlayMemories Camera Apps icon, also shown in Figure 9-37. With that method, you need to connect the camera to a wireless network and then sign in to the playmemoriescameraapps.com site with your username and password. That can be a laborious process using the on-screen keyboard, but the system does work effectively for downloading apps if you are not able to use a computer for that purpose.

Once you have installed an app and highlighted its icon on the camera's screen, press the Center button and follow the on-screen instructions to use the app.

If you press the camera's Menu button while the app is running, the camera may display a special menu with options that apply while that app is in use. For example, when the Smart Remote Control app is running, if you press the Menu button you will see one of the five menu screens for that app, as shown in Figure 9-38.

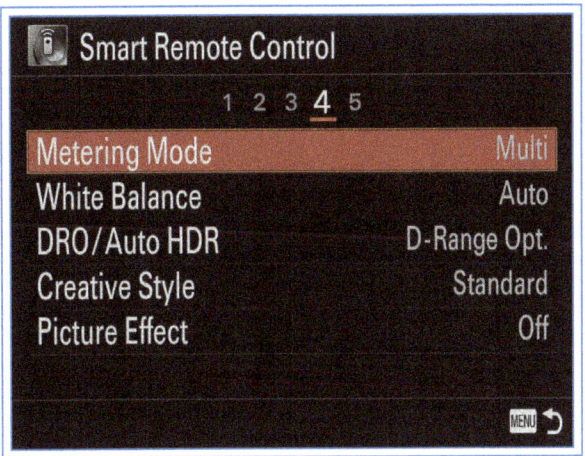

Figure 9-38. Menu Screen for Smart Remote Control App

The other four menu screens for this app display standard camera options that can be controlled when the app is in use, such as Image Size, Quality, ISO, and the like. In other cases, an app may just use icons to let you choose various functions. If you expect to use in-camera apps often, you can assign the Application List menu item to the Custom, Center, Left, or Right button so it can be called up quickly.

The second line of the Application menu, Introduction, provides some general information about applications.

Other Topics

Using the Superzoom Lens

One of the most outstanding features of the HX80 and HX90V is the lens, which has a large range of focal lengths at both the wide-angle and telephoto ends of its zoom. The focal length of a lens is a measure of how wide is its view of a scene and how powerfully it enlarges the view.

A "normal" lens—used for everyday shooting of family scenes, portraits, and the like—is often considered to be a 50mm lens. A "wide-angle" lens is in the range of 35mm or lower, and a "telephoto" lens is one with a focal length of 100mm or greater. The HX80 and HX90V, of course, have a zoom lens, which means the lens can change its focal length. The focal lengths of this lens range from a very wide 24mm to a powerful 720mm at the telephoto end, for an overall range of 30 times optical zoom. (None of this discussion will involve digital zoom, which is not a "real" zoom capability, as discussed in Chapter 7.)

Of course, there are trade-offs for having this great zoom range. It is not possible to provide the same quality in a zoom lens of this type as in lenses used by professional photographers at major sporting events, for example. A good zoom lens for a DSLR can easily cost more than $1,000, and a top-quality professional telephoto (non-zoom) lens can cost more than $10,000. However, for everyday photography, the HX90V provides you with the ability to capture scenes with an array of focal lengths that is among the best in the world of consumer cameras.

At the wide-angle end, the camera's lens gives you several millimeters more than many cameras in its class. A wide-angle range starting at 28mm is often considered quite adequate, and not all compact digital cameras offer a zoom range starting as low as 24mm. The 24mm focal length is very useful when you need to photograph a large group of people without standing back a great distance. Also, if you need to photograph the interiors of rooms, this focal length is a great bonus, because you will likely be able to capture an excellent view of the entire room by standing in one corner.

But the telephoto power of its lens is probably its most dramatic feature, so I will concentrate on using the telephoto capability.

First, this zoom lens is so powerful it can capture details you barely see, if at all, with the naked eye. For example, I took the shot of distant buildings in Figure 9-39 with the lens zoomed out to its 24mm wide-angle setting. In this image, you cannot see many details in the distance.

Now, look at Figure 9-40. This shot was taken at the same time and place as the wide-angle shot. This time, though, the lens was zoomed in to the full 720mm extent of the optical zoom. In this image, you can see the flag as a prominent feature. In the previous image, the flag, located in the center of the image, is practically invisible. The telephoto shot includes a level of detail that is not even hinted at in the first image.

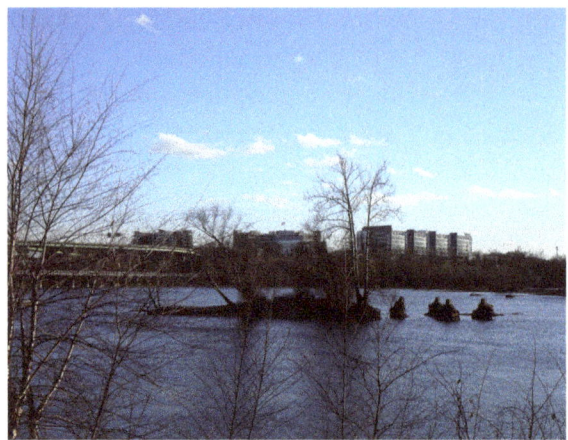

Figure 9-39. Zoom Comparison: 24 mm

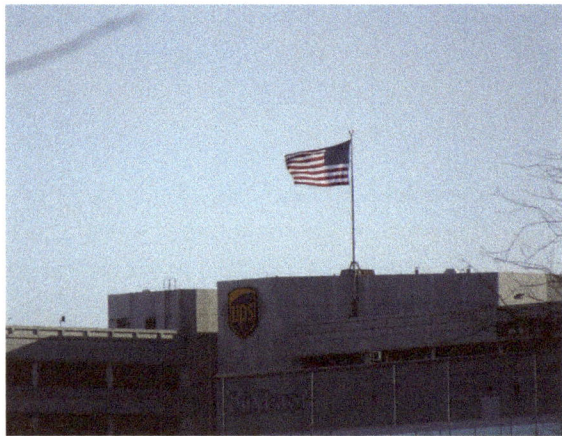

Figure 9-40. Zoom Comparison: 720mm

When you use this powerful zoom lens at its highest power, you will encounter some issues that you should take into account when deciding whether to rely on the long reach of the lens rather than trying to get closer to your subject.

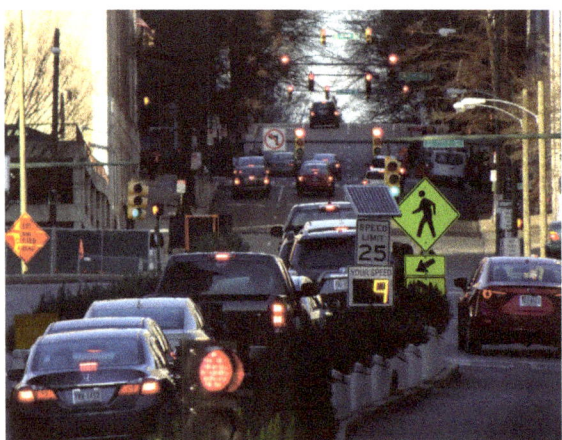

Figure 9-41. Flattening Effect of Long Zoom Shot

For one thing, as you may be able to tell from Figure 9-41, a telephoto shot of cars on a busy street, images shot at this power can exhibit flattening or foreshortening of the objects you are photographing. The result of using such a powerful zoom in this case is that cars and other objects appear compressed into a single level, so that it looks as if they are located close to each other, even though they are more widely separated in reality.

However, you very well may find good uses for this effect, which can give a distinctive look to a scene.

Another positive side of the super-long zoom range is its ability to isolate a single subject. If you use the zoom to focus on a particular person in a crowd or on a particular animal in a pack, you can fill the frame with that single subject, thereby limiting extraneous objects and emphasizing the subject you want to concentrate on. Another advantage can be the ability to take a photo of a subject from a distance without disturbing her, as was the case with Figure 9-42.

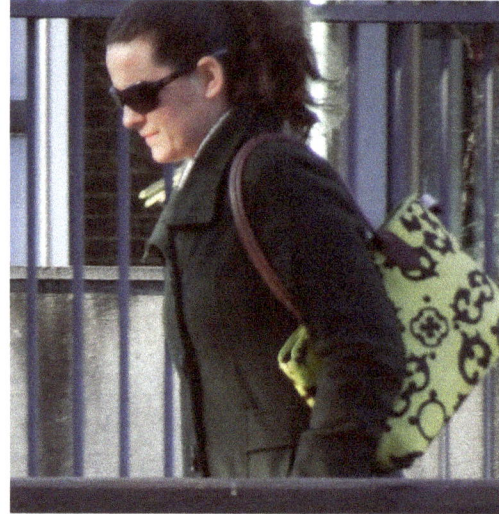

Figure 9-42. Isolating Effect of Long Zoom Shot

When I spotted this woman through the lens, I wanted to get a picture of her but did not want to get close enough to disturb her. Using the long zoom range of the HX90V, I took this shot from a considerable distance, which isolated her from other objects and resulted in an image with the scenery flattened into a somewhat indistinct background.

Another benefit from using the camera's zoom lens in its telephoto range is that, when the lens is zoomed in, it has a very shallow depth of field. As a result, when you take a picture at the long end of the zoom range, particularly when the lens is fairly close to the subject, the background will be blurred to the point of becoming indistinct. This effect, often called "bokeh," as discussed in Chapter 3, can reduce distractions from the background and emphasize your primary subject in the foreground. This was the case with Figure 9-43, in which I took a shot of a mannequin with the lens zoomed in to a long focal length of 425mm, thereby blurring the background of trees and bushes.

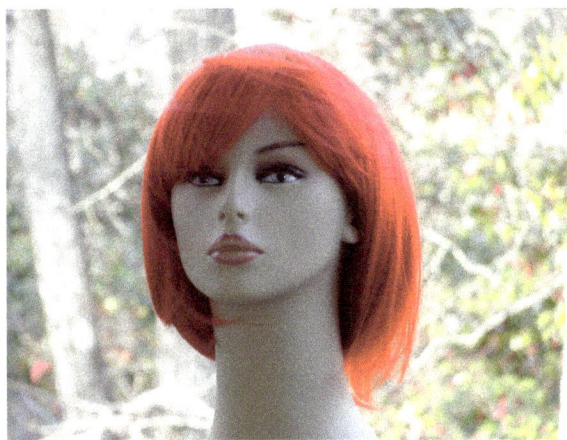

Figure 9-43. Bokeh Effect of Long Zoom Shot

Beyond the specific advantages from the long reach of the zoom lens, perhaps the greatest overall benefit of the superzoom lens on the HX80 and HX90V is that it gives you the equivalent of a whole range of focal lengths without the need to carry around a bag filled with heavy lenses. In practical terms, with the HX90V you have at your fingertips every focal length that a photographer could reasonably want or need for everyday photography, ranging from the wide-angle 24mm with a strong macro capability to the super 720mm telephoto.

If you have an opportunity to go on a safari or a cruise around the world and you want to be able to bring back a complete photographic record of your trip using one lightweight, easy-to-use camera, the HX80 or HX90V can do the job nicely.

There also is a definite problem that comes along with a superzoom capability—image blur caused by camera movement. When the lens is zoomed in to its full 720mm focal length or close to that range, any motion of the camera is multiplied because of the magnification of the image. You will notice how jittery the image looks on the display, and it will be hard to keep the picture steady.

There are several steps you can take to reduce the effects of camera movement. First, if possible, use a tripod. It can be inconvenient to do, but using a solid tripod is one of the best ways to ensure high-quality images. If you can't manage a full-blown tripod, use a lightweight travel tripod, a monopod, or any support available, such as a fence post, or just sit on a bench and hold the camera steady on your lap, folding the LCD display up toward your face to view the image.

Suppose, though, that you are walking through a field in search of wildlife shots and there is no physical support available. There are several things you can do to minimize the effects of camera shake. First, you may find you can keep the camera steadier if you use the electronic viewfinder, so you can hold the camera against your forehead and look into that window, rather than using the LCD display at some distance from your face.

Next, use the fastest shutter speed you can. If the shutter is open for only a brief instant, there will not be time for camera motion to register on the image. According to one rule of thumb, when handholding a zoom lens you should use a shutter speed no slower than the fraction of a second with the focal length of the lens as the denominator. So, if the lens is zoomed all the way in to 720mm, you would use a shutter speed of 1/800 second or faster, including choices of 1/1000, 1/1250, 1/1600, or 1/2000 second.

If you want to control the shutter speed, you should use Shutter Priority as your shooting mode, as discussed in Chapter 3. You also could use Manual mode, if you are willing to accept the added task of setting the aperture correctly. Or, if you would like to use Program mode, you can let the camera set the shutter speed and aperture initially, and then use the Flexible Program feature, which lets you turn the command dial to select new combinations of shutter speed and aperture that are equivalent to what the camera selected.

However, you are likely to run into a problem if you use the camera's standard settings and try to set a fast shutter speed. One of the limiting characteristics of the superzoom lens on the HX80 and HX90V is that, as was discussed in Chapter 3, its maximum aperture when zoomed in is quite narrow. When the lens is zoomed all the way out to wide-angle, the maximum (widest open) aperture is f/3.5, which is not exceptionally wide to start with, though it is wide enough for most purposes. But, when the lens is zoomed in, it rapidly loses the ability to use a wide aperture.

When the lens is zoomed all the way in, the maximum aperture is f/6.4. In order to use a shutter speed of 1/1500 second or faster at that rather narrow aperture, there will have to be a good deal of light, unless you change some other settings.

Your best option probably is to increase the ISO sensitivity of the camera, which will mean that the camera's image sensor will require less light to expose the picture, at the risk of increased visual noise in the image. Using the ISO setting on the Shooting menu, you may want to try setting ISO to Auto, with ISO Auto Maximum set to a level such as 1600. If you want to be sure a high ISO is set, you should use a specific level, such as ISO 800, ISO 1600, or even ISO 3200.

If you prefer not to boost the ISO, which likely will introduce noise into the image, one strategy you can use is to zoom back out until the camera can use a wider aperture, such as, say, f/5.0 or f/4.5. Later on, when editing your photos with software, you can crop them to achieve the same field of view you originally saw with the zoomed-in lens, though with some loss of quality because of the cropping.

Another possible strategy for getting good, clear images with the superzoom lens is to take advantage of the camera's continuous-shooting options. With those options, the camera will take multiple shots in rapid succession, increasing the likelihood that one or more shots will be usable.

Finally, don't forget that the HX80 and HX90V offer the convenient MR slot on the Mode dial, for the Memory Recall mode. If you use the lens zoomed in frequently, you may want to save your preferred settings for those occasions, so you can quickly call them up just by turning the mode dial to the MR setting. For example, you may want to set up the camera in Shutter Priority mode, with a shutter speed of 1/800 second, with an ISO setting of 1600, with the lens zoomed out to its wide-angle setting, and with high-speed continuous shooting enabled.

Macro Photography

Macro photography is the art or science of taking photographs when the subject is shown at actual size (1:1 ratio between size of subject and size of unenlarged image) or slightly magnified (greater than 1:1 ratio). So, if you photograph a flower using macro techniques, the image on the camera's sensor will be about the same size as the actual flower. You can get wonderful detail in your images using macro photography, and you may discover things about the subject you hadn't noticed before taking the photograph.

There are two basic ways to take macro photographs with the HX80 and HX90V. First, you can set the Mode dial to the Intelligent Auto or Superior Auto mode setting and rely on the camera's scene-recognition capability to recognize a macro shot and make appropriate settings. However, you will not be able to select several important Shooting menu items, including Focus Area, ISO, White Balance, Metering Mode, Creative Style, and others. I took the shot of the orchid in Figure 9-44 using Intelligent Auto mode. The camera exposed the image for 1/50 second at f/4.0 using ISO 125.

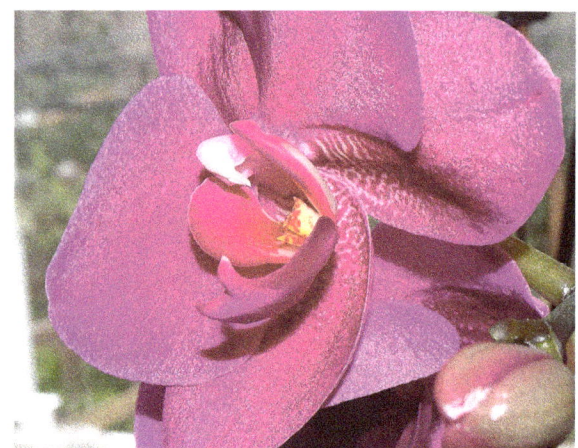

Figure 9-44. Macro Shot with Intelligent Auto Mode

The other way to take macro shots with the HX80 and HX90V is to use one of the advanced shooting modes—Program, Aperture Priority, Shutter Priority, or Manual exposure, and use the camera's natural macro focusing ability. In that way, you will have the full range of Shooting menu options available. Also, depending on the subject, you can choose a shooting mode that makes the most sense.

For example, if you are photographing flowers or other items that are not moving significantly, you may want to use Aperture Priority for one of two reasons: so you can use a wide aperture to focus sharply on the subject while blurring the background, or so you can use a more narrow aperture to get the whole subject in focus, with expanded depth of field. In other cases you may prefer to use another shooting mode.

I took the shot in Figure 9-45 using Aperture Priority mode with a shutter speed of 1/10 second, aperture of f/8.0, and ISO set to 3200. I wanted good depth of field with a narrow aperture, and I wanted to use a shutter speed fast enough that I could hand-hold the camera.

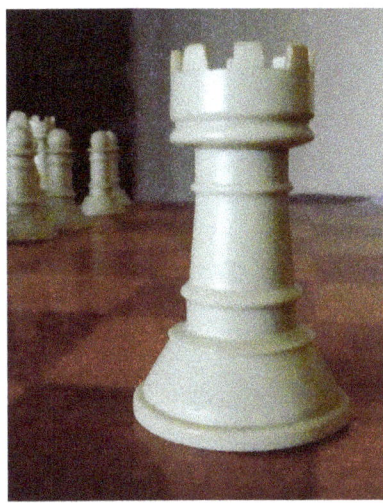

Figure 9-45. Macro Shot with Aperture Priority Mode

There is one aspect of the camera's focusing system that makes macro photography particularly easy: There is no special "macro" focusing mode, as there is on many other cameras. In the camera's normal autofocus mode (which is automatically set on the HX80 and is set from the Focus Mode menu option on the HX90V), the camera will focus on objects as close as 2 inches (5 cm) when the lens is zoomed out. The lens quickly loses the ability to focus on close subjects as it is zoomed in. When the lens is zoomed in to its maximum telephoto range, it can focus only on subjects no farther away than about eight feet (250 cm).

(HX90V only) With the HX90V, you don't have to use autofocus to take macro shots. If you set the camera to manual focus, you can focus on objects as close as 2 inches (5 cm). You do, however, lose the benefit of automatic focus, and it can be tricky finding the correct focus manually. If you use the DMF setting, you have the ability to check your manual focusing by pressing the Shutter button halfway and having the camera use its autofocus system. You also can take advantage of the several excellent aids to manual focusing that the HX90V provides: Peaking, MF Assist, and the Focus Magnifier option, discussed in Chapter 4 and Chapter 7.

When shooting extreme close-ups, you should use a tripod if possible because the depth of field is very shallow and you need to keep the camera steady to take a usable photograph. It's also a good idea to take advantage of the two-second self-timer setting. If you take the picture using the self-timer, you will not be touching the camera when the shutter is activated, so the chance of camera shake is minimized. You also can use Sony's wired remote control, discussed in Appendix A.

If you need artificial illumination, consider using some sort of diffuser over the built-in flash, such as a handkerchief or piece of translucent plastic. Using the flash without some diffusion may result in uneven illumination at such a close range. You might consider using a small lamp that can illuminate the subject without overwhelming it.

STREET PHOTOGRAPHY

The HX80 and HX90V cameras are well suited for street photography—that is, shooting candid pictures in public settings, often without the subject being aware of your activity. They are small, lightweight, and unobtrusive in appearance, so they can easily be held casually or hidden in the photographer's hand. Their 24mm wide-angle lens takes in a broad field of view, so you can shoot from the hip without framing the image carefully on the screen. You can tilt up the LCD screen and look down at it to frame your shot, which further hides your actions. You can silence the camera by turning off its beeps and shutter sounds.

If you want to produce your street images in black and white, which is often the practice for this sort of photography, you can use the Black and White setting of the Creative Style option on the Shooting menu. You can tweak it by increasing (or decreasing) contrast and sharpening if you want. Also, try turning on continuous shooting, so you'll get several images to choose from for each shutter press.

You also can experiment with exposure settings. I recommend you shoot in Shutter Priority mode at a fairly fast shutter speed, 1/100 second or faster, to stop action on the street and to avoid blur from camera movement. You can set ISO to Auto, or use a high ISO setting, in the range of 800 or so, if you don't mind some noise.

To get a gritty "street" look, try using the High Contrast Monochrome setting of the Picture Effect item on the Shooting menu, with ISO set somewhat high, in the range of 800 or above, to include some grain in the image while boosting sensitivity enough to stop action with a fast shutter speed. You also can use the High Sensitivity setting of Scene mode to convey a gritty feeling. You cannot shoot in monochrome with that setting, though.

One different approach is to take advantage of the camera's ability to shoot HD video. You can shoot video in an exposure mode such as Shutter Priority that lets you use a fast shutter speed to avoid motion blur, and record a street scene for several seconds, or even a minute or two. You can then use video-editing software to extract a single frame. The resolution of the still image will not be great, but the results may be quite interesting.

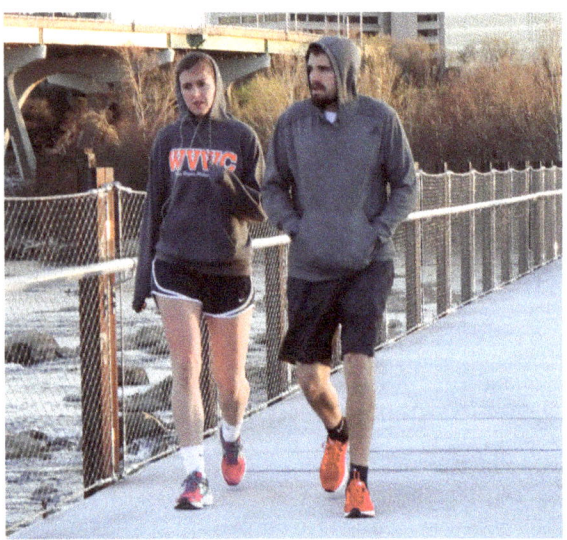

Figure 9-46. Street Photography Example

For Figure 9-46, I was taking pictures using the Advanced Sports Shooting setting of Scene mode when I spotted this couple walking along the pedestrian bridge. I made sure continuous shooting was turned on and fired off a burst of shots, capturing this image.

Connecting to a Television Set

The HX80 and HX90V can play back their still images and videos on an external television set, as long as the TV has an HDMI input jack. The camera does not come with any audio-video cable as standard equipment, so you have to purchase your own cable, with a micro HDMI connector at the camera end and a standard HDMI connector at the TV end. These cables are available from online retailers and electronics stores.

To connect the cable to the camera, just plug the micro HDMI connector into the port on the bottom of the camera, as shown in Figure 9-47.

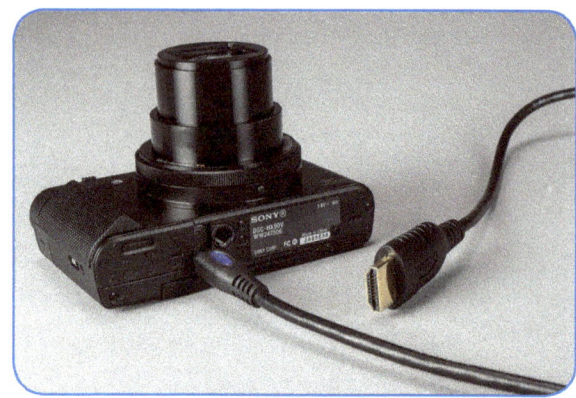

Figure 9-47. HDMI Cable Connected to Camera

Then connect the large connector at the other end of the cable to an HDMI input port on an HDTV set.

Once you have connected the camera to the set, the camera not only can play back images and videos; it also can record. When the camera is hooked up to a TV while in recording mode, you can see on the TV screen the live image being seen by the camera. In that way, you can use the TV as a large monitor to help you compose your photographs and videos.

You also can use this port and cable to output a "clean" video signal to another device, such as a video recorder. To do that, you have to turn off the HDMI Information Display option under the HDMI Settings item on the Setup menu, as discussed in Chapter 7.

As noted earlier in this chapter, the HX80 and HX90V also have an option on the Wi-Fi menu called View on TV, which lets you view your images on a Wi-Fi–enabled TV. As I discussed in that chapter, I have found that option to be difficult to use effectively. Unless you are familiar with setting up the special type of network that is needed for that sort of setup, I recommend that you stick to using an HDMI cable for the connection.

Appendix A: Accessories

When people buy a new camera, they often ask what accessories they should buy to go with it. I will discuss several options, with an emphasis on items I have used personally.

Cases

The HX80 and HX90V are so small that you may find you don't need a case. There is no separate lens cap to deal with as there is with some models in this class, and when the camera turns off and its lens retracts, the camera is ready to stow easily in your pocket, purse, or other handy location. But I often use a case with my camera, and I know that other users do also, so I will provide some suggestions.

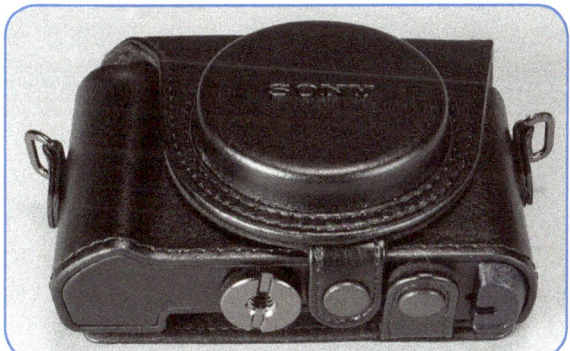

Figure A-1. Sony Case LCJ-HWA - Closed

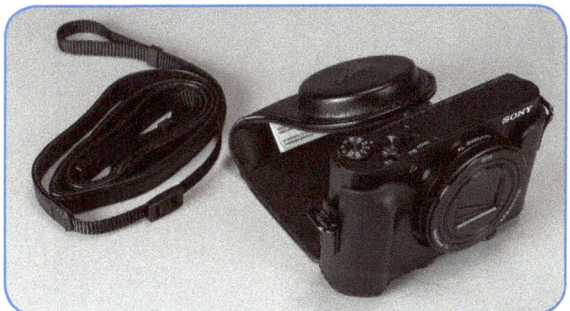

Figure A-2. Sony Case LCJ-HWA - Open

The Sony case designated for the HX80 and HX90V cameras, model number LCJ-HWA, is shown in Figures A-1 and A-2. This case is roomy enough to hold either camera with its tilting LCD.

This is an attractive case made of synthetic material that looks like leather. It holds the camera securely and comes with a matching shoulder strap. It does not have room for holding an extra battery or other items.

A less expensive option is the MegaGear case, shown in Figures A-3 and A-4.

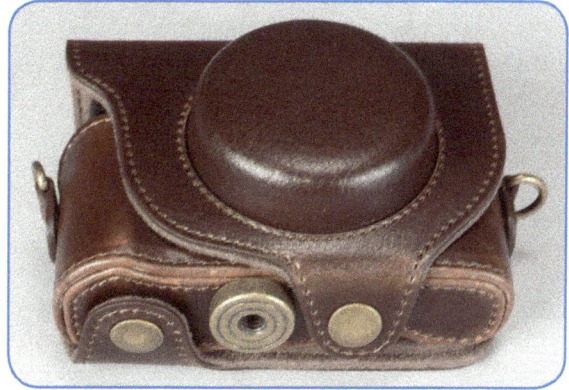

Figure A-3. MegaGear Case - Closed

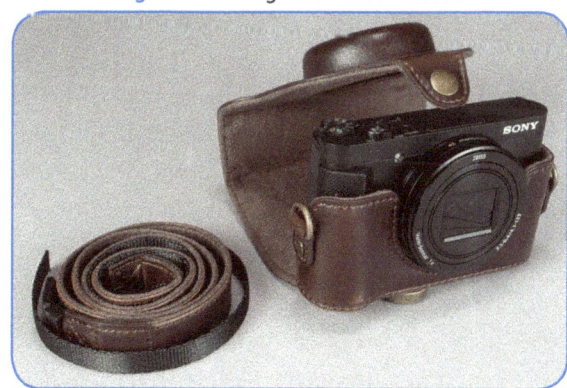

Figure A-4. MegaGear Case - Open

This brown leather case comes with a matching strap and can hold the camera, but not much else. It has a nice appearance and feel and does not display the Sony label, so it may provide a degree of security because it does not reveal the brand of your camera.

If you want a case with room for other items besides the camera, there are many choices. One I have used successfully is the Lowepro Rezo 110 AW, shown in Figure A-5. This case can hold the camera easily, with room for other items such as extra batteries or a USB charger. It has a belt loop, or you can carry it by the padded handle on top. You also could fit in a small bottle of water and some snacks for a short trip.

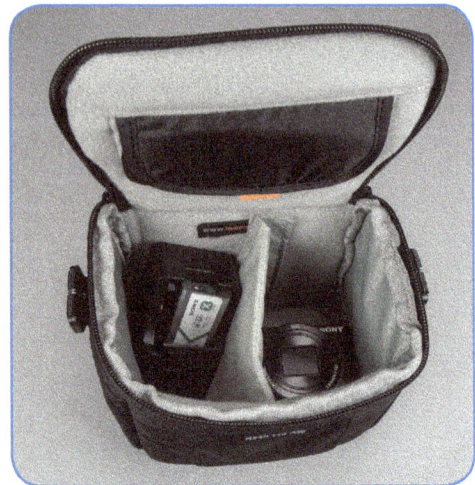

Figure A-5. Lowepro Rezo 110 AW Case

When I am going on a day trip to take photos, I often use a larger pack, such as the Lowepro Inverse 100 AW waist pack, shown in Figure A-6.

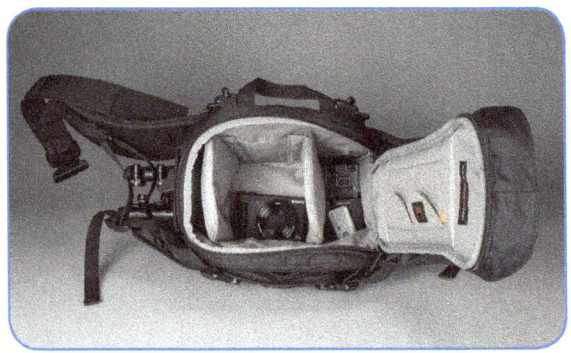

Figure A-6. Lowepro Inverse 100 AW Waist Pack

You can fasten this case around your waist or use its shoulder strap. It holds the camera along with water bottles, batteries, chargers, and other items. One feature I appreciate is that it has straps for attaching a tripod to the bottom of the case.

Another good option is a standard waist pack, not designed just for photography, such as the Eagle Creek pack shown in Figure A-7. It can readily accommodate the camera and some small accessories, and it has two mesh pockets for holding small water bottles.

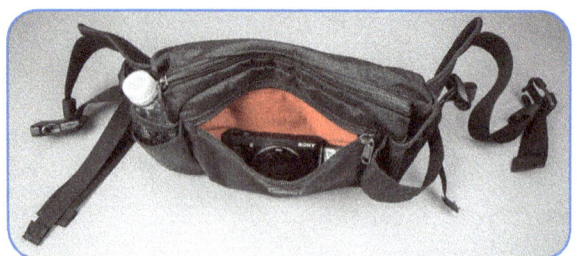

Figure A-7. Eagle Creek Waist Pack

Batteries and Chargers

This is a category of items that I recommend you purchase along with the camera or soon after getting the camera. You can't use disposable batteries, so if you're out taking pictures and the battery dies, you're out of luck unless you have a spare battery (or another power source, as discussed below). The model number of the Sony battery is NP-BX1. You can get a spare Sony battery for about $33 as I write this. It won't do you a great deal of good by itself, though, because the battery is designed to be charged in the camera.

One solution to this problem is to purchase generic replacement batteries, as well as a charger to charge the batteries outside the camera, from an online seller. I purchased a package including a generic replacement battery and a charger for about $20 on eBay. You also can get the official Sony external charger, model number BC-TRX. Besides charging a battery externally, the Sony charger can be used with its included USB cable to charge a battery inside the camera. Both the Sony charger and a generic charger are shown in Figure A-8, along with a generic battery and a Sony battery.

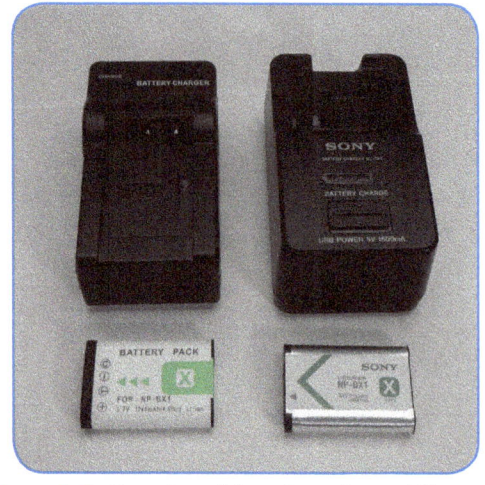

Figure A-8. Generic and Sony Batteries and Chargers

Another option for powering the camera is to use the AC adapter that comes with the camera, which, in the United States, is model number AC-UUD12 for the HX80 and AC-UB10C for the HX90V. If you plug the micro USB end of the camera's USB cable into the Multi port on the camera and plug the other end into the AC adapter, and then plug the adapter into an electrical outlet, the adapter will provide constant power to the camera. If the camera is turned off, the battery inside the camera will be charged. If the camera is turned on, you can operate the camera normally. The AC-UUD12 charger will power the camera even if no battery is currently installed in the camera. However, the AC-UB10C charger will not power the camera unless a battery is installed in the camera.

Of course, it is usually not convenient to have the camera plugged into an electrical outlet, unless you are taking shots in a studio or otherwise using the camera indoors. If you want to power the camera from an external source when you are in the field, you can get a good-quality USB power source and connect it to the camera, either for charging the camera's battery or for powering the camera.

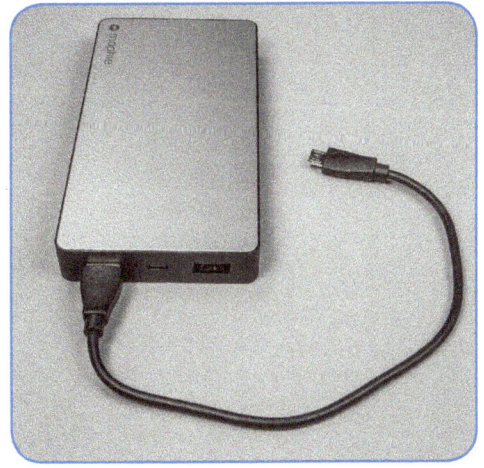

Figure A-9. Mophie PowerStation XL USB Power Supply

Figure A-9 shows the Mophie PowerStation XL. This device has two standard-sized USB ports. You can plug the camera's USB cable into one of those ports and connect the other end to the camera to provide a long-lasting source of power (even with no battery in the camera), or to charge the camera's battery. You can charge the power supply through its own micro USB port, using any compatible AC adapter. In fact, you can use the HX80's or HX90V's own AC adapter to recharge the Mophie device. The Mophie unit is slightly more than 5 inches (130mm) long and weighs about 7.65 ounces (217 grams).

Another device I have found very useful for providing power for the camera is the Anker 40-watt desktop USB charger, shown in Figure A-10, which has five slots for charging devices such as smartphones and tablets.

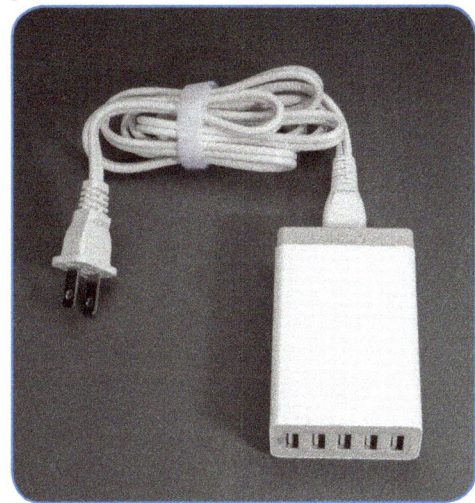

Figure A-10. Anker 40-Watt Desktop USB Charger

I have used it to charge my iPhone and iPad, and it does a good job of charging the Sony battery inside the HX80 or HX90V camera at the same time. You also can use it to charge the Mophie device, discussed above. There undoubtedly are other USB chargers that can handle this process; just make sure the charger meets the necessary specifications.

Remote Controls

In several situations, it is useful to control a camera remotely. For example, when you are using a slow shutter speed, doing closeup photography, or using a very long focal length, any camera motion during the exposure is likely to blur the image. If you put the camera on a tripod and control it remotely, you lessen the risk of blurred images from moving the camera as you press the shutter button. Remote control also is helpful when you need to be located away from the camera, as for taking self-portraits or images of wildlife.

As I discussed in Chapter 9, the HX80 and HX90V have built-in Wi-Fi capability for connecting a computer, smartphone, or tablet to the camera wirelessly. Besides using that feature to transfer images from the camera to the other device, you can use a smartphone or tablet as a wireless remote control. However, it can be tricky to establish and maintain the connection between the camera and the phone or tablet.

Fortunately, Sony offers several remote controls that are compatible with both of these camera models.

Sony's model number RM-VPR1 is shown in Figure A-11.

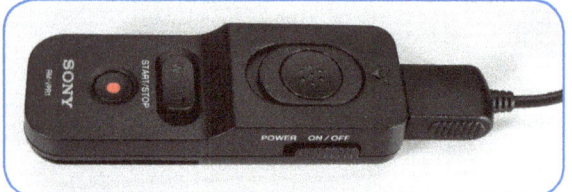

Figure A-11. Sony Remote Control RM-VPR1

You connect this device to the Multi port on the right side of the camera. With this remote, you can turn the camera on and off, use the autofocus system, zoom the lens in and out, take a still image, lock the shutter down for a long exposure, and start and stop video recording.

You can half-press the shutter button to cause the autofocus system to operate, and press the button fully down to take a still picture. You can press the shutter button down and then slide it back toward the other controls to lock it in place. This locking may be useful when you are taking continuous shots using the Drive Mode settings. Press the shutter button back up in its original direction to release it.

The red button labeled Start/Stop is similar to the Movie button on the camera. Press it once to start recording a movie and press it again to stop the recording.

The power button on the side of the remote control can be used to turn the camera on and off, and to wake it up from power-saving mode. Press the switch back toward yourself as you hold the control to power the camera either on or off.

A more sophisticated remote, Sony model number RMT-VP1K, is shown in Figure A-12 with the HX90V camera. This remote comes with an infrared receiver that plugs into the camera's Multi port. The receiver, a small cylinder, has a foot for attaching to a camera's shoe, but, of course, neither the HX80 nor the HX90V has a shoe, so you have to let the receiver dangle or attach it somewhere else. The remote kit comes with a clip that you can use to attach the receiver to a tripod leg or other support.

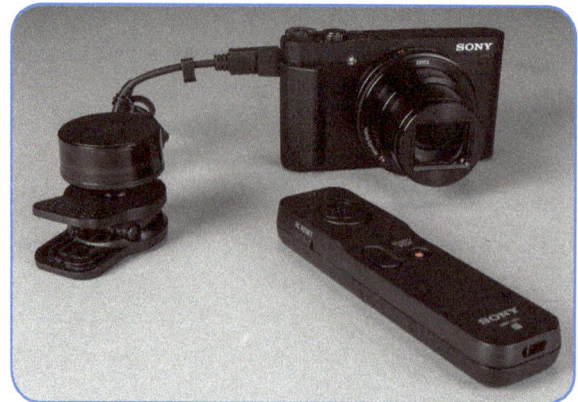

Figure A-12. Sony Remote Control RMT-VP1K

The remote control itself is similar in operation to the wired remote discussed earlier, RM-VPR1. You can press the shutter button, zoom the lens, and start and stop a video recording.

Figure A-13 shows another option, Sony model number RM-SPR1. This device is a very simple wired remote that also connects to the Multi port. It has only one large button, which acts as a remote shutter button.

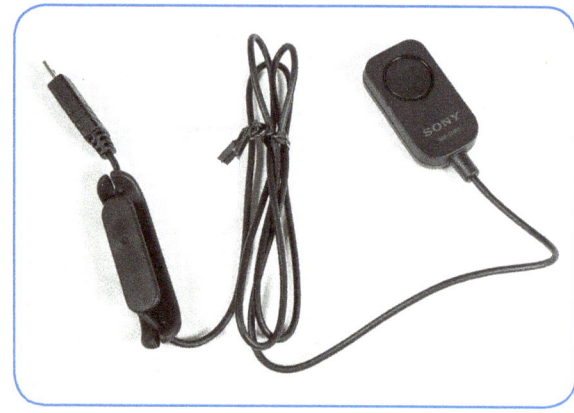

Figure A-13. Sony Remote Control RM-SPR1

You can press it halfway to evaluate focus and exposure, press it all the way to take a still image, or hold it down to fire a burst of shots if Drive Mode is set for continuous shooting. You cannot use this remote to record a movie or carry out any other functions.

One more device, which has more functionality than an ordinary remote control, is the Vello ShutterBoss II, shown in Figure A-14. This versatile device can act as a remote control, similar to the Sony devices discussed above. In addition, it can serve as a powerful intervalometer, for setting up the camera for a time-lapse sequence. Using the controls and the small LCD screen on the device, you can set up a sequence of up to 399 shots, or an indefinite series, until you command it to stop. You can set the interval between shots to any value from one second up to 99 hours, 59 minutes, and 59 seconds.

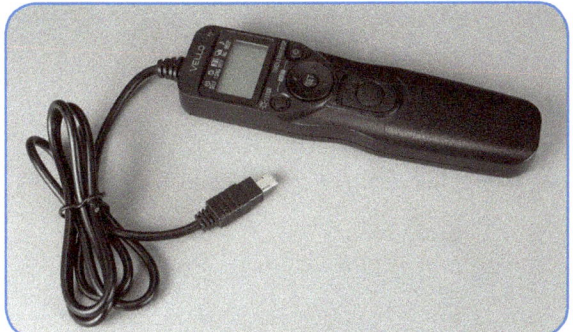

Figure A-14. Vello ShutterBoss II Remote Control

External Flash and LED Light

When Sony designed the HX80 and HX90V, they included the desirable feature of a built-in viewfinder that pops up, but, probably because of that feature, they omitted a hot shoe where you can attach an external flash unit. So, if you want to use an external flash unit to supplement the light from the camera's small pop-up flash, you have to use an optical slave.

An optical slave is a flash unit that includes a sensor that triggers the flash when it senses the light from the camera's built-in flash. (You also can use a separate optical slave that can be attached to any compatible flash unit.)

One problem with this system is that the camera fires one or more pre-flashes before it fires the main flash burst to expose the image. The automatic exposure system uses the pre-flashes to measure the amount of light being reflected from the subject so the image can be exposed properly. If the optical slave is not set to ignore the pre-flashes, it will fire as soon as it "sees" a pre-flash, and the external flash will not be synchronized with the actual exposure.

The solution to this problem is to use an optical slave that can be set to ignore the pre-flashes. One of the best ones I have found for use with these cameras is the LumoPro LP180, shown in Figure A-15.

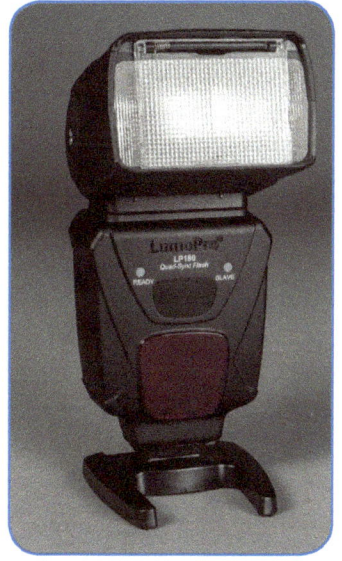

Figure A-15. LumoPro LP180 Flash

This powerful unit has a head that swivels and rotates, a built-in diffuser, variable power, and settings that allow it to ignore a variable number of pre-flashes. I have had good success using this flash with the HX80 and HX90V by setting the flash to its S2-1 mode.

With this flash, as with any optical slave, you have to use Manual exposure mode on the camera and determine the proper exposure by trial and error or by using a light meter. You can set up the external flash on a light stand or tripod at any location where it can sense the light from the camera's built-in flash.

Another good unit for use as an optical slave is the Yongnuo YN560-IV, shown in Figure A-16, which also has a built-in optical slave capability.

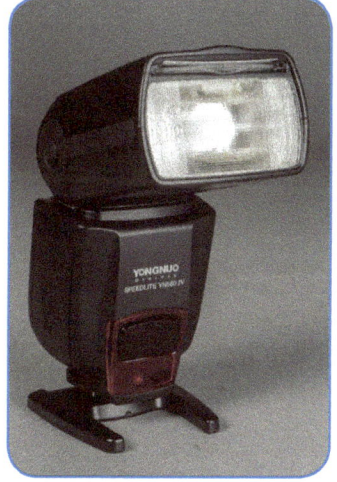

Figure A-16. Yongnuo YN560-IV Flash

I had success using this unit with the HX80 and HX90V with the flash set to either its S1 or its S2 optical slave mode. You can attach this, or any, external flash to the camera using a standard flash bracket with a tripod socket.

Finally, Figure A-17 shows the HX90V camera with the Genaray LED light, model number LED-2100. This compact and inexpensive unit has 36 LED lights, and comes with the bracket shown here, which attaches easily to the camera's tripod socket. This light, or one like it, is a good option for video shooting or any situation in which you need a moderate amount of lighting to brighten your images or movies.

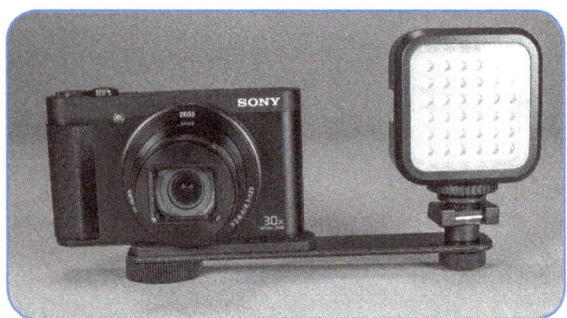

Figure A-17. Genaray LED-2100 Light with HX90V Camera

External Video Recorder

In Chapter 7, in connection with the HDMI Settings option on the Setup menu, I noted that the HX80 and HX90V can output their HD video signal via the HDMI port to an external video recorder. I have tested this process with the Atomos Shogun 4K recorder, a very capable device though an expensive one, available at this writing for $1,495.00.

As you can see from Figure A-18, the recorder is considerably larger than the camera, and it can be tricky to mount the two devices together. One issue is that the camera's tripod socket is very close to its HDMI port, so it is difficult to attach the camera firmly to a tripod or other support while it is connected to an HDMI device such as a video recorder. I found a way to make a secure connection between the two devices by attaching the camera to a Puroma universal cell phone tripod adapter, which includes a tripod socket at its base. I then connected that adapter to a Pearstone 4.2-inch articulating arm.

With this setup, shown in Figure A-18, the camera's LCD screen was partially blocked, but it was still possible to connect the camera to the recorder and operate both devices effectively. Another possibility is to use the Rock Solid Easy Grip, XL size, from tethertools.com. That device includes a large clamp that can hold the camera, leaving the camera's HDMI port free for making the connection to the recorder.

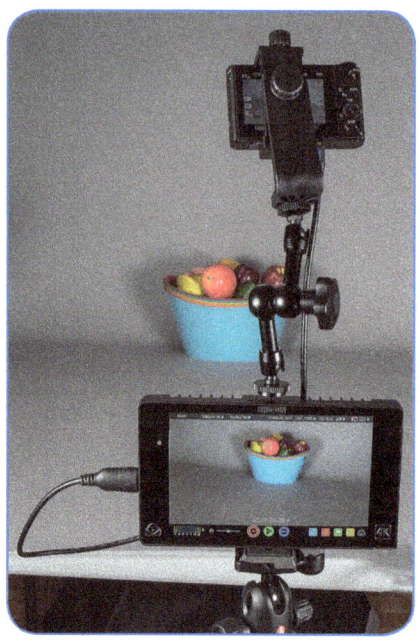

Figure A-18. HX90V Camera Attached to Shogun Recorder

Apart from the mounting issues, the combination of HX90V and Shogun performed well in producing HD video files. The menu system is easy to work with and the recorder produces high-quality files. At the highest quality, the files can be quite large (about 17 GB for a five-minute recording in one case), so be prepared with a strong computer capability for editing. However, I was not able to record any audio signal through the HDMI cable. To record audio, it would be necessary to connect one or more microphones to the Shogun recorder and record the sound through those channels.

External Audio Recorder

The HX80 and HX90V have very good video features but no provision for connecting an external microphone for high-quality audio. Although the built-in microphone records good-quality audio, you can get better results if you use an external audio recorder and synchronize the audio track from that recorder with the sound recorded by the camera.

Appendix A: Accessories

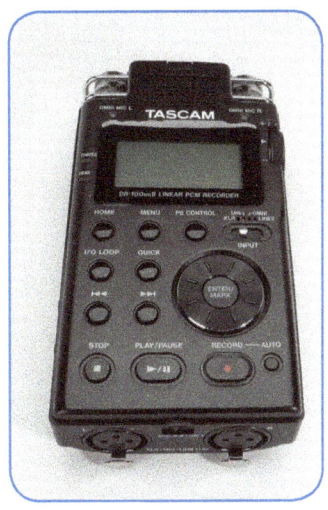

Figure A-19. Tascam DR-100MkII Audio Recorder

One excellent piece of equipment for this purpose is the Tascam DR-100MkII recorder, shown in Figure A-19. This recorder includes two sets of high-quality microphones, one set that is omnidirectional for recording lectures or classes, and another that is directional for recording concerts or other performances. The recorder also has two XLR inputs where you can connect high-quality microphones of your choice.

There are many other options that will work for this purpose, depending on your budget and needs, including the Shure VP83F, the Tascam DR-40, the Zoom H1, and the Zoom H6. Also, if you use the Atomos Shogun video recorder discussed above, you can connect high-quality microphones to that device using an audio connection cable from Atomos.

Once you have recorded high-quality audio with a recorder of this sort, you have to synchronize that audio with the video file produced by the camera. With current versions of video-editing software, that process is not complicated. When the recording is done, load the video file and its attached sound track into a video-editing program such as Adobe Premiere Pro CC, Final Cut Pro, or others. You also can use Plural Eyes, a program from redgiant.com that synchronizes audio and video. The software will compare the waveforms from the camera's sound track and the external audio track to move them into sync. With Premiere Pro CC, which I use, the procedure is to select the video track

and the two audio tracks, right-click on them, and select Synchronize-Audio-Mix Down. The software will move the external audio track into sync with the video track. Once the external audio track has been synchronized with the video track, you can delete the audio track recorded by the camera.

Tripods

I will mention two tripods that I have found to be excellent for traveling with the Sony HX80 and HX90V cameras. They are both Manfrotto BeFree tripods, shown in Figures A-19 and A-20.

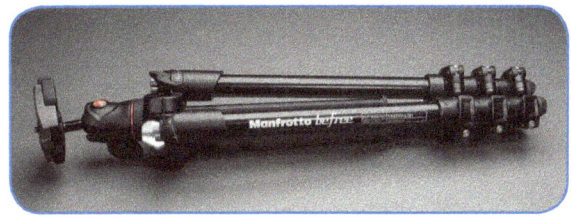

Figure A-20. Manfrotto BeFree Aluminum Tripod

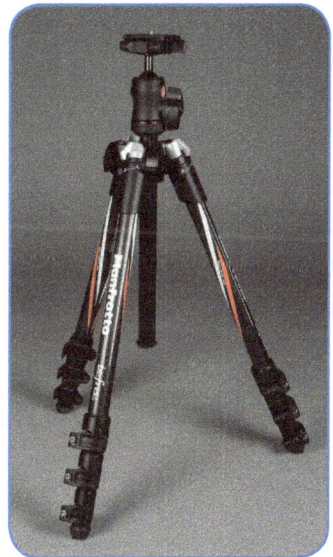

Figure A-21. Manfrotto BeFree Carbon Fiber Tripod

The tripod shown in Figure A-20 is the aluminum version, model no. MKBFRA4-BH. It includes a versatile head, reduces to about 20 inches (50 cm) long just by collapsing the legs, and to about 16 inches (40 cm) if you take the trouble to fold the legs backward. It weighs about three pounds five ounces (1.5 kg). The tripod in Figure A-21 is the carbon-fiber version, model no. MKBFRC4-BH, which is lighter and more expensive than the aluminum one.

Appendix B: Quick Tips

In this section, I will list some tips and facts that might be useful as reminders. I have tried to include points that you might not remember from day to day, especially if you don't use the HX80 or HX90V constantly.

Move the focus frame quickly. To adjust the focus frame for use with autofocus, choose Flexible Spot or Expand Flexible Spot for the Focus Area menu option and Standard for the Center Button option of the Custom Key Settings item on the last screen of the Custom menu. Then, when the camera is in shooting mode, press the Center button to put the movable focus frame on the screen. Use the direction buttons to move it around the display.

Use Auto ISO with Manual exposure mode. With these settings, you can set the shutter speed and aperture and let the camera choose the ISO value to produce a good exposure. This is like having a new shooting mode that lets you stop action and control depth of field at the same time.

Use continuous shooting. Consider turning burst shooting on as a matter of routine, unless you are running out of storage space or battery power, or have a particular reason not to use it. Even with portraits, you may get the perfect expression on your subject's face with the fourth or fifth shot. Press the Left button (or use the menu system) to call up Drive Mode, scroll to Continuous Shooting, and turn it on. With the High speed setting, the camera can shoot at up to 10 frames per second. Continuous shooting is not available when the camera is set to iSweep Panorama mode or to any Scene mode setting other than Advanced Sports Shooting.

Use shortcuts. Speed up access to many settings by placing them on the Function menu for recall with a press of the Function button. In some cases, as with flash settings and Drive Mode, you can press a button (the Right and Left buttons, respectively) to get access to the features you need. Speed through the Shooting menu using the Control wheel to move rapidly through the items on a screen. Use the Right and Left buttons to move through the menus a screen at a time by highlighting the icons at the top of the screen.

Take advantage of the help system. The HX80 and HX90V do a good job of advising you about conflicts between settings. If a menu option is unavailable for selection, you can still highlight it and press the Center button. The camera will display a message telling you what setting is causing the highlighted item to be unavailable. Press the In-Camera Guide button, which is marked with a question mark, when a menu item is highlighted, to get information about the item, if In-Camera Guide is assigned to that button through the Custom Key Settings menu option.

Use the Memory Recall shooting mode. The MR position on the Mode dial lets you save three favorite groups of settings. You also can use it for more specific purposes. I like to have one slot set up to remove all "special" settings, such as Creative Style, Picture Effect, and self-timer, so I can quickly set up the camera to take a shot with no surprises. You can use one slot to set the camera at a particular zoom range, such as, say, 50mm. To do this, press the zoom lever to move the lens, so you see the desired range below the zoom scale in the upper right corner of the display. When the range is set as you want it, save the settings to one of the MR slots. (With the HX90V, you also can use the Step Zoom feature to set a particular zoom amount; to do that, set the Control ring to control zoom, and set the Zoom Function on Ring option on the Custom menu to Step.)

Use an external power source to power the camera. These cameras can be powered by any compatible USB battery, such as the Mophie unit discussed in Appendix A. A device like that is useful when you need to do extensive photography in the field.

Use the extra settings for White Balance and Creative Style. When you set White Balance, even to Auto White Balance, you can press the Right button and use the amber-blue and green-magenta axes to further adjust the color of your shots. Remember to undo any color shift when you no longer need it. Also, you can press the Right button after selecting a Creative Style option and then adjust the contrast, saturation, and sharpness settings. (Saturation is not adjustable for the Black and White and Sepia settings.)

Play your movies in iTunes, and on iPods, iPhones, and iPads. If you record movies using the MP4 extension (including XAVC S HD movies), you can use iTunes to copy the MP4 files to an iTunes-compatible device, such as an iPad. After transferring the files to your computer, open iTunes on that computer and drag an .mp4 file from the computer's Explorer or Finder window to the Home Movies panel in iTunes. You can then play the movie from iTunes. To play it on an iPod, iPhone, or iPad, select the video in iTunes, and, on the iTunes menu, select File—Convert—Create iPod or iPhone version, or Create iPad or AppleTV version, as appropriate. Then sync iTunes with your device, and the converted movie will play on that device. (If you have trouble locating the .mp4 files on your computer, see the last part of Chapter 8.)

Diffuse your flash. If the built-in flash produces light that's too harsh for macro or other shots, try using translucent plastic pieces from milk jugs or broken ping-pong balls as diffusers. Hold the plastic between the flash and the subject. When using Fill-flash outdoors, use the Flash Compensation setting on the Shooting menu to reduce the intensity of the flash by -2/3 EV. You can bounce the light from the built-in flash off of the ceiling or a wall by holding it back gently with a finger.

Use the self-timer to avoid camera shake. The self-timer is not just for group portraits; you can use the two-second or five-second self-timer whenever you use a slow shutter speed and need to avoid camera shake. It also is useful for macro photography. Don't forget that you can set the self-timer to take multiple shots, which can increase your chances of getting more great images.

With the HX90V, use DMF for focusing. The direct manual focus option combines the camera's autofocus ability with your own manual focus adjustments, to achieve precision for critical focus tasks. You can use the MF Assist option, which enlarges the display when you turn the Control ring to adjust focus, but, with DMF, you have to half-press the shutter button as you turn the Control ring for MF Assist to work.

Try time-lapse photography. With time-lapse photography, a camera takes a series of images at regular intervals, several seconds, minutes, or even hours apart, to record a slow-moving event such as the rising of the moon or sun or the opening of a flower. The images are played back at a much faster rate to show the whole event unfolding quickly. The HX80 and HX90V do not have this feature built in, but you can use the Vello ShutterBoss II intervalometer, discussed in Appendix A.

Use the self-timer for bracketed exposures. To do this, use the Bracket Settings option on screen 2 of the Shooting menu and select the first sub-option, Self-timer During Bracketing.

Use the camera's automatic HDR option. To do this, go to the Shooting menu and select DRO/Auto HDR, then HDR. You cannot use certain other settings with HDR, including Picture Effect.

Use the Playback button to turn on the camera. This is useful if you only need to look at menu items or view your images or videos. The lens will not be activated.

Be aware of the camera's focusing options. These options can be confusing if you are used to a focusing system in a different camera. With the HX80, when shooting still images, the camera is always set to the single autofocus mode, which means that the camera attempts to focus when you press the shutter button halfway down. When shooting movies, the camera always uses the continuous autofocus mode, which means that the camera continuously adjusts the focus as the distance to the subject changes. With the HX90V, for still images you can use the Focus Mode menu option to choose single autofocus, manual focus, or DMF (direct manual focus). For movies, when the Mode dial is at the Movie position, you can use the Focus Mode menu option to choose either continuous autofocus or manual focus.

Appendix C: Resources for Further Information

Books

There are many excellent books about photography. Rather than trying to compile a long bibliography, I will list a few especially useful books that I consulted while writing this guide.

C. George, *Mastering Digital Flash Photography* (Lark Books, 2008)

C. Harnischmacher, *Closeup Shooting* (Rocky Nook, 2007)

H. Horenstein, *Digital Photography: A Basic Manual* (Little, Brown, 2011)

H. Kamps, *The Rules of Photography and When to Break Them* (Focal Press, 2012)

Websites and Videos

Since websites come and go and change their addresses, it's impossible to compile a list of sites that discuss the HX80 and HX90V cameras that will be accurate far into the future.

I will include below a list of some of the sites or links I have found useful, with the caveat that some of them may not be accessible by the time you read this.

Digital Photography Review

Listed below is the current web address for the "Sony Cyber-shot Talk" forum at dpreview.com. Dpreview.com is one of the most useful sites for reviews, discussion forums, technical information, and other resources concerning digital cameras.

http://www.dpreview.com/forums/1009

Reviews of the HX80 and HX90V

The links below lead to reviews or previews of the HX80 and HX90V by dpreview.com, imaging-resource.com, and others.

https://www.dpreview.com/products/sony/compacts/sony_dschx80

http://www.imaging-resource.com/PRODS/sony-hx80/sony-hx80A.HTM

http://streamleaf.com/magical-sony-cyber-shot-dsc-hx80-digital-camera/

https://www.dpreview.com/products/sony/compacts/sony_dschx90v

http://www.imaging-resource.com/PRODS/sony-hx90v/sony-hx90vA.HTM

http://www.cameralabs.com/reviews/Sony_Cyber-shot_HX90V/

http://www.pcmag.com/article2/0,2817,2487125,00.asp

http://www.photographyblog.com/reviews/sony_cybershot_dsc_hx90v_review/

http://www.whatdigitalcamera.com/reviews/compact-cameras/sony-hx90v-review

http://www.amateurphotographer.co.uk/reviews/compacts/sony-cyber-shot-dsc-hx90v-review

Finally, my own site, White Knight Press, provides updates, offers support for download of PDFs and eBooks, and provides a way to contact me with questions or comments.

http://whiteknightpress.com

Appendix C: Resources for Further Information | 197

THE OFFICIAL SONY SITE

Sony provides resources on its websites, including the downloadable user's manual for the HX90V and other information.

The link below provides general support for the HX80 camera:

https://esupport.sony.com/US/p/model-home.pl?mdl=DSCHX80&LOC=3#/manualsTab

Here is a link to the downloadable Sony user's guide for the HX80:

https://docs.sony.com/release//Help_4591308111.pdf

The link below is to the official specifications for the HX80 camera:

https://docs.sony.com/release//Specs_DSCHX80.pdf

The link below provides general support for the HX90V camera:

https://esupport.sony.com/US/p/model-home.pl?mdl=DSCHX90V&LOC=3#/manualsTab

Here is a link to the downloadable Sony user's guide for the HX90V:

https://docs.sony.com/release//DSC-HX90V_help.pdf

The link below is to the operating instructions for the PlayMemories Mobile app for Android and iOS:

http://support.d-imaging.sony.co.jp/www/disoft/int/playmemories-mobile/en/operation/index.html

The link below leads to the site for downloading camera apps for Sony cameras:

https://www.playmemoriescameraapps.com/portal/

Below is a link to a support document for the PlayMemories Home computer app:

http://support.d-imaging.sony.co.jp/www/disoft/int/playmemories-home/en/index.html

OTHER RESOURCES

If you're interested in using the Atomos Shogun external video recorder, which is discussed in Appendix A, the video in the link below gives a helpful introduction to using that recorder with the Sony A7S and the Panasonic GH4. A lot of this discussion is helpful for users of the HX90V.

http://nofilmschool.com/2014/12/helpful-crash-course-using-atomos-shogun-4k-recorder-gh4-a7s

Finally, the last link below is to a site that has excellent tutorials on many photographic topics.

http://www.cambridgeincolour.com

Index

Symbols

4K Still Image Playback menu item 111
24p/60p Output menu item 142
35mm-equivalent zoom range 10, 123

A

Access lamp 11, 102
Access Point Settings menu item 169, 178
Adobe Premiere Elements software 20
Adobe Premiere Pro software 20
Advanced Sports Shooting scene type setting 32
AF Illuminator menu item 61, 90
AF Illuminator/Self-timer Lamp 10, 89
  controlling operation of 61
Airplane Mode menu item 168, 178
Anker 40-watt desktop USB charger 189
Anti Motion Blur scene type setting 34–35
  compared to Hand-held Twilight setting 35
Aperture
  range of available settings 23, 25, 30
    effect of focal length on 26
Aperture Priority exposure mode for movies 154
Aperture Priority mode 24–26
Apple Computer devices and software
  playing movies with 195
Application List menu item 173–174
Application Management app 180
Application menu 173–174, 180–181
Area Setting menu item 145
Aspect Ratio menu item 45–46
  incompatibility with other settings 46
  relationship to Image Size menu item 43–44
  relationship to zoom range 125
Atomos Shogun video recorder 192
Audio Signals menu item 136
Autoflash setting 12, 52
Auto ISO setting
  setting minimum and maximum values for 62–63
  using with Manual exposure mode 29, 64, 194
    for movies 156
Auto Object Framing menu item 32, 83–84
  incompatibility with other settings 84
Auto Review menu item 19, 118–119
  deleting an image in Auto Review 119
Auto Slow Shutter menu item 84, 157–158
  works only when Auto ISO is in effect 158
AVCHD format for movies 151

B

Battery
  charging 3–4
    indicator light 4
    time for full charge 4
    when camera connected to computer 4
  generic replacement 188
  Sony NP-BX1 3, 188
Battery charger
  generic external charger 188
  Sony AC-UB10C 4, 189
  Sony AC-UUD12 189
  Sony BC-TRX external charger 188
  using as external power source 3
Battery/memory card compartment 102
Beach scene type setting 35
Beauty Effect menu item 113
Bit rates of video formats 153
Black and white
  shooting in 73
    for street photography 185
Blinking highlights in playback mode
  indicating overexposure 106
Blurred background
  how to achieve 25
    using long zoom range 183
Bokeh 25, 183
Bounce flash 88, 195
Bracket Order menu item 51–52
Bracket Settings menu item 51–52
Brightness setting for Photo Creativity 14

C

Calendar display of images 19, 104, 108
Camera apps 180
Cases for HX80 and HX90V cameras
  Eagle Creek Waist Pack 188
  Lowepro Inverse 110 AW Waist Pack 188
  Lowepro Rezo 110 AW 187–188
  MegaGear leather case 187
  Sony LCJ-HWA 187
Center button 10, 97
  assigning a function to 131–132
  Standard setting for 60–61, 97, 132
  using to activate focus tracking 97
  using to adjust location of Flexible Spot focus frame 60, 97
  using to determine reason for setting conflict 194
  using to magnify focus area 58, 80, 97
  using to play a panorama at larger size 97
  using to play a video 97, 164
  using to return enlarged image to normal size 97, 104
Center Button menu item 131–132
  using Standard setting 132
Center Lock-on AF menu item 81
  incompatibility with other settings 81
Center option for Focus Area 59–60

Index | 199

distinguishing focus frame from Spot metering circle 65
Center option for Metering Mode 64–65
Clean HDMI signal output 143, 186
Clear Image Zoom 123, 124–125
   incompatibility with other settings 125
Clipping of highlights 105
Clipping of shadow areas 105
Color temperature 65
   using to set white balance 66
Compression of JPEG images 46
Continuous AF setting 56, 195
   limited availability of 56
Continuous shooting option 17, 48, 194
   incompatibility with other settings 48
   selecting speed of 48
Contrast
   adjusting 71–72
Control ring 9, 90–91
   assigning functions to 90, 130–131
   icon on display screen 130
   speeding up zoom operation 133
   Standard option for settings 90, 131
   using during movie recording 162
   using to adjust exposure compensation 29, 99
   using to adjust manual focus 91
   using to select panorama direction 38, 46
   using to select scene type setting 31, 84
   using to set aperture 25, 28
   using to set shutter speed 27
   using to zoom the lens 88, 133
Control Ring option of Custom Key Settings menu item 90
Control wheel 10, 96
   icon on display screen 96
   using to control both aperture and shutter speed 96
   using to move to other enlarged images 104
   using to select scene setting 31, 84, 96
   using to set aperture 96
   using to set panorama direction 38, 46, 96
   using to set shutter speed 96
Creative Style comparison chart 72
Creative Style menu item 71–73
   adjusting contrast, saturation, and sharpness 71–72, 195
   comparison of settings to Scene mode settings 73
   incompatibility with other settings 72
CTRL for HDMI menu item 143
Custom Key Settings menu item 90, 97, 129–133
   list of items that can be assigned to a button 131
   list of items that can be controlled during movie recording 162
Custom menu 114–134
Custom white balance
   how to set 66–67

D

Date
   recording permanently on image 128

Date and Time
   setting with Setup menu 7–8, 144–145
Date Format menu option 7, 144
Date/Time Setup menu item 7, 144
Day for night movie recording 156
Daylight Savings Time adjustment 7, 144
Delete Confirmation menu item 139
Delete menu item 107
Deleting images or videos 95, 106, 107
Demo Mode menu item 141
Depth of field
   relationship to aperture setting 24
Digital Zoom 123, 124–125
   incompatibility with other settings 125
Dimmed menu items 43
Diopter adjustment lever 88–89
Display button 97
   using to cycle through display screens 19
Display Button menu item 89, 119–121
Display MAC Address menu item 179
Display Media Information menu item 147–148
Display Quality menu item 140
Display Rotation menu item 109
Display screens
   playback mode 105–106
   shooting mode
      selecting with Display button menu item 119–121
DLNA streaming media server 177
DMF (direct manual focus) 56, 91, 195
   requirement to hold shutter button down halfway with MF Assist 57, 91, 115, 195
Down button 98–99
   assigning a function to 133
   using to activate Photo Creativity options 98
   using to adjust exposure compensation 98–99
   using to adjust volume for movies 99, 136
   using to switch functions of Control wheel 27, 98
Download Application option 132
DPOF (Digital Print Order Format) printing 112
Drive Mode 13, 47–51
   basic procedure for using 17–18
DRO/Auto HDR menu item 68–71
   incompatibility with other settings 71
DRO bracketing 51
   incompatibility with other settings 50

E

Edit Device Name menu item 179
Electronic viewfinder 9, 88–89
   adjusting brightness of 89, 135
   adjusting color temperature 135
   does not function during Wi-Fi remote control operation 89
   pulling into position for use 11, 88
   setting camera to power off when EVF closed 89, 141
   setting information display screens for 89
   switching between EVF and LCD screen 89, 126

turning on camera by popping up EVF 88
Enlarge Image menu item 111
Enlarging images with zoom lever 19, 104
Expand Flexible Spot setting for Focus Area 60
Exposure bracketing
   continuous 49–50
   incompatibility with other settings 50
   order of bracketed exposures 50
     changing 50, 51–52
   single 50
   using exposure compensation with 50
   using flash with 50
   using self-timer with 51
Exposure compensation 98–99
   limited adjustment range for movies 62, 161
   using with iSweep Panorama mode 38
   using with Manual exposure mode 29, 61
Exposure Compensation menu item 29, 61–62
Exposure Settings Guide menu item 122
External audio recorder
   Tascam DR-100MkII 192
External flash
   LumoPro LP180 190
   using with HX80 or HX90V camera 191
   Yongnuo YN560-IV 191
Eye-Fi card
   setting upload options for 138
Eye sensor 10, 89

F

Face Detection On menu item 82
Face Detection On (Registered Faces) menu item 81–82, 127
Face Registration menu item 127
Fadeout
   in-camera effect for movies 154–155
Fade to white
   in-camera effect for movies 154–155
File Format menu option 18, 47, 151
File Number menu item 146
Fill-flash setting 16, 52–53
Final Cut Express software 20
Final Cut Pro software 20
Finder Color Temperature menu item 135
Finder/Monitor menu item 89, 126
Finder switch 10, 88, 101
Fireworks scene type setting 36
Firmware
   checking for updates 148
   displaying version 148
Flash
   basic procedure for using 16–17
   incompatibility with other settings 16
Flash Compensation menu item 54–55
   incompatibility with other settings 55
Flash Mode menu 12, 16, 52–54, 88
Flash Off setting 16, 52

Flash pop-up switch 9, 88
Flash unit 9, 88
   cannot be used until manually popped up 9, 16, 98
   moving for bounce flash 88
   using diffuser with 195
Flattening effect of long zoom shot 182
Flexible Spot option for Focus Area 60–61
Focus Area menu item 59–61
Focus frame
   changing size and location of 60–61, 194
Focusing on off-center subject 56, 60
Focus Magnification Time menu item 58–57, 80, 115–116
Focus Magnifier menu item 58, 79–80
   assigning to a control button 80
   compared to MF Assist option 58, 80, 115
   using for recording movies 80, 164
Focus Mode menu item 55, 90
Folder Name menu item 147
Format item on Setup menu 7, 145
For Viewfinder display screen 93, 119, 120
Function button 10, 92–94
   using during movie recording 161–162
   using to activate Send to Smartphone option 10, 94
Function for VF Close menu item 11, 89, 101, 141
Function menu 90, 92–93
   assigning options to 92, 128–129
   using to adjust settings 92–93
Function Menu Settings menu item 92, 128–129

G

Genaray LED light 192
Gourmet scene type setting 35
GPS Area Adjustment menu item 137
GPS assist data
   using 137
GPS Auto Correction menu item 137
GPS logo on HX90V 11
GPS Log Recording menu item 137–138
GPS On/Off menu item 136
GPS Settings menu item 136–138
Grid Line menu item 116

H

Hand-held Twilight scene type setting 34
   compared to Anti Motion Blur setting 34
HDMI cable
   using to connect camera to HDTV 186
HDMI Information Display menu item 142, 186
HDMI port 11, 102
HDMI Resolution menu item 142
HDMI Settings menu item 141–143
HDR (high dynamic range) photography 68, 69–70
HDR setting in camera 69–70, 195
Help system 95, 194
High ISO Noise Reduction menu item 81
   incompatibility with other settings 81

Index

High Sensitivity scene type setting 36–37
    compared to Anti Motion Blur and Hand-held Twilight settings 36
Histogram
    activating in shooting mode 106, 120
    playback mode 105–106

I

Icon for menu items for still images or movies 43
Illustrations
    controls on back of camera 9
    controls on top of camera 9, 87
    Electronic viewfinder 89
    items on bottom of camera 11, 102
    items on front of camera 10, 89
    items on left side of camera 10, 101
    port on right side of camera 10, 101
    tilting LCD screen 100
Image blur from long zoom shots 183
Image Index menu item 108–109
Image size
    relationship to aspect ratio 43–44
Image Size menu item 43–44
iMovie software 20, 151, 166
In-Camera Guide/Delete button 10, 94–96
    assigning function to 133
    using for In-Camera Guide option 95
    using to call up help screens 10
    using to delete images or videos 10, 95, 106, 139
    using to reset Photo Creativity settings 95
In-Camera Guide option 95, 132, 194
Index screen of images 19, 103–104, 108–109
Intelligent Auto Mode 21–22
    settings unavailable with 21
Interlaced video formats 151
ISO 62–64
    basic procedure for setting 28, 62–63
    MFNR setting 63
        incompatibility with other settings 64
    range of available settings 62
    setting minimum and maximum values for Auto ISO 62–63
ISO Auto Minimum and Maximum settings 62
Isolating effect of long zoom shot 182
iSweep Panorama mode 37–39
    incompatibility with other settings 37

J

JPEG images 46

K

Kelvin units of color temperature 65
Key icon for protected image 111

L

Landscape scene type setting 33

Language
    selecting on Setup menu 8, 144
Large focus frame 125
    indicating focusing difficulty or non-optical zoom 59
LCD screen
    ability to tilt up or 180 degrees forward 100–101, 127
    adjusting brightness of 135
    in general 100
    setting information display screens for 119–121
    switching between LCD screen and EVF 126
Left button
    assigning a function to 132
    using to activate Drive Mode 100
Lens
    focal length range of 10, 123, 181
    focusing distance for closeup shots 185
    using the superzoom capability of 181–184
Level display screen 120
Locations of still images and videos on memory card 166
Locking focus 56

M

Macro photography 184–185
Manfrotto BeFree tripods 193
Manual exposure mode 27–30
    using for HDR photography 30, 70
Manual Exposure mode for movies 155–156
Manual focus 57
    focusing aids 57–58
    using for macro shots 185
Marker Display menu item 117, 159
Marker Settings menu item 117–118
Memory cards
    capacity for storing images and videos 6
    cards suitable for use with XAVC S HD video format 150
    Eye-Fi cards 6
    formatting in camera 7, 145
    inserting into camera 6
    micro-SD cards 5
    operating camera without card 4, 126
    SD, SDHC, and SDXC cards 5
    Sony Memory Stick cards 5
        inserting into camera 7
    special requirements for XAVC S HD video format 5, 150, 151
    types of 4–6
Memory menu item 40, 85
Memory Recall menu item 85
Memory Recall mode 39–40, 85, 194
Menu button 10, 91
    using to return enlarged image to normal size 91
Menu items
    dimmed because of conflicting settings 42
    preceded by icons: Stills, Movies 42
Menu system
    navigating through 41–42

Metering Mode menu item 64–65
  incompatibility with other settings 65
MF Assist menu item 57, 91, 115
  compared to Focus Magnifier option 58, 80, 115
  not available for movies 164
  using with DMF 91, 115
MFNR (Multi Frame Noise Reduction) setting 63
Micref Level menu item 84, 158
Microphone, built-in 9
M.M. icon for metered manual value 28
Mode dial 9, 87
  effect of position on movie recording 158–160
Mode Dial Guide menu option 11, 30–31, 85, 139
Monitor Brightness menu item 135
Mophie PowerStation XL portable USB power supply 189
Motion Interval Adjustment menu item 111–112, 166
Motion Shot feature for movie playback 165–166
Movie button 10, 91
  limiting operation to Movie mode 87, 91, 134, 159
Movie Button menu item 87, 91, 134, 159
Movie (exposure mode selection) menu item 84, 153–156
MOVIE option for assignment to control button 132, 134
Movie position on Mode dial
  reasons for using 159
Movies
  adjusting playback volume 135–136
  editing 166
  recording
    basic procedure 17–18, 163
    functions that work from control buttons during video recording 162
    time limits 150
MP4 format for movies 18, 151
Multi option for Metering Mode 64–65
Multi port 10, 101
  uses of 10, 101
My Best Portrait camera app 180

N

New Folder menu item 146–147
NFC area on left side of camera 11, 101, 173, 177
NFC (near field communication) protocol 11, 101, 177
  using to connect camera to Android device 172–173
Night Portrait scene type setting 34
Night Scene scene type setting 33
NO CARD warning message 4, 126
Not Set option for assignment to control button 97, 132
NTSC/PAL Selector menu item 140–141
  effect on Record Setting menu option 140

O

One-touch NFC menu item 175, 177–178
Optical slave flash 191
Optical zoom 123
Overlay icon
  indicator of burst of shots in Superior Auto mode 23

P

Panorama Direction menu item 37–38, 46
Panorama Size menu item 37–38, 46
Panoramas, playback 39, 97
Panoramas, shooting 38–39
Peaking Color menu item 58, 122
Peaking Level menu item 58, 121–122
  using with DMF 58, 121, 122
  using with MF Assist 122
Pearstone 4.2-inch articulating arm 192
Pet scene type setting 35
Photo Creativity feature 13–16
  combining multiple settings 15
  not available during movie recording 163
  resetting to default values 16
Photomatix software 30
PictBridge printer 112
Picture Effect comparison charts 74
Picture Effect menu item 73–79
  HDR Painting setting 77–78
  High Contrast Monochrome setting 77
    using for street photography 185
  Illustration setting 79
  incompatibility with other settings 73, 79
  Miniature Effect setting 78
  Off setting 74
  Partial Color setting 76–77
    adjusting range of colors recognized 76–77
  Pop Color setting 75
  Posterization setting 75
  Retro Photo setting 76
  Rich-tone Monochrome setting 78
  Soft Focus setting 77
  Soft High-key setting 76
  Toy Camera setting 74–75
  using for movies 79, 161
  Watercolor setting 79
Picture Effect setting for Photo Creativity feature 15, 79
Playback
  movies
    basic procedure 19–20, 164–165
  still images
    basic procedures 19, 103
Playback button 10, 91
  using to turn on camera 10, 91, 106, 195
Playback menu 106–113
PlayMemories Camera Apps app 180
PlayMemories Home software 20, 166
  where to download 3, 168
PlayMemories Mobile app 171–176
Pole aerial photography 101, 176
Portrait scene type setting 32
Power button 9, 88
Power Save Start Time menu item 140
Printing images directly to printer 112
Program Auto exposure mode for Movies 154

Index

Program mode 23–24
Program Shift feature 23–24
　not available for movie recording 163
Progressive video formats 151
Protect menu item 111

Q

QR code
　scanning with phone 174
Quality menu item 46
Quick Navi system 90, 93–94, 121
QuickTime software 151

R

Rear Sync flash setting 53–54
Record Setting menu item 47, 151–153
Recover Image Database menu item 147
Red Eye Reduction menu item 55
Release Without Card menu item 4, 126
Remote control devices 10
　Sony RM-SPR1 wired remote 190
　Sony RMT-VP1K infrared remote 190
　Sony RM-VPR1 wired remote 190
　Vello ShutterBoss II intervalometer 190
Reset Network Settings menu item 179
Resetting camera settings 148
Resolution of images 43
Right button
　assigning a function to 133
　using to activate Flash Mode menu 88, 97–98
Rotate menu item 110

S

Saturation
　adjusting 71–72
Scene mode 30–37
　incompatibility with other settings 30
　methods of selecting a scene type 30–31
Scene recognition feature 21
　requires face detection to be on to recognize faces 22
　using for macro shots 184
Scene Selection menu item 31, 84
Sekonic C-700 color meter 66
Select REC Folder menu item 146
Self-portrait Timer menu item 100, 127
Self-timer 49, 195
　basic procedure for using 17, 49
　incompatibility with other settings 49
　using for closeup photography 49
　using with exposure bracketing 51
Self-timer (Continuous) 49
　using to take multiple shots 49
Self-timer During Bracket menu option 51
Send to Computer menu item 168–170, 176
Send to Smartphone menu item 10, 171, 176
　activating with Function button 94

Setting Reset menu item 148–149
Setup menu 134–149
Sharpness
　adjusting 71–72
Shooting menu
　in general 42
　navigating through 42
Shooting modes
　list of 21
Shooting Tip List menu item 85
　summoning with In-Camera Guide button 85, 95
Shutter Priority exposure mode for movies 155
Shutter Priority mode 26–27
Shutter release button 9, 87
Shutter speed
　range of available settings 23, 26, 30
　range of available settings for movies 155
Single shooting setting for Drive Mode 47
Single-shot AF setting 55–56, 195
Slide Show menu option 109–110
　incompatibility with other settings 109
Slow Sync flash setting 34, 52–53
Smart Remote Control app 174, 175
Smart Remote Embedded app 174
Smart Zoom 123
Smile/Face Detection menu item 81–82
　incompatibility with other settings 82
Smile Shutter menu item 82
Snow scene type setting 36
Soft Skin Effect menu item 82
　requirement to have Face Detection turned on 82
Soft Skin scene type setting 36
Sony HX80 and HX90V cameras
　differences between 1
　general features of 1
　items supplied with in box 3
Sony HX90 camera
　same as HX90V but without GPS 1
Speaker 102
Specify Printing menu item 112
Spot option for Metering Mode 64–65
SSID/PW Reset menu item 179
SteadyShot (Movies) menu item 84, 156–157
　cropping of video image with 156
Step-by-step guides
　connecting with NFC 172–173
　sending images to a computer 168–170
　sending images to a smartphone 170–171
　taking pictures in Auto mode 11
　using smartphone as remote control for camera 173–175
Step Zoom option 88, 133–134
　not available for movies 133, 164
Street photography 185–186
　extracting still frames from HD video for 185
Sunset scene type setting 33
Superior Auto mode 22–23
　difference from Intelligent Auto mode 22

Sweep Panorama mode. See iSweep Panorama mode

T

Tables
  behavior of camera for video recording in various modes 160
  functions of Control ring with Standard setting 131
  maximum zoom range at various image sizes 125
  number of images that fit on 16 GB memory card 44
  Shooting menu items that can be adjusted during video recording 160
  suggested control assignments for movie recording 163
  suggested settings for Auto Mode still images 12
  suggested settings for movies in Intelligent Auto mode 18
  suggested settings for panoramas 38
  suggested Shooting menu settings for recording movies in Movie mode 163
Television set, playing images and videos on 185
Tile Menu menu option 41, 138–139
Time-lapse photography 195
Time zone
  selecting 145
Tripod socket 102
Tv notation for shutter speed 27

U

Upload Settings menu item 138
USB Connection menu item 143, 168
  using MTP option for downloading camera apps 143
USB LUN Setting menu item 143
USB Power Supply menu item 144
Use GPS Assist Date menu item 137

V

Version menu item 148
VGA setting for Image Size 44
  available only with 4:3 aspect ratio 44
Viewfinder Brightness menu item 89, 135
View Mode menu item 19, 108
View on TV menu item 177
Vividness setting for Photo Creativity feature 15
Volume setting for movies
  changing 20, 135–136
Volume Settings menu item 135–136

W

WD TV Live media player 177
White balance bracketing 50–51
  changing order of exposures 51, 52
  incompatibility with other settings 50
White balance comparison chart 67–68
White Balance menu item 65–68
  adjusting setting with color axes 67, 195
  incompatibility with other settings 67
Wide option for Focus Area 59

Wi-Fi menu 176–179
Wi-Fi router
  using to send images to computer from camera 169
Wind Noise Reduction menu item 84, 158
Windows Movie Maker software 20, 151–153, 166
WPS button on router 169, 178
WPS Push menu item 169, 178
Write Date menu item 128

X

XAVC S HD format for movies 151
  editing with computer 20

Z

Zebra menu item 114–115
Zoom Function on Ring menu item 123, 133–134, 164
Zoom lever 9, 87–88
  adjusting speed of zooming 88, 122–123
  using to display index screen 19, 88
  using to enlarge images 19, 88
  using to zoom in and out when shooting 13, 87
Zoom Setting menu item 123–125
  incompatibility with other settings 125
Zoom Speed menu item 122–123

www.ingramcontent.com/pod-product-compliance
Lightning Source LLC
Chambersburg PA
CBHW040539220526
45473CB00016B/2978